# Contributions to Economics

The series *Contributions to Economics* provides an outlet for innovative research in all areas of economics. Books published in the series are primarily monographs and multiple author works that present new research results on a clearly defined topic, but contributed volumes and conference proceedings are also considered. All books are published in print and ebook and disseminated and promoted globally. The series and the volumes published in it are indexed by Scopus and ISI (selected volumes).

Fadil Sahiti

# Catching Up in the Digital Age

## Capabilities, Governance and Industrial Policy in Transitional Europe

Springer

Fadil Sahiti
Rochester Institute of Technology Kosovo
Prishtinë, Kosovo

ISSN 1431-1933 ISSN 2197-7178 (electronic)
Contributions to Economics
ISBN 978-3-032-17058-3 ISBN 978-3-032-17059-0 (eBook)
https://doi.org/10.1007/978-3-032-17059-0



This Springer imprint is published by the registered company Springer Nature Switzerland AG.
The registered company address is: Gewerbestrasse 11, 6330 Cham, Switzerland

# Foreword

The question of how countries catch up in an age of global technological acceleration has re-emerged as a central dilemma in development economics. Classical accounts of late industrialization—ranging from Gerschenkron's insights into backwardness to the developmental state analyses of Japan and East Asia—highlighted how capable states, coherent bureaucracies, and embedded industrial policies can accelerate transformation. Yet, the conditions of development in the 21st century have changed profoundly. The rise of digital technologies, fragmented production networks, and the constraints of ecological transition have rendered traditional blueprints increasingly inadequate.

It is precisely this gap that *Catching Up in the Digital Age* addresses. Fadil Sahiti's book represents a major conceptual and empirical innovation in the study of latecomer development. It extends the intellectual lineage of the developmental state into the twenty-first century by reconceptualizing *governance as a dynamic capability* rather than as a static institutional endowment. It is not seen as a precondition but as an evolving capability that can emerge given the confluence of favourable factors, each of which can be nurtured individually. In doing so, it reframes catch-up not as a once-off leap through state intervention or market opening, which dominated much of transition economics thinking in the 1990s and early 2000s, but as an ongoing process of learning, coordination, and adaptation under constraint.

The concept of the *Developmental Network State (DNS),* which represents the core analytical framework, builds on and extends a rich lineage in development theory. From Chalmers Johnson's account of the hierarchical Japanese developmental state (1982[1]) to Peter Evans' notion of *embedded autonomy* (1995[2]), the central question has been how states coordinate transformation. Fred Block's later

[1] Johnson, Chalmers (1982). MITI and the Japanese Miracle. Stanford, CA: Stanford University Press.

[2] Evans, Peter (1995) Embedded Autonomy, States and Industrial Transformation. Princeton, NJ: Princeton University Press.

reinterpretation of the United States as a *developmental network state* (Block 2008[3]; Block et al., 2020[4]) marked a decisive shift: development was no longer driven by a central bureaucracy but by distributed networks linking mission-oriented agencies, firms, and research institutions. In this view, governance operates through learning, feedback, and relational coordination rather than command.

Fadil Sahiti's book advances this tradition into new empirical and conceptual territory. It shows how the *DNS* can function under conditions of *low capacity, donor dependence, and digital transition*, such as in the Western Balkans. By reframing governance itself as a *dynamic capability*, Sahiti extends Block's model of innovation-driven coordination into the domain of constrained, transitional economies—transforming the DNS from a hidden feature of advanced systems into an explicit framework for governing catch-up under uncertainty.

## Conceptual Novelty: From Developmental State to DNS

The book's most original theoretical move is its elaboration of the DNS. This framework neither rejects the insights of the classical developmental state nor accepts the minimalist prescriptions of market governance. Instead, it synthesizes both within a model of *adaptive, networked governance* that can operate in contexts where bureaucratic capacity is partial, authority is dispersed, and institutional coherence is fragile—the normal conditions of many contemporary latecomers.

The DNS retains the developmental state's emphasis on directionality and strategic coordination, but reinterprets these functions through the logic of networks, feedback, and embedded experimentation. In place of a Weberian bureaucracy, it imagines a learning-oriented state that orchestrates coalitions of ministries, firms, donors, diaspora actors, and civic organizations. In contrast to traditional policy compliance models, it treats governance as a *meta-capability*: the ability of societies to learn, coordinate, and adapt across institutional boundaries.

This conceptual shift is both timely and profound. It links the literature on developmental states with newer streams of thinking in *innovation systems, experimentalist governance, and mission-oriented industrial policy.* By integrating these traditions, Sahiti offers a framework capable of explaining transformation in contexts that are neither fully developmental nor fully neoliberal—the "grey zones" of real-world development where most latecomers now operate.

---

[3] Block, F. (2008), 'Swimming Against the Current: The Rise of a Hidden Developmental State in the United States', Politics & Society, 36 (2), pp. 169–206.

[4] Fred Block & Matthew R. Keller & Marian Negoita (2020) Network Failure and the Evolution of the US Innovation System, Journal of Industry, Competition and Trade, 20:235–247.

## Empirical Novelty: Bringing the Western Balkans into the Development Debate

Equally significant is the book's empirical contribution. Few regions of the world have been as systematically neglected in the comparative literature on development as the *Western Balkans*. Despite their strategic position between the EU and the global periphery, and their experience of post-socialist transition, donor dependency, and EU conditionality, these countries rarely figure in analyses of industrial policy, innovation, or governance capabilities.

Sahiti's research fills this void with a rich and rigorously constructed comparative study of *Kosovo, Albania, and North Macedonia*. Through detailed fieldwork, institutional mapping, and more than thirty stakeholder interviews, the book shows how these economies navigate transformation within tight structural constraints. Each case illustrates a distinct configuration of governance, capability building, and external dependence:

- In *Kosovo*, donor-funded ICT programmes, diaspora mentorship, and local entrepreneurship create dynamic but fragile digital ecosystems.
- In *Albania,* agri-food modernization proceeds through fragmented coordination and selective value-chain upgrading.
- In *North Macedonia*, automotive suppliers are gradually bridging the gap between foreign-led enclaves and the development of domestic capabilities.

These case studies move beyond the familiar dichotomy of success and failure. They reveal the *mechanisms* through which transformation occurs even in low-capacity systems: informal coalitions, learning-by-doing, and feedback loops across donor, public, and private spheres. By treating governance itself as a capability that can evolve through practice, Sahiti brings to life the micro-foundations of catch-up that conventional datasets or policy diagnostics rarely capture.

This is more than a regional contribution. The Western Balkans became a *laboratory for rethinking development in constrained settings,* where limited capacity, high volatility, and external dependence expose the real tensions of governing transformation in the digital age. In this sense, the book places the region within the global comparative debate alongside East Asia, Latin America, and Sub-Saharan Africa, thus enriching the geography of development economics and innovation studies.

## Policy Relevance: A Framework for Action, not just Analysis

Beyond its theoretical and empirical depth, this book stands out for its *policy relevance*. It generates a wealth of insights directly applicable to policymakers, donors, and practitioners grappling with the challenges of industrial transformation in constrained environments.

Sahiti's analytical architecture—built around *feedback loops, experimental spaces, and coordination platforms*—translates directly into actionable tools. It shows how governments can institutionalize learning, link short-term donor programmes with long-term industrial strategies, and mobilize transnational resources such as diaspora networks for capability upgrading.

Rather than prescribing yet another reform template, the book proposes a *learning-by-governing* approach. It recognizes that the central problem in many transition economies is not the absence of strategies but the lack of adaptive mechanisms to adjust and realign them. Its five guiding principles—reflexivity, relational capital, learning infrastructures, strategic anchoring with local flexibility, and activation of polycentric networks—provide a practical compass for reformers seeking to navigate complexity without the illusion of control.

For international organizations, the book offers a constructive critique. It demonstrates how donor-driven alignment with EU or OECD standards, while administratively useful, often produces *formal convergence without functional depth*. Sahiti argues persuasively that development partners should shift from compliance monitoring to *capability mentoring*, helping domestic institutions 'learn to learn' rather than merely adopt procedural templates.

## Bridging Scholarship and Policy Practice

Perhaps the book's most valuable contribution lies in its ability to *bridge analytical rigour with pragmatic realism*. It brings together insights from evolutionary economics, political economy, and policy studies into a coherent framework that speaks to both scholars and practitioners. Its conceptual ambition is matched by a clear recognition of empirical constraint—a rare combination in contemporary development debates.

For researchers, the *DNS* offers a fertile conceptual terrain for comparative studies of adaptive governance. It invites extensions to other regions—Central Asia, the Caucasus, or parts of Africa—where similar combinations of donor dependence, digitalization, and institutional fragmentation prevail. For policymakers, it offers a diagnostic toolkit for assessing where and how capabilities can be strengthened, coordinated, and aligned with strategic missions.

## A Forward-looking Intellectual Contribution

In reinterpreting the developmental state for the digital and ecological age, Sahiti's book makes three lasting contributions. First, it *redefines state capability* from bureaucratic control to collective learning. Second, it *broadens the empirical base* of development theory by bringing the Western Balkans into comparative conversation. Third, it *reclaims industrial policy* as a practical process of orchestration under uncertainty rather than a rigid plan.

These contributions make *Catching Up in the Digital Age* not only an important scholarly achievement but also a guide for those seeking to govern transformation in the absence of ideal conditions. It reminds us that development is never a matter of replication; it is a matter of adaptation.

This book significantly advances our understanding of *industrial policy* by reframing it through the lens of *capabilities and network governance*. Yet, it also opens new and challenging questions for future research. If coordination is itself a *developmental capacity*, how is it created and sustained? What kinds of institutional environments and political incentives encourage actors—ministries, firms, donors, or intermediaries—to share information, pool resources, and collaborate rather than compete or disengage? How do *network coordinators*—the actors who provide direction, convene coalitions, and sustain trust—actually emerge? Are they the result of deliberate strategy and state design, or do they evolve spontaneously through iterative problem-solving? And in whose interest is it to play this coordinating role when short-term political or commercial rewards may be limited?

By raising these questions, the book pushes the debate on industrial and innovation policy beyond traditional state-versus-market dichotomies. It invites scholars and policymakers alike to examine the *political economy of coordination*—the incentives, legitimacy, and institutional conditions that underpin the durability of developmental networks as engines of learning and transformation.

In a nutshell, the book thus stands at the frontier of contemporary development thinking—deeply grounded in theory and empirics and profoundly relevant for policy.

Slavo Radosevic
Professor of Industry and Innovation Studies
University College London

**Acknowledgements** This book is the outcome of sustained engagement with the challenges of structural transformation, capability building, and governance under constraint. It reflects not only years of research but also many dialogues, field encounters, and shared reflections.

Fieldwork across Kosovo, Albania, and North Macedonia was essential to this project. I am deeply grateful to the policymakers, entrepreneurs, donor representatives, educators, and local actors who offered their time and insights. Their openness and generosity brought the abstract language of coordination, learning, and embeddedness into clear and practical focus.

Colleagues across institutions provided valuable critiques that sharpened the analytical clarity of this book. Exchanges in seminars, working groups, and informal conversations played a vital role in refining both argument and structure. I also wish to acknowledge the support of the Visegrad Fund and Jagiellonian University, whose hospitality and intellectual environment enabled focused writing during a crucial phase of the project.

I owe special thanks to my family and friends for their quiet and unwavering support. This book was written across many contexts and seasons, and their presence was the one constant.

The author used AI-assisted tools to support the preparation of this book. These tools were employed under the author's direction for language refinement, stylistic consistency, and the generation of illustrative figures, as noted below each figure. All conceptual content, analytical interpretation, and argumentation are entirely the author's own. The author retains full responsibility for the accuracy, integrity, and originality of the book.

What follows is not a blueprint but a navigational tool. If it provokes reflection or helps others act with greater clarity and purpose, it will have fulfilled its aim. Any errors of judgment or interpretation are mine alone.

**Competing Interests** The author has no competing interests to declare that are relevant to the content of this manuscript.

# Contents

# List of Acronyms and Abbreviations

| | |
|---|---|
| ADB | Asian Development Bank |
| AI | Artificial Intelligence |
| ARISE | Accelerating Research and Innovation in the South-East Europe |
| ASEAN | Association of Southeast Asian Nations |
| B2B | Business-to-Business |
| CEO | Chief Executive Officer |
| CIM | Computer Integrated Manufacturing |
| CSO | Civil Society Organization |
| DNS | Developmental Network State |
| ECA | Europe and Central Asia |
| EIB | European Investment Bank |
| ENP | European Neighbourhood Policy |
| EU | European Union |
| FDI | Foreign Direct Investment |
| GVC | Global Value Chain |
| ICT | Information and Communication Technology |
| ILO | International Labour Organization |
| IMF | International Monetary Fund |
| IPA | Instrument for Pre-Accession Assistance |
| IPR | Intellectual Property Rights |
| IT | Information Technology |
| KIESA | Kosovo Investment and Enterprise Support Agency |
| LED | Local Economic Development |
| MESAP | Multi-Enterprise Sectoral Action Programme |
| MNE | Multinational Enterprises |
| MoU | Memorandum of Understanding |
| NATO | North Atlantic Treaty Organization |
| NGO | Non-Governmental Organization |
| OECD | Organization for Economic Co-operation and Development |
| PPP | Public–Private Partnership |
| R&D | Research and Development |

| | |
|---|---|
| SDG | Sustainable Development Goals |
| SEE | South-Eastern Europe |
| SME | Small and Medium-sized Enterprise |
| STEM | Science, Technology, Engineering, and Mathematics |
| UNDP | United Nations Development Programme |
| UNECE | United Nations Economic Commission for Europe |
| UNESCO | United Nations Educational, Scientific and Cultural Organization |
| UNIDO | United Nations Industrial Development Organization |
| USAID | United States Agency for International Development |
| WB | Western Balkans |
| WTO | World Trade Organization |

# List of Figures

# List of Tables

# Chapter 1
# Introduction

## 1.1 The Paradox of Governing Catch-Up in the Digital Age

Governments across transitional Europe have placed digitalization at the centre of their development strategies. National plans often combine trade liberalization, macroeconomic stabilization, and regulatory convergence with the European Union (EU), alongside donor-supported investments in broadband infrastructure, government technology (GovTech), and start-up ecosystems. For instance, Kosovo's Digital Agenda Observatory outlines a roadmap to position the country as a regional digital hub by 2030 (Open Data Kosovo, 2021). Similarly, the OECD's Western Balkans (WB) Competitiveness Outlook highlights digital transformation as a key lever for closing productivity and infrastructure gaps with advanced EU member states (OECD, 2024).

Despite this focus, implementation remains uneven and fragmented. In capital cities, co-working spaces host start-ups working in artificial intelligence, blockchain, and fintech, supported by donor-backed innovation hubs. Policymakers often promote these initiatives as evidence that digital services can leap over the physical constraints of traditional industrialization. The dominant assumption is that intangible, skill-intensive sectors offer a faster route to development in settings where industrial capacity remains limited.

At the same time, firms operating in industrial zones still rely on outdated equipment, analogue processes, and legacy production systems. Small and medium-sized enterprises (SMEs) face skills mismatches, unreliable infrastructure, and limited access to finance. Donor programmes unfold in short cycles, often disconnected from long-term strategies. While digital initiatives have proliferated, few have scaled or translated into measurable productivity gains. The promise of leapfrogging through technology frequently rests on fragile institutional foundations.



F. Sahiti, *Catching Up in the Digital Age*, Contributions to Economics,
https://doi.org/10.1007/978-3-032-17059-0_1

This disjuncture reveals a deeper paradox in latecomer development. Classical theories of catch-up suggested that, through strategic imitation and access to foreign technologies, countries could close the development gap with advanced economies (Fagerberg et al., 2010; Gerschenkron, 1962). Yet long-term upgrading requires more than access to tools. It depends on institutional and organizational capabilities that allow societies to adapt, learn, and reshape technologies to local conditions (Lall, 1992). In environments marked by weak state capacity and fragmented authority, neither liberal markets nor centralized planning has consistently delivered these capabilities (Stiglitz & Greenwald, 2014).

A comparison of two solar energy projects on the outskirts of Pristina illustrates this point. In one case, a coalition of returnee entrepreneurs, local NGOs, and informal farmer groups pooled remittances to address persistent electricity shortages. They sourced second-hand photovoltaic panels from Germany, held technician workshops, modified inverters to cope with grid instability, and produced bilingual manuals to enable replication. Within 18 months, several neighbouring villages secured stable electricity and signed a micro-grid agreement with the municipality.

By contrast, a larger EU-funded solar initiative in central Pristina stalled. Despite a budget twice as large and a technically sound design, the project failed to adapt to local constraints. Regulatory bottlenecks, grid incompatibilities, and limited stakeholder engagement prevented implementation beyond the planning phase.

The difference between the two efforts was not technical capacity or financial size. It was the mode of governance. The grassroots initiative approached capability formation as a process of embedded learning and collaborative problem-solving. It relied on decentralized coordination and local adaptation. The donor-led project was structured around formal planning and external expertise, assuming that compliance and capital could substitute for situated knowledge.

These contrasting outcomes point to a broader insight. Economic catch-up should be understood as a dynamic process of capability formation, rather than merely the deployment of equipment. Innovation emerges through sustained interactions among firms, users, and institutions. For latecomer economies, effective governing the catching-up process requires institutionalizing mechanisms that facilitate learning, coordination, and adaptation.

A central challenge for many transitional economies lies in steering transformation under conditions of weak bureaucracies, donor dependence, and institutional fragmentation. Both market reforms and hierarchical state planning have proven insufficient. What is required is a governance model that supports decentralized learning, embedded experimentation, and the strategic use of transnational linkages to foster adaptation.

This book addresses this paradox. Catching up in the digital age cannot be achieved by simply replicating existing institutional templates. Instead, it requires the construction of governance systems capable of learning, coordinating, and adapting under conditions of uncertainty and constraint. The framework presented here is not a prescriptive blueprint; rather, it functions as a diagnostic lens for examining how learning, coordination, and embedded engagement interact to produce developmental outcomes in fragmented, low-capacity settings. By focusing on understanding processes rather than applying fixed problem solutions, this approach highlights the critical role of adaptive governance in enabling latecomer economies to navigate complex and dynamic development challenges.

The next section revisits the conceptual foundations of catch-up, exploring how governance, institutional learning, and technology interact in digitally mediated environments.

### *1.1.1 Rethinking Catch-Up in the Digital Age*

In today's digital age, the prospect of catching up with wealthier economies can appear to be only "one click away." Across transitional Europe, governments often view digital technologies as an opportunity to leap ahead—a shortcut that promises to bypass the long, sequential stages of industrialization and accelerate progress toward prosperity. In practice, however, these aspirations frequently collide with structural realities. Latecomer economies continue to struggle with persistent barriers to convergence with advanced economies. Their production systems tend to occupy the lower tiers of global value chains, constraining opportunities for technological upgrading and learning. Without solid foundations such as technical expertise, responsive policy frameworks, and institutions that are both embedded and supportive, digital initiatives seldom advance beyond small-scale pilot projects. They remain isolated experiments, unable to generate system-wide transformation (Andreoni & Chang, 2019; Lee, 2019).

Recent analyses suggest that, far from lowering the barriers to development, digitalization has in fact raised them. Rather than making industrial upgrading easier, it has established a higher threshold for success (Lee, 2024). In the current context, countries require greater capabilities, stronger institutions, and more adaptive forms of governance to transform digital technologies into genuine drivers of development. Catching up is no longer a matter of simply adopting the latest technologies; it depends on cultivating the capabilities, institutional arrangements, and governance systems necessary to sustain progress over time (Lee & Lim, 2001; Fagerberg et al., 2010; UNIDO, 2024).

In this sense, catching up is not simply about acquiring new equipment or software. It involves developing the deeper capabilities that allow societies to absorb new ideas, adapt them to local conditions, and mobilise collective action around them. Real progress depends on institutions that encourage experimentation, support learning from failure, and coordinate the efforts of governments, businesses, schools, and communities. The key test is not whether such institutions exist in theory, but whether they function effectively in practice and help societies learn, adapt, and solve problems together.

At this point, governance emerges as the central concern. Drawing on established definitions, it can be understood as the manner in which state authority is exercised through institutions and processes to manage collective affairs (UNDP, 1997; World Bank, 1994). In this book, governance is defined more specifically as the way societies make and implement decisions, coordinate diverse actors, and adapt to rapid change in pursuit of collective goals. State authority operates not only through laws and regulations, but also through the institutions, administrative systems, and practices that shape these interactions and translate them into action.

Governance, in this sense, is not limited to formal rules or rigid institutional structures. It can be understood as the operating system of development—a meta-capability that enables societies to learn continuously, coordinate diverse actors, and adapt to rapid change (Cimoli et al., 2009; Rodrik, 2010; Sabel & Zeitlin, 2012). Just as an operating system allows different applications to function and interact, governance provides the foundation for experimentation, feedback, and flexibility. In fast-changing and uncertain environments, the factor that most sustains development efforts is the capacity to learn from experience, coordinate across levels of organization, and revise and improve practices over time.

Policies, in turn, can be viewed as the applications that run on this operating system. Their effectiveness depends not only on sound design but also on the capacity of governance systems to implement them, adjust them to changing conditions, and integrate them across sectors. Well-designed policies without strong governance often remain unimplemented, while even modest policies can generate significant impact when supported by governance that encourages experimentation, feedback, and coordination.

This perspective carries important implications. In the digital era, the central question is not which technologies a country adopts, but how those technologies are governed, managed, and adapted. Effective catch-up depends on the ability to identify bottlenecks, adjust strategies in real time, and mobilise knowledge distributed across sectors and institutions. It also requires policies embedded within governance frameworks that promote cross-sector learning, support experimentation, and respond flexibly to emerging challenges.

This book therefore approaches catch-up as a dynamic process of capability building rather than a linear progression toward a single endpoint. Governance is understood as a practical instrument that can enable progress even in weak or fragmented systems. By leveraging transnational linkages, fostering local experimentation, and mobilizing diverse coalitions, societies can gradually develop the technological, organizational, and institutional capacities required to sustain transformation.

These arguments are grounded in empirical evidence rather than abstract theory. Case studies from Kosovo, Albania, and North Macedonia illustrate how meaningful progress can occur even under conditions of limited resources and fragile institutions. In Kosovo, digital entrepreneurs are creating new opportunities within a challenging environment. In Albania, farmers and food producers are experimenting with innovative methods to modernise agriculture. In North Macedonia, suppliers are learning to strengthen their positions within international production networks. Together, these examples demonstrate that economic transformation is achievable, even under constraint, when societies adopt adaptive governance, continuous learning, and deliberate experimentation.

The discussion now turns to a broader perspective on how these challenges intersect with global restructuring and regional transition. Post-socialist legacies, fragmented institutions, and shifting production regimes continue to shape the space for capability development and define the conditions under which development unfolds in the twenty-first century.

## 1.2 Structural Transformation Under Twenty-First Century Constraints

In the previous section, catching up in the digital age was described as a process that depends less on acquiring technology and more on building the capabilities and governance systems that enable societies to use it effectively. To explore this more fully, the discussion now situates the argument within a broader structural context. It examines how global disruptions, regional legacies, and institutional configurations shape the opportunities and constraints that affect efforts to develop the technological, organizational, and governance capabilities needed for structural transformation.

For transitional economies in Europe, these dynamics are influenced by post-socialist reform trajectories, evolving patterns of global production, and widening socio-technical divides. As countries in the region navigate EU accession, donor dependency, and persistent capability gaps, they provide a valuable perspective for rethinking development strategies in the twenty-first century.

### *1.2.1 A Complex Global Landscape*

Globally, the development landscape has grown more complex and volatile. Climate change, inequality, geopolitical instability, and rapid technological change are not isolated trends but interconnected pressures reshaping the very terrain on which development takes place. For latecomer economies, this means that older strategies such as export-led industrialization, institutional imitation, or reliance on donor-driven policy conditionality now yield diminishing returns. The central dilemma becomes: how can societies build competitive capabilities when global value chains and ecological constraints are in constant flux?

### 1.2.2 Climate Change as Constraint

Climate change represents one of the most pressing structural barriers. Economic upgrading remains essential for social development, yet it must now occur within the limits of a shrinking global carbon budget. Historically, structural transformation relied on fossil-fuel-based infrastructure and carbon-intensive expansion. Today, green industrialization is not an option but a necessity.

However, many latecomer economies face major obstacles: high public debt, underdeveloped renewable energy sectors, and weak regulatory systems. According to UNIDO (2024), without targeted support for clean technology diffusion, green skills, and institutional reform, these economies risk becoming locked into obsolete, high-emission growth paths that diverge from climate obligations and EU integration benchmarks. Moreover, climate shocks such as floods, droughts, and heatwaves place additional stress on infrastructure, agriculture, and public services, compounding risks of stagnation and institutional fragility.

### 1.2.3 Inequalities Deepening Under Transition

The legacy of transition-era reforms and rapid technological change has also widened social and spatial inequalities. Many countries dismantled social protections while exposing firms and workers to global competition, often without parallel investments in reskilling or innovation systems.

Digitalization and financial integration have benefitted urban centres, capital-intensive firms, and digitally skilled elites, while large segments of the workforce remain in low-wage, low-skill sectors. The World Inequality Report highlights that income and wealth disparities in Southeastern Europe exceed those of most Western European countries (Alvaredo et al., 2021). These inequalities not only undermine social inclusion but also weaken the political coalitions required to sustain long-term investments in education, innovation, and infrastructure.

### 1.2.4 Geopolitical Instability and Shocks

Geopolitical tensions add further uncertainty to development processes. The war in Ukraine has disrupted supply chains for critical commodities such as wheat, fertilizers, and energy, creating volatility that disproportionately impacts developing economies. Similarly, rivalry between major powers such as the United States and China has shifted trade routes and investment flows, while conflicts in other regions continue to threaten stability.

For latecomer economies, these dynamics complicate the catching-up process by forcing governments to adapt to external shocks while simultaneously attempting domestic capability formation. Adaptive governance frameworks, capable of responding flexibly, coordinating diverse actors, and supporting collective learning, are essential for resilient development (Cimoli et al., 2009; Rodrik, 2010; Sabel & Zeitlin, 2012).

### *1.2.5 Digitalization and Thin Modernization*

Digitalization adds another layer of complexity. It opens opportunities for smaller economies to participate in high-value services and creative industries, but adoption requires more than improved infrastructure. It demands capabilities in data management, platform integration, and organizational learning.

Although broadband access has expanded, many firms still lack the routines and linkages necessary to translate digital access into productivity. As Radosevic (2017) argues, this results in a pattern of "thin modernization," where visible progress in infrastructure coexists with persistent capability deficits. A dual economy often emerges, where donor-funded start-ups and digital-native firms exist alongside a larger industrial base that operates with outdated processes, weak coordination, and limited innovation capacity.

### *1.2.6 Industrial Policy Under Pressure*

These structural pressures have brought industrial policy back into the development debate. In advanced economies, it is increasingly reframed around missions—strategies to steer innovation toward goals such as decarbonization, digital sovereignty, and supply chain resilience (Mazzucato, 2021).

In contrast, industrial policy in latecomer economies often remains fragmented and subordinate to donor agendas. The gap between development ambitions and practical outcomes reflects not only financial and technical deficits but also deeper institutional challenges. As Andreoni and Chang (2019) emphasise, effective industrial policy requires governance capabilities—the ability to align interests, manage conflict, and coordinate across policy domains and timeframes. In the absence of such capabilities, reforms are often undermined by political turnover, bureaucratic competition, and disjointed implementation.

### *1.2.7 Innovation Systems and Fragmentation*

Innovation systems mirror these governance shortcomings. There are now many programs that help new businesses and tech ideas grow, like start-up contests and hackathons. But often, these efforts are not well connected to larger industries or the real economy around them. Public research institutions remain underfunded and poorly linked to global networks. Technology transfer offices frequently lack the resources or mandates to connect science with industry.

The outcome is fragmented excellence without systemic coherence. As the European Innovation Scoreboard shows, countries in the region consistently underperform on indicators such as R&D intensity, university–industry collaboration, and firm-level innovation (European Commission, 2024).

### *1.2.8 A Regional Lens on Global Challenges*

These constraints are not unique to Southeastern Europe. Similar patterns exist across the Global South and post-socialist regions more broadly. What makes Southeastern Europe especially significant is the convergence of EU integration pressures, donor dependency, and fragmented governance. This combination highlights how capability gaps, governance fragility, and external dependencies interact to shape development trajectories.

This book does not treat these conditions as exceptions. Instead, it views them as part of a broader development condition in the twenty-first century. Structural transformation is not simply a question of adopting the right policies or copying institutions. It is a relational and iterative process shaped by how states, firms, and institutions learn, coordinate, and adapt under constraint.

Addressing these challenges requires governance architectures that can absorb feedback, facilitate cooperation, and support cumulative capability-building. For transitional economies, the critical question is not only which policies to adopt, but how to create systems that can learn to govern in real time.

## 1.3 The Capabilities Imperative in a Digital World

The ability of countries to achieve structural transformation increasingly depends on their capacity to develop and mobilise a broad set of capabilities. These are not peripheral to development; they are its foundation (Lall, 1992; Cimoli et al., 2009). Capabilities determine whether economies can adapt to shifting global conditions, absorb new technologies, and generate innovation over time (Teece et al., 1997; Andreoni & Chang, 2019). In today's digital economy—shaped by automation, digital platforms, and the governance of data—the process of building capabilities has grown more intricate and pressing, as societies must continuously learn and adapt to remain competitive. For latecomer economies, capability formation is not simply a precondition for convergence; it constitutes the central mechanism through which convergence unfolds (Mazzucato, 2021).

This book posits four interdependent capabilities (technological, institutional, organizational, and transformative) as the foundations of sustained upgrading.

Collectively, they constitute the analytical framework for the case studies that follow. These categories offer both a conceptual lens for interpreting structural change and a practical tool for diagnosing constraints and identifying viable pathways across diverse sectors and contexts. Whether analysing digital entrepreneurship in Kosovo, agri-food modernization in Albania, or supplier integration in North Macedonia, each case examines how capabilities are built, constrained, and leveraged in practice.

### *1.3.1 Technological Capabilities*

Technological capabilities refer to the knowledge, skills, infrastructure, and systems that enable firms and economies to absorb, adapt, and eventually create new technologies. They are the foundation of productivity growth and innovation. Such capabilities emerge through cumulative investments in education, research and development (R&D), technical training, and learning by doing. As Lall (1992) and Bell and Pavitt (1993) argue, they do not arise automatically through trade or foreign investment but must be deliberately cultivated through targeted policy interventions and institutional support.

In many transitional contexts, technological capabilities remain shallow and uneven. Firms frequently operate with outdated equipment, face shortages of skilled labour, and lack access to applied research. Weak innovation networks and fragmented supply chains further constrain their ability to move into higher-value segments of global markets. Strengthening technological capabilities is therefore critical to escaping low-productivity traps and embedding innovation more deeply within national development strategies.

### *1.3.2 Institutional Capabilities*

Institutional capabilities refer to the rules, routines, and coordination mechanisms embedded in public agencies and policy networks that enable stability and coherence in governance. This includes coherence among ministries, integration between education and innovation systems, and the use of feedback mechanisms to revise strategies. Institutional capabilities are especially important for navigating the transitions associated with climate change, digitalization, and geopolitical volatility.

As Evans (1995), Chang (2002), and Rodrik (2008) note, institutional quality is not defined by formal rules alone but by learning processes, adaptive capacity, and institutional memory. In many latecomer economies, institutions are shaped by donor templates and external benchmarks, leading to formal convergence without functional depth. Strengthening institutional capabilities thus requires building learning-oriented cultures, flexible routines, and durable coalitions capable of sustaining long-term coordination.

### 1.3.3 Organizational Capabilities

Organizational capabilities refer to the internal systems, routines, and learning processes within firms, agencies, and intermediary organizations that allow them to adapt, coordinate, and improve performance over time. These capabilities underpin quality upgrading, process innovation, and strategic coordination across networks.

Drawing on evolutionary theories of the firm (Nelson & Winter, 1982; Teece et al., 1997), organizational capabilities are cumulative and context-specific. They depend on tacit knowledge, trial-and-error learning, and the ability to manage complexity. In many transitional economies, SMEs lack the managerial depth and technical expertise needed to sustain upgrading. Building organizational capabilities therefore requires investment in managerial and technical training, support for collective learning, and the creation of coordination platforms such as business associations and industrial clusters.

### 1.3.4 Transformative Capabilities

Transformative capabilities represent higher-order capacities to reconfigure existing institutions and networks, enabling experimentation, cross-sectoral learning, and systemic adaptation. They involve not merely reacting to external pressures but actively steering institutional and technological transitions toward inclusive and sustainable outcomes.

This concept draws on the work of Sen (1999) and Appadurai (2004), as well as on mission-oriented innovation approaches (Mazzucato, 2021). Transformation depends on governance systems capable of organizing shared visions, enabling experimentation, and coordinating action across domains. In many latecomer contexts, public discourse invokes transformation, but implementation remains fragmented and short-term. Strengthening transformative capabilities thus entails developing governance architectures that align policy agendas with long-term commitments, foster inclusive participation, and enable societies to learn and adapt collectively over time.

These four dimensions—technological, institutional, organizational, and transformative—constitute the capabilities imperative in the digital age. They highlight that successful development is not a linear sequence of reforms or technology transfers but a cumulative, learning-based process of building systems that can adapt, coordinate, and innovate in response to shifting challenges and opportunities.

### *1.3.5 Interdependent Capabilities and the Systemic Logic of Catch-Up*

The four capabilities discussed above are deeply interdependent. Their significance lies not only in their individual functions but also in how they reinforce and enable one another. Structural transformation depends on the alignment of these capabilities across institutions, firms, and policy domains. When one capability lags behind, it can constrain the performance of the others and weaken the system as a whole.

Figure 1.1 illustrates this interdependence by showing how weaknesses in one domain, such as skills, finance, or coordination, can undermine performance across

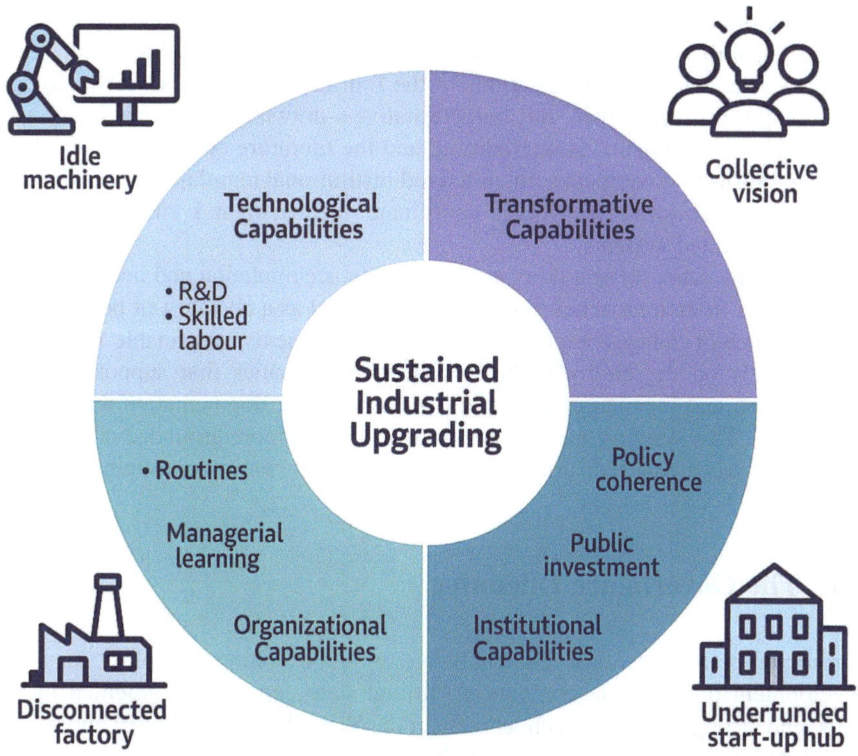


**Fig. 1.1** Capabilities and constraints in industrial upgrading. *Note* The diagram visualises four mutually reinforcing capability domains: technological, institutional, organizational, and transformative. Each contributes to sustained industrial upgrading. Arrows indicate reciprocal relationships, while icons around the circle highlight typical failure points that arise when capabilities are misaligned or absent. The model emphasises the need for systemic coordination and continuous learning across all domains to prevent fragmentation and enable long-term transformation. *Source* Author's elaboration, generated with DALL · E using Microsoft Copilot (2025)

the system. For example, advanced technologies may remain underutilized without sufficient organizational capacity to manage them, while ambitious national strategies may fail in the absence of institutional mechanisms for implementation and feedback.

When capabilities evolve in isolation, they tend to reproduce fragmentation rather than enable upgrading. Catch-up, in this framework, is not a linear progression through predefined stages but a dynamic process of building and aligning multiple capabilities in response to structural constraints and shifting global pressures.

This book positions these interdependent capabilities as the central analytical lens for understanding catch-up in the digital era. The chapters that follow apply this framework to three sectoral case studies drawn from transitional economies: Kosovo's ICT sector, Albania's agri-food processing industry, and North Macedonia's automotive supply base. Each case examines how different combinations of capability strengths and weaknesses shape distinctive trajectories of upgrading under constraint.

The capability lens also structures the organization of the book. Chapter 2 elaborates the conceptual foundations of the four capability types—technological, institutional, organizational, and transformative—drawing on innovation systems theory, the developmental state tradition, and the literature on economic catch-up. Chapter 3 turns to governance, not as a fixed institutional template but as a dynamic capacity to orchestrate networks, coordinate feedback, and enable adaptation across fragmented systems.

By framing catch-up as a process of capability accumulation and interaction, this book departs from approaches that treat development as a checklist of best practices or a sequence of policy compliance. In latecomer contexts, sustainable transformation depends on the ability to build collective capacities that support learning, coordination, and innovation in the face of institutional fragmentation and external uncertainty. This systems-oriented perspective offers a more grounded and adaptive strategy for advancing industrial upgrading under 21st-century constraints.

## 1.4 The Governance Dilemma

Latecomer economies face the challenge of coordinating complex, long-term development processes in contexts of limited state capacity, fragmented institutions, and strong external dependencies. In the WB, alignment with EU norms and the adoption of donor-driven reforms have not translated into effective developmental governance. This section explains why conventional governance models often fail under such conditions and identifies alternative principles better suited to steering structural transformation when ideal institutional environments are absent.

In the digital age, technologies evolve rapidly, and production is increasingly organized through platforms and data infrastructures. Effective governance therefore requires faster feedback loops, openness to experimentation, and the ability to manage complexity without relying on rigid hierarchies. Governance can no longer be confined to formal bureaucracies; it must extend across digital systems, multi-actor networks, and flexible coalitions of public, private, and civic actors.

### *1.4.1 The Challenge of Uncertainty, Complexity, and Partial Capacity*

Structural transformation depends on coordinated action across sectors, sustained investment in technology, and continuous learning through experimentation (UN DESA, 2018). In settings where public agencies lack autonomy and coordination mechanisms are weak, neither markets nor hierarchies generate the feedback and risk-sharing systems needed for upgrading (Evans, 1995; UNESCAP, 2023). Political mandates and funding cycles are short, while development processes unfold over decades. Governments struggle to align innovation, education, and industrial policies, creating a persistent mismatch between long-term goals and short-term institutional rhythms.

These challenges are particularly acute in latecomer economies, where hybrid institutional arrangements combine formal and informal rules, weak bureaucratic capacity, and overlapping authorities. Formal mandates coexist with informal practices, while accountability mechanisms remain inconsistently applied. Donor-led reforms often emphasise procedural alignment with external standards rather than building domestic problem-solving capacity. Strategic coherence is frequently traded for administrative compliance, and learning occurs sporadically rather than systematically. This reactive governance culture struggles to manage complexity or sustain long-term developmental coalitions.

### *1.4.2 Limits of Market-Based Coordination*

Market-oriented governance relies on competition and openness to drive innovation and structural change. In theory, market signals reward efficiency and allocate resources effectively. In practice, many latecomer economies lack the institutional and infrastructural foundations for markets to foster long-term capability development.

Without public mechanisms for risk-sharing, research and development support, or collaboration among firms, universities, and suppliers, private actors tend to underinvest in foundational capabilities (Rodrik, 2008; Chang, 2002). Productivity gaps in emerging economies often stem less from capital scarcity than from misallocation and coordination failures (Hsieh & Klenow, 2010). Markets alone cannot address these failures. In contexts characterized by weak capital markets, skills mismatches, and limited technological ecosystems, strategic foresight remains constrained. Capability building requires targeted coordination and policy instruments designed to overcome structural and informational barriers.

### *1.4.3 Limits of Hierarchical Planning*

Developmental state models historically relied on strong bureaucracies and centralized leadership to coordinate investment and policy. This approach proved effective in several East Asian economies, where public agencies combined autonomy with deep engagement in productive networks (Evans, 1995; Johnson, 1982).

In donor-dependent and politically fragmented contexts, however, hierarchical planning faces serious constraints. In Southeast Europe, for instance, EU accession frameworks have promoted legal harmonization and alignment with the acquis communautaire. Yet formal compliance often outpaces implementation capacity. Policy models imported from high-capacity contexts may be technically sound, but without political ownership, inter-ministerial coordination, or sustained funding, they fail to achieve operational traction.

Moreover, the absence of embedded feedback systems prevents adaptation when reforms fall short. Planning becomes rigid rather than responsive, and strategies stagnate instead of evolving. In such environments, hierarchical governance can produce formal convergence without building functional capability.

### *1.4.4 Principles of Adaptive, Networked, and Experimentalist Governance*

The limits of both market and hierarchical models are magnified by the speed and complexity of digital transformation. Traditional governance architectures cannot easily manage the uncertainty and decentralization that define platform-based and data-driven economies. These evolving conditions have renewed interest in governance approaches that emphasise iterative learning, adaptability, and collaborative problem-solving across distributed networks of actors.

Emerging frameworks of adaptive, networked, and experimentalist governance are built on decentralized learning, continuous feedback, and iterative review (Ostrom, 2005; Sabel & Zeitlin, 2012). Four principles are particularly relevant.

First, anticipatory scanning and foresight enable governments to identify emerging risks and capability gaps early, allowing for pre-emptive intervention (UNESCAP, 2023). Second, agile decision-making gives local actors room to experiment with context-specific solutions, assess results in real time, and adjust policies accordingly (Hatfield-Dodds et al., 2007). Third, distributed authority allows public agencies, firms, universities, donors, and diaspora networks to share responsibility, reduce risk, and accelerate collective learning (Sabel & Zeitlin, 2012). Fourth, embedded experimentation links formal institutions with informal networks, enabling successful practices to diffuse through voluntary adoption and peer recognition (Mazzucato, 2021; Andreoni & Chang, 2019).

Adaptive governance treats policies as working hypotheses that evolve through implementation. It aligns with mission-oriented strategies that mobilise actors around shared challenges, such as decarbonization or digital upgrading, while accommodating local experimentation and feedback. Rather than serving as a blueprint, it represents a practice of continuous reflection, coordination, and adaptation.

### *1.4.5 Implications for Latecomer Economies*

For latecomer economies in latecomer economies, networked governance offers a pragmatic approach to overcoming structural constraints. By treating governance as a capability to be developed, these states can move beyond compliance checklists and rigid institutional templates. They can instead cultivate routines, trust-based coalitions, and feedback mechanisms that support coordinated upgrading under constraint.

Experience from donor-supported industrial clusters in the region shows that when local governments, SMEs, and diaspora actors co-design and co-finance initiatives, learning accelerates and ownership deepens (Sabel & Zeitlin, 2012). Institutionalizing such practices, however, is a gradual process. It requires tolerance for failure, mechanisms for scaling success, and institutional memory to retain lessons over time.

Without these enabling conditions, adaptive governance risks becoming a rhetorical label. The challenge is to embed learning, sustain dialogue among fragmented actors, and maintain momentum despite political volatility.

The following chapters build on this analysis. Chapter 2 deepens the capability-based framework introduced earlier, while Chap. 3 presents a model of networked governance suited to constrained environments. It outlines how structural transformation can be governed through iterative learning, distributed coordination, and collaborative experimentation, even when formal state capacity is weak or fragmented.

## 1.5 The Developmental Network State and Digital-Era Catch-Up

In latecomer economies marked by institutional fragmentation and external dependency, conventional development models have struggled to generate sustained structural transformation. Market-based strategies emphasise openness and competition, while hierarchical planning depends on centralized coordination and bureaucratic control. In environments where capabilities are uneven and coordination failures systemic, both approaches have produced limited results.

This book introduces an alternative governance model, the *Developmental Network State* (DNS). It serves as both a metaphor and an analytical framework for reimagining how structural transformation can be governed under constraint. Rather than functioning as a commanding authority or a passive facilitator, the DNS positions the state as a strategic orchestrator embedded within a web of actors: public agencies, private firms, universities, civil society organizations, and transnational partners such as donors and diaspora networks. Within this networked configuration, learning, coordination, and feedback can emerge even where formal institutional capacity remains limited.

The conceptual foundations of this approach are deeply influenced by Karl Popper's philosophy of *piecemeal social engineering*. Writing in *The Open Society and Its Enemies* (Popper, 1945 (2002), p. 158), Popper argued that meaningful progress in complex societies cannot be achieved through utopian design but through incremental reform guided by continuous learning and critical self-correction. His rejection of grand, deterministic planning in favour of adaptive experimentation provides a philosophical anchor for the DNS perspective. The framework developed in this book builds on that logic: it views development not as the implementation of fixed blueprints, but as a process of discovery shaped by feedback, coordination, and institutional learning. In this sense, the DNS translates Popper's epistemology of open, adaptive systems into the political economy of late development, offering a model of governance that learns and evolves under constraint.

### *1.5.1 Rethinking Governance from Blueprint to Orchestra*

Governance models frequently draw on metaphors to render complex systems intelligible. The blueprint metaphor portrays development as a pre-designed sequence executed through hierarchical, top-down planning (Evans, 1995; Amsden, 2001). In contrast, the market metaphor conceives development as an emergent outcome of decentralized decision-making and competitive dynamics (Hayek, 1945; Rodrik, 2008). Both perspectives, however, rest on the assumption of stable conditions and robust institutional frameworks.

The DNS instead draws on the orchestra metaphor. Here, the state is neither a soloist acting in isolation nor a composer dictating every note, but a conductor who coordinates diverse actors—ministries and public agencies, private firms, educational institutions, civil society organizations, and transnational partners such as donors and diaspora networks—to perform in concert toward shared developmental objectives. Each actor brings distinct capabilities, and the state's task is to ensure coordination and coherence without suppressing diversity. This metaphor captures the essence of adaptive governance: development as an interactive process of experimentation, learning, and adjustment across institutional boundaries.

The orchestral model is especially relevant in contexts where no single actor possesses the authority or resources to lead transformation alone. It enables the mobilization of distributed capabilities and fosters responsiveness to evolving technological and political conditions.

### *1.5.2 Beyond Markets-Only and Plans-Only Approaches*

Market-centred governance assumes that once distortions are removed, firms will naturally upgrade through competition. In reality, however, foundational capabilities such as research and development, quality certification, and skills formation seldom emerge through market incentives alone. Without mechanisms for risk-sharing and coordination, private actors underinvest in innovation and long-term learning (Stiglitz & Greenwald, 2014; Andreoni, 2020). In many latecomer economies, competition fragments rather than consolidates collective capabilities.

Hierarchical planning, by contrast, assumes that the state can steer development through strategic vision and central control. While this model succeeded in several high-capacity East Asian economies (Johnson, 1982), it has proven difficult to replicate in fragmented or donor-dependent settings. Plans that appear coherent on paper often fail due to weak implementation, limited political commitment, and the absence of adaptive feedback mechanisms (Mahoney & Thelen, 2010).

The DNS does not reject either model. It seeks instead to recombine their strengths. It retains the dynamism of markets and the strategic orientation of planning, embedding them within adaptive governance systems that mobilise collective intelligence, coordinate across institutions, and respond flexibly to changing realities.

### *1.5.3 Core Components of the Developmental Network State*

The DNS is grounded in three interrelated governance functions: learning, coordination, and embeddedness. Each plays a distinct yet complementary role in enabling development under conditions of uncertainty and limited capacity.

Learning treats policy not as a fixed prescription but as a working hypothesis that must be tested, revised, and refined through ongoing feedback. This requires mechanisms such as pilot programmes, monitoring platforms, and participatory review processes that enable continuous adaptation and adjustment. Through learning, governance becomes an iterative process of experimentation and evidence-based revision rather than compliance with static models.

Coordination involves aligning the efforts of ministries, firms, training institutions, civil society and transnational actors (donors and diaspora) around shared developmental objectives. Effective coordination ensures that public investment supports firm-level upgrading and that education and innovation systems are linked to industrial strategies. It establishes coherence across policy domains and creates a framework through which dispersed actors can collectively pursue long-term transformation.

Embeddedness refers to grounding governance within real-world relationships and social networks. It entails building trust among public and private actors, drawing on diaspora expertise, and ensuring that donor-supported initiatives are adapted to domestic needs and priorities. Embeddedness provides the relational foundation for collaboration, legitimacy, and the sustained exchange of knowledge across institutional boundaries.

These three functions constitute the operational core of the DNS. They enable governance systems to coordinate collective action, learn from experience, and remain connected to the social and economic realities they aim to transform (Fig. 1.2).

To operationalise these pillars, DNS governance relies on three mechanisms: feedback loops, experimental spaces, and coordination platforms.

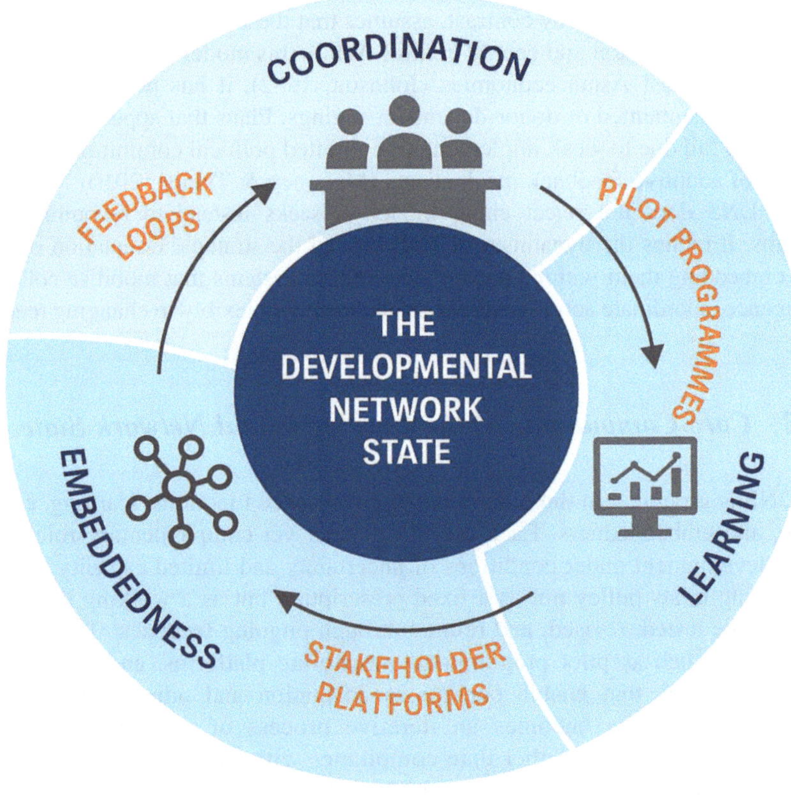


**Fig. 1.2** Interdependent Capabilities and Systemic Constraints in Industrial Upgrading. The developmental network state: pillars and mechanisms. *Source* Author's elaboration, generated with DALL · E using Microsoft Copilot (2025)

#### 1.5.3.1 Feedback Loops

Adaptive governance depends on continuous learning. Feedback loops—implemented through dashboards, monitoring systems, and stakeholder forums—allow policies to be adjusted in real time. Sectoral scorecards can track innovation adoption, skills mismatches, or productivity shifts. Regular review forums involving government agencies, firms, training centres, and donors can generate shared diagnostics and co-create corrective strategies.

Digital platforms that connect firms to technical advisory services or capture user feedback on training outcomes further accelerate information flows. These mechanisms transform governance from periodic evaluation into continuous problem-solving.

#### 1.5.3.2 Experimental Spaces

Transformation requires room to experiment. Pilot programmes, innovation labs, and regulatory sandboxes allow actors to test new policies, technologies, or business models in controlled conditions. In digital sectors, such spaces have facilitated experimentation in areas such as platform regulation and artificial intelligence. Mission-oriented funding schemes can support collaborative responses to challenges such as green industrialization or workforce reskilling.

The objective is not perfection but learning. Experimental spaces de-risk innovation, generate evidence, and institutionalise flexibility in governance routines.

#### 1.5.3.3 Coordination Mechanisms

Effective transformation also requires orchestration. Coordination platforms—public-private councils, regional innovation boards, or diaspora advisory groups—connect fragmented actors and align their actions. Inter-ministerial task forces can synchronise strategies across domains such as skills, energy, and industry, while diaspora networks can link domestic firms to global knowledge and markets.

Rather than relying on formal mandates, these platforms cultivate relational trust and ensure consistency of purpose across institutions and time horizons.

### *1.5.4 Building Governance as a Dynamic Capability*

The DNS views governance not as a fixed structure but as a dynamic capability that must be cultivated through practice. This involves developing reflexivity—the ability to question routines and revise them—and building relational trust among diverse actors.

Relational capital plays a critical role. When officials, business leaders, researchers, and donors share a common language and a history of collaboration, coordination becomes more effective. Learning infrastructures such as policy labs, data dashboards, and secondment schemes help circulate knowledge across sectors and institutions.

What distinguishes the DNS is not a rigid blueprint but a learning orientation. It recognises that capability development is uncertain and iterative, requiring institutions that can listen, adapt, and evolve over time.

Chapter 3 develops the DNS framework in greater depth, tracing its intellectual lineage within developmental state theory, innovation systems, and network governance. It elaborates the three core mechanisms—feedback, experimentation, and coordination—and specifies the enabling conditions under which these mechanisms foster technological and institutional upgrading.

The sectoral case studies that follow illustrate how the DNS operates in practice across diverse settings. In Kosovo's ICT sector, diaspora mentorship, municipal councils, and donor-funded bootcamps have stimulated digital entrepreneurship and enhanced the local skills base. In Albania's agri-food industry, value chain committees, certification schemes, and regional innovation hubs have strengthened product diversification and compliance with international standards. In North Macedonia's automotive cluster, inter-firm learning, supplier development programmes, and cross-sectoral councils have helped firms escape capability traps and integrate more effectively into global production networks.

These cases demonstrate how adaptive and networked governance can facilitate upgrading even in environments of limited capacity, institutional fragmentation, and external dependency. They provide an empirical foundation for assessing how the DNS framework enables coordination, learning, and experimentation under real-world conditions.

## 1.6 Research Agenda and Contributions

This study investigates the role of governance in fostering economic catch-up and structural transformation in latecomer economies characterized by institutional fragmentation, limited state capacity, and extensive external dependence. Rather than treating governance as a static institutional backdrop, the book conceptualizes it as a dynamic capability that facilitates learning, coordination, and adaptation in contexts where conventional models often prove inadequate. The research agenda delineates the central questions, identifies key gaps in the literature, clarifies the study's principal contributions, and links the conceptual framework to the overall structure of the volume.

### 1.6.1 Principal Research Questions

The analysis centres on four interrelated questions that collectively address the challenge of governing transformation under conditions of constraint and digital disruption. The first concerns how governance systems in donor-dependent, post-socialist contexts shape the development of technological, organizational, institutional, and transformative capabilities. This question is explored through the sectoral case studies presented in Chaps. 5 to 7, which examine how learning is orchestrated through coalitions, digital tools, and policy mechanisms.

The second question asks what conditions enable or hinder coordination, learning, and institutional adaptation in settings characterized by low administrative capacity and misaligned external incentives. This issue is analysed through pilot initiatives, cross-sectoral experimentation, and feedback loops, themes that are elaborated in Chaps. 8 to 10.

The third question investigates which governance functions support sustained upgrading in polycentric environments where authority is dispersed and bureaucratic autonomy is limited. This aspect is addressed through an assessment of decentralized orchestration and adaptive coalitions, offering comparative insights in Chaps. 11 and 12.

The fourth question examines how digital instruments such as dashboards, data platforms, and regulatory sandboxes can be integrated into governance frameworks to accelerate capability formation. This theme recurs throughout the book, with particular emphasis in Chap. 4 and in the Kosovo ICT case. Together, these questions structure an inquiry into the governance of transformation in systems characterized by constraint, fragmentation, and rapid change.

### 1.6.2 Gaps in the Literature

A substantial body of literature addresses the intersections of governance, innovation, and development, yet significant blind spots persist regarding capability formation in fragmented and donor-saturated contexts. The developmental state tradition elucidates how late-industrializing countries coordinated structural transformation, but its central assumptions of cohesive bureaucracies and embedded state–business relations seldom hold in the WB. The innovation systems literature explains how firms, states, and research institutions generate and diffuse knowledge, yet it gives limited consideration to the distortions produced by fragmented donor ecosystems, institutional voids, and entrenched power asymmetries. Research on networked governance and complexity emphasizes decentralized learning and experimentalist approaches, but it provides little guidance for environments characterized by weak trust, low administrative capacity, and volatile political conditions. Moreover, there is a scarcity of empirically grounded studies that conceptualize governance as a capability in its own right, while the roles of diaspora networks, hybrid coalitions, and informal institutions in small, externally constrained economies remain insufficiently explored.

### 1.6.3 Key Contributions of the Book

The book makes five interrelated contributions to debates on development, governance, and capabilities in transitional contexts. First, it reconceptualizes governance as a capability that enables coordination, learning, and adaptation, shifting analytical attention to the mechanisms through which actors address problems under constraint. Second, it bridges theoretical traditions by integrating insights from the developmental state, innovation systems, and network governance literatures, thereby offering a more comprehensive account of transformation in donor-dependent and low-capacity environments. Third, it operationalizes adaptive governance through three practical functions that underpin capability formation in fragmented systems: feedback loops, experimental spaces, and coordination platforms. Fourth, it reintroduces political economy into capability debates by highlighting the roles of external conditionalities, institutional fragmentation, and path dependence. Finally, it grounds the framework in comparative case studies of Kosovo's ICT sector, Albania's agri-food industry, and North Macedonia's automotive suppliers, demonstrating that transformation can emerge even where formal institutions are weak. Collectively, these contributions converge in the DNS framework.

### 1.6.4 Guiding Principles for Governing Catch-Up in the Twenty-First Century

Catch-up in the digital era is inherently non-linear. It entails navigating uncertainty, institutional gaps, and global pressures. The book advances five guiding principles. First, governance should institutionalize reflexivity through feedback mechanisms that facilitate real-time learning, such as policy labs, digital dashboards, and pilot initiatives. Second, it should cultivate relational capital to sustain cross-sectoral collaboration through transparent incentives, shared ownership, and repeated engagement, particularly in contexts where formal credibility is limited. Third, governance should embed learning infrastructures by using monitoring for problem-solving rather than compliance, thereby enabling cumulative learning over time. Fourth, it should combine strategic anchoring with local flexibility, aligning national priorities with the discretion required for context-sensitive implementation. Fifth, governance should leverage polycentric networks by activating municipal authorities, sectoral organizations, diaspora groups, and donor coalitions as interconnected nodes in a broader system of learning and innovation. Collectively, these principles signify a shift from static reform templates toward dynamic capability building and constitute the foundation of the DNS framework developed in this book.

## 1.7 Methodological Compass

The study employs a comparative case study approach to examine how governance systems in donor-dependent, latecomer economies influence industrial upgrading and capability development. Curated secondary datasets are integrated with targeted stakeholder interviews. WB cases are benchmarked against selected EU and Baltic economies to generate context-sensitive insights into how capabilities evolve under constraint rather than to prescribe best practices.

### *1.7.1 Research Design*

The study adopts a multiple-case comparative design to analyse governance and capability development under constraint. Kosovo, Albania, and North Macedonia are selected for their shared post-socialist legacies, extensive donor involvement, and ongoing EU integration trajectories, yet they differ in governance performance and institutional reform outcomes. The Baltic states serve as benchmark cases, offering useful contrasts due to comparable starting conditions and relatively successful transitions. Additionally, EU-15 averages provide a broader baseline for contextualizing performance across dimensions such as innovation, workforce development, and regulatory capacity.

This design enables both in-depth within-case analysis and cross-case comparison, balancing empirical specificity with the potential for cautious generalization about governance dynamics in resource-constrained and institutionally fragmented settings.

### *1.7.2 Case Selection and Benchmarking*

The WB cases were chosen purposively for theoretical relevance. All are small transitional economies that pursued liberalization and EU alignment yet continue to face persistent capability gaps. Despite broadly similar structural conditions, governance outcomes diverge, which makes these cases analytically valuable for tracing variation in institutional performance. Baltic countries provide contrasts that highlight the roles of strategic coordination and learning. The benchmarking exercise is used to reveal where and why particular institutional configurations succeed or falter, not to extract policy blueprints.

### 1.7.3 Data Sources

The analysis draws on quantitative and qualitative evidence. Quantitative data were compiled from national enterprise and labour force surveys, Eurostat indicators on regional innovation and competitiveness for 2023, World Bank Development Indicators and Doing Business reports for 2022, UNIDO Industrial Development Reports for 2024, and OECD science, technology, and innovation scoreboards. These datasets capture trends in productivity, research and development intensity, training, and governance quality. Data harmonization followed international cross-country research protocols, with gaps addressed through interpolation and triangulation. Qualitative data were collected through semi-structured interviews with more than thirty stakeholders across selected cases, including representatives of ICT firms, agri-food processors, automotive suppliers, chambers of commerce, donor agencies, innovation intermediaries, and relevant ministries. Interviews examined implementation dynamics, coordination, digital infrastructure, and learning processes. Thematic coding and anonymization ensured confidentiality and analytical consistency.

### 1.7.4 Analytical Procedures

The analysis proceeds in two stages. The first stage conducts within-case tracing of how governance interventions, such as industrial strategies, skills programmes, or innovation initiatives, relate to observed changes in technological, organizational, and institutional capabilities. Documentary analysis of strategies and donor reports is combined with interview evidence to assess intent, execution, and outcomes. The second stage undertakes cross-case benchmarking that compares the WB cases with Estonia, Latvia, and EU-15 baselines. Visual tools, including radar charts, heat maps, and cluster analyses, are used to depict disparities in capability performance and to identify performance cohorts and governance traits associated with more successful upgrading. Qualitative insights inform interpretation of informal practices, such as diaspora engagement or donor coordination platforms, that shape observed outcomes.

### *1.7.5 Validity, Reliability, and Reflexivity*

Construct validity is strengthened by triangulating quantitative indicators, documentary evidence, and interview narratives. Internal validity is supported through process tracing that links interventions to capability changes. Reliability is addressed through transparent documentation of coding procedures, data sources, and analytical steps. Reflexivity is incorporated by acknowledging the limits of available data and of interview-based evidence. Many governance functions, for example informal learning, networked coordination, and political negotiation, are not fully captured by standard indicators. Where formal data are insufficient, qualitative insights guide interpretation of how governance operates in practice.

### *1.7.6 Limitations*

Several limitations remain. Aggregate national indicators can obscure subnational variation and sector-specific dynamics, which is why sectoral case studies are employed to recover granularity. Time-series gaps and differences in indicator definitions complicate longitudinal analysis; harmonized variables and qualitative triangulation are used to mitigate these concerns. Benchmarking risks overgeneralization: structural and institutional differences are carefully contextualized to avoid misplaced comparisons. Elite interviews provide critical insights yet are susceptible to bias; triangulation with policy documentation, donor evaluations, and performance data helps to correct for this. These methodological choices support the broader objective of understanding how transformation can be governed in contexts of fragmentation, constraint, and rapid technological change.

## 1.8 Roadmap of the Book

The book advances the argument that catching up in the digital age depends on governance systems capable of building and aligning technological, organizational, institutional, and transformative capabilities. The structure moves from theoretical foundations to sectoral case studies, comparative synthesis, and policy directions.

The Introduction presents the developmental puzzle of formal convergence without structural transformation in transitional Europe. It introduces the DNS as a governance framework suited to contexts of donor dependence and institutional fragmentation and outlines the research questions, methodological design, and chapter structure.

Part I: Theoretical Foundations develops the conceptual scaffolding. Chapter 2 reframes development as cumulative capability formation and introduces the four interdependent capability domains. Chapter 3 analyses the governance dilemma in latecomer settings, explaining why market-based and hierarchical models perform poorly in fragmented environments. Chapter 4 sets out the DNS framework, specifies three core governance functions of coordination, learning, and embeddedness, and presents operational tools such as feedback loops, pilot initiatives, and coordination platforms.

Part II: Sectoral Case Studies in Transitional Europe applies the framework. Chapter 5 examines Kosovo's ICT sector, where digital skills programmes, donor initiatives, and diaspora networks have generated rich feedback but remain institutionally fragile. Chapter 6 analyses Albania's agri-food sector, tracing local coordination efforts, donor interventions, and selective value chain upgrading that often proceed without systemic learning. Chapter 7 studies North Macedonia's automotive components industry, showing how export-oriented foreign investment has created enclaves and how supplier development and inter-firm coordination are beginning to bridge capability gaps.

Part III: Synthesis and Emerging Challenges draws cross-cutting insights and addresses new governance challenges. Chapter 8 synthesises patterns across the cases, highlighting institutional bricolage, fragmented learning systems, and the emergence of experimental practices. Chapter 9 examines how digitalization and artificial intelligence reshape upgrading possibilities, arguing that digital tools require adaptive governance rather than regulation alone and that iterative learning, institutional responsiveness, and coordinated investment are essential for inclusive upgrading. Chapter 10 considers the future of industrial policy under technological, ecological, and geopolitical disruption, calling for a shift from reactive reform to adaptive industrial policy grounded in the DNS.

Part IV: Conclusion and Policy Directions consolidate the theoretical and empirical contributions. Chapter 11 revisits the DNS within development theory and offers a governance model that combines institutional learning, coordination, and capability building under uncertainty. Chapter 12 outlines strategic policy recommendations and advances five principles that guide transformation in low-capacity, donor-dependent states: institutional reflexivity, relational capital, embedded learning infrastructures, strategic anchoring with local flexibility, and the activation of polycentric networks. The book concludes that industrial catch-up is not a product of best-practice templates. It is a process of cumulative learning and coordination across fragmented systems, for which the DNS provides a realistic and adaptive governance framework.

## References


Alvaredo, F., Chancel, L., Piketty, T., Saez, E., & Zucman, G. (2021). *World inequality report 2022*. Paris: World Inequality Lab. Available at: https://wir2022.wid.world/. Accessed July 14, 2025.

Amsden, A. H. (2001). *The rise of 'The Rest': Challenges to the west from late-industrializing economies*. Oxford University Press.

Andreoni, A. (2020). Technical change, the shifting 'terrain of the industrial', and digital industrial policy. In A. Oqubay, C. Cramer, H. J. Chang, & R. Kozul-Wright (Eds.), *The Oxford handbook of industrial policy*. Oxford University Press. https://doi.org/10.1093/oxfordhb/9780198862420.013.15

Andreoni, A., & Chang, H.-J. (2019). The political economy of industrial policy: Structural interdependencies, policy alignment and conflict management. *Structural Change and Economic Dynamics*, *48*, 136–150. https://doi.org/10.1016/j.strueco.2018.10.007

Appadurai, A. (2004). The capacity to Aspire: Culture and the terms of reconition. In V. Rao & M. Walton (Eds.), *Culture and Public Action* (pp. 59–84). Stanford University Press.

Bell, M., & Pavitt, K. (1993). Technological accumulation and industrial growth: Contrasts between developed and developing countries. *Industrial and Corporate Change*, *2*(2), 157–210. https://doi.org/10.1093/icc/2.2.157

Chang, H.-J. (2002). *Kicking away the ladder: Development strategy in historical perspective*. London: Anthem Press. https://anthempress.com/kicking-away-the-ladder-pdf. Accessed July 14, 2025.

Cimoli, M., Dosi, G., & Stiglitz, J. E. (2009). *Industrial policy and development: The political economy of capabilities accumulation*. Oxford University Press. https://doi.org/10.1093/acprof:oso/9780199235261.001.0001

European Commission. (2024). *European innovation scoreboard 2024*. Brussels: Publications Office of the European Union. Available at: https://research-and-innovation.ec.europa.eu/statistics/performance-indicators/european-innovation-scoreboard_en. Accessed July 14, 2025.

Evans, P. (1995). *Embedded autonomy: States and industrial transformation*. Princeton University Press.

Fagerberg, J., Srholec, M., & Verspagen, B. (2010). Innovation and economic development. *Handbook of the Economics of Innovation*, *2*, 833–872. https://doi.org/10.1016/S0169-7218(10)02004-6

Gerring, J. (2004). What is a case study and what is it good for? *American Political Science Review*, *98*(2), 341–354. https://doi.org/10.1017/S0003055404001182

Gerschenkron, A. (1962). *Economic backwardness in historical perspective: A book of essays*. Belknap Press of Harvard University Press. https://www.hup.harvard.edu/catalog.php?isbn=9780674226005

Hatfield-Dodds, S., Nelson, R., & Cook, D. C. (2007). 'Adaptive governance: An introduction and implications for public policy', *CSIRO Sustainable Ecosystems Working Paper*, 2007–01. Available at: https://doi.org/10.22004/ag.econ.10440. Accessed July 14, 2025.

Hayek, F. A. (1945). The use of knowledge in society. *American Economic Review*, *35*(4), 519–530.

Hsieh, C. T., & Klenow, P. J. (2010). Development accounting. *American Economic Journal: Macroeconomics*, *2*(1), 207–223. https://doi.org/10.1257/mac.2.1.207

Johnson, C. (1982). *MITI and the Japanese miracle: The growth of industrial policy, 1925–1975*. Stanford University Press.

Lall, S. (1992). Technological capabilities and industrialization. *World Development*, *20*(2), 165–186. https://doi.org/10.1016/0305-750X(92)90097-F

Lee, K. (2019). *The art of economic catch-up: Barriers, detours and leapfrogging in innovation systems*. Cambridge: Cambridge University Press. Available at: https://doi.org/10.1017/9781108588232. Accessed July 14, 2025.

Lee, K. (2024). Economics of technology cycle time (TCT) and catch-up by latecomers: Micro-, meso-, and macro-analyses and implications. *Journal of Evolutionary Economics*, *34*, 253–290. https://doi.org/10.1007/s00191-024-00847-9

Lee, K., & Lim, C. (2001). Technological regimes, catching-up and leapfrogging: Findings from the Korean industries. *Research Policy*, *30*(3), 459–483. https://doi.org/10.1016/S0048-7333(00)00088-3

Mahoney, J., & Thelen, K. (2010). *Explaining institutional change: Ambiguity, agency, and power*. Cambridge University Press. https://doi.org/10.1017/CBO9780511806414

Mazzucato, M. (2021). *Mission economy: A moonshot guide to changing capitalism*. Penguin.

Nelson, R. R., & Winter, S. G. (1982). *An evolutionary theory of economic change*. Belknap Press of Harvard University Press.

OECD. (2024). *Western balkans competitiveness outlook 2024: Regional profile, competitiveness and private sector development*. https://doi.org/10.1787/170b0e53-en

Open Data Kosovo. (2021). *Kosovo digital agenda observatory: Country report and roadmap for digital agenda advancement in Kosovo*. Pristina: ICEDA Project Partners. Available at: https://opendatakosovo.org/wp-content/uploads/2021/12/Kosovo-DAO-2021.pdf. Accessed July 14, 2025.

Ostrom, E. (2005). *Understanding institutional diversity*. Princeton University Press.

Popper, K. (2002). *The open society and its enemies* (7th). Routledge. https://doi.org/10.4324/9780203820377

Radosevic, S. (2017). Upgrading technology in Central and Eastern European economies. *IZA World of Labor*, *338*, https://doi.org/10.15185/izawol.338

Rodrik, D. (2008). *Normalizing industrial policy*. Washington, DC: World Bank (Commission on Growth and Development Working Paper No. 3). Available at: https://drodrik.scholar.harvard.edu/files/dani-rodrik/files/normalizing-industrial-policy.pdf. Accessed July 14, 2025.

Rodrik, D. (2010). Diagnostics before prescriptions. *Journal of Economic Perspectives*, *24*(3), 33–44. https://doi.org/10.1257/jep.24.3.33

Sabel, C. F., & Zeitlin, J. (2012). Experimentalist governance. In D. Levi-Faur (Ed.), *The Oxford handbook of governance* (pp. 169–183). Oxford University Press. https://doi.org/10.1093/oxfordhb/9780199560530.013.0012

Sen, A. (1999). *Development as freedom*. Oxford University Press.

Stiglitz, J. E., & Greenwald, B. C. (2014). *Creating a learning society: A new approach to growth, development, and social progress*. Columbia University Press. https://doi.org/10.7312/stig15214

Teece, D. J., Pisano, G., & Shuen, A. (1997). Dynamic capabilities and strategic management. *Strategic Management Journal*, *18*(7), 509–533. https://doi.org/10.1002/(SICI)1097-0266(199708)18:7<509::AID-SMJ882>3.0.CO;2-Z

UN DESA. (2018). *The sustainable development goals report 2018*. New York: United Nations Department of Economic and Social Affairs. Available at: https://unstats.un.org/sdgs/report/2018/. Accessed July 14, 2025.

UNDP. (1997). Governance for sustainable human development: A UNDP policy document. New York: United Nations Development Programme. Available at: https://www.undp-aciac.org/publications/other/undp/governance/undppolicydoc97-e.pdf. Accessed October 2, 2025.

UNESCAP. (2023). *Rethinking Development through Anticipatory, Agile and Adaptive Governance*. Bangkok: United Nations Economic and Social Commission for Asia and the Pacific. Available at: https://www.unescap.org/blog/rethinking-development-through-anticipatory-agile-and-adaptive-governance. Accessed July 14, 2025.

UNIDO. (2024). *Industrial development report 2024: Turning challenges into sustainable solutions–the new era of industrial policy*. Vienna: United Nations Industrial Development Organization. Available at: https://www.unido.org/sites/default/files/unido-publications/2024-06/Industrial%20Development%20Report%202024.pdf. Accessed July 14, 2025.

World Bank. (1994). *Governance: The World Bank's experience*. Washington, DC: The World Bank. Available at: https://documents.worldbank.org/en/publication/documents-reports/documentdetail/711471468765285964/governance-the-world-banks-experience. Accessed October 2, 2025.

World Bank. (2022). *World Development Indicators*. Washington, DC: World Bank. Available at: https://databank.worldbank.org/source/world-development-indicators. Accessed July 14, 2025.

# Part I
# Theoretical Foundations: Capabilities, Governance, and Structural Transformation

Part I establishes the analytical foundations for understanding how latecomer economies can pursue industrial upgrading and technological learning under the constraints of the digital age. It moves beyond conventional paradigms that equate development with GDP growth, institutional templates, or policy adoption. Instead, it places development at the centre of *productive capability accumulation*, encompassing technological, institutional, organizational, and transformative dimensions. It also examines how governance systems shape, enable, or hinder this process.

Chapter 2 introduces capability accumulation as the core of structural transformation. It critiques narrow growth-focused approaches and situates *technological capabilities* as the main mechanism through which countries advance within global value chains. Drawing on evolutionary and structuralist perspectives, it frames development as an endogenous and long-term process of learning and upgrading.

Chapter 3 addresses the governance dilemmas faced by latecomer economies, particularly in post-socialist and donor-dependent contexts. It traces the historical shift from state-led to market-oriented paradigms and argues for a reorientation toward adaptive and networked forms of governance. The chapter emphasizes coordination, learning, and embeddedness as critical functions that support capability formation in constrained institutional environments.

Chapter 4 presents the *Developmental Network State (DNS)* as a conceptual framework for governing catch-up in the digital era. It outlines the DNS's core pillars of coordination, learning, and integration and explains how this model can support transformation where state capacity is limited, authority is dispersed, and external actors play a central role.

Taken together, these three chapters establish the theoretical lens through which the sectoral case studies in Part II are analysed. They form the conceptual backbone of the book's argument, reframing catch-up not as the replication of institutional blueprints but as a continuous, context-specific process of capability building through adaptive governance.

# Chapter 2
# Technological Capabilities and the Architecture of Catch-Up

## 2.1 Introduction

This chapter revisits the challenge of economic catch-up in the digital age by placing capability development at the center of structural transformation. It argues that latecomer economies cannot rely solely on market liberalization, digital connectivity, or alignment with international standards to achieve sustainable progress. While these measures may create enabling conditions, they are insufficient to generate the processes of learning, adaptation, and innovation that underpin long-term upgrading.

Instead, the chapter contends that durable transformation depends on the coordinated accumulation of four interrelated types of capabilities: technological, organizational, institutional, and transformative. These capabilities shape not only how firms produce and innovate but also how institutions foster learning, how coordination across sectors is achieved, and how societies navigate technological change. While all four are essential and mutually reinforcing, particular emphasis is placed on technological capabilities, which form the production-oriented core of structural transformation. They determine how effectively knowledge is applied in practice, how rapidly firms can upgrade within value chains, and how innovation translates into competitive advantage. In latecomer economies, where resource constraints, institutional gaps, and market volatility are acute, technological capabilities are often the most tangible lever for accelerating productivity growth and enabling higher-value activities. Strengthening them thus becomes both a driver of change and a catalyst for progress in other capability domains, forming the foundation for more dynamic, resilient, and inclusive economic systems.

Drawing on insights from development economics, innovation systems theory, and governance studies, the chapter presents an integrated framework for understanding how skills are built, supported, and scaled. Focusing on the experience of European economies in transition, particularly those in the Western Balkans (WB),



F. Sahiti, *Catching Up in the Digital Age*, Contributions to Economics,
https://doi.org/10.1007/978-3-032-17059-0_2

it shows how fragmented innovation systems, skills mismatches, and weak institutional coherence have constrained the region's capacity to absorb and advance technology.

The analysis identifies six interrelated pathways for capability development: learning by doing, supplier upgrading, vocational education reform, strengthening innovation systems, fostering cross-sectoral enablers, and sequencing governance reforms. These pathways are inherently context-sensitive and adaptive, reflecting the cumulative nature of skills formation and the iterative process of institutional learning.

The chapter concludes by arguing that industrial policy can more effectively support capability development when it functions as a platform for learning, coordination, and strategic adaptation. Structural transformation depends not on replicating external models but on cultivating locally grounded institutions that evolve alongside the challenges they seek to address.

## 2.2 The Problem of Catch-Up Without Capabilities

For many years, developing or "latecomer" economies have tried to close the gap with richer countries. The main strategy has been to open markets, adopt foreign technologies, and align national policies with international standards, especially those of the European Union (EU). These reforms were meant to speed up growth and help countries integrate into the global economy.

However, the results have been uneven. Even after major reforms, many countries in Southeast Europe still face low productivity, weak competitiveness, and limited progress in modernizing their industries.

Kosovo, for example, has made impressive advances in digital government and EU integration, yet its economy still depends heavily on remittances and low-value services. Albania has opened its markets and expanded access to digital tools, but a shortage of skilled workers and poor connections between universities and businesses continue to hold it back. North Macedonia has attracted foreign investors, but much of its industry remains focused on low-complexity assembly work with few benefits for local firms.

These examples reveal a common problem. Economic growth remains fragile, innovation systems are fragmented, and progress toward higher-value industries is limited. In other words, countries are following the right policies on paper, but real transformation on the ground is still missing.

The roots of this gap run deeper. In today's digital economy, progress depends not only on adopting new technologies or enacting formal policy reforms, but on the ability to learn, coordinate, and adapt under conditions of uncertainty and change. In this book, these abilities are described as capabilities. Capabilities encompass not just the technical knowledge and skills found within firms, but also the broader institutional and organizational systems that enable societies to experiment, collaborate, and learn over time.

This perspective represents a shift from earlier development theories. Classical approaches tended to attribute progress either to a strong state directing industrialization or to open markets driving natural convergence (Gerschenkron, 1962; Solow, 1956). Experience has shown that neither approach is sufficient on its own. Research by Cimoli et al. (2009), Rodrik (2011), and others show that market liberalization and donor-led reforms rarely foster the learning and innovation capacities required for sustained growth. As a result, countries remain trapped in low-value production, unable to upgrade or adapt foreign technologies effectively.

This challenge is evident in the WB. Governments have introduced digital and innovation strategies and aligned many regulations with EU standards. Yet industries continue to rely on outdated technologies, links between education and business remain weak, and public institutions often lack the capacity to implement policies effectively. These are not only political or administrative shortcomings; they reflect a deeper shortage of capabilities—the collective ability to absorb, coordinate, and sustain technological and institutional upgrading.

This book therefore adopts a capability-focused perspective. Building on the work of Lall (1992), Bell and Pavitt (1993), Sen (1999), Andreoni and Chang (2019), and others, it views development not as a question of resources or policy templates, but as a continuous process of learning. Progress depends on how societies, through the actions of economic actors, generate, share, and apply knowledge, and how they adapt to emerging challenges. Capabilities evolve gradually through experience, collaboration, and cumulative learning.

From this perspective, governance is not simply about designing good rules or ensuring their enforcement. It is about enabling learning by mobilizing people and resources, aligning incentives, and creating opportunities for feedback and experimentation. Effective governance connects innovation, education, and industry, allowing knowledge to circulate and expand across these domains.

In a rapidly changing digital environment, national success depends less on following predetermined policy models and more on building and applying capabilities effectively. Without the capacity to understand and adapt to new technologies, countries risk falling further behind in global value chains. Policy alignment alone cannot deliver progress; what matters most is the ability to develop and sustain technological capabilities that drive inclusive and lasting transformation.

This understanding also calls for a new approach to industrial policy. Traditional tools such as subsidies or investment incentives have limited impact when technological capabilities are weak. Industrial policy should therefore focus on strengthening capabilities—fostering cooperation among firms, universities, and public institutions; supporting continuous learning and experimentation; and adapting to technological change.

In this view, industrial policy becomes a living and adaptive process. Its effectiveness depends not only on design, but also on trust, coordination, and the capacity to learn over time. Successful policies evolve through collaboration, feedback, and incremental improvement rather than through rigid planning.

The diagram below illustrates this approach. It depicts how capabilities, governance, and structural transformation interact in a continuous cycle of learning and adaptation. Governments create the conditions for collaboration and knowledge exchange; capabilities develop through experience and innovation; and as economies upgrade, governance must adjust to new challenges. This cycle forms the engine of sustainable and inclusive development in the digital age (Fig. 2.1).

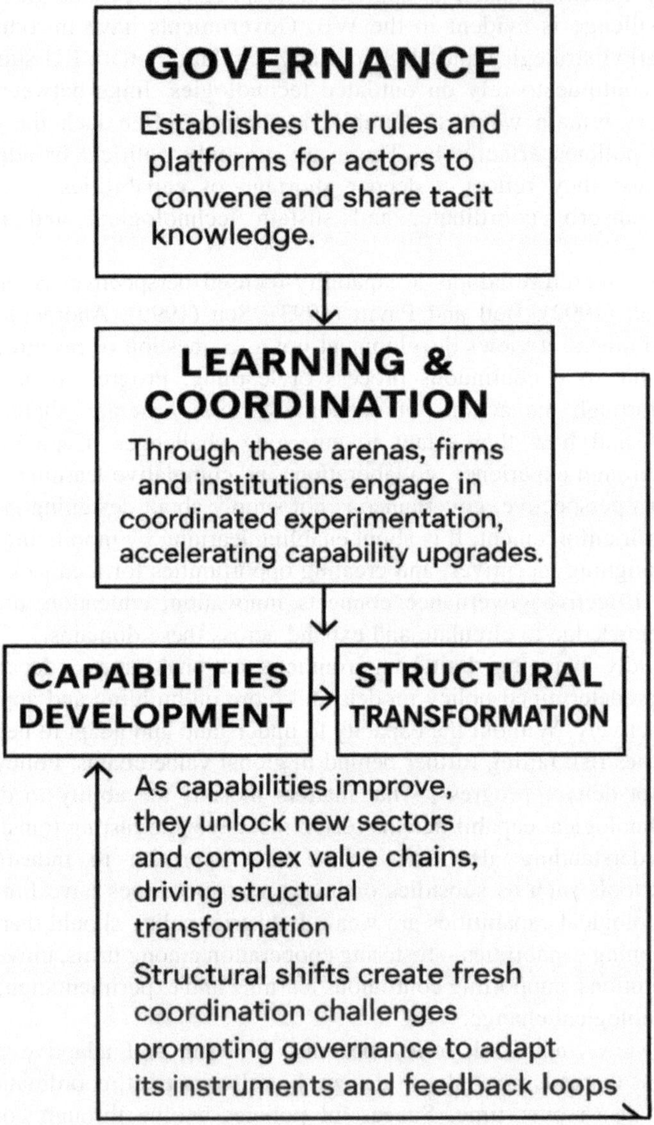


**Fig. 2.1** Capabilities for development. *Source* Adapted and illustrated by the author, based on the capability-centred framework discussed in the manuscript, generated with DALL · E using Microsoft Copilot (2025)

The following sections build on this framework by examining technological capabilities in more detail and explaining how they drive productivity growth, innovation, and value chain upgrading.

## 2.3 Why Technological Capabilities Matter

### *2.3.1 The Role of Technological Capabilities*

In many latecomer economies, technological capabilities remain weak. Firms may acquire modern machinery, subscribe to digital platforms, or participate in donor-supported programmes, yet their operations often remain confined to routine, low-productivity tasks. Technologies are adopted but rarely adapted or improved. Organizational practices may be followed but seldom refined. What is missing is not access to tools, but the ability to integrate them—to transform external knowledge into embedded capabilities through problem-solving, iterative practice, and experiential learning.

Researchers describe this process as the transformation of external knowledge into local capability. Cohen and Levinthal (1990) referred to this as absorptive capacity: the ability of a firm to recognize, understand, and apply new knowledge. It depends on prior experience and established learning routines and cannot be built overnight. Later, Teece et al. (1997) introduced the concept of dynamic capabilities, which capture how firms restructure and renew their resources and skills as conditions change. Both perspectives point to the same conclusion: access to technology alone is insufficient. What matters most is the ability to learn, adapt, and improve over time.

This challenge is particularly evident across the WB. Despite years of reforms aimed at aligning with EU standards, many economies in the region continue to struggle with upgrading. Productivity gains remain limited, innovation systems are fragmented, and participation in global value chains is concentrated in low-value segments. Weak connections between firms, universities, and research institutions hinder the translation of policy reforms into tangible improvements in productivity (World Bank, 2023a; OECD, 2024a).

The fundamental problem is that technological capabilities cannot simply be imported or legislated into existence. As Radosevic (2017) observes, they evolve gradually through iterative learning, feedback loops, adaptation, and institutional support. Building these capabilities requires more than skilled individuals; it demands networks that connect people, organizations, and ideas. It also depends on effective coordination between government and industry, and on mechanisms that enable learning across sectors and regions.

This perspective shifts the focus away from technology adoption as a one-time objective toward the systems that allow firms and institutions to use, improve, and eventually transform technologies. Technological capabilities are not merely technical skills; they are also social and relational, built through cooperation, experimentation, and trust among actors. Their strength depends on how effectively people and organizations share knowledge, learn from mistakes, and respond to new challenges.

In this context, governance plays a central role. Market forces alone cannot sustain learning or structural transformation. Governments, firms, educational institutions, and transnational actors—including donors and diaspora networks—must work together to align industrial and education policies, strengthen institutions that link firms with researchers and training centres, and create incentives that promote innovation rather than imitation. As Cimoli et al. (2009) note, capabilities are embedded in the rules, networks, and incentives that shape how knowledge circulates within an economy. Andreoni and Chang (2019) similarly emphasize that without policy coherence and coordination, even well-designed reforms are unlikely to generate lasting change.

In conclusion, technological capabilities form the backbone of structural transformation. They enable firms to raise productivity, move into more sophisticated activities, and adapt to emerging technologies. Yet, as noted earlier, such capabilities do not evolve automatically. They develop through learning by doing, experimentation, and sustained collaboration among firms, institutions, and policymakers. Without this enabling environment, technology remains underutilized and its transformative potential unrealized.

The next section examines how technological capabilities can be developed, measured, and strengthened across different sectors.

### 2.3.2 *Defining Technological Capabilities*

Technological capabilities encompass the technical, managerial, and institutional skills that enable firms to use technology effectively and improve it over time (Lall, 1992). They are fundamental for an economy to move beyond simple production tasks toward more advanced, knowledge-based activities that drive innovation, competitiveness, and long-term growth.

Access to new machinery, digital tools, or participation in global production networks is not, by itself, sufficient to transform an economy. As Lall (1992) argues, genuine progress requires deliberate effort through sustained investment in technical training, support for experimentation, and an environment that fosters learning and problem-solving.

A key distinction exists between *production capabilities* and *technological capabilities*. Production capabilities refer to the efficient use of existing techniques, while technological capabilities involve improving and adapting those techniques by learning how to make products more efficiently, at higher quality, or in new ways. Bell and Pavitt (1993) argue that deeper learning arises from solving practical problems, experimenting with new ideas, and integrating knowledge across functions and disciplines. Such learning depends on skilled people, access to relevant knowledge, and strong institutional support.

Teece and colleagues (Teece et al., 1997) expanded this concept through the idea of *dynamic capabilities*, which describe how firms adapt and restructure their resources as conditions change. In today's digital economy, where technologies evolve rapidly, this adaptability is essential. Firms must not only learn how to use new tools but also how to upgrade processes, redesign products, and respond to data-driven production systems. These abilities develop through internal learning routines and strong connections with universities, research institutes, and other firms.

Research on global value chains (GVCs) reinforces this view. To upgrade within these international networks, firms must meet demanding standards for quality, delivery, and coordination while managing complex relationships with global buyers (Gereffi, 1999; Gereffi et al., 2005). Many latecomer economies face challenges in this regard. Their firms often remain confined to low-value activities because they lack the skills, organizational structures, and institutional support needed to move up the value chain. Radosevic (2017) describes this as the *technology upgrading trap*, a situation where firms have access to advanced technologies but cannot translate them into higher productivity or greater value creation.

The development of technological capabilities is therefore not only a technical challenge but an institutional and systemic one. It depends on how firms learn, how knowledge circulates through the economy, and how incentives are structured to promote long-term investment in skills and innovation. As Cimoli et al. (2009) argue, the strength of national innovation systems and the quality of coordination between public and private actors largely determine whether capabilities expand or stagnate. Andreoni and Chang (2019) further emphasize that effective governance is essential, not only to provide policy support but also to align diverse actors around shared strategic objectives.

This book adopts a three-tier framework that distinguishes among *operational*, *intermediate*, and *advanced* capabilities. Each level represents a different stage of learning and complexity, helping to identify where firms or sectors currently stand and what forms of support are needed to move forward (Table 2.1).

This framework offers a practical approach for identifying capability gaps and designing policies to address them. Capability development is a gradual and continuous process. Firms rarely move from basic production to advanced innovation quickly; progress occurs through experience, problem-solving, and targeted support.

Technological capabilities evolve through constant interaction among firms, universities, training systems, and production networks, as well as through the interplay of public policies and market incentives. Their development depends both on firm-level initiative and on institutions that promote learning, facilitate knowledge sharing, and align incentives for long-term growth.

In many transitional European economies, where public institutions are fragmented and firms often lack absorptive capacity, strengthening technological capabilities requires more than access to digital tools or imported knowledge. It demands deliberate strategies that build institutional linkages and establish

**Table 2.1** Levels of technological capabilities

| Capability tier | Core functions | Typical activities | Systemic enablers |
|---|---|---|---|
| Advanced capabilities | Create and extend technologies; innovate strategically | R&D, product design, AI model training, patenting, participation in international standards | Public R&D funding, innovation policy, strong research–industry linkages |
| Intermediate capabilities | Adapt and improve technologies | Process redesign, product upgrading, quality enhancement, integration of new tools | Vocational training, supplier development, learning-by-doing programmes |
| Operational capabilities | Use and maintain technologies efficiently | Equipment operation, software use, basic quality control, routine maintenance | Basic technical skills, infrastructure access, digital literacy initiatives |

*Source* Author's elaboration based on Lall (1992); Bell and Pavitt (1993); Teece et al. (1997); Radosevic (2017); Andreoni and Chang (2019)

feedback mechanisms for continuous learning. In this sense, capabilities are not only attributes of individual firms but also outcomes of system-wide coordination.

This understanding provides the foundation for the following sections, which examine how technological capabilities influence productivity growth, value chain upgrading, and innovation. These dimensions shed light on how firms and economies learn, adapt, and evolve in the context of global technological change.

### *2.3.3 Technological Capabilities and Productivity Growth*

Productivity growth is one of the clearest indicators of structural transformation. It reflects how effectively firms use knowledge and resources to produce output and how well they adapt to changes in technology, markets, and production standards. Technological capabilities lie at the heart of this process. They enable firms to refine their routines, improve product quality, and introduce innovations that enhance the efficiency of resource use.

In an increasingly digital environment, tools such as enterprise resource planning systems, automated workflows, and data-driven management platforms can significantly raise efficiency. However, their impact depends on a firm's ability to implement, adapt, and integrate them effectively. Without these capabilities, even the most advanced technologies often remain underutilized.

Research consistently links productivity growth to the strength of technological capabilities. Fagerberg et al. (2010) show that differences in innovation and learning systems help explain why some countries achieve higher productivity than others. Similarly, UNIDO (2024) finds that investments in equipment or infrastructure yield limited returns when firms lack the skills and learning systems needed to use them effectively. This challenge is particularly evident in latecomer economies, where new technologies often fail to translate into meaningful performance improvements.

The WB provide a clear example of this pattern. Despite considerable investment in infrastructure, digital connectivity, and modern machinery, productivity growth has remained modest (OECD, 2022; World Bank, 2023a). The primary constraint is the absence of complementary capabilities such as technical skills, feedback mechanisms, and adaptive management practices. Many firms operate modern software alongside manual processes or use new equipment below capacity due to limited training and inadequate process design.

Productivity outcomes are also shaped by the wider institutional environment. Suppliers, training institutions, regulators, and business intermediaries all influence whether technology adoption leads to real performance gains. In digital contexts, bottlenecks frequently arise from fragmented data systems, inconsistent regulatory frameworks, and limited access to technical support.

Technological capabilities should therefore be viewed as system-wide capacities rather than attributes of individual firms. Productivity growth depends not only on internal efficiency but also on the quality of infrastructure, institutional linkages, and policy frameworks that foster learning and adaptation. Evidence from the WB and other latecomer economies shows that without coordinated learning systems and institutional support, productivity gains from digital investments remain limited and uneven (Radosevic, 2017; OECD, 2022; World Bank, 2023a).

### *2.3.4 Technological Capabilities and Value Chain Participation*

Participation in GVCs is an important step for latecomer economies, but it is not sufficient on its own to achieve structural transformation. The real challenge lies in upgrading within these value chains, moving from simple, low-value activities to more complex, knowledge-intensive functions that generate higher economic returns.

Upgrading can follow several interconnected pathways, each representing a stage in capability development. Process upgrading focuses on improving efficiency and productivity through better technologies, refined production methods, or workflow innovations. Product upgrading builds on these gains by enabling firms to produce higher-quality, more sophisticated goods that meet evolving market standards. Functional upgrading involves a strategic shift toward higher-value activities within the value chain, such as design, branding, or logistics, allowing firms to capture a greater share of value. Finally, inter-sectoral upgrading occurs when the skills and knowledge developed in one sector are successfully applied to new industries, fostering diversification and broader structural change.

These forms of upgrading create a cumulative path of capability development that enables firms and economies to progress from basic production toward innovation-driven growth. Figure 2.2 illustrates this capability ladder and its role in supporting long-term structural transformation.

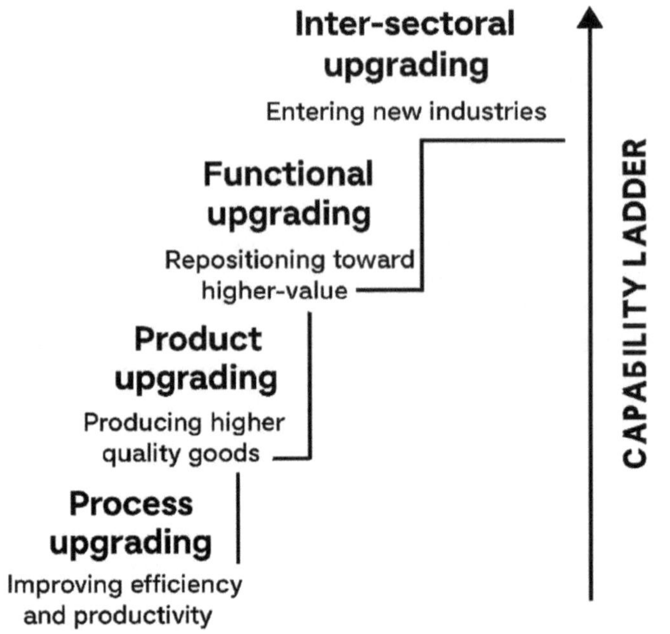


**Fig. 2.2** Capability ladder of upgrading trajectories in global value chains. *Source* Author's synthesis based on literature on global value chains and economic upgrading, generated with DALL · E using Microsoft Copilot (2025)

This pattern of limited upgrading is widespread across the WB. Firms in Kosovo, Albania, and North Macedonia often operate as subcontractors or assemblers for global lead firms. While such participation offers access to export markets and international production standards, it rarely translates into strategic autonomy. Lead firms typically retain control over design, branding, and customer relationships, leaving local suppliers dependent and vulnerable to contract shifts or relocation. This situation exemplifies the technology upgrading trap, where participation in GVCs fails to produce deeper capability development.

Upgrading is not a linear or automatic process. It requires deliberate and coordinated capability building that allows firms to meet evolving standards, manage complex production processes, and assume more advanced functions. These efforts operate at both the firm and system levels. Without workforce development, knowledge transfer, and collaborative problem-solving, GVC integration remains a transactional rather than developmental process.

In the WB, institutional fragmentation, limited absorptive capacity, and weak policy coordination frequently undermine upgrading efforts. Although foreign direct investment can facilitate access to global networks, these linkages often remain shallow, leaving many firms confined to routine, low-value tasks with limited opportunities for advancement.

The potential for upgrading nonetheless exists. Realizing it requires targeted strategies to strengthen technological capabilities across the value chain. This includes building robust local supplier networks, integrating technical and vocational training into industrial ecosystems, and fostering regional cooperation to overcome scale constraints and share learning infrastructure. Such measures are essential for shifting from passive participation to more autonomous, value-generating roles within the global economy.

### 2.3.5 Innovation as an Expression of Technological Capabilities

Innovation represents a more advanced stage in the way firms create and apply knowledge. While upgrading enables firms to improve production processes or move into higher-value segments of GVCs, innovation reflects their ability to generate new value through experimentation, adaptation, and problem-solving. It allows firms to redesign technologies, refine routines, and respond creatively to evolving market conditions and technological opportunities. In this sense, innovation is one of the most advanced expressions of technological capability.

In latecomer economies, innovation seldom takes the form of major inventions or large-scale research breakthroughs. More often, it emerges as incremental improvements and practical solutions developed through daily operations rather than formal research and development (Nelson & Winter, 1982). This process is gradual and cumulative. It depends on the ability of firms and workers to learn by doing, share tacit knowledge, and build routines that support continuous experimentation and improvement.

In increasingly digital economies, innovation frequently involves adapting software tools, integrating digital platforms, or redesigning business models in response to user feedback. Open-source technologies, cloud services, and agile working methods now enable even small firms to innovate effectively. Although these activities often fall outside conventional innovation statistics, they are critical for strengthening technological capabilities and maintaining competitiveness.

Across the WB, however, innovation remains uneven. Public investment in research and development is limited, and institutional linkages between universities, research centres, and private firms are often weak or temporary. Collaboration tends to occur within donor-funded projects rather than through stable, long-term partnerships. As a result, much innovation happens informally within networks of entrepreneurs, start-ups, and diaspora actors rather than through formal institutions.

Innovation is part of a broader learning system. It draws on the same underlying capabilities that enable technological upgrading—experimentation, feedback, co-ordination, and adaptation. Where these capabilities and networks of trust are strong, innovation becomes continuous and scalable. Where they are weak or fragmented, innovation tends to remain isolated and unsustainable.

In the WB, fragmented institutions and limited absorptive capacity continue to constrain the transformative potential of innovation. This is a central argument of this book: innovation is not merely the outcome of technological progress, but a reflection of how effectively the broader system of capabilities, learning, and governance supports continuous adaptation and improvement.

Understanding this relationship between innovation and capability formation requires systematic analysis. Because capabilities evolve gradually and are not easily captured by conventional indicators, policymakers and researchers need practical tools to make them visible and measurable. The next section presents several analytical tools designed to identify capability gaps, assess learning potential, and inform strategic interventions for technological upgrading.

### 2.3.6 Illustrative Tools for Capability Analysis

As previously stated, technological capabilities play a crucial role in driving productivity, innovation, and value chain upgrading. Recognizing their importance is only the starting point. Effective policymaking requires an understanding of *where capabilities are strong, where they are weak,* and *why they fail to develop.* This section introduces a set of practical tools designed to *visualize capability gaps,* identify coordination problems, and guide more targeted policy responses.

These tools do not provide definitive answers but serve as *frameworks for structured analysis.* They move beyond general indicators to explore how capabilities are distributed within firms, evolve across sectors, and interact within broader institutional systems. By making these patterns visible, policymakers and analysts can better identify where learning and upgrading stall, and which interventions are needed to restore progress.

The first tool, the *Capability Ladder Diagram* (Fig. 2.3), maps firms according to three levels of capability development. At the base are firms with *operational capabilities* that use existing technologies and digital tools but make few modifications. The intermediate level represents *intermediate capabilities,* where firms begin to enhance processes, upgrade products, and learn from experience. At the top are *advanced capabilities,* where firms innovate, conduct research and development, design new products, and contribute to broader knowledge and industry standards.

The ladder illustrates how firms are distributed across these levels and where progress tends to slow. In many latecomer economies, most firms remain at the operational level, with only a few advancing further. This pattern raises critical questions: are the barriers primarily financial, institutional, regulatory, or related to skills? The purpose is not to evaluate firms against a fixed model of success but to understand *where and why learning trajectories are interrupted* and which enabling conditions are missing.

The second tool, the *Capability Matrix* (Fig. 2.4), links firm capabilities to their position in global and regional production systems. It recognizes that a firm's role

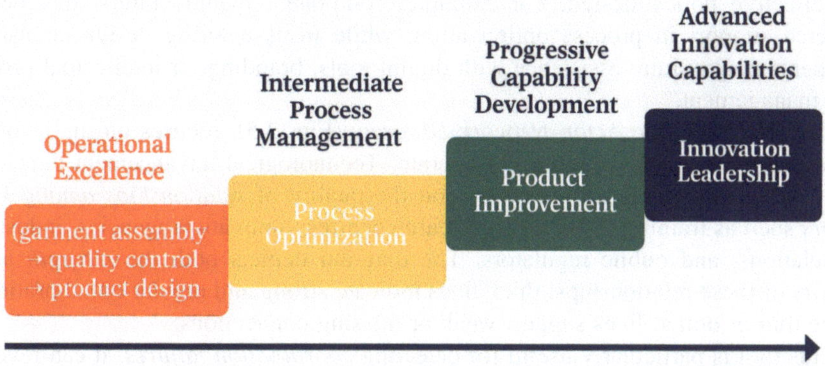


**Fig. 2.3** Capability ladder diagram. *Source* Author's illustration (adapted from Andreoni & Chang, 2019; Sabel & Zeitlin, 2012), generated with DALL · E using Microsoft Copilot (2025)

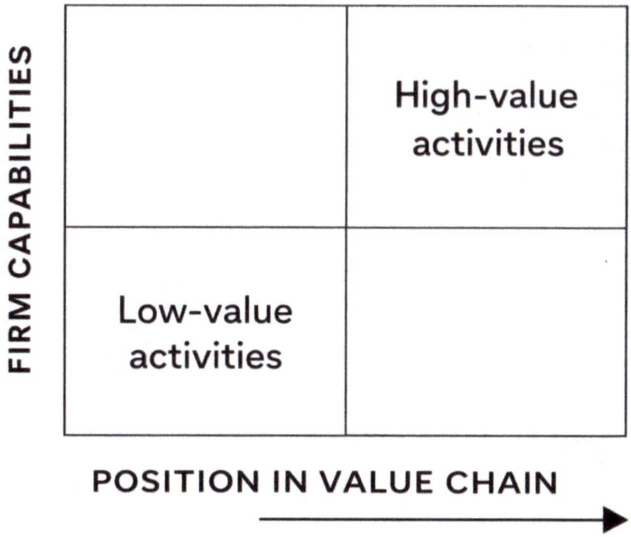


**Fig. 2.4** Capability–GVC matrix. *Source* Author's illustration (adapted from Gereffi et al., 2005; Humphrey & Schmitz, 2002), generated with DALL · E using Microsoft Copilot (2025)

in a value chain does not always correspond to its internal capability level. Some firms may possess strong production skills yet remain confined to low-value assembly activities, while others operate in higher-value segments but lack the capabilities to sustain or expand their position.

The matrix helps identify whether upgrading barriers stem from *external constraints* such as market access or buyer control, or from *internal weaknesses* such as limited design capacity or poor-quality management. This distinction is essential for effective policy design. For example, component manufacturers may need targeted support in process optimization, while firms entering design-intensive segments may require assistance with digital tools, branding, or intellectual property management.

The third tool, the *Actor–Network Diagram* (Fig. 2.5), focuses on the institutional environment in which firms operate. Technological advancement depends not only on firm-level skills but also on the quality of *relationships among key actors* such as training institutions, research centres, innovation agencies, industry associations, and public regulators. The diagram depicts both the *strength* and *density* of these relationships: thick lines indicate strong and regular collaboration, while thin or dotted lines suggest weak or missing connections.

This tool is particularly useful for detecting *coordination failures.* It can reveal where institutions operate in isolation, where firms are disconnected from knowledge providers, or where support systems exist but remain underutilized. In the WB, for instance, numerous organizations involved in innovation and industrial support often work in parallel with limited communication. The diagram can highlight potential linkages, overlapping mandates, and weak learning systems. Faded nodes may also indicate *underused actors* such as diaspora networks, training centres, or emerging digital communities.

Technological capabilities often remain invisible without the right analytical tools. These diagnostic frameworks do not replace strategy *but make it more evidence-based and responsive to real conditions.* By revealing how firms, institutions, and networks interact, they provide a foundation for designing policies that

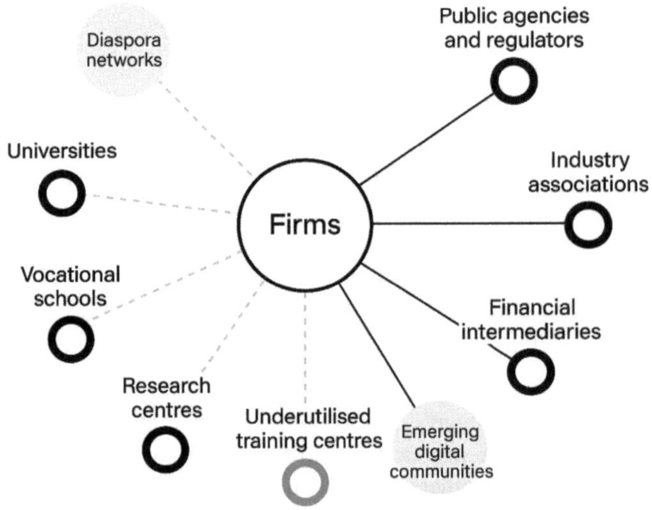


**Fig. 2.5** Actor-network diagram. *Source* Author's actor-network diagram of the national innovation ecosystem (2025), generated with DALL · E using Microsoft Copilot (2025)

are *coherent, targeted, and sustainable*. The next chapter develops this approach further by examining how capability formation depends on governance systems that can *learn, coordinate, and adapt* over time.

## 2.4 Structural Barriers to Capability Development in the WB

The earlier framework in this book redefined *structural transformation* in latecomer economies by placing *capability development* at the centre of analysis, rather than focusing solely on formal compliance with external standards.

The experience of the WB reveals a mixed picture. The region has achieved progress in macroeconomic stability, trade liberalization, and regional cooperation, yet deeper capability development remains limited. Despite ongoing digitalization efforts and closer cooperation with the EU, productivity growth remains modest, innovation systems are weak, and industrial upgrading is slow. Participation in GVCs has expanded, but movement toward higher-value, knowledge-based activities is rare.

According to the OECD (2024a), digital infrastructure has improved, but the transformation is *fragmented.* Regulatory reforms exist, but they are often disconnected from learning systems and institutional coordination. These patterns reveal persistent weaknesses that hinder the emergence of *coherent capability systems.*

This section identifies five major barriers that reinforce one another: *underinvestment in research and development (R&D), skills mismatches and gaps in human capital, weak firm-level learning, a shallow digital transformation,* and *institutional fragmentation with limited governance capacity.* These challenges are deeply interrelated. Firms' ability to absorb and apply new knowledge depends on supportive institutions, yet underinvestment limits opportunities for learning and innovation, while fragmented governance reduces coordination and policy consistency. Addressing these obstacles requires *integrated and sustained strategies* that treat them as parts of a single systemic issue rather than as separate reform areas.

### *2.4.1 Underinvestment in R&D and Fragmented Innovation Systems*

The first major barrier is the persistent *underinvestment in research and development.* Domestic expenditure on R&D remains below 0.5% of GDP across the region, far below the European Union's target of 3%. Kosovo and Albania invest approximately 0.2%, and North Macedonia slightly more at around 0.35%, while the Baltic states invest between 1 and 1.8%—see the Fig. 2.6.

Low spending, however, is only part of the problem. Collaboration between *research institutions, universities,* and *firms* remains limited. Mechanisms for

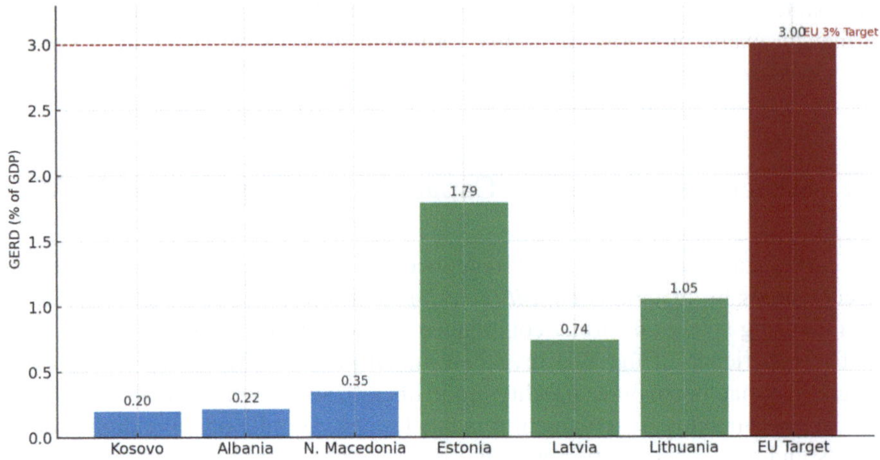


**Fig. 2.6** R&D spending (% of GDP) in WB vs. Baltics and EU Target. *Source* OECD (2024a); Eurostat (2023)

*technology transfer* and *joint R&D* are inadequate, and many initiatives are short-term and donor-driven. National innovation policies often exist formally, but with insufficient budgets, weak coordination, and limited implementation capacity.

This *fragmentation* undermines the links between research, training, and production systems. It contributes to low patenting rates, minimal participation in international research networks, and a shortage of durable public–private partnerships. As a result, firms have few opportunities to integrate foreign technologies or generate their own innovations.

## 2.4.2 *Skills Mismatches and Human Capital Gaps*

Nelson and Phelps (1966) observed that a country's ability to absorb new technologies depends on the education and adaptability of its workforce. In the WB, *education and labour market systems* have not kept pace with the demands of digital and knowledge-based economies. This shortfall has weakened the region's foundation for *research, innovation,* and *technological upgrading.*

*Skills mismatches* are widespread. Although more students are completing university degrees, many graduates lack the *practical* and *digital skills* required by employers. Curricula are frequently outdated and rarely developed in consultation with industry partners. As a result, there is an oversupply of general qualifications and a shortage of applied expertise in areas such as *data analytics, cloud computing,* and *cybersecurity* (OECD, 2024a, 2024b; ETF, 2022).

Opportunities for *lifelong learning* and *adult training* remain limited. Participation in continuing education is among the lowest in Europe, at around

9.6% in Kosovo, 9.8% in Albania, and 5% in North Macedonia, compared with more than 20% in the EU-27—see the Fig. 2.7. Digital literacy rates range from 45 to 55% (UNICEF, 2021), and fewer than one in six adults participate in structured workplace training (OECD, 2024b).

*Vocational education and training (VET)* systems face similar challenges. Instruction remains largely theoretical, equipment is outdated, and collaboration with employers is limited. The absence of *dual training models*—which combine classroom learning with practical work placements—means that graduates often lack the applied skills required for modern industrial roles in fields such as *mechatronics, diagnostics,* and *automation.*

These challenges are compounded by *high youth unemployment* and the *emigration of skilled workers.* In 2023, youth unemployment reached 33.9% in Kosovo, 30.3% in North Macedonia, and 25.1% in Albania (World Bank, 2024)—see the Fig. 2.7. Many science and engineering graduates seek employment abroad, reducing the domestic talent pool and eroding the return on public investment in education (ETF, 2022). Although donor programmes and mobility agreements exist, few mechanisms are in place to *retain* or *reintegrate* skilled workers (OECD, 2022).

In sum, skills mismatches, weak adult learning systems, and persistent *brain drain* have created a significant *human capital bottleneck.* Addressing it requires coordinated reforms that modernize curricula and equipment, strengthen linkages between education providers and employers, expand opportunities for lifelong learning, and create incentives for *talent retention.* These initiatives must also be aligned with broader *R&D* and *firm learning strategies* to sustain innovation and competitiveness over time.

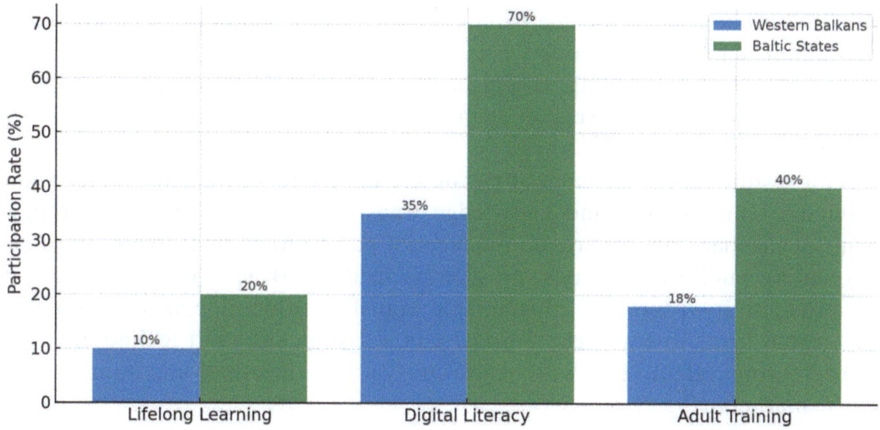


**Fig. 2.7** Participation rates in lifelong learning, digital literacy and adult training. *Source* OECD (2024b); ETF (2022); Eurostat (2023)

### 2.4.3 Weak Firm-Level Learning and Limited Upgrading

Firm-level learning is essential for strengthening technological capabilities and achieving sustained productivity growth. Through experimentation, problem-solving, and process improvement, firms build the knowledge and techniques necessary to absorb new technologies, enhance quality, and innovate. In the WB, however, most firms remain focused on basic operations with limited capacity to upgrade. This reinforces the skills and research weaknesses discussed in earlier sections.

Only around 14% of manufacturing firms in Albania, Kosovo, and North Macedonia conduct in-house research and development, compared with more than 40% in comparable EU economies (World Bank, 2023a). Structured on-the-job training is rare: fewer than one in five small and medium-sized enterprises offer regular upskilling programmes, while nearly half do so in the EU (ETF, 2022). Innovation performance is also low, with fewer than 12% of firms introducing a new or improved product or process between 2021 and 2023, less than half the EU-27 average (OECD, 2024a).

These shortcomings reflect systemic barriers rather than isolated firm weaknesses. In 2022, 45% of WB firms were classified as credit-constrained, compared with only 6% in the EU (OECD, 2025a). Bank lending and venture capital remain underdeveloped, while equity financing is scarce (EIB & EBRD, 2022). More than half of small and medium-sized enterprises operate without formal business planning or quality assurance systems (OECD, 2023a, 2023b). Institutional linkages are also weak, with only about 8% of firms collaborating with universities or research institutes (OECD, 2024b).

While participation in GVC has expanded, it has created limited learning opportunities. Firms in the region often act as subcontractors performing low-skill tasks, with backward linkages accounting for only 15% of activity compared with 28% in the EU-10 (Vienna Institute, 2021). Local sourcing by multinational corporations tends to be transactional, offering little access to higher-value functions such as design, branding, or logistics. Supplier development programmes and industrial clusters remain weak or fragmented, restricting spillovers from foreign investment.

As a result, functional upgrading, or the ability to move into higher-value activities, remains rare, and knowledge transfer is limited. Without stronger financial mechanisms, improved managerial capabilities, and better coordination among public institutions, most firms in the WB are likely to remain in low-productivity segments. Sustainable transformation depends on policies that enable firms to *learn continuously*, invest in people and technology, and connect more effectively with research systems, financial institutions, and global markets (Fig. 2.8).

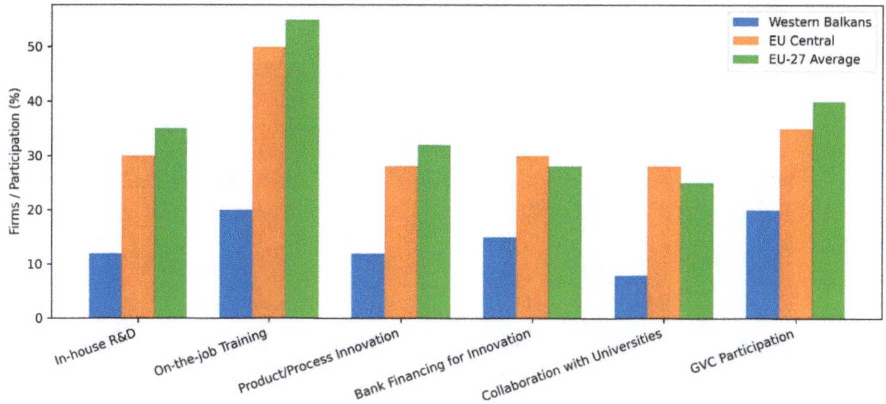


**Fig. 2.8** Firm-Level learning and innovation metrics: WB vs EU benchmarks. *Note* EU-27 and Central Europe benchmarks are provided for comparative reference. *Source* World Bank (2023a); OECD (2024a, 2024b); ETF (2022); Vienna Institute (2021)

### 2.4.4 Shallow Digital Transformation and Low Absorptive Capacity

Over the past decade, countries in the WB have made significant investments in digital infrastructure. Broadband coverage has expanded, e-government services have improved, and online public platforms have become more accessible. These achievements are noteworthy, yet their economic impact remains limited. Many economies in the region have experienced what can be described as a *digital bump* —visible progress in digital access but little improvement in productivity or innovation (OECD, 2024a). The Western Balkan economies cluster at the lower end of the digital adoption scale (0.45–0.52) and simultaneously record modest productivity growth (1.3–1.6 %). In contrast, the Baltic states, with much higher digital adoption (0.69–0.74), achieve significantly stronger productivity growth (2.4–2.7 %). This suggests that the digital divide translates into a productivity divide, reinforcing existing income and competitiveness gaps.—see the Fig. 2.9.

The main reason for this gap lies in what economists term *limited absorptive capacity* (Cohen & Levinthal, 1990). Many firms invest in new software or hardware but struggle to integrate these tools into their daily operations. Without skilled personnel, clear strategies, or effective learning systems, technologies are often underused or eventually abandoned. The lack of structured planning and feedback mechanisms prevents firms from translating digital access into measurable productivity gains.

Support systems that could help firms manage this transition are also weak. Businesses, training providers, and chambers of commerce rarely offer practical digital advisory services. Public subsidy programmes often provide financial assistance but not the complementary guidance required for successful implementation

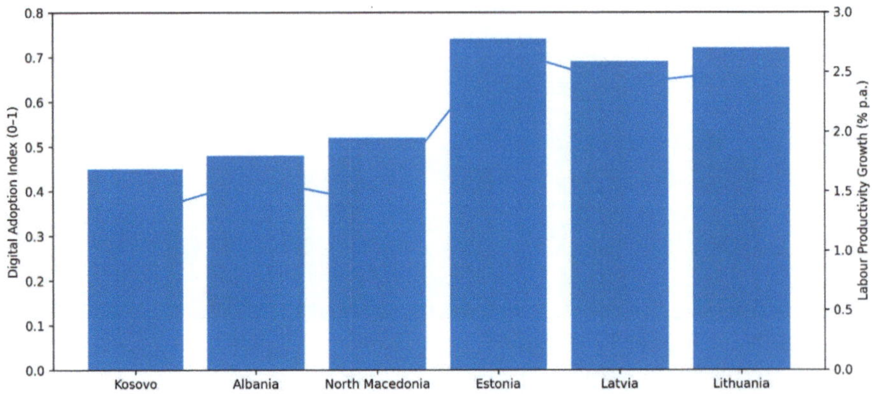


**Fig. 2.9** Digital infrastructure Index vs. productivity growth. *Note* Digital adoption is measured using the World Bank's Digital Adoption Index (DAI, scale 0–1). Labour productivity growth refers to average annual growth in GDP per hour worked. *Source* OECD (2023c); World Bank (2023b)

(OECD, 2025a; EBRD & EU, 2025). As a result, many SMEs adopt digital technologies without understanding how to adapt them to their specific business models.

Radosevic (2017) argues that building infrastructure alone does not lead to technological advancement. Without simultaneous investment in skills, organizational change, and institutional coordination, digital technologies may amplify inefficiencies rather than drive transformation.

In the WB, this *digital bump* both reflects and reinforces the broader challenges outlined earlier: weak research and development systems, skill shortages, and limited firm-level learning. Unless digital investments are accompanied by strategies that strengthen capabilities, support experimentation, and promote continuous learning, they will yield only temporary improvements rather than lasting structural transformation.

## *2.4.5 Structural and Institutional Barriers*

Governance challenges continue to constrain innovation, entrepreneurship, and capability development across the WN. Despite repeated reform efforts, the institutional environments in Kosovo, Albania, and North Macedonia remain significant obstacles to sustained transformation.

Regulatory systems are often opaque, fragmented, and costly, discouraging long-term investment and weakening business confidence. According to the OECD (2025b), WB economies lag behind their Central European peers in business entry and regulatory quality. Corruption and informality further erode trust. Transparency International (2023) scores for the region range from 35 to 40 on a 100-point scale, indicating widespread bribery, nepotism, and inconsistent rule enforcement.

Institutional fragmentation compounds these problems. Responsibilities for regulation and policy implementation are spread across multiple ministries, municipalities, and agencies, creating overlaps, gaps, and conflicting requirements. Public administration capacity is also limited. Governments allocate only 0.15% of total expenditure to training civil servants, compared with the OECD median of 0.45% (OECD, 2024a).

The gap between the WB and the Baltic states is striking. The Baltic economies consistently score above + 1.0 on World Bank indicators for regulatory quality and rule of law, while Kosovo, Albania, and North Macedonia remain below zero. These differences reflect variations in governance quality, institutional learning, and policy coherence, which in turn influence investor confidence and the sustainability of reforms.

Weak governance also explains why many promising initiatives, such as digital skills programmes, innovation grants, and research support schemes, fail to achieve lasting results. Policies are often fragmented, poorly coordinated, and lack effective monitoring and feedback systems. As a result, their impact is short-lived and rarely scaled up.

Ultimately, capability development is not only a technical or economic challenge but also a political and institutional one. Without transparent, coordinated, and learning-oriented governance systems, capability formation remains limited and fragile. Sustainable transformation depends on building trust, improving policy coherence, and ensuring consistent implementation across all levels of government and society (Fig. 2.10).

The preceding diagnostic has mapped the systemic barriers that constrain capability accumulation in the WB. The next section shifts focus from identifying these constraints to examining how latecomer economies can build capabilities amid institutional complexity through governance arrangements, coordination mechanisms, and policy instruments that foster learning, enable upgrading, and stimulate innovation in fragmented systems.

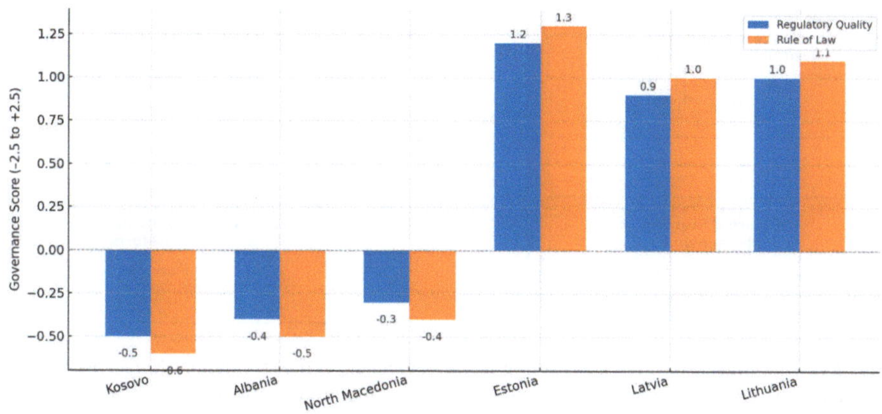


**Fig. 2.10** Regulatory quality vs. Rule of Law (2023). *Source* World Bank (2023a); Transparency International (2023)

## 2.5 Understanding the Dynamics of Capability Formation

This section examines how technological capabilities are built and expanded over time. It focuses on the dynamics that drive capability development once key structural and institutional constraints begin to be resolved.

Rather than viewing policy instruments in isolation, the discussion highlights six interconnected mechanisms observed in successful cases of industrial upgrading: experiential learning through production, functional upgrading within value chains, skills adaptation and vocational training, innovation system linkages, external support mechanisms, *and* sequenced and coherent reform.

Figure 2.11 illustrates how these mechanisms interact to drive capability formation. The process is cumulative and non-linear, resulting from continuous interaction among firms, public institutions, infrastructure, and knowledge systems. Development occurs through practical problem-solving, learning from experience, and adaptation to new opportunities and challenges.

By tracing these processes, the section provides a grounded understanding of how capabilities evolve in real-world contexts. It also prepares the ground for the next chapter, which explores how governance systems can coordinate learning, support upgrading, and sustain long-term transformation.

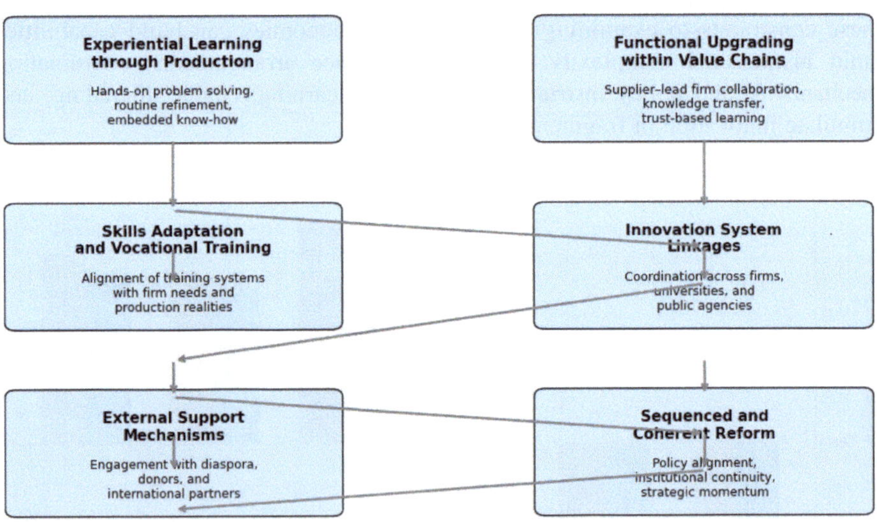


**Fig. 2.11** Interlinked mechanisms driving technological capability formation. *Note* This conceptual diagram synthesizes insights from case studies and literature on industrial policy, innovation systems, and vocational reform in latecomer contexts. *Source* Author's elaboration based on comparative analysis of sectoral upgrading and capability development in transitional economies, generated with DALL · E using Microsoft Copilot (2025)

### 2.5.1 Experiential Learning Through Production

*Experiential learning* refers to the acquisition of knowledge through direct engagement in production. By repeating tasks, refining routines, and addressing practical challenges, firms gradually develop technical know-how and operational efficiency (Arrow, 1962). Even small improvements—such as reorganizing workflows or adjusting tools—contribute to cumulative learning.

This learning is dynamic and practice-based. It evolves through daily problem-solving rather than through formal training programmes. It is particularly important in late-industrializing economies, where firms must adapt under conditions of uncertainty, limited resources, and rapidly changing technologies (Cimoli et al., 2009; Lall, 2001).

In the WB, frequent production disruptions, weak infrastructure, and poor contract enforcement often interrupt the feedback loops that transform production into a learning environment. Recognizing production as a learning process reframes industrial policy: progress depends not only on investment or equipment but on institutional conditions that allow lessons to be shared, refined, and scaled.

### 2.5.2 Functional Upgrading Within Value Chains

Technological capabilities also depend on the relationships firms maintain within value chains. In advanced production systems, suppliers and lead firms collaborate in planning, quality control, and process improvement, creating opportunities for knowledge transfer and mutual learning (Gereffi et al., 2005).

When trust and clear standards exist, lead firms share technical expertise and co-develop products, enabling suppliers to move into higher-value functions such as design, logistics, and branding. For smaller firms, this cooperation provides access to resources and experience that would otherwise be out of reach.

In the WB, however, supplier networks are often transactional rather than developmental. Many firms compete mainly on price, and structural barriers such as outdated equipment, limited certification, and fragmented institutions hinder upgrading. Strengthening inter-firm collaboration is therefore essential for promoting learning and building collective capabilities.

### 2.5.3 Skills Adaptation and Vocational Training

Technological upgrading requires a skilled workforce capable of applying and adapting knowledge in practice. *Vocational training* plays a crucial role in aligning education with industrial needs. It combines design with production, ensures precision, and enables real-time problem-solving.

Vocational education is most effective when classroom learning is integrated with workplace experience. In well-functioning systems, training institutions and firms collaborate to design curricula, provide work placements, and update teaching in line with technological change (Lall, 2001).

In the WB, many vocational systems remain disconnected from industry. Outdated curricula, limited equipment, and weak partnerships with employers have led to persistent skill gaps. Graduates often lack practical experience, and firms struggle to recruit skilled professionals. Viewing vocational education as a bridge between human capital and production underscores its strategic role: it must evolve alongside industrial development to sustain continuous learning and innovation.

### 2.5.4 Innovation System Linkages

An *innovation system* encompasses the institutions and networks that create, adapt, and share knowledge. When effective, it connects firms with universities, research centres, and public agencies, allowing ideas to circulate between science and production (Lundvall, 1992; Nelson, 1993).

Strong linkages encourage collaboration on research, problem-solving, and product development. Innovation in this sense is not limited to formal R&D; it emerges through continuous interaction and learning by doing.

In the WB, these linkages are weak. Research institutions often operate in isolation, and collaboration with industry is sporadic. Feedback loops between science, training, and production are rare, preventing knowledge from being applied or diffused. Strengthening these connections is essential for building a resilient innovation ecosystem that supports technological capability development.

### 2.5.5 External Support Mechanisms

Capability development also relies on *external enablers* that mobilize resources and foster coordination. Public–private partnerships, diaspora networks, and donor programmes can play an important role when aligned with national strategies.

Public–private partnerships bring together governments, firms, and service providers to co-invest in infrastructure, training, or applied research. When transparently managed and outcome-oriented, they help reduce fragmentation and share risks (ADB, 2018; World Bank Group & IFC, 2022).

Diaspora networks contribute through the transfer of knowledge, technology, and investment. Structured mechanisms—such as fellowships, innovation platforms, or co-financing schemes—help align these contributions with domestic development priorities (Kapur & McHale, 2005; Riddle & Brinkerhoff, 2011; ICMPD, 2023).

Donor programmes are also influential, particularly in aid-dependent economies. Their impact increases when initiatives are coordinated, locally owned, and embedded within systems of monitoring and learning (OECD, 2020; UNDP, 2021).

External mechanisms work best when they *reinforce*, rather than replace, domestic institutions. Their value lies in strengthening coordination, building coherence, and sustaining learning over time.

### *2.5.6 Sequenced and Coherent Reform*

The mechanisms outlined above are most effective when combined in a coherent and well-sequenced manner. Successful late-industrializing countries show that capability development evolves in stages, supported by institutions that provide continuity and feedback.

Early stages typically focus on expanding production capacity and infrastructure. Intermediate phases strengthen vocational training, supplier upgrading, and organizational learning. At more advanced stages, innovation systems and policy coordination become central, linking firms with research institutions and global markets.

In the WB, many initiatives have struggled due to fragmented or poorly implemented reforms. Vocational reforms lacked strong industrial demand, supplier upgrading was constrained by weak market access, and innovation programmes often operated in isolation from production needs.

Achieving systemic coherence requires coordination among ministries, agencies, firms, and intermediaries, supported by monitoring mechanisms that enable adaptation and learning. Without this alignment, reforms remain isolated and capability accumulation uneven.

This discussion leads directly to Chap. 3, which examines governance arrangements that sustain sequencing, enable coordination, and foster learning in complex and uncertain policy environments.

## 2.6 Concluding Reflections on Building Capabilities for Transformation

Technological transformation in latecomer regions such as the WB requires more than digital tools or policy reform. At its core, it depends on the accumulation of *technological capabilities*, the skills, routines, and institutional relationships that enable firms to learn, adapt, and move into higher-value activities.

Despite progress in digitalization, regulatory reform, and market liberalization, deep structural gaps persist. The main constraint is not ambition or funding, but the absence of coherent systems that sustain *continuous learning*. Technologies adopted without supporting learning frameworks yield only temporary gains. Participation in global value chains without upgrading traps firms in low-value segments, and donor projects without strong local ownership risk fragmenting already fragile innovation systems.

This chapter identified six interconnected pathways for building capabilities: learning through production, strengthening supplier relationships, reforming vocational training, improving innovation systems, mobilizing external enablers such as diaspora networks and donors, and sequencing governance reforms over time. Together, these mechanisms enhance firm-level knowledge, strengthen institutional linkages, and make learning more systematic and productive.

*Governance* emerges as a *meta-capability*, a coordinating function that enables adaptation, feedback, and experimentation under uncertainty. Capabilities develop not through isolated interventions but through processes that are context-sensitive, multidimensional, and strategically aligned.

Transformation is rarely linear or automatic. It depends on how systems are organized to learn, how actors interact, how trust is built, and how strategies remain aligned across public and private sectors. For the WB, the key challenge is to create systems that learn continuously, respond effectively, and coordinate across fragmented institutions, shifting from reform as a formal obligation to transformation as an ongoing, capability-driven process of development.

Chapter 3 builds on this foundation. It presents an operational framework for *governance for learning*, a model that supports capability accumulation by structuring experimentation, facilitating coordination, and institutionalizing feedback. Through this lens, governance becomes the central mechanism for fostering adaptive, collaborative, and locally grounded development.

## References

ADB. (2018). *Public—private partnership operational plan 2012–2020*. Asian development bank. Available at https://www.adb.org/documents/public-private-partnership-operational-plan-2012-2020. Accessed 14 July 2025.

Andreoni, A., & Chang, H.-J. (2019). The political economy of industrial policy: Structural interdependencies, policy alignment and conflict management. *Structural Change and Economic Dynamics*, *48*, 136–150. https://doi.org/10.1016/j.strueco.2018.10.007

Arrow, K. J. (1962). The economic implications of learning by doing. *Review of Economic Studies*, *29*(3), 155–173. https://doi.org/10.2307/2295952

Bell, M., & Pavitt, K. (1993). Technological accumulation and industrial growth. *Industrial and Corporate Change*, *2*(2), 157–210. https://doi.org/10.1093/icc/2.2.157

Cimoli, M., Dosi, G., & Stiglitz, J. E. (2009). *Industrial policy and development: The political economy of capabilities accumulation*. Oxford University Press. https://doi.org/10.1093/acprof:oso/9780199235261.001.0001

Cohen, W. M., & Levinthal, D. A. (1990). Absorptive capacity: A new perspective on learning and innovation. *Administrative Science Quarterly*, *35*(1), 128–152. https://doi.org/10.2307/2393553

EBRD & EU. (2025). *EBRD launches €417 million programme to help WB go digital*. Retrieved from https://www.reuters.com/markets/europe/ebrd-launches-417-million-programme-help-western-balkans-go-digital-2025-04-10

EIB & EBRD. (2022). *The impact of the EIB's intermediated lending to businesses in the WB*. European Investment Bank. Available at https://www.eib.org/attachments/lucalli/20230344_impact_of_the_eibs_intermediated_lending_to_businesses_in_the_western_balkans_en.pdf. Accessed 14 July 2025.

ETF. (2022). *Skills and innovation in the WB: Country assessments and regional overview*. Turin: European training foundation. Available at https://www.etf.europa.eu. Accessed 14 July 2025.

European Commission. (2024). *Digital economy and society index 2024: Country report for Estonia*. Brussels: European commission. Available at https://digital-strategy.ec.europa.eu Accessed 14 July 2025).

Eurostat. (2023). *Science, technology and innovation statistics*. Publications Office of the EU. Available at https://ec.europa.eu/eurostat/statistics-explained/index.php?title=Science,_technology_and_innovation_statistics Accessed 13 July 2025.

Fagerberg, J., Srholec, M., & Verspagen, B. (2010). Innovation and economic development. In B. H. Hall & N. Rosenberg (Eds.), *Handbook of the economics of innovation* (Vol. 2, pp. 833–872). North-Holland. https://doi.org/10.1016/S0169-7218(10)02004-6

Gereffi, G. (1999). International trade and industrial upgrading in the apparel commodity chain. *Journal of International Economics*, *48*(1), 37–70. https://doi.org/10.1016/S0022-1996(98)00075-0

Gereffi, G., Humphrey, J., & Sturgeon, T. (2005). The governance of global value chains. *Review of International Political Economy*, *12*(1), 78–104. https://doi.org/10.1080/09692290500049805

Gerschenkron, A. (1962). *Economic backwardness in historical perspective*. Belknap Press of Harvard University Press. Available at https://www.hup.harvard.edu/catalog.php?isbn=9780674226005. Accessed 14 July 2025.

Humphrey, J., & Schmitz, H. (2002). How does insertion in global value chains affect upgrading in industrial clusters? *Regional Studies*, *36*(9), 1017–1027. https://doi.org/10.1080/0034340022000022198

ICMPD. (2023). *Study on the diasporas' contributions to the socio-economic development in the WB (ECONDIAS). Final Report and Policy Brief*. International Centre for Migration Policy Development.

Kapur, D., & McHale, J. (2005). *Give us your best and brightest: The global hunt for talent and its impact on the developing world*. Center for Global Development. Available at. https://www.cgdev.org/publication/give-us-your-best-and-brightest-global-hunt-talent-and-its-impact-developing-world. Accessed 14 July 2025.

Lall, S. (1992). Technological capabilities and industrialization. *World Development*, *20*(2), 165–186. https://doi.org/10.1016/0305-750X(92)90097-F

Lall, S. (2001). *Competitiveness, technology and skills*. Edward Elgar.

Lundvall, B.-Å. (1992). *National systems of innovation: Towards a theory of innovation and interactive learning*. Pinter.

Nelson, R. R., & Phelps, E. S. (1966). Investment in Humans, Technological Diffusion, and Economic Growth. *The American Economic Review*, *56*(1/2), 69–75. http://www.jstor.org/stable/1821269

Nelson, R. R. (1993). *National innovation systems: A comparative analysis*. Oxford University Press.

Nelson, R. R., & Winter, S. G. (1982). *An evolutionary theory of economic change*. Harvard University Press.

OECD. (2020). *Financing SMEs and entrepreneurs 2020: An OECD scoreboard.* https://doi.org/10.1787/061fe03d-en
OECD. (2022). *Labour migration in the WB: Mapping patterns, addressing challenges and reaping benefits.* https://doi.org/10.1787/af3db4f9-en
OECD. (2023a). *OECD science, Technology and innovation outlook 2023: Enabling transitions in times of disruption.* https://doi.org/10.1787/0b55736e-en
OECD. (2023b). *Economic convergence scoreboard for the WB.* OECD Publishing. Retrieved from https://www.oecd.org/content/dam/oecd/en/regions/grc/see/economic-convergence-scoreboard-for-the-western-balkans-2023.pdf
OECD. (2023c). *Labour productivity growth (GDP per hour worked) [Data set].* OECD Data. https://data.oecd.org/lprdty/gdp-per-hour-worked.htm
OECD. (2024a). *WB competitiveness outlook 2024: Regional profile, competitiveness and private sector development.* https://doi.org/10.1787/170b0e53-en
OECD. (2024b). *WB digital economy and society outlook 2024.* OECD Publishing. Available at https://www.oecd.org/south-east-europe/programme/wb6-digital-2024.htm. Accessed 14 July 2025.
OECD. (2025a). *Economic convergence scoreboard for the WB 2025.* https://doi.org/10.1787/bc0babf3-en
OECD. (2025b). *Digital and green SMEs: Accelerating the twin transitions in the WB – Tirana peer dialogue report.* OECD Publishing. Retrieved from https://www.oecd.org/content/dam/oecd/en/events/2025/02/grc_see_tirana/Tirana-Peer-Dialogue-Activity-Report.pdf
Radosevic, S. (2017). Upgrading technology in central and Eastern European economies. *IZA World of Labor, 338*, https://doi.org/10.15185/izawol.338
Riddle, L., & Brinkerhoff, J. M. (2011). Diaspora entrepreneurs as institutional change agents: The case of Thamel.com. *International Business Review, 20*(6), 670–680. https://doi.org/10.1016/j.ibusrev.2011.02.013
Rodrik, D. (2011). *The globalization paradox: Democracy and the future of the world economy.* New York: W.W. Norton & Company. Available at https://wwnorton.com/books/9780393071610. Accessed 14 July 2025.
Sabel, C. F., & Zeitlin, J. (2012). Experimentalist governance. In D. Levi-Faur (Ed.), *The Oxford handbook of governance* (pp. 169–183). Oxford University Press. https://doi.org/10.1093/oxfordhb/9780199560530.013.0012
Sen, A. (1999). *Development as freedom.* Alfred A. Knopf.
Solow, R. M. (1956). A contribution to the theory of economic growth. *The Quarterly Journal of Economics, 70*(1), 65–94. Available at https://www.jstor.org/stable/1884513. Accessed 14 July 2025.
Teece, D. J., Pisano, G., & Shuen, A. (1997). Dynamic capabilities and strategic management. *Strategic Management Journal, 18*(7), 509–533. https://doi.org/10.1002/(SICI)1097-0266(199708)18:7<509::AID-SMJ882>3.0.CO;2-Z
Transparency International. (2023). *Corruption perceptions index 2023.* Transparency International. Available at https://www.transparency.org/en/cpi/2023. Accessed: 14 July 2025.
UNDP. (2021). Innovation acceleration labs: Learning and experimentation in development practice. United Nations Development Programme. Available at https://acceleratorlabs.undp.org. Accessed 14 July 2025.
UNICEF. (2021). *Education and digital skills in the WB.* UNESCO Publishing.
UNIDO. (2024). *Industrial development report 2024: Turning challenges into sustainable solutions – the new era of industrial policy.* United Nations Industrial Development Organization. Available at https://www.unido.org/sites/default/files/unido-publications/2023-11/IDR24-OVERVIEW_1.pdf. Accessed 14 July 2025.
Vienna Institute. (2021). *WB labor market trends 2021.*
World Bank. (2023a). *Enterprise surveys: WB data highlights.* World Bank. Available at https://www.enterprisesurveys.org. Accessed 14 July 2025.

World Bank. (2023b). Digital Adoption Index (DAI) [Data set]. World Bank Open Data. https://www.worldbank.org/en/publication/wdr2016/Digital-Adoption-Index

World Bank. (2024). *World development indicators*. Retrieved from https://data.worldbank.org/indicator/SL.UEM.1524.ZS

World Bank Group and IFC. (2022). *Creating markets in Albania: Taking advantage of new trade and investment opportunities for a more robust private sector—country private sector diagnostic*. World Bank. https://doi.org/10.1596/37868

# Chapter 3
# Governance in Latecomer Contexts

## 3.1 Introduction

This chapter reconceptualizes governance as a core driver of economic transformation in latecomer economies. Traditional indicators of good governance, such as the rule of law, regulatory efficiency, and institutional alignment, often fail to translate into structural transformation or sustained capability development. Formal institutions may exist, but they often struggle to perform the developmental tasks required in an era of digital complexity and economic fragmentation.

This chapter shifts the focus from institutional form to functional capability. It draws on three key traditions: the political economy of developmental states, innovation systems theory, and adaptive governance. Together, these perspectives frame governance as a meta-capability—the ability of institutions to learn through experimentation, coordinate diverse actors, and embed policies within local institutional and social contexts. This view reflects the practical realities of the Western Balkans (WB), where overlapping mandates, fragmented donor programs, and rapid digital transitions often hinder conventional planning practices.

The chapter begins by questioning conventional assumptions regarding governance in transitional economies and by proposing a functional approach. It then identifies recurring constraints that hinder capability accumulation and introduces the concept that governance functions through three interdependent functions: learning, coordination, and embeddedness. These functions are located within relevant theoretical frameworks derived from developmental state theory, innovation systems, and adaptive governance. The discussion shows how the absence of these functions hinders the transformation of Kosovo, Albania, and North Macedonia. The chapter concludes by reframing governance not as a comprehensive checklist of institutions, but as an evolving capability essential for fostering economic learning, technological advancement, and structural change in latecomer contexts.



F. Sahiti, *Catching Up in the Digital Age*, Contributions to Economics,
https://doi.org/10.1007/978-3-032-17059-0_3

## 3.2 Governing Transformation from Form to Function

In the digital age, latecomer economies are facing a dual challenge. They must develop the technological and industrial capabilities necessary to compete in fast-changing global value chains while operating within bureaucratic systems that are often weak, donor-dependent, and fragmented. Under these circumstances, conventional governance models rarely provide the flexibility or coherence necessary for sustained transformation.

This gap has led to the search for guiding models, two of which have shaped much of the reform thinking. The first is the East Asian developmental state model, exemplified by Japan, South Korea, and later Taiwan and China. It emphasizes a strong and strategically oriented state that maintains close cooperation with the private sector while preserving autonomy to set long-term objectives (Johnson, 1982; Amsden, 1989; Evans, 1995). Transformation in this model is achieved through coordinated industrial policy, targeted credit, selective protection, and disciplined bureaucracies. Institutions such as Japan's Ministry of International Trade and Industry or Korea's Economic Planning Board were able to change by sequencing interventions and withdrawing support from underperforming areas. This model assumes strong bureaucracy and a stable political arrangement capable of sustaining long-term planning.

The second model, liberal institutionalism, was influenced by the work of North (1990) and policy frameworks promoted by the World Bank (1993). It emphasizes "good governance" principles such as regulatory convergence, property rights, rule of law, transparency, and administrative efficiency. The assumption is that open markets and predictable institutions create incentives for investment and innovation. In practice, this has led many reform programmes to prioritize legal harmonization and anti-corruption measures, expecting improved rules to produce better economic outcomes.

However, both models rely on preconditions that are rarely present in the WB. Ministries and agencies often overlap in their mandates, donor programmes operate independently, and policy agendas are shaped more by EU accession requirements or external conditionalities than by locally defined priorities (Elbasani, 2009; Bartlett, 2020). The result is a hybrid governance landscape that is neither strategically coordinated in the East Asian sense nor institutionally consolidated in the liberal sense, leaving limited capacity to steer transformation effectively.

This chapter therefore adopts a different lens. Governance is not viewed simply as the existence of formal institutions but as a higher-order capability through which states and other actors learn from experience, coordinate diverse interests, and design policies grounded in local realities (Cimoli et al., 2009; Chang & Andreoni, 2020). The critical question is not whether the right structures exist, but whether governance systems can perform essential functions under real-world constraints.

Digitalization makes this shift even more relevant. Rapid technological change increases interdependence across sectors and challenges traditional, linear planning methods. Successful development now depends on the ability to adapt quickly, share knowledge, and respond to emerging needs in real time. This requires governance that is flexible, interactive, and capable of continuous learning.

A functional perspective also explains why many reforms in the WB have produced limited results. Innovation councils, digital strategies, and reform plans often align with international best practices, yet they fail to generate sustained impact because they lack feedback mechanisms, cross-institutional coordination, and genuine stakeholder engagement. Pritchett et al. (2013) describe this phenomenon as isomorphic mimicry—copying institutional forms without embedding their developmental functions.

The core problem, therefore, lies not in the absence of institutions but in the lack of profound interaction, alignment, and adaptability among them. As Ostrom (2010) notes, systems perform best when actors share norms, exchange information, and learn iteratively. Institutions that do not foster these dynamics may appear robust on paper but remain ineffective in practice.

This analysis does not dismiss the importance of institutions; it clarifies their role. Institutions matter to the extent that they enable experimentation, coordination, and the localization of reform. These capacities are particularly crucial in fast-evolving sectors such as information technology, digital manufacturing, and data-driven services.

In the WB, formal institutions are numerous, but functional governance remains weak. Strategies are rarely revised based on evidence, ministries often act in isolation, and public consultations are largely procedural. The result is a governance system that appears structured but lacks the dynamic capabilities needed to guide transformation.

The discussion begins from this paradox. It redefines governance as an evolving capability and lays the foundation for the framework developed in the following section, which focuses on three interdependent functions: learning, coordination, and embeddedness.

## 3.3 Why Systems Break Down: Seven Interlinked Constraints

Governance failures in the WB are not the result of a single weakness but of a network of interrelated constraints. These factors operate together, reinforcing one another and undermining institutional performance and policy outcomes. They shape how reforms are designed, implemented, and sustained, often eroding even well-intentioned initiatives before they take root.

While these problems overlap—for instance, fragmentation can worsen coordination failures, and donor dependence can weaken policy ownership—treating them as distinct functional weaknesses allows for clearer diagnosis and reform strategies. The key is to recognize how they interact and compound each other, rather than viewing them as isolated issues. Understanding these interconnections is essential for designing governance reforms that work in practice as well as on paper.

### 3.3.1 Institutional Fragmentation

One of the most visible challenges is fragmentation across ministries, agencies, and public bodies. In many post-socialist states, institutions have overlapping mandates and weak coordination. This results in confusion, duplicated programmes, and policy fatigue. In North Macedonia, for example, multiple economic councils operate with unclear mandates, creating uncertainty about who is leading development strategy. Similar overlaps occur in Albania and Kosovo, particularly in areas such as digital policy, education, and innovation (World Bank, 2017; Bartlett, 2020; OECD, 2023). Fragmentation not only wastes resources but also weakens the state's ability to engage stakeholders, respond to change, and maintain reform momentum.

### 3.3.2 Donor Dependence

External funding plays a central role in shaping the policy agenda across the region. Donor programmes have supported valuable reforms and experimentation but often contribute to fragmentation. Initiatives are frequently designed to meet donor reporting requirements rather than national priorities. In Kosovo, for instance, many digital skills projects supported by donors are not aligned with national education or labour strategies. The result is a collection of short-term projects that lack systemic impact (Grindle, 2004; Booth, 2011; UNDP, 2021). When donor efforts are not well integrated, they dilute local ownership and make long-term planning difficult.

### 3.3.3 Political Volatility

Frequent government changes disrupt continuity and institutional learning. Ministries are reorganized, senior staff replaced, and new administrations often rewrite existing strategies. In Albania, repeated institutional restructuring has blurred mandates and eroded institutional memory. This instability weakens focus and interrupts reform cycles. When politics changes faster than policies can be implemented, long-term development priorities are sidelined (Ganev, 2005; European Commission, 2023).

### 3.3.4 Low Absorptive Capacity

Even when clear plans exist, governments often struggle to implement them effectively. Public administrations are typically under-resourced and lack the skills needed for complex projects. This problem is evident in the management of EU funds: across the WB, countries regularly fail to absorb available resources due to weak coordination and limited follow-through (European Court of Auditors, 2022; World Bank, 2023; OECD, 2025). Low absorptive capacity means that good ideas remain unimplemented and potential gains unrealized.

### 3.3.5 Capability Traps

Many institutions are created to meet international standards or donor requirements but remain hollow in practice. They have formal mandates and strategies yet lack the internal routines and learning systems needed for real implementation. This is known as a capability trap (Radosevic, 2017). Reforms often look impressive on paper but fail to function in practice. Without mechanisms for reflection and adjustment, institutions become static and ineffective (Pritchett et al., 2013; Andrews et al., 2017).

### 3.3.6 Policy Incoherence

Fragmentation leads directly to incoherence. Different ministries, agencies, or donors may work on similar issues—such as innovation, skills, or agriculture—without coordination. In Albania, for instance, vocational training and agricultural value chain initiatives are managed by separate institutions and donors, often with little communication. As a result, potentially complementary efforts work at cross-purposes (Borrás & Edquist, 2013; FAO, 2020; OECD, 2025). Without shared frameworks or joint planning, even well-designed policies can undermine one another.

### 3.3.7 Weak Embeddedness

Governance systems also struggle to build lasting relationships with the actors they aim to serve. Consultations with businesses, civil society, or local communities are often symbolic and occur too late to influence decisions. In North Macedonia, business associations were invited to contribute to cluster reforms, but their input was not reflected in the final policy. In Kosovo, diaspora entrepreneurs are praised publicly but rarely engaged in formal policymaking. In Albania, employer councils exist but have little influence over vocational training decisions. Without mechanisms for ongoing engagement, trust remains low and implementation suffers (Khan, 2018; FAO, 2020; IOM, 2021; World Bank, 2023).

In sum, what makes these barriers particularly challenging is their interdependence. Donor dependence deepens fragmentation; political volatility weakens institutional learning; and shallow embeddedness amplifies incoherence. Together, they produce a governance system that may appear institutionally dense but remains functionally fragile. It struggles to coordinate actors, build trust, and respond effectively to feedback.

Reform, however, is possible. Progress depends on shifting the focus from institutional form to institutional function. Governance systems that can perform three essential functions—learning, coordination, and embeddedness—can make progress even in settings of limited capacity. These functions provide the foundation for an adaptive and realistic approach to building state capability in complex, digitally evolving economies.

The next section introduces each of these governance functions and explains their role in supporting transformation in latecomer contexts.

## 3.4 Toward a Functional Conception of Governance as Meta-Capability

The previous discussion showed that conventional institutional reforms in the WB have often produced limited results. New ministries are created, strategies written, and donor programmes launched, yet governance systems frequently fail to deliver on their core developmental functions. Coordination mechanisms remain weak, learning processes are irregular, and stakeholder engagement is mostly symbolic. The problem is not the absence of institutions, but the inability of governance systems to function effectively in practice.

To move beyond this impasse, governance needs to be understood differently. Instead of focusing on whether formal institutions exist, attention should be directed to what governance actually enables. Does it foster learning from experience? Does it coordinate fragmented actors around shared goals? Does it build and sustain trust between the state, businesses, and civil society?

This section develops a functional conception of governance, viewing it not as a fixed institutional design but as a meta-capability: the capacity of the state to perform three interconnected functions—learning, coordination, and embeddedness. These functions are the foundation of capability development, particularly in settings marked by uncertainty, limited administrative capacity, and institutional fragmentation.

### *3.4.1 Learning as a Governance Function*

In an environment shaped by rapid technological change and evolving global value chains, learning is not optional; it is central to effective governance. Learning allows governments to adapt policies, respond to emerging challenges, and improve performance over time. Along with coordination and embeddedness, it enables the state to align diverse actors, sustain collaboration, and pursue shared developmental goals.

In high-capacity systems, learning is often institutionalized through foresight units, monitoring frameworks, or policy evaluation mechanisms. In lower-capacity settings, learning needs to occur through more flexible instruments such as pilot programmes, innovation labs, or mission-driven teams that can test ideas and adjust policies based on real-time feedback (Andrews et al., 2017).

This adaptive approach is particularly relevant in fast-changing sectors such as ICT, green manufacturing, and digital skills development, where technologies evolve faster than traditional planning cycles. The ability to learn by experimenting, adjusting, and scaling what works forms the backbone of a state's capacity to govern effectively in uncertain environments.

### 3.4.2 Coordination Across Sectors and Institutions

The second essential governance function is coordination—the ability to align multiple actors, including ministries, agencies, donors, firms, and universities, around common objectives. Coordination does not imply centralized control, but rather a capacity to connect and align different efforts across sectors and institutions.

In fragmented systems, responsibilities often overlap and mandates conflict, leading to duplication or paralysis (Borrás & Edquist, 2013). Effective coordination mechanisms can take many forms: joint funding platforms, cross-sectoral councils, or intermediary bodies that bridge public and private actors.

Some WB countries have experimented with such mechanisms through smart specialization strategies, where governments, researchers, and business leaders jointly identify strategic investment areas. Although implementation remains uneven, these examples show that coordination can work when structured around shared priorities and ongoing dialogue.

Coordination is not purely administrative; it is also political. It requires managing incentives, negotiating trade-offs, and building coalitions among actors with different interests and degrees of power (Khan, 2018). Effective coordination therefore depends as much on relationships and trust as on institutional design.

### 3.4.3 Embeddedness and Relational Governance

The third function of governance is embeddedness—the ability of the state to build lasting, trust-based relationships with economic and social actors. The concept, developed by Evans (1995), highlights the importance of interaction between public institutions and the communities they serve.

Embeddedness goes beyond consultation. It requires continuous exchange, joint problem-solving, and shared responsibility for outcomes. When institutions engage stakeholders only superficially, policies lose legitimacy and impact. This remains a persistent challenge in the WB. Business associations and civil society groups are often invited to participate in consultations, but their contributions rarely influence final decisions. Diaspora entrepreneurs and employer councils are celebrated rhetorically but seldom integrated into policymaking or implementation.

Building embeddedness requires dedicated platforms for engagement, such as regional innovation councils, sectoral advisory boards, or intermediary organizations that connect government and stakeholders (Fritz & Levy, 2014; Chaminade & Padilla-Pérez, 2017). Even in low-capacity contexts, these mechanisms can improve coordination, strengthen credibility, and foster accountability through mutual exchange.

### *3.4.4 The Governance Triangle*

Learning, coordination, and embeddedness are most effective when they work together. Learning without coordination results in fragmented initiatives. Coordination without embeddedness risks creating top-down mandates that lack legitimacy. Embeddedness without learning fosters relationships but delivers limited progress.

Together, these functions form what can be described as the governance triangle—a conceptual framework that shifts the focus from institutional form to system performance. The relevant question is not whether the right ministries or laws exist, but whether the system can adapt, align, and anchor reforms within the realities of its political and economic environment.

This functional perspective provides a more realistic benchmark for assessing governance in latecomer economies. It emphasizes that formal structures alone are insufficient for transformation. What matters is whether they enable learning that supports adaptation, coordination that builds credibility, and embeddedness that ensures participation and ownership (Fig. 3.1).

This conceptualization draws on several theoretical traditions. The next section traces these roots, linking the political economy of collective action, innovation systems theory, and adaptive governance to explain how the governance triangle helps latecomer economies organize learning and steer transformation.

## 3.5 Theoretical Roots of Functional Governance

The idea that governance should be judged by what it does, rather than by how it looks, comes from a broad and evolving body of scholarship. Although the shift from institutional form to institutional function may appear conceptually simple, it

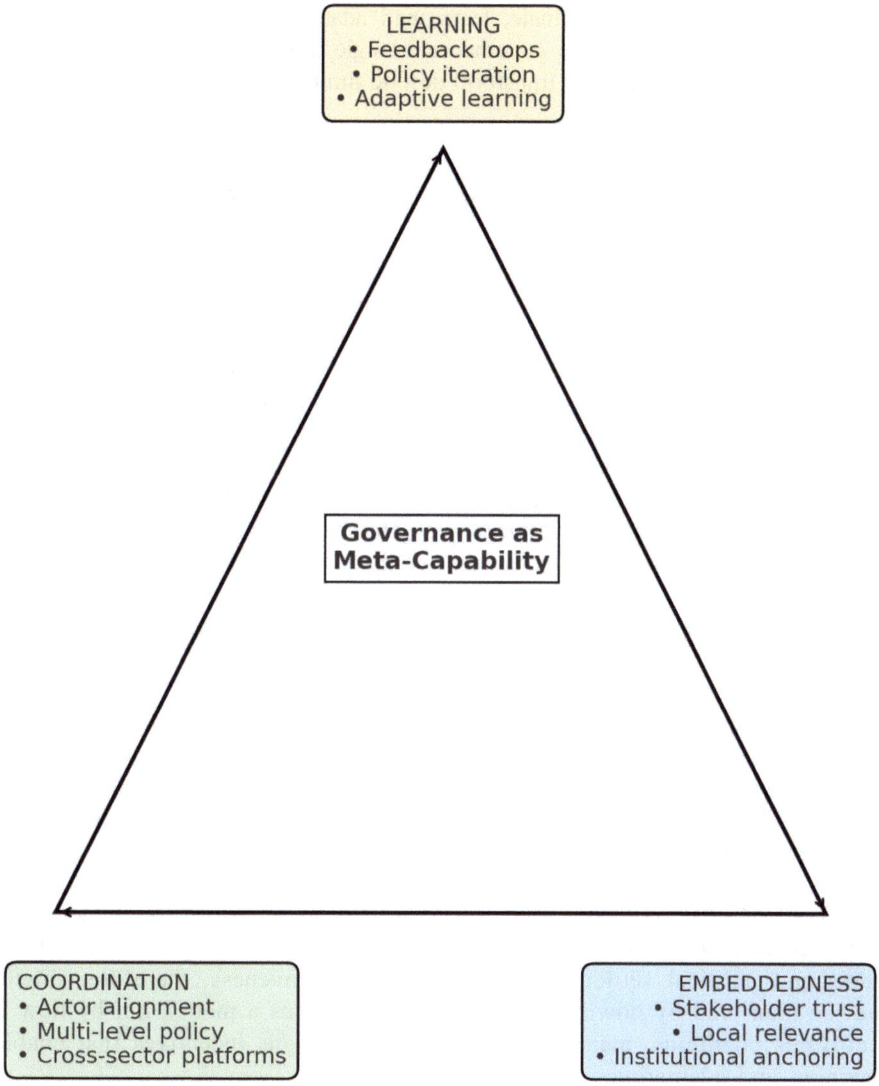


**Fig. 3.1** The governance triangle. *Source* Author's illustration, based on Andrews et al. (2017), Evans (1995), Sabel and Zeitlin (2012a, 2012b), generated with DALL·E using Microsoft Copilot (2025)

represents a significant departure from mainstream reform thinking, especially in post-socialist and aid-dependent contexts.

This section outlines the theoretical roots of this functional perspective, drawing on three interrelated traditions: the political economy of developmental states, innovation systems theory, and adaptive governance. Each offers a dual contribution: a critique of institutional formalism and a framework for understanding governance through its capacity to coordinate, learn, and adapt. Together, they provide the intellectual foundation for the governance triangle introduced earlier and explain how latecomer economies can transform despite limited institutional capacity.

### *3.5.1 Developmental States and the Politics of Capability*

The first foundation lies in the political economy of developmental states, a literature shaped by studies of Japan, South Korea, and Taiwan. In these countries, state institutions played a central role in driving industrial transformation. They combined professional bureaucracies, performance-based incentives, and close but disciplined relationships with business to promote structural change (Johnson, 1982; Amsden, 1989; Wade, 1990).

Evans' (1995) concept of embedded autonomy captures this model well. It describes the state's ability to maintain professional independence while remaining closely connected to key economic actors. This balance allowed governments to support private sector growth while ensuring that national development goals were not captured by narrow interests.

However, attempts to reproduce this model in Latin America, Sub-Saharan Africa, and post-socialist Europe often fell short. Instead of fostering strategic coordination, these efforts frequently produced fragmented bureaucracies, politicized appointments, and externally driven policy agendas (Leftwich, 2000; Doner et al., 2005). These experiences led scholars to adopt a more context-sensitive political economy perspective—one that asks not whether countries have high-capacity institutions, but whether their governance systems can perform essential functions within existing political and organizational constraints.

As Khan (2018) argues, the success of coordination and embeddedness depends on how institutional strategies align with prevailing incentive structures and political settlements. Governance effectiveness, therefore, should not be measured by how closely a country replicates a model, but by how it cultivates coalitions, manages trade-offs, and designs incentives that enable learning and adaptation.

### *3.5.2 Innovation Systems and Institutional Interdependence*

The second foundation comes from the theory of national innovation systems. This approach shifts attention from individual firms or sectors to the broader institutional environment that shapes how knowledge is created, shared, and applied. Pioneering work by Lundvall (1992), Nelson (1993), and Edquist (2005) redefined innovation as a system-level process driven by the quality of interaction among firms, universities, research institutes, and intermediary organizations.

In this view, learning is not simply an internal capability of individual organizations but a collective process structured by shared routines, feedback loops, and trust (Nelson & Winter, 1982). Governance, therefore, matters not only for setting rules but also for organizing relationships that allow learning to spread and deepen. Instruments such as innovation councils, cluster networks, and public–private partnerships help align incentives and enable coordination across institutional boundaries (Borrás & Edquist, 2013).

This tradition also highlights the importance of embeddedness. Effective innovation systems are grounded in regional capabilities and social trust. They succeed when institutions are anchored in local realities and capable of supporting continuous interaction and feedback (Chaminade & Lundvall, 2019).

For latecomer economies, especially in digitally intensive sectors, the lesson is clear: building innovation capacity is not just about investing in research or creating new agencies. It requires developing systems that promote collaboration, information exchange, and adaptive learning across fragmented institutional landscapes.

### *3.5.3 Adaptive Governance and Experimentalist Reform*

The third foundation is the growing literature on governance in complex and uncertain environments. This body of work emerged in response to the repeated failure of "blueprint" reforms that attempted to transfer institutional models wholesale. It argues instead for governance systems that evolve through problem-solving, experimentation, and iterative learning (Grindle, 2004; Rodrik, 2008; Andrews et al., 2017).

A leading approach in this tradition is Problem-Driven Iterative Adaptation (PDIA). PDIA starts from locally defined problems, encourages small-scale experimentation, and embeds learning through continuous feedback and course correction (Andrews et al., 2017). Rather than importing ready-made solutions, it builds capability by connecting reform efforts to real challenges and allowing adaptation as experience accumulates.

A related perspective, experimentalist governance, conceptualizes institutions as operating through flexible goal-setting, decentralized implementation, and regular review (Sabel & Zeitlin, 2012a, 2012b). Instead of treating governance as a system of rigid rule enforcement, it sees it as an ongoing cycle of exploration, evaluation, and adjustment.

Both frameworks share a set of assumptions: uncertainty is unavoidable, capacity develops through practice, and progress depends on mechanisms that enable experimentation and responsiveness. They also point to practical instruments—such as innovation labs, challenge funds, and learning platforms—that can be institutionalized even where capacity is limited.

### *3.5.4 Convergence and Implications*

These three traditions converge on a central insight: governance effectiveness depends less on institutional design and more on the capacity to coordinate, learn, and embed. Whether expressed as embedded autonomy, system orchestration, or iterative problem-solving, they all highlight the importance of relational, adaptive, and context-sensitive approaches to reform.

For transitional economies facing digital disruption, fragmented authority, and donor dependence, this insight is particularly relevant. Governance should be assessed not by the formal existence of institutions, but by their ability to perform the functions that drive transformation.

The next section applies this functional lens to analyse how the absence of these core capabilities—learning, coordination, and embeddedness—creates persistent barriers to upgrading and innovation in Kosovo, Albania, and North Macedonia.

## 3.6 Functional Deficits in the Western Balkans

Although the WB have adopted many institutions associated with good governance, such as innovation councils, vocational training agencies, and digital strategies, these structures often fall short in practice. The challenge is not institutional absence but institutional underperformance. Systems exist, yet they struggle to coordinate, adapt, and engage effectively.

This section illustrates how the three core governance functions, learning, coordination, and embeddedness, remain weak in Kosovo, Albania, and North Macedonia, and how these weaknesses limit capability development and structural transformation.

### *3.6.1 Learning: Episodic Experiments, Weak Feedback Loops*

Across the region, learning processes are fragmented and largely reactive. Policies are designed and implemented but seldom reviewed or adapted based on experience. Pilot projects are common, yet they rarely include mechanisms for continuous evaluation or feedback. Information is collected but not circulated across institutions, leaving learning episodic rather than systematic.

In Kosovo, the Digital Skills Strategy (2021–2024) was developed with donor support and broad consultation. Despite an inclusive design phase, it lacked mechanisms to monitor implementation or integrate feedback from employers, educators, or learners. Learning relied on external evaluations rather than internal review cycles (UNDP, 2021).

In Albania, modular reforms in vocational education were aligned with EU standards but introduced without a system to track outcomes or employer satisfaction. A 2020 FAO review found that lessons from donor-funded agri-food programmes were rarely shared across institutions, leading to repeated mistakes and fragmented innovation (FAO, 2020).

In North Macedonia, stakeholder workshops helped identify priorities for smart specialization. However, the absence of institutional mechanisms to act on these insights meant that findings were disconnected from national development planning (OECD, 2023).

These cases reflect a broader pattern: experimentation occurs, but learning is not institutionalized. Without structured feedback loops, successful practices are not scaled, and ineffective ones are repeated.

### 3.6.2 Coordination: Fragmentation Across Actors and Levels

Coordination remains one of the most persistent governance challenges in the WB. Ministries operate in silos, donor programmes follow separate agendas, and subnational institutions struggle to align with national strategies. Even when objectives overlap, such as improving digital skills or supporting export competitiveness, efforts often remain fragmented and duplicative.

In Albania, overlapping mandates in the agriculture, economy, and EU integration ministries create confusion. Donor initiatives in vocational training, value chain development, and export promotion are rarely aligned, leading to conflicting interventions and wasted resources. National strategies for industry, digitalization, and education coexist without shared goals or frameworks for implementation (European Commission, 2023).

In Kosovo, the Ministry of Economy, the Ministry of Education, and various SME support agencies each run digital skills and innovation programmes, often with donor backing. Coordination meetings are infrequent, and data systems remain incompatible. Firms tend to engage with whichever agency is most accessible rather than through an integrated support structure. Civil servants lack platforms to pool insights or plan collectively (World Bank, 2023).

In North Macedonia, coordination gaps are especially visible in regional development. Municipalities, regional agencies, and national ministries operate independently, with limited communication. Business support organizations exist formally but lack capacity and authority to connect stakeholders. The OECD (2023) observed that entrepreneurial discovery processes were launched without clear channels to integrate results into national policy or budgeting.

These examples show that coordination failures are not only administrative but also political. Ministries compete for visibility, donors pursue separate reporting requirements, and incentives for collaboration are weak or misaligned.

### 3.6.3 Embeddedness: Shallow Consultation, Weak Anchoring

The third governance function, embeddedness, is also underdeveloped across the region. Although stakeholder consultations are now standard practice, they often occur late in the policy process and have little influence on final outcomes. Engagement is typically procedural rather than substantive.

In North Macedonia, cluster development and vocational training reforms included consultation meetings, but participants reported that their contributions were rarely reflected in the results. Business associations are invited to discussions but often lack the capacity or leverage to shape outcomes. Without sustained dialogue, trust remains low and implementation uneven (World Bank, 2023).

In Kosovo, diaspora networks are increasingly active in digital entrepreneurship but remain outside formal policymaking. Public events and campaigns celebrate their contributions, yet there are few institutional mechanisms to integrate them into innovation or export strategies (IOM, 2021).

In Albania, employer engagement in vocational education shows both progress and limitation. Sectoral skills councils meet regularly, but their recommendations have little influence on curricula, budgets, or performance evaluation. This weakens incentives for ongoing participation (FAO, 2020).

Across the region, embeddedness suffers from weak networks, limited trust, and low continuity. Many engagement platforms are donor-initiated and collapse when funding ends. Without durable mechanisms linking institutions to real users and implementers, policies remain disconnected from practice and lack legitimacy.

### 3.6.4 Implications

These functional deficits explain why well-designed reforms often fail to produce lasting change. Learning does not accumulate, coordination remains weak, and engagement lacks substance. Strategies are launched with ambition but lose momentum without follow-up, alignment, or co-ownership.

The problem is not simply administrative inefficiency. It reflects a deeper absence of governance as a meta-capability, the systemic capacity to learn, coordinate, and adapt. Institutions exist, but the system as a whole fails to integrate experience, align incentives, or sustain collaboration. Reforms therefore remain isolated and their impact short-lived.

Recognizing this pattern opens the door to more practical reform strategies. Instead of creating new institutions, governments and development partners can focus on strengthening functional capacities, building pilot programmes with built-in review cycles, establishing coordination platforms with cross-sector mandates, and designing stakeholder mechanisms with real influence. These approaches may not transform systems overnight, but they provide realistic pathways for rebuilding trust, embedding learning, and fostering adaptation over time (Table 3.1).

**Table 3.1** Governance gaps in learning, coordination, and embeddedness

| Country | Learning | Coordination | Embeddedness |
|---|---|---|---|
| Kosovo | The Digital Skills Strategy lacked built-in review or feedback mechanisms | Digital initiatives dispersed across ministries and donors with little integration | Diaspora networks active but not formally engaged in policy processes |
| Albania | Vocational education reforms piloted without systematic tracking or feedback | Agri-food policy fragmented across ministries with weak cross-sector alignment | Employer councils exist but have little influence on curricula or funding decisions |
| North Macedonia | Smart specialization workshops initiated but disconnected from follow-up | Regional agencies and ministries act independently on industrial upgrading | Business associations consulted late in the process with limited impact |

*Source* Author's elaborations based on UNDP (2021), World Bank (2023), IOM (2021), FAO (2020), European Commission (2023), and OECD (2021a, 2021b)

The next chapter builds on these insights by outlining a governance framework capable of performing these functions under constraint. The Developmental Network State (DNS), introduced in this chapter, provides a structured approach for aligning actors, fostering learning, and embedding reforms in ways that reflect the institutional realities of transitional economies.

## 3.7 Conclusion: Why Reimagining Governance as Capability

This chapter has argued that governance in latecomer economies should be understood not as a collection of formal institutions, but as a meta-capability: the ability of a system to learn, coordinate, and embed policies within its social and institutional environment. This perspective is particularly relevant in transitional economies such as those of the WB, where institutions often exist on paper but lack the functionality needed to drive transformation.

Across Kosovo, Albania, and North Macedonia, governance systems display recurring weaknesses. Learning is sporadic and disconnected from implementation. Coordination is undermined by overlapping mandates and fragmented donor agendas. Embeddedness remains shallow, with stakeholder engagement often reduced to consultation without real influence. The result is a pattern of reform that is ambitious in design but fragile in practice.

These shortcomings are not only technical. They reflect deeper systemic issues such as political instability, donor dependence, and institutional fragmentation. Reforms are frequently well-intentioned but lack mechanisms for alignment, adaptation, or continuity. Strategies are introduced without feedback loops, agencies work in isolation, and dialogue between public and private actors remains limited and procedural.

However, these challenges also reveal a path forward. Shifting the focus from institutional form to governance function allows reformers to identify more realistic entry points for change. Rather than building new structures, attention can be directed toward strengthening the capabilities that enable existing institutions to perform more effectively. Pilot programmes can include built-in feedback and evaluation mechanisms. Coordination platforms can be given clear cross-sector mandates and shared funding pools. Stakeholder participation can be embedded within institutions that have stability, authority, and accountability.

This functional approach does not downplay the importance of institutions but clarifies their purpose. Institutions matter when they help systems adapt, align, and build trust over time. This is particularly crucial in areas shaped by rapid technological change, such as digital skills development, innovation, and industrial upgrading. In these contexts, governance must evolve from enforcing static rules to facilitating dynamic learning and collaboration.

By framing governance as a meta-capability, this chapter provides the conceptual foundation for what follows. In this chapter builds on these insights by introducing the DNS, a governance framework designed to operationalize learning, coordination, and embeddedness in low-capacity, digitally evolving environments. Where traditional models of governance have struggled, the DNS offers a practical structure for building capabilities through iterative, networked, and context-sensitive solutions.

## References

Amsden, A. H. (1989). *Asia's next giant: South Korea and late industrialization*. Oxford University Press.

Andrews, M., Pritchett, L., & Woolcock, M. (2017). *Building state capability: Evidence, analysis, action*. Oxford University Press.

Bartlett, W. (2020). International assistance, donor interests, and state capture in the Western Balkans. *Journal of Contemporary European Studies, 29*(2), 184–200. https://doi.org/10.1080/14782804.2020.1794801

Booth, D. (2011). Aid, institutions and governance: What have we learned? *Development Policy Review, 29*(S1), S5–S26. https://doi.org/10.1111/j.1467-7679.2011.00518.x

Borrás, S., & Edquist, C. (2013). The choice of innovation policy instruments. *Technological Forecasting and Social Change, 80*(8), 1513–1522. https://doi.org/10.1016/j.techfore.2013.03.002

Chaminade, C., & Lundvall, B.-Å. (2019). Science, technology and innovation policy—Old patterns and new challenges. *Oxford Research Encyclopedia of Business and Management*. https://doi.org/10.1093/acrefore/9780190224851.013.179

Chaminade, C., & Padilla-Pérez, R. (2017). The challenge of alignment and barriers for the design and implementation of science, technology and innovation policies. In S. Kuhlmann & G. Ordoñez-Matamoros (Eds.), *Research handbook on innovation governance for emerging economies* (pp. 181–204). Edward Elgar. https://doi.org/10.4337/9781783471911.00013

Chang, H. J., & Andreoni, A. (2020). Industrial policy in the twenty-first century. *Development and Change, 51*(2), 324–351. https://doi.org/10.1111/dech.12570

Cimoli, M., Dosi, G., & Stiglitz, J. E. (Eds.). (2009). *Industrial policy and development: The political economy of capabilities accumulation*. Oxford University Press.

Doner, R. F., Ritchie, B. K., & Slater, D. (2005). Systemic vulnerability and the origins of developmental states. *International Organization, 59*(2), 327–361. https://doi.org/10.1017/S0020818305050113

Elbasani, A. (2009). *EU administrative conditionality and domestic downloading: The limits of Europeanization in challenging contexts*. KFG Working Paper Series No. 2. Freie Universität Berlin.

European Commission. (2023). *Enlargement Package: Western Balkans Progress Reports*. Directorate-General for Neighbourhood and Enlargement Negotiations (DG NEAR).

European Court of Auditors. (2022). *Special report: Implementation of EU pre-accession assistance in the Western Balkans*. ECA. Available at: https://www.eca.europa.eu/en/Pages/DocItem.aspx?did=60213. Accessed July 18, 2025.

Evans, P. B. (1995). *Embedded autonomy: States and industrial transformation*. Princeton University Press.

FAO. (2020). *The state of food and agriculture 2020: Overcoming water challenges in agriculture*. Food and Agriculture Organization. Available at: http://www.fao.org/3/cb1447en/CB1447EN.pdf. Accessed July 18, 2025.

Fritz, V., & Levy, B. (2014). *Problem-driven political economy analysis: The World Bank's experience*. World Bank.

Edquist, C. (2005). Systems of Innovation: Perspectives and Challenges. In J. Fagerberg, D. Mowery, & R. R. Nelson (Eds.), *Oxford Handbook of Innovation* (pp. 181–208). Oxford University Press.

Gallup. (2022). *Balkan monitor survey results*. Available at: https://www.gallup.com. Accessed July 18, 2025.

Ganev, V. I. (2005). Post-communism as an episode of state-building: A reversed Tillyan perspective. *Communist and Post-Communist Studies, 38*(3), 425–445. https://doi.org/10.1016/j.postcomstud.2005.09.008

Grindle, M. S. (2004). Good enough governance: Poverty reduction and reform in developing countries. *Governance, 17*(4), 525–548. https://doi.org/10.1111/j.0952-1895.2004.00256.x

IOM. (2021). *Mapping and Profiling of the Albanian Diaspora*. International Organization for Migration. Available at: https://albania.iom.int/sites/g/files/tmzbdl1401/files/documents/Mapping%20and%20Profiling%20of%20Albanian%20Diaspora%20Research.pdf. Accessed July 18, 2025.

Johnson, C. (1982). *MITI and the Japanese miracle: The growth of industrial policy, 1925–1975*. Stanford University Press. https://doi.org/10.1515/9780804765602

Khan, M. (2018). Political settlements and the analysis of institutions. *African Affairs, 117*(469), 636–655. https://doi.org/10.1093/afraf/ady018

Leftwich, A. (2000). *States of development: On the primacy of politics in development*. Polity Press.

Lundvall, B.-Å. (1992). *National Systems of Innovation: Towards a Theory of Innovation and Interactive Learning*. Pinter.

Nelson, R.R. & Winter, S.G. (1982). *An Evolutionary Theory of Economic Change*. Belknap Press of Harvard University Press.

Nelson, R.R. (1993). *National Innovation Systems: A Comparative Analysis*. Oxford University Press.

North, D. C. (1990). *Institutions, institutional change and economic performance*. Cambridge University Press. https://doi.org/10.1017/CBO9780511808678

OECD. (2021a). *Digital government index: Western Balkans pilot report*. Available at: https://www.oecd.org/governance/digital-government-index-western-balkans-pilot-report.pdf. Accessed July 18, 2025.

OECD. (2021b). *Multi-level governance of economic development in the Western Balkans*. Available at: https://www.oecd.org/regional/regional-policy/multi-level-governance-of-economic-development-in-the-western-balkans-49b0776a-en.htm. Accessed July 18, 2025.

OECD. (2023). Global trends in government innovation 2023. *OECD Public Governance Reviews*. https://doi.org/10.1787/0655b570-en
OECD. (2025). *Economic convergence scoreboard for the Western Balkans 2025*. https://doi.org/10.1787/bc0babf3-en
Ostrom, E. (2010). Beyond markets and states: Polycentric governance of complex economic systems. *American Economic Review, 100*(3), 641–672. https://doi.org/10.1257/aer.100.3.641
Pritchett, L., Woolcock, M., & Andrews, M. (2013). Looking like a state: Techniques of persistent failure in state capability for implementation. *Journal of Development Studies, 49*(1), 1–18. https://doi.org/10.1080/00220388.2012.709614
Radosevic, S. (2017) 'Upgrading technology in Central and Eastern European economies', *IZA World of Labor*, 338. https://doi.org/10.15185/izawol.338
Rodrik, D. (2008). Thinking about governance. In D. C. North, D. Acemoglu, F. Fukuyama, & B. Weingast (Eds.), *Governance, growth, and development decision-making* (pp. 17–24). World Bank.
Sabel, C. F., & Zeitlin, J. (2012a). *Experimentalist governance in the European Union: Towards a new architecture*. Oxford University Press.
Sabel, C. F., & Zeitlin, J. (2012b). Experimentalist governance. In D. Levi-Faur (Ed.), *The Oxford handbook of governance* (pp. 169–183). Oxford University Press.
UNDP. (2021). *Innovation in governance: The case of the UNDP accelerator labs*. United Nations Development Programme. Available at: https://www.undp.org/sites/g/files/zskgke326/files/2022-07/2021_AnnualReport_UNDPAcclabs_Reimagining_Development_through_a_Global_Learning_Network.pdf. Accessed July 18, 2025.
Wade, R. (1990). *Governing the market: economic theory and the role of government in East Asian industrialization*. Princeton University Press.
World Bank. (1993). *The East Asian miracle: Economic growth and public policy*.
World Bank. (2017). *World development report 2017: Governance and the law*. https://doi.org/10.1596/978-1-4648-0950-7
World Bank (2023). *Enterprise Surveys: WB Data Highlights*. World Bank. Available at: https://www.enterprisesurveys.org (Accessed: 14 July 2025).

# Chapter 4
# Governing Capability Accumulation

## 4.1 Introduction

In the Digital Age, structural transformation unfolds within an ecosystem defined by rapid technological change, global interconnectivity, and shifting value chains. Latecomer economies must navigate these dynamics while managing resource constraints and continued donor dependence. This chapter introduces the Developmental Network State (DNS), a governance framework designed to build capabilities within this complex environment.

Rather than offering rigid blueprints or prescribing new digital infrastructures, the DNS works through the defining features of the modern ecosystem: interconnected actors, continuous feedback, and fluid knowledge flows. It seeks to coordinate collective action and accelerate industrial upgrading by using existing networks more effectively.

Building on Chaps. 2 and 3, this chapter pursues four goals. First, it defines the DNS at the intersection of developmental state theory, innovation systems, and adaptive governance, reinterpreted for a world where data and networks shape every sector. Second, it explores the DNS's three core functions, learning, coordination, and embeddedness, and explains how each is strengthened by digital connectivity and information-rich environments. Third, it outlines practical mechanisms such as multi-stakeholder councils, learning consortia, and mission-driven coalitions that translate these functions into sustained development without requiring new technology investments. Finally, it highlights the DNS's relevance for post-socialist economies in the Western Balkans (WB), where conventional industrial policy has struggled amid institutional fragmentation and rapidly changing digital contexts.

By situating the DNS within the realities of the Digital Age, characterized by rapid knowledge exchange, cross-border linkages, and adaptive governance, this chapter provides a foundation for the case studies that follow. These cases will



F. Sahiti, *Catching Up in the Digital Age*, Contributions to Economics,
https://doi.org/10.1007/978-3-032-17059-0_4

illustrate how a network-oriented state can harness digital connectivity to promote capability accumulation and catch-up growth in transitional, donor-dependent settings.

## 4.2 Conceptual Foundations of the DNS

Latecomer economies in the WB continue to face deep structural constraints, including institutional fragmentation, weak bureaucratic capacity, and limited state legitimacy. These weaknesses have undermined both traditional state-led development models and market-based reforms, leaving sustained structural transformation difficult to achieve.

The DNS offers a new way to approach this challenge. It reimagines governance for settings where neither centralized control nor fully autonomous markets function effectively. Instead, it treats governance as a dynamic network of relationships among public agencies, private firms, universities, donors, and diaspora actors. These actors are not bound by rigid hierarchies but connected through adaptive collaboration and shared problem-solving.

At the heart of the DNS is flexibility. Institutions are seen as evolving arrangements that must adapt to changing opportunities and constraints. This approach draws on ideas from network governance, institutional adaptation, and experimental policymaking to describe how fragmented states can still foster coordination, innovation, and learning through relationships and feedback.

The conceptual framework unfolds in three steps. First, it traces the intellectual origins of the DNS across several traditions, including embedded autonomy, networked governance, mission-oriented policy, political settlements, and dynamic capabilities. Second, it situates the DNS within current debates on governance, contrasting it with both the East Asian developmental state and the Washington Consensus, which have limited relevance in fragmented, low-capacity contexts. Third, it synthesizes insights from experimentalist governance, adaptive learning, and political economy to articulate a coherent model of governance suited to transitional environments.

Through this synthesis, the DNS emerges as a context-sensitive framework for cultivating the technological and organizational capabilities that latecomer economies need to compete and adapt.

### *4.2.1 Intellectual Lineage of the DNS*

The DNS builds on a diverse but complementary set of ideas from governance, innovation, and political economy. These perspectives explain how development can advance even when institutions are fragmented or under-resourced.

Peter Evans's concept of embedded autonomy (1995) shows how capable states can combine professional independence with close engagement with economic actors. The DNS extends this logic to contexts where bureaucratic cohesion is limited, suggesting that collaboration and feedback can still emerge through relational networks and shared learning.

Network governance theory (Rhodes, 1997; Provan & Kenis, 2008) emphasizes policymaking as a polycentric process where multiple actors, public, private, and civic, interact to address complex challenges. This view underpins the DNS's focus on horizontal coordination, cross-sector linkages, and iterative experimentation.

Manuel Castells's network society framework (1996) further demonstrates that decentralized knowledge flows can substitute for top-down control. This insight reinforces the DNS principle that effective governance can arise from connectivity and interaction rather than hierarchy.

In innovation studies, Mariana Mazzucato's work on mission-oriented innovation policy (2013; 2021) redefines the state as an active shaper of markets and technological direction. The DNS applies this concept to resource-constrained environments, encouraging public agencies to take calculated risks and mobilize coalitions for long-term capability building.

Slavo Radosevic's research on post-socialist innovation systems (1999; 2011) shows that weak inter-organizational linkages hinder coordination and learning. His findings support the DNS emphasis on stitching together dispersed actors to create coherence in fragmented settings.

Joseph Stiglitz (2015) highlights the importance of feedback and learning under uncertainty. The DNS incorporates this by embedding real-time review and adaptive mechanisms into governance processes. Similarly, Justin Lin's New Structural Economics (2011; 2021) calls for development strategies aligned with evolving comparative advantage. The DNS aligns with this by promoting interventions that connect local capabilities with global opportunities.

These intellectual strands converge on a common insight: development is sustained not by rigid blueprints but by governance systems that enable learning, coordination, and collaboration (Table 4.1).

### *4.2.2 Situating the DNS in Contemporary Governance Debates*

The DNS addresses the limitations of two dominant development paradigms: the East Asian Developmental State (EADS) and the Washington Consensus (WC). Both have proven difficult to apply in contexts characterized by weak capacity, political instability, and donor dependence.

The EADS model, exemplified by Japan, South Korea, and Taiwan, relied on strong, meritocratic bureaucracies capable of long-term industrial coordination (Evans, 1995; Johnson, 1982). It succeeded where elite cohesion and bureaucratic autonomy were sustained. In contrast, such conditions are rarely

**Table 4.1** Intellectual foundations of the DNS

| Intellectual tradition | Key insights | Implications for DNS |
|---|---|---|
| Embedded autonomy (Evans, 1995) | States can coordinate development while maintaining social engagement | Adapts autonomy to fragmented contexts through proximity and feedback-based learning |
| Network governance (Rhodes, 1997; Provan & Kenis, 2008) | Policy outcomes emerge from networks rather than hierarchies | Promotes multi-actor collaboration and horizontal coordination |
| Network society (Castells, 1996) | Decentralized knowledge flows can replace top-down directives | Emphasizes distributed information and inter-organizational connectivity |
| Mission-oriented policy (Mazzucato, 2013, 2021) | The state can shape markets and guide innovation | Encourages public agencies to build coalitions and develop capabilities strategically |
| Post-socialist innovation systems (Radosevic, 1999, 2011) | Weak linkages hinder learning and coordination | Focuses on integrating fragmented actors into coherent networks |
| Learning under uncertainty (Stiglitz, 2015) | Feedback and adaptation are essential for effective policy | Embeds iterative learning and review within governance routines |
| New structural economics (Lin, 2011, 2021) | Industrial policy must align with evolving advantages | Promotes context-specific interventions connected to global markets |

*Source* Author's elaboration based on different literature strands

present in donor-dependent or politically fragmented settings, where clientelism and institutional fragility undermine consistent policy direction (Khan, 2010; Leftwich, 2010).

The WC, by contrast, advocates market liberalization, fiscal restraint, and deregulation, assuming markets allocate resources more efficiently than governments (Williamson, 1990; Rodrik, 2004). While this approach can deliver macroeconomic stability, it often weakens state capacity and fails to address coordination failures or capability gaps, particularly in latecomer economies (Chang, 2002; Radosevic, 2017).

The DNS provides a middle path for such contexts. It treats governance as an adaptive, networked process that connects government agencies, firms, universities, donors, and diaspora actors in cycles of learning and collective problem-solving. Instead of depending on top-down control or pure market mechanisms, the DNS mobilizes practical instruments such as donor coordination forums, diaspora investment platforms, and cross-ministerial task forces to align agendas, build trust, and institutionalize cooperation even **under conditions of limited formal capacity** (Table 4.2).

**Table 4.2** Governance models for capability development—a comparative overview

| Model | Governance logic | Typical strengths | Limitations in low-capacity environments |
|---|---|---|---|
| East Asian developmental state | Centralized, meritocratic bureaucracy steering private sector | Long-term planning, effective coordination, rapid industrialization | Requires political stability and elite cohesion; vulnerable to clientelism |
| Washington consensus | Market liberalization and deregulation | Macro stability, improved efficiency | Weakens state capacity, fails to address coordination gaps |
| Developmental network state | Adaptive, networked governance | Flexible problem-solving, embedded learning, diverse collaboration | Requires sustained coordination among varied actors and effective intermediaries |

*Sources* Adapted from Williamson (1990), Evans (1995), Teece et al. (1997), Rodrik (2004), Khan (2010), Sabel and Zeitlin (2012), Andrews et al. (2017)

### *4.2.3 Core Theories Underpinning the DNS*

The DNS draws from three complementary theoretical traditions: experimentalist governance, political settlements theory, and the dynamic capabilities approach. These theoretical traditions explain how adaptive governance can function in low-capacity environments.

Experimentalist governance views policymaking as an ongoing cycle of setting goals, experimenting locally, learning from results, and adjusting accordingly (Sabel & Zeitlin, 2012). It highlights the importance of feedback and iteration where uncertainty and limited capacity prevail. The DNS applies this by creating "sandbox" environments in which agencies and firms test solutions, identify early problems, and refine approaches continuously.

Political settlements theory emphasizes that power dynamics and elite bargains shape how institutions function (Khan, 2018, 2010). The DNS works within these realities by building coalitions that align reform agendas with the interests of influential actors, ensuring that governance innovations are politically feasible and sustainable.

The dynamic capabilities approach (Teece et al., 1997) explains how organizations sense opportunities, seize them through experimentation, and reconfigure resources to embed new learning. Within the DNS, this theory helps explain how governance systems can reorganize their structures and relationships to adapt as challenges evolve.

Taken together, these perspectives reinforce the DNS as a governance system built on adaptive learning, political feasibility, and institutional flexibility.

Figure 4.1 illustrates this convergence, showing how DNS weaves adaptive learning, relational networks and political economy navigation into a unified model of governance.

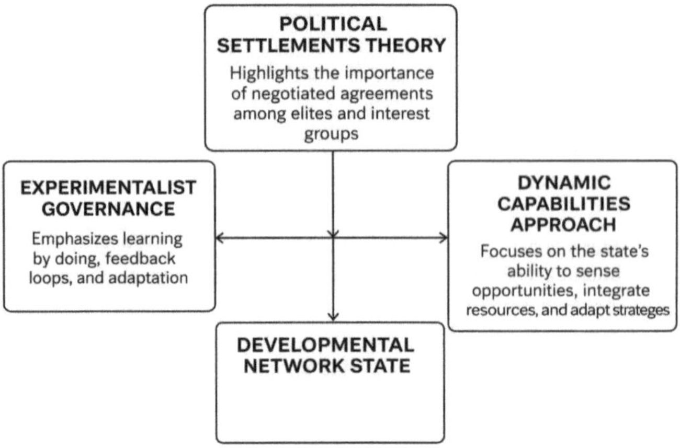


**Fig. 4.1** The theoretical pillars of the DNS. *Note* Conceptual diagram showing DNS at the intersection of experimentalist governance, political settlements theory and dynamic capabilities approach, highlighting adaptive learning cycles, boundary-spanning networks and political feasibility in low-capacity states. *Sources* Adapted from Sabel and Zeitlin (2012), Khan (2010; 2018), Teece et al. (1997)

Building on these theoretical foundations, the next section examines DNS in action through three interlocking principles: coordination, learning and embeddedness.

## 4.3 Learning, Coordination, and Embeddedness as Drivers of Capability Development

This section operationalizes the conceptual foundations of the DNS by analysing these three governance functions as interdependent mechanisms that support technological upgrading in latecomer economies. The DNS treats them not as separate policy tools but as mutually reinforcing capabilities that enable adaptive problem solving in contexts of institutional fragmentation, limited administrative capacity, and high uncertainty.

In environments where formal rules are applied unevenly and public bodies struggle to act in unison, these functions become essential. Coordination lowers transaction costs and aligns diverse stakeholders around shared missions. Learning spreads new practices and embeds collective routines. Embeddedness roots collaboration in local institutions and strengthens trust. Crucially, DNS effectiveness depends on cultivating these capabilities through relationships and local anchoring rather than solely on technical design.

Figure 4.2 offers a visual overview of how coordination, learning and embeddedness interact in the DNS framework. It illustrates the dynamic engagement between state and non-state actors that forms the operational core of governance

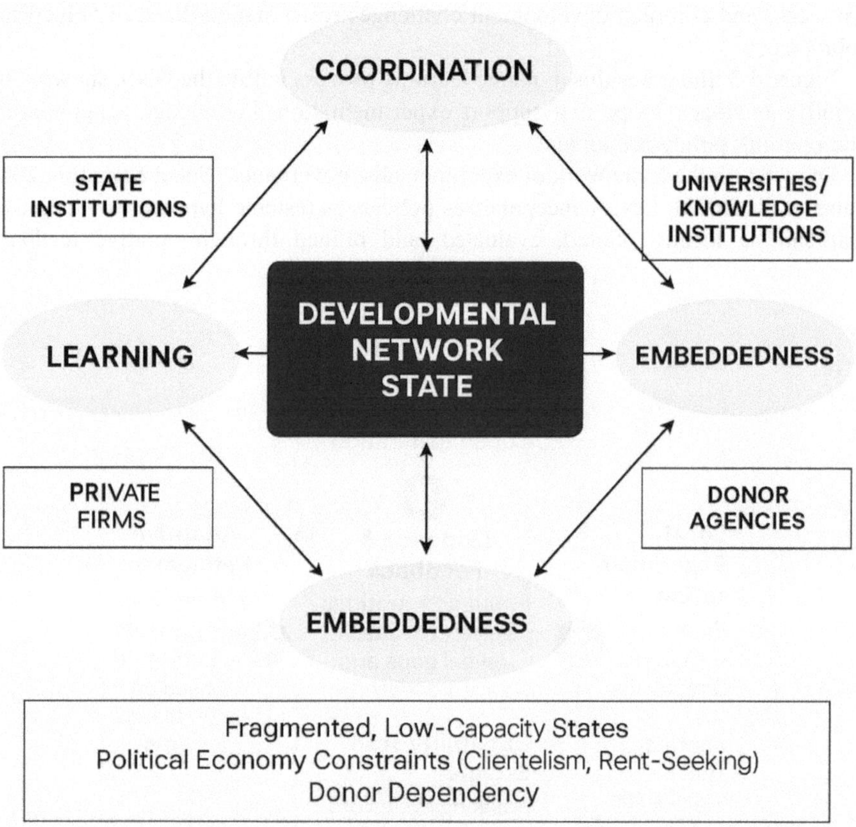


**Fig. 4.2** Operational overview of the DNS (DNS) framework. *Source* Author's elaboration, *generated with the aid of DALL · E using Microsoft Copilot (2025)*

where traditional models fall short. This diagram serves as a roadmap for the detailed analysis that follows, unpacking each function and its role in driving capability-centred development.

## *4.3.1 Learning, Feedback, and Adaptive Experimentation*

Learning is the driving force behind the DNS. It transforms governance from a static sequence of rules and procedures into a recursive cycle of experimentation, reflection, and continuous adjustment. This adaptive approach enables policymakers to refine solutions based on emerging evidence and evolving conditions, rather than relying solely on pre-defined plans. Such a mindset is especially critical in low-capacity states, where uncertainty is high, formal governance mechanisms are weak, and complex development challenges resist standardized or "blueprint" solutions.

Figure 4.3 illustrates this dynamic learning process within the DNS, showing the iterative feedback loops that support experimentation, knowledge accumulation, and ongoing policy refinement.

Drawing on the framework of experimentalist governance (Sabel & Zeitlin, 2012; Sabel et al., 2023), DNS conceptualizes policies as testable hypotheses—initiatives that can be locally piloted, evaluated, and refined through iterative feedback.

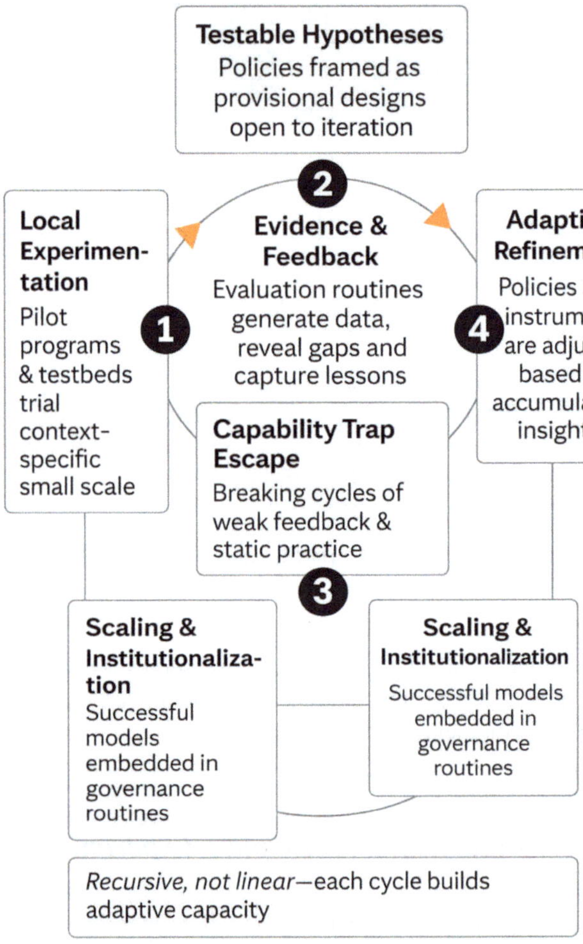


**Fig. 4.3** DNS governance as a learning and adaptation cycle. *Source* Author's own elaboration, adapted from the experimentalist governance literature (e.g., Sabel & Zeitlin, 2012; Sabel et al., 2023), generated with DALL · E using Microsoft Copilot (2025)

By institutionalizing learning mechanisms such as pilot programs, innovation funds, systematic evaluations, and knowledge-sharing platforms, latecomer countries can overcome capability traps, where weak feedback loops and fragmented information impede adaptive improvement.

Figure 4.3 illustrates the conceptual cycle of recursive learning, while Table 4.3 details the operational instruments and mechanisms through which this learning process is embedded in DNS implementation.

Examples from the WB illustrate these principles. Kosovo's Innovation Centre functions as a digital entrepreneurship lab that supports startups, provides training, and connects diaspora mentors. Albania's agri-food pilots use phased co-financing to align producer incentives with export standards. In both cases, iterative design and review allow for timely adjustment.

Performance metrics in the DNS prioritize learning. Adaptive indicators, stakeholder reviews, and embedded diagnostics replace rigid monitoring frameworks. When linked to incentives and integrated into administrative routines, these practices build a culture of continuous improvement.

### *4.3.2 Coordination for Aligning Fragmented Systems*

Coordination is the foundational pillar of the DNS framework. It aligns public agencies, private firms and civil-society actors around shared development goals. In many latecomer contexts, fragmented authority, siloed ministries and uncoordinated reform agendas undermine even well-designed interventions. Without strategic alignment, actors work at cross-purposes and implementation lacks cohesion.

**Table 4.3** Strengthening learning systems in DNS

| Instrument/ mechanism | Function in DNS | Illustrative outcome |
|---|---|---|
| Pilot programs & testbeds | Trial new policies or technologies before wider rollout | Context-specific solutions that scale credibly |
| Innovation funds | Flexible finance for experimental and adaptive initiatives | Support for startups, sector pilots, and grassroots efforts |
| Evaluation routines | Systematic feedback on performance and gaps | Mid-course corrections and incremental refinement |
| Knowledge-sharing platforms | Exchange of practices and lessons across actors and regions | Collective problem solving and faster diffusion of learning |
| Embedded diagnostics & reviews | Discovery-oriented indicators and stakeholder reviews | Governance routines that favor learning over compliance |

*Source* Author's own compilation, drawing on experimentalist governance literature and DNS practice cases (e.g., Innovation Centre Kosovo; Albania agri-food pilots)

The DNS departs from top-down, command-and-control models by favouring networked coordination mechanisms grounded in relational trust, iterative dialogue and collective problem solving. These mechanisms operate along three dimensions: horizontal, vertical and cross-sectoral coordination. Each dimension reinforces the others, creating a cohesive governance system despite low administrative capacity and high uncertainty.

Horizontal coordination aligns institutions operating at the same administrative level, such as the Ministry of Economy, Ministry of Education, and Ministry of Digital Affairs. Instruments typically include joint planning boards, inter-ministerial task forces, and shared funding pools, which facilitate integrated action across departments. An illustrative outcome is the co-development of national innovation strategies that link vocational training systems to evolving industrial needs. Similarly, collaboration between the Ministry of Trade and the Ministry of Education to align export promotion with skills development demonstrates the potential of horizontal mechanisms to bridge sectoral gaps within government.

Vertical coordination connects central and subnational levels of government, ensuring coherence between national strategies and local implementation. Mechanisms such as regional platforms, structured feedback channels, and decentralized pilot frameworks allow local insights to inform central policymaking while safeguarding consistency with overarching national priorities. For example, national digital strategies may be localized through regional skills programs and municipal infrastructure investments, thereby ensuring alignment across governance tiers.

Cross-sectoral coordination integrates domains often treated in isolation, including skills, finance, infrastructure, trade, technology, and environmental policy. Instruments such as multi-stakeholder councils, cross-sectoral challenge funds, and hybrid innovation platforms foster systemic responses to complex development challenges. A typical example is the design of blended programs in which SMEs simultaneously receive financing, technical training, and improved logistics access to enhance their competitiveness in export markets. Likewise, cross-sectoral approaches have been applied to address regional digital skills gaps, where training is combined with infrastructure expansion and market linkages.

Collectively, these three dimensions provide a comprehensive framework for coordinating digital national strategies. This framework is illustrated in Fig. 4.4: DNS Coordination Framework, which depicts the interplay of coordination mechanisms across governance levels and sectors.

Coordination in the DNS is a dynamic process that evolves through continuous feedback. Shared data infrastructures, real-time dashboards, and outcome-based metrics reveal misalignments and guide mid-course corrections. Adaptive planning cycles and learning-oriented monitoring systems embed iterative refinement into governance routines. A practical example is Croatia's sectoral innovation councils (SICs), established under the EU's Smart Specialisation Strategy (S3) (European Commission Joint Research Centre, 2025). SICs convene government agencies, firms, and universities to co-identify investment priorities and co-design research agendas. Although not formally labelled DNS, they exemplify multi-actor coordination, iterative adjustment, and strategic alignment.

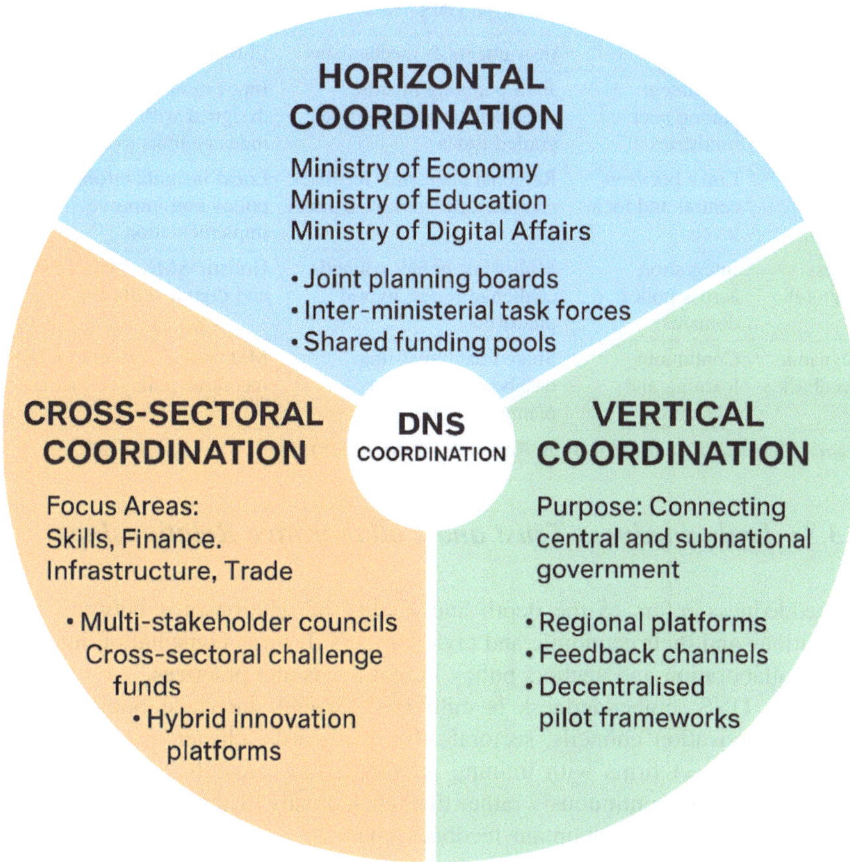


**Fig. 4.4** DNS coordination framework. *Source* Author's own elaboration, adapted from the experimentalist governance literature, generated with DALL · E using Microsoft Copilot (2025)

Table 4.4 presents the key dimensions of coordination in Dynamic Networked Systems (DNS), where relational and adaptive mechanisms drive learning and capability accumulation. The four dimensions—horizontal, vertical, cross-sectoral, and dynamic feedback—highlight how focus areas, instruments, and outcomes interact to align actors, integrate knowledge, and support iterative refinement. Croatia's sectoral innovation councils (SICs) exemplify this approach, demonstrating how multi-actor platforms can co-shape priorities, adjust strategies in real time, and embed coordination as a core function of governance

In summary, coordination in the DNS is relational and adaptive. It relies on shared agendas, mutual accountability, and iterative adjustment. When combined with learning and embeddedness, coordination becomes the connective tissue of a governance system that supports capability accumulation under constraint.

**Table 4.4** Coordination dimensions in the DNS

| Dimension | Focus | Instruments & mechanisms | Illustrative outcome |
|---|---|---|---|
| Horizontal | Alignment among peer ministries | Joint planning boards; interministerial task forces; pooled funds | Innovation strategies co-designed with skills and industry links |
| Vertical | Links between central and local levels | Regional platforms; feedback channels; decentralized pilots | Local insights inform national policy and improve implementation |
| Cross-sectoral | Integration across policy domains | Multi-stakeholder councils; challenge funds; hybrid platforms | Holistic SME export readiness and digital skills convergence |
| Dynamic feedback | Continuous learning and adaptation | Shared data; real-time dashboards; adaptive planning cycles | Mid-course corrections and recursive policy refinement |

*Source* European Commission Joint Research Centre (2025)

### *4.3.3 Embeddedness Trust and Collaborative Relationships*

Embeddedness refers to the depth and quality of relationships between public institutions and their economic and civic partners. It turns consultation into structured collaboration and anchors policy in real needs and practices.

In the DNS, embeddedness is cultivated through interface bodies such as regional innovation councils, sectoral advisory boards, cluster associations, and hubs that connect firms with training providers and research institutions. These platforms operate continuously rather than episodically. They convene actors, co-produce priorities, and maintain feedback channels that ensure learning informs decisions.

Embedding learning in everyday routines is essential. Feedback loops, evaluation practices, and knowledge exchange need to be part of administrative workflows and incentive systems. This institutional anchoring helps practices persist beyond individual projects or funding cycles and builds trust through repeated, productive interaction.

The recursive, iterative nature of DNS is illustrated in Fig. 4.5, which visualizes the continuous cycle of experimentation, reflection, and policy adjustment. The figure highlights how learning loops are reinforced through embedded administrative routines and incentive structures, demonstrating how adaptive practices are institutionalized and sustained over time.

Table 4.5 complements this conceptual model by detailing the concrete instruments and mechanisms through which DNS learning is operationalized. It summarizes how pilot programs, innovation funds, evaluation routines, and knowledge-sharing platforms embed learning into governance practice, linking each instrument to illustrative outcomes that reflect adaptive coordination.

DNS performance metrics shift the focus from compliance to discovery. Adaptive indicators, stakeholder reviews, and embedded diagnostics are linked to

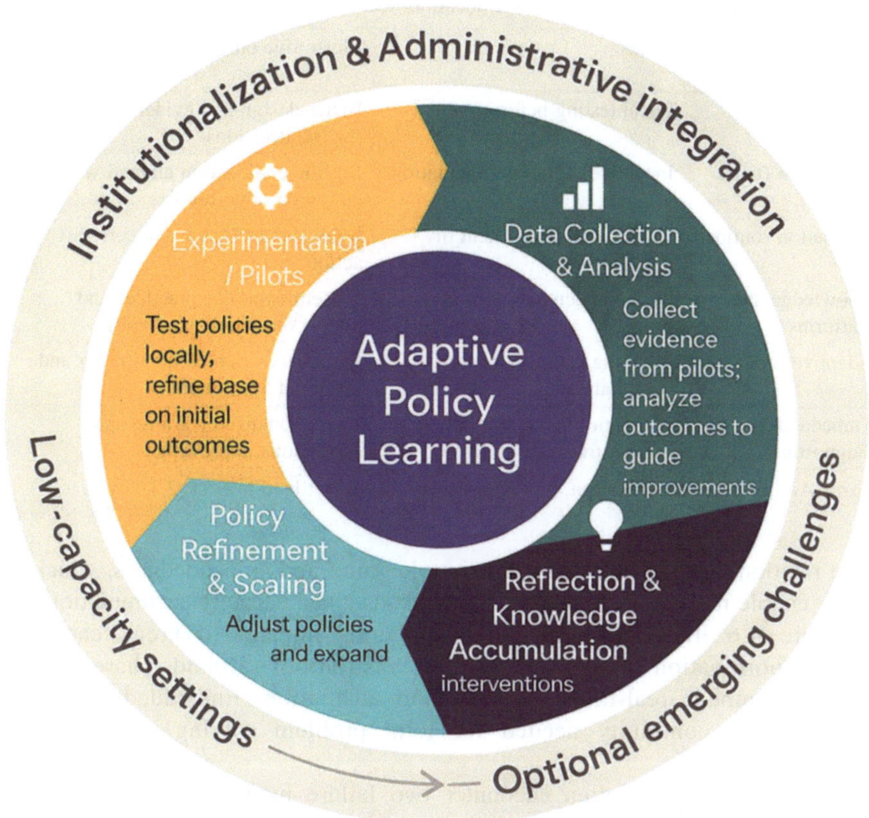


**Fig. 4.5** The recursive learning cycle in the DNS. *Source* Adapted from OECD, 2022. 'Assessing national digital strategies and their governance', *generated with DALL · E using Microsoft Copilot (2025)*

incentives and incorporated into administrative routines, fostering a culture of continuous improvement. By embedding learning into institutional practices, DNS ensures that coordination and experimentation become enduring drivers of governance innovation.

### *4.3.4 Addressing Capability Traps in Low-Capacity States*

Latecomer contexts often fall into two failure modes: isomorphic mimicry, where best-practice forms are adopted without real functionality; and premature load-bearing, where weak institutions bear unsustainable reform demands (PDIA Network, 2017). The DNS tackles both through the combined operation of its

**Table 4.5** Instruments and mechanisms embedding learning in DNS

| Instrument/ mechanism | Focus | Illustrative outcome |
|---|---|---|
| Pilot programs | Local testing before scaling | Better design and evidence-based scaling decisions |
| Innovation funds | Incentives for experimentation | Resource allocation aligned with emerging opportunities |
| Evaluation routines | Continuous assessment of performance | Real-time feedback and corrective action |
| Knowledge-sharing platforms | Learning across actors and places | Dissemination of practices and networked problem solving |
| Adaptive indicators | Tracking progress beyond compliance | Discovery-oriented monitoring and informed adjustment |
| Embedded diagnostics | Evaluation integrated in administrative routines | Institutionalized learning and continuous improvement |

*Source* Author's own compilation, based on the principles outlined in Sect. 2.3.3

three relational capabilities, coordination, learning and embeddedness, which together enable modest, iterative steps toward sustained capacity accumulation.

Figure 4.6 illustrates how these functions interact to break capability traps. Coordination aligns actors and institutions around shared goals. Learning embeds real-time feedback and adaptation. Embeddedness builds the trust and continuity needed for joint problem solving and long-term commitment.

Latecomer contexts often encounter two failure modes identified by PDIA (Andrews et al., 2017). The first is isomorphic mimicry, adopting best-practice forms without real functionality. The second is premature load-bearing, placing heavy reform demands on weak institutions. The DNS sidesteps both isomorphic mimicry and premature load-bearing by combining three relational capabilities, coordination, learning and embeddedness, to build capacity through modest, iterative steps.

Table 4.6 maps each capability to its theoretical source, core mechanism and the specific failure mode it neutralizes.

In combination, these functions create a relational capability system. Coordination builds shared goals in practice, not only on paper. Learning treats policy as a hypothesis and uses feedback to steer adaptation. Embeddedness weaves durable relationships that allow institutions to take on greater responsibilities over time. Together, they support gradual capacity accumulation and the emergence of governance routines suited to fragmented, low-capacity environments.

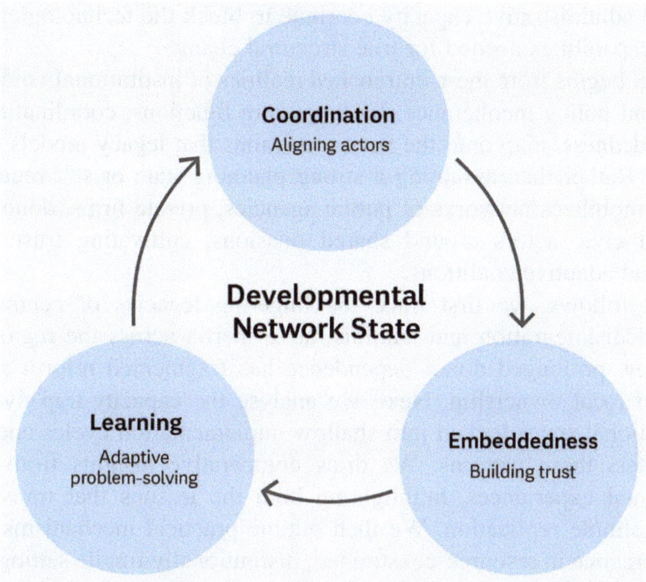


**Fig. 4.6** The enabling functions of the DNS. *Note* A conceptual diagram illustrating how coordination, learning, and embeddedness interact to address capability traps in fragmented, low-capacity states. *Source* Adapted from Sabel and Zeitlin (2012), Khan (2010), Ostrom (1990), Teece et al. (1997), Andrews et al. (2017), and Mazzucato (2021), generated with DALL · E using Microsoft Copilot (2025)

**Table 4.6** Relational capability functions in DNS

| Function | Theory & source | Mechanism | Pitfall addressed |
|---|---|---|---|
| Coordination | Polycentric governance | Networked councils, task forces, pooled funds | Counters isomorphic mimicry through real collaboration |
| Learning | Problem-Driven Iterative Adaptation (PDIA) | Pilots, adaptive indicators, evaluation routines | Avoids premature load-bearing by testing before scaling |
| Embeddedness | Embedded autonomy | Interface bodies and reciprocity incentives | Reduces fragmentation through durable trust |

*Source* Adapted from (Ostrom 1990; Evans 1995; Andrews et al. 2017)

## 4.4 Relevance for Post-Socialist Economies

We believe the DNS framework speaks directly to the predicament of late-comer economies, where decades of institutional reform and external aid have failed to shift persistently low-productivity equilibria. In post-socialist Europe, nowhere more so than in the WB, fragmented state structures, enduring donor dependence and limited administrative capacity continue to block the technological and organizational capabilities needed for true structural change.

The DNS begins from these entrenched realities of institutional voids, contested authority and policy incoherence. Its three core functions, coordination, learning and embeddedness, map onto the very constraints that legacy models overlook or exacerbate. Rather than assuming a strong planning state or self-regulating markets, DNS mobilizes networks of public agencies, private firms, donors, diaspora groups and civic actors around shared missions, cultivating trust, continuous feedback and adaptive coalitions.

In what follows, we first trace the lingering legacies of central planning, institutional disintegration and administrative inertia across the region. We then examine how prolonged donor dependence has fragmented reform agendas and undermined local ownership. Next, we analyse the capacity-trap dynamics that keep transitional states locked into shallow implementation cycles and show how DNS counters these patterns. We draw comparative insights from East-Asian developmental experiences, highlighting both the lessons that transfer and the barriers to simple replication. We then outline practical mechanisms for putting DNS into practice in resource-constrained, institutionally fragile settings. We close by positioning DNS as a context-sensitive alternative for governing capability accumulation across transitional Europe

### *4.4.1 Historical Legacies and Institutional Voids*

More than thirty years after the collapse of socialist regimes, the WB still lack the institutional foundations needed for capability-driven transformation. Instead of cohesive governance systems to guide technological upgrading in a digital era, these post-socialist economies continue to wrestle with fragmented authority, weak administrative learning and chronic coordination gaps. These challenges are rooted in a history of centralized planning followed by abrupt liberalization and donor-led reform trajectories (Elster et al., 1998; Offe, 1996).

The early 1990s saw the disbanding of planning ministries and state-owned industrial agencies, leaving a vacuum that neither market institutions nor new developmental structures filled. Privatization proceeded rapidly, yet the regulatory frameworks and capability-building systems to support competitive industries never materialized (Kikeri & Nellis, 2002; Grzymała-Busse, 2007). Ministries of economy, education and innovation were often renamed rather than restructured, operating in silos with overlapping mandates and minimal coordination. Although national strategies proliferated, implementation remained episodic and disconnected, undermining sustained commitment to capability accumulation (Fritz & Menocal, 2007).

A second layer of constraint comes from weak accountability mechanisms. High turnover among senior officials, political appointments that override merit-based recruitment and short strategic horizons have all stymied administrative learning

(Meyer-Sahling, 2009; World Bank, 2020). Civil-service reforms lagged, leaving policy evaluation capacities underdeveloped and incentives for cross-ministerial collaboration absent. The result is a governance architecture overloaded with formal rules yet starved of the coordination capacity required for complex, multi-actor initiatives (Andrews et al., 2017).

Equally persistent is the normative legacy of top-down governance imported from state socialism. Decades of prescriptive, blueprint-style reforms, often driven by donor conditionality—have discouraged experimentation and suppressed bottom-up feedback (Kitschelt et al., 1999; Schmitter & Karl, 1991). This path-dependent mindset favours input-driven programming over adaptive policymaking, making cross-sector integration and digital responsiveness difficult to achieve.

The DNS offers a pragmatic response to these legacies. It does not assume high-capacity institutions but builds coordination, learning and embeddedness into existing constraints. Horizontal and vertical coordination platforms align fragmented ministries without requiring formal mergers. Iterative learning loops—pilot initiatives, joint monitoring frameworks and adaptive policy reviews—compensate for limited strategic foresight. And intermediary bodies such as diaspora networks, innovation hubs and sectoral councils foster the relational trust needed for sustained collaboration (Rodrik, 2008; Sabel & Zeitlin, 2012).

The institutional realities of post-socialist Europe are not anomalies but emblematic of twenty-first-century development dilemmas: fragmentation, donor complexity and eroding capabilities in the face of rapid technological change. Figure 4.7 visualizes the three core voids, fragmented mandates, weak accountability and hierarchical control norms, that inhibit effective policy coordination and learning. These voids are precisely the spaces the DNS navigates, not by eliminating them through top-down reform but by introducing connective tissue across otherwise disconnected nodes.

### *4.4.2 Donor Dependence and Policy Coherence*

Because the DNS aligns diverse stakeholders around shared missions and embeds continuous feedback, it offers a way out of the policy incoherence that plagues many latecomer economies. In the WB, since the 1990s the European Commission's Instrument for Pre-Accession funds (IPA), the World Bank, USAID, GIZ and other development partners have provided vital support for reconstruction, institution building and policy reform. At the same time, this assistance has created structural distortions—such as fragmented donor-driven priorities, weak coordination, high political interference and shallow administrative capacity—that complicate governance and undermine coherent strategies for capability development (Bartlett, 2020; European Court of Auditors, 2022; OECD, 2025).

One major challenge has been the proliferation of parallel structures. Donor-funded initiatives often establish separate project implementation units, bespoke

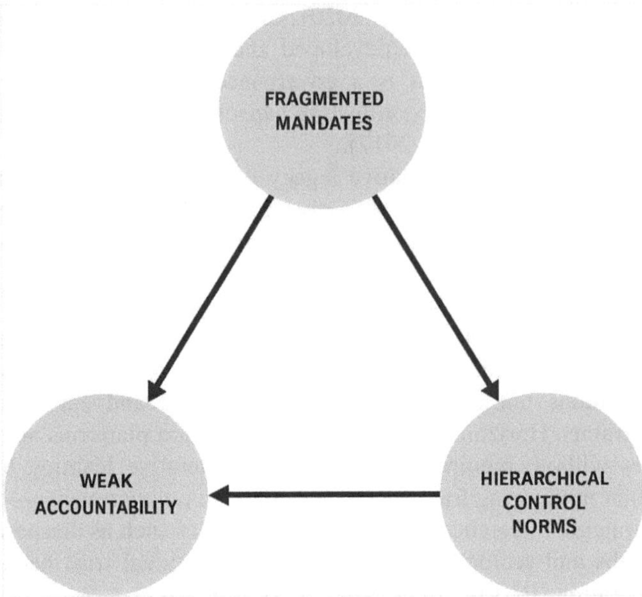


**Fig. 4.7** Institutional voids in post-socialist governance. *Note* This diagram visualizes three persistent features of governance in the Western Balkans and other transitional contexts: fragmented mandates, weak accountability and hierarchical control norms. Together they form a structural triad that inhibits coordinated, learning-based. *Source* Author's elaboration, based on Radosevic (2017), Andrews et al. (2017), and Khan (2022), generated with DALL · E using Microsoft Copilot (2025)

monitoring and evaluation templates and standalone governance mechanisms that operate outside existing state bodies. Line ministries find themselves managing multiple projects at once, each following its own logic, reporting requirements and timelines. This patchwork of procedures diverts administrative energy from core functions and frustrates strategic alignment (OECD, 2019).

Policy fragmentation poses a second problem. Donor priorities range from judicial reform and rule of law to SME competitiveness, education, social protection, and digital infrastructure. In the absence of robust state-led coordination, these agendas often compete for ministerial attention and budget lines. Vertical fragmentation arises when national and local objectives diverge, while horizontal fragmentation occurs when initiatives in skills, infrastructure, and enterprise support fail to align into a coherent upgrading strategy (Lawson, 2013).

The DNS framework tackles these issues by reshaping the interface between external assistance and domestic governance. Its coordination function creates inclusive platforms, multi-stakeholder councils and inter-ministerial task forces, in which donor representatives join national actors in setting priorities and aligning resources. These bodies foster harmonization between international programmes and domestic plans, reduce duplication and strengthen local ownership.

Through its learning function, the DNS embeds iterative feedback loops into donor programmes. Ministries and development partners co-design pilot projects that share a unified monitoring and evaluation framework. As results emerge, stakeholders use real-time data to identify design flaws and make mid-course corrections. This approach builds local capacities for adaptive learning instead of perpetuating one-size-fits-all reforms (Andrews et al., 2017).

The embeddedness pillar ensures that donor engagement contributes to long-term system building. By institutionalizing external actors in permanent governance bodies—such as innovation councils or diaspora coordination boards, temporary projects feed into enduring networks for technological and institutional upgrading. Donors thus become active participants in capability formation rather than stand-alone financiers (Rodrik, 2008; Khan, 2018).

Figure 4.8 illustrates how the DNS model redirects donor interventions from isolated policy islands toward integrated governance ecosystems that leverage coordination, learning and embeddedness.

### 4.4.3 *Capability Traps in Transitional Economies*

Many post-socialist states in the WB find themselves caught in self-reinforcing cycles of weak implementation, stalled reforms and minimal institutional learning,

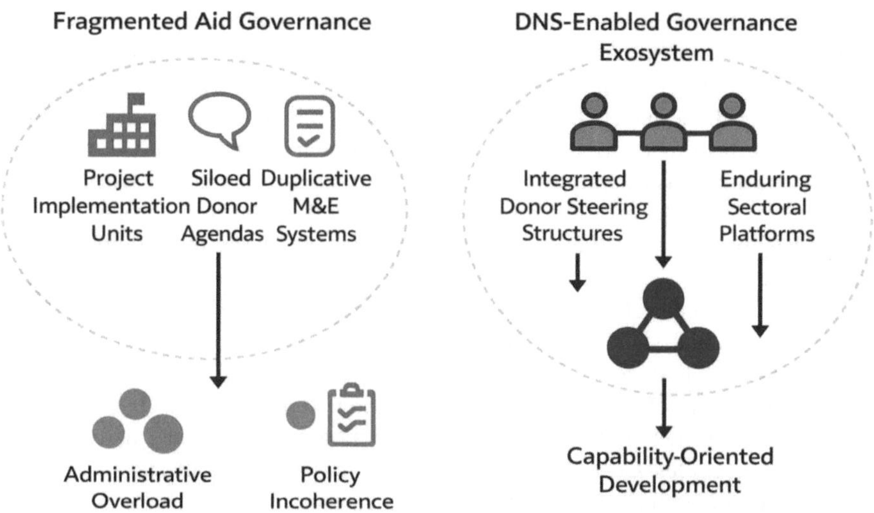


**Fig. 4.8** Aligning donor support with capability-oriented governance. *Note* This conceptual diagram contrasts a fragmented donor-driven landscape, characterized by isolated project units and parallel agendas, with a DNS-inspired ecosystem where all actors engage in iterative, networked processes *Source* Author's elaboration, based on OECD (2019), Fritz and Levy (2014), and Andrews et al. (2017), generated with DALL · E using Microsoft Copilot (2025)

what Radosevic (2017) terms "capability traps." Despite elaborate reform designs, new laws and strategic plans often fail to translate into better outcomes or deeper change. Four interlinked dynamics lie at the heart of these traps.

First, reforms suffer from shallow institutionalization. Pilot programmes and donor-driven initiatives routinely dissolve once external funding ends. Because these interventions are never fully integrated into core planning, budgeting or regulatory processes, civil servants lack the incentives and mandates needed to sustain them. A new digital skills training unit may operate effectively for a year under a grant, only to be folded back into an overburdened ministry once that grant expires, leaving local actors cynical about the value of further experimentation.

Second, siloed information flows prevent lessons from spreading across agencies. The studies, evaluations and pilot results generated by labour market observatories, innovation labs or sector-specific projects tend to remain locked within individual ministries. As a result, data on emerging skill gaps or successful production methods never informs curriculum reform or enterprise support programmes elsewhere in government. Without shared data platforms and structured inter-agency dialogue, knowledge stays fragmented and institutional learning stalls.

A third constraint arises from short political horizons. Governments in transitional settings often govern through unstable coalitions and face high turnover among senior officials. Ministers and senior bureaucrats focus on quick, visible wins that can be delivered before the next election or reshuffle. Long-term reform agendas, such as overhauling inspection systems or redesigning vocational education, are abandoned midway when fresh appointees prioritize their own pet projects. This discontinuity disrupts the incremental improvement and strategic alignment that capability building demands.

Finally, policy communities remain fragmented and under-engaged. Universities, think tanks, business associations and civil society organizations rarely participate meaningfully in policy design or implementation. Consultation tends to be formalistic and late-stage, often confined to donor-led workshops or post-hoc reviews. As a result, reforms are insulated from on-the-ground realities and fail to benefit from the diverse expertise and networks that could reinforce sustained change.

The DNS framework offers a pathway out of these capability traps by weaving together coordination, learning and embeddedness into an institutional learning architecture. Its first corrective measure is to embed pilot programmes within existing state structures. Rather than creating separate project units, DNS approaches link new initiatives directly to national budget lines and medium-term planning cycles. Co-financing requirements ensure that domestic actors maintain a stake in continuation once donor funding tapers off.

Next, DNS champions interoperable learning systems. Shared data infrastructures, such as national innovation observatories and inter-ministerial dashboards, aggregate evidence across multiple pilots and programmes. Regular cross-agency workshops and sectoral councils provide forums for ministers, civil servants and private-sector representatives to discuss emerging findings, compare experiences and agree on mid-course corrections. By breaking down silos, these mechanisms turn isolated experiments into a cumulative repertoire of proven practices.

To address political discontinuities, DNS builds enduring coalitions that transcend electoral cycles. Governance platforms bring together political appointees, career civil servants, diaspora networks and industry associations. These coalitions embed reforms in relational ties and shared commitments that survive changes in leadership. As one minister departs and another arrives, the coalition's common agenda remains anchored by long-term technical experts and community stakeholders.

Finally, DNS establishes boundary-spanning institutions, innovation hubs, digital observatories and hybrid councils, that broker collaboration between government, academia and the private sector. These bodies serve as custodians of institutional memory, translating the results of pilot initiatives into standard operating procedures and training curricula. By holding regular peer-learning events and public-private hackathons, they nurture a culture of experimentation and ensure that successful approaches scale beyond their original contexts.

Figure 4.9 depicts how these DNS mechanisms counteract the dynamics of shallow institutionalization, siloed information flows, short political horizons and fragmented policy communities. By transforming discrete reform inputs into a cohesive process of cumulative learning and networked collaboration, the DNS provides a realistic blueprint for breaking capability traps and driving sustained structural transformation in fragmented, low-capacity environments.

### 4.4.4 *Comparative Insights from East Asia*

East Asian economies such as South Korea and Taiwan show how latecomer countries can transform themselves into high-technology powerhouses. Their

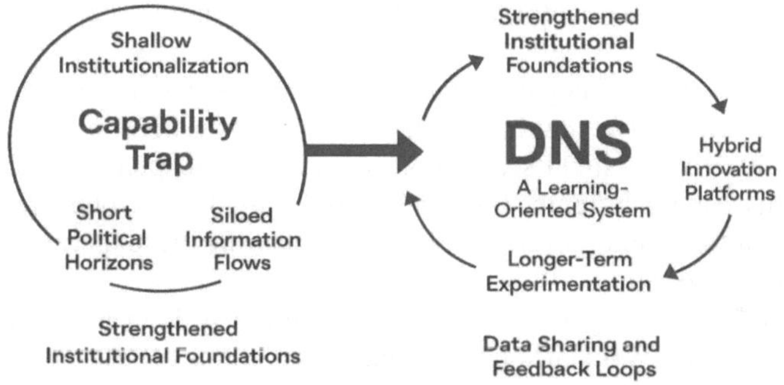


**Fig. 4.9** DNS as an institutional learning architecture. *Source* Author's elaboration, based on Andrews et al. (2017), Meyer-Sahling et al. (2019), and Kmezic (2016), generated with DALL · E using Microsoft Copilot (2025)

success rests on a developmental state model in which a meritocratic bureaucracy enjoyed strategic autonomy and deep links to industry. In South Korea, state planners set clear export targets, disciplined large conglomerates and directed subsidized credit to emerging sectors like steel, shipbuilding and semiconductors. In Taiwan, public research institutions such as the Industrial Technology Research Institute combined independence from short-term politics with close collaboration with small and medium-sized firms.

Three conditions underpinned these experiences. First, bureaucratic capacity was strong: civil servants were recruited on merit, career paths were stable and internal coherence was high. Second, elite consensus coalesced around national development goals, reinforced by cohesive ruling coalitions. Third, strategic external alignment, particularly with the United States during the Cold War, ensured favourable trade terms and institutional support from multilateral development banks.

By contrast, post-socialist Europe faces very different governance constraints. Bureaucratic capacity varies widely and often suffers from politicization and weak incentives for performance. Elite coalitions are fragmented by electoral volatility, ethnic divisions and clientelist networks. External assistance, while substantial, is dispersed among multiple donors, each pursuing its own priorities rather than a coherent national agenda.

Despite these differences, several lessons from the East Asian experience can guide a DNS approach. The first lesson is polycentric coordination. In South Korea, regional agencies and industrial parks operated under national guidelines yet retained autonomy to adapt to local conditions. A networked governance model in the WB could replicate this logic through inter-ministerial task forces, regional councils and cross-sector steering bodies that align priorities without requiring wholesale institutional mergers.

The second lesson is embedded autonomy. Taiwan's research institute balanced political insulation with active engagement in industrial innovation. Similarly, post-socialist economies can create semi-autonomous interface bodies, such as innovation labs, diaspora councils and digital skills observatories, that foster trust and knowledge exchange across public and private spheres.

The third lesson is strategic learning. East Asian states did not rigidly follow blueprints. Korea's drive into heavy and chemical industries in the 1970s began with feasibility studies, small-scale pilots and iterative adaptation. A DNS institutionalizes this pattern by embedding pilot projects, adaptive budgeting and joint monitoring platforms into governance routines, ensuring that experimentation leads to refined policy designs.

Where the DNS diverges from the East Asian model is in its starting assumptions. It accepts that WB states operate under conditions of low trust, fragmented authority and donor dependence, rather than presuming a unified and highly capable bureaucracy. The emphasis therefore shifts to building governance capabilities incrementally, through coalition-building, continuous feedback loops and embedded learning, rather than importing strong-state templates wholesale.

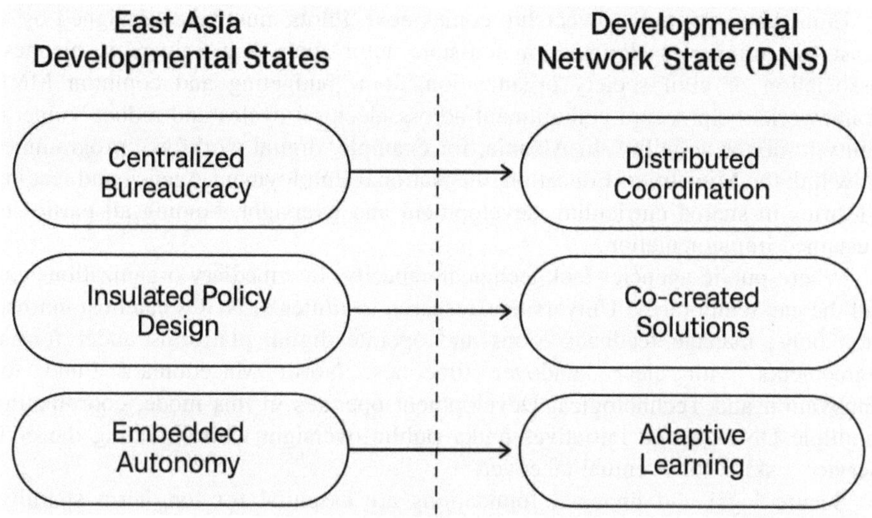


**Fig. 4.10** Learning from East Asia: convergences and divergences. *Source* Author's elaboration, based on Evans (1995), Amsden (1989), Wade (1990, 2018), Kim (1997), and Meyer-Sahling et al. (2019), generated with DALL · E using Microsoft Copilot (2025)

Figure 4.10 contrasts the governance conditions and strategies of East Asian developmental states with those of post-socialist economies. It highlights how coordination, learning and embeddedness can be selectively adapted to the political and institutional realities of transitional Europe.

### *4.4.5 Practical Implementation Considerations*

Translating the abstract pillars of the DNS into functioning institutions in the WB requires careful sequencing, genuine domestic ownership, realistic assessments of capacity and an eye on political economy constraints. The following implementation principles provide a roadmap for embedding DNS in fragmented, donor-saturated settings.

One effective entry point is to leverage quick-win pilots in sectors where broad consensus exists and resistance is minimal. Fields such as digital skills development, SME export readiness or green innovation combine high demonstration value with limited political opposition. The Kosovo Digital Economy Project, co-financed by the World Bank and the national government, illustrates this approach by connecting technology hubs, municipal authorities and diaspora mentors in a phased, multi-stakeholder effort that delivered visible results within one implementation cycle.

Embedding domestic ownership comes next. Pilots must be co-designed by at least two ministries alongside a non-state actor such as a university, business association or civil society organization. Joint budgeting and common M&E frameworks help secure commitment across electoral cycles and reduce vulnerability to donor volatility. In Albania, for example, digital workforce programmes now link the Ministry of Education, the National Employment Agency and leading IT firms in shared curriculum development and oversight, binding all parties to sustained implementation.

Where public agencies lack technical capacity, intermediary organizations can fill the gap temporarily. Universities, research institutes or NGOs can host innovation hubs, manage feedback loops and operate digital platforms under formal agreements with clear handover timelines. North Macedonia's Fund for Innovation and Technological Development operates in this mode, coordinating multiple DNS-aligned initiatives under public oversight while building the civil service's skills for eventual takeover.

Secure legal and financial foundations are essential for long-term stability. Governments should enact enabling legislation that establishes sectoral councils, innovation boards and diaspora engagement platforms with multi-year mandates and rotating leadership. Budget lines for DNS instruments, such as challenge funds or pilot initiatives, must be embedded in medium-term expenditure frameworks and shielded from ad hoc reallocation. Estonia's digital governance boards offer a useful precedent, showing how permanent legal status can reinforce experimental and adaptive governance structures.

Finally, DNS platforms must guard against political capture. Rotating leadership among public, private and academic stakeholders strengthens legitimacy. Transparent appointment processes, regular public reporting and parliamentary oversight of major structural revisions reinforce accountability. Performance dashboards and public innovation reviews can stimulate reputational incentives while fostering civic engagement. The EU's 2024 Growth Facility links transparency mechanisms to conditional budget support, demonstrating how reputational stakes can bolster resilience against capture.

Figure 4.11 synthesizes these mechanisms, showing how coordination, learning and embeddedness translate into structured institutional designs. Strategic entry points (for example, digital skills), practical tools (such as co-design mandates and shared learning platforms) and safeguards (including rotating leadership and statutory anchoring) together reinforce an adaptive, inclusive governance architecture.

By following these five principles, WB states can construct DNS architectures that respect domestic political realities, harness latent institutional capital, and incrementally build indigenous capacity. Structural transformation does not require ideal conditions. It requires iterative, networked governance that treats reform as a process of collaborative learning and embedded experimentation.

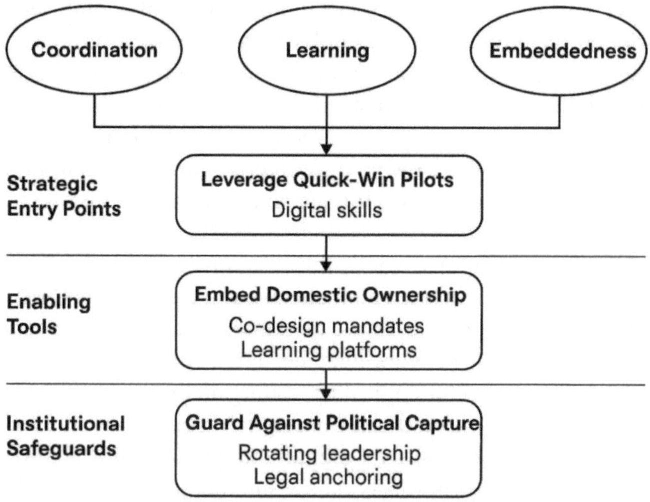


**Fig. 4.11** Translating DNS principles into practice. *Source* Author's elaboration, adapted from Andrews et al. (2017), Fritz and Levy (2014), and World Bank (2020), generated with DALL · E using Microsoft Copilot (2025)

## 4.5 Conclusion: Charting the Path Ahead With DNS

Post-socialist economies continue to wrestle with fragmented legacies, donor-driven incoherence and self-reinforcing cycles of weak implementation. Traditional paradigms, whether an interventionist developmental state or unfettered markets, have proven poorly suited to contexts marked by contested authority, limited administrative capacity and high uncertainty. In response, the DNS offers a governance paradigm that starts from these very constraints rather than from idealized preconditions.

At its core, DNS reconceives governance as a networked, adaptive process. Drawing on embedded autonomy, network-society theory, mission-oriented innovation, political-settlements analysis and dynamic capabilities, it shows that state capacities can emerge through iterative problem solving among public agencies, firms, universities, donors and diaspora groups rather than through monolithic hierarchies or pure market forces alone.

This synthesis materializes in three mutually reinforcing pillars. Learning treats each policy experiment as a hypothesis, embedding real-time feedback and structured adaptation. Coordination aligns fragmented actors and institutions around shared development goals. Embeddedness forges the relational trust and continuity necessary for collaboration to endure across electoral cycles and donor timelines. The three functions dismantle the capability traps, shallow institutionalization, siloed information flows and short political horizons, that keep transitional states stuck in low-productivity equilibria.

Comparative lessons from East Asia highlight how late-comer economies can scale industry and technology through polycentric coordination, embedded autonomy and strategic experimentation. Unlike those strong-state templates, however, DNS eschews wholesale mimicry. Instead, it offers tools calibrated for pluralistic, low-capacity environments: quick-win pilots to build momentum; co-designed programmes to secure domestic ownership; intermediary bodies to bridge capacity gaps; legal and budgetary anchoring for sustainability; and transparent governance safeguards against capture.

In the WB, where institutional voids, donor complexity and urgent development imperatives intersect, DNS provides a practicable roadmap for inclusive, capability-driven growth. By treating reform as a cumulative process of collaborative experimentation and trust-based networking, the DNS offers latecomer economies a realistic pathway toward technological upgrading and sustainable transformation.

Looking ahead, Part II moves from conceptual foundations to hands-on implementation. We will explore Kosovo's digital entrepreneurship lab, Albania's agri-food upgrading pilots and North Macedonia's automotive sector initiatives, showing how DNS principles translate into concrete governance architectures. Each chapter unpacks the institutional designs, feedback mechanisms and trust-building strategies that have turned isolated experiments into sustained routines.

## References

Andrews, M., Pritchett, L., & Woolcock, M. (2017). *Building state capability: Evidence, analysis, action*. Oxford: Oxford University Press. Available at: https://bsc.cid.harvard.edu/book/building-state-capability. Accessed June 4, 2025.

Bartlett, W. (2020). International assistance, donor interests, and state capture in the Western Balkans. *Journal of Contemporary European Studies*, *29*(2), 184–200. https://doi.org/10.1080/14782804.2020.1794801

Castells, M. (1996). *The rise of the network society*. Blackwell.

Chang, H. J. (2002). *Kicking away the ladder: Development strategy in historical perspective*. London: Anthem Press. Available at: https://www.jstor.org/stable/40722165. Accessed June 4, 2025.

Elster, J., Offe, C., & Preuss, U. K. (Eds.). (1998). *Institutional design in post communist societies: Rebuilding the ship at sea*. Cambridge University Press. https://doi.org/10.1017/CBO9780511628351

European Commission Joint Research Centre (JRC). (2025). *Smart Specialisation Platform: Croatia*. Available at: https://s3platform.jrc.ec.europa.eu/croatia. Accessed June 13, 2025.

European Court of Auditors. (2022). *EU support for the rule of law in the Western Balkans: Despite efforts, fundamental problems persist. Special Report No. 01/2022*. Luxembourg: European Court of Auditors. Available at: https://www.eca.europa.eu/en/publications/SR22_01. Accessed July 12, 2025.

Evans, P. (1995). *Embedded autonomy: States and industrial transformation*. Princeton: Princeton University Press. Available at: https://www.jstor.org/stable/j.ctt7t0sr. Accessed July 12, 2025.

Fritz, V., & Rocha Menocal, A. R. (2007). Developmental states in the new millennium: Concepts and challenges for a new aid agenda. *Development Policy Review*, *25*(5), 531–552. https://doi.org/10.1111/j.1467-7679.2007.00384.x

Fritz, V. & Levy, B. (2014). *Problem-Driven Political Economy Analysis: The World Bank's Experience*. World Bank.

Grzymała-Busse, A. (2007). *Rebuilding leviathan: Party competition and state exploitation in post communist democracies*. Cambridge University Press. https://doi.org/10.1017/CBO9780511618819.001

Johnson, C. (1982). *MITI and the Japanese miracle: The growth of industrial policy, 1925–1975*. Stanford University Press. https://doi.org/10.1086/ahr/88.1.158

Khan, M. (2018). 'Political settlements and the analysis of institutions', *African Affairs*, 117(469), 636–655. https://doi.org/10.1093/afraf/adx044. Accessed May 15, 2025.

Khan, M. H. (2010). 'Political settlements and the governance of growth-enhancing institutions'. In D. North, J. Wallis, S. Webb, & B. Weingast (Eds.), *In The shadow of violence: Politics, economics, and the problems of development* (pp. 285–323. Cambridge: Cambridge University Press. Available at: https://www.researchgate.net/publication/265567069. Accessed May 15, 2025.

Kikeri, S., & Nellis, J. R. (2002). *Privatization in competitive sectors: The record to date*. World Bank Policy Research Working Paper No. 2860. Washington, DC: World Bank. Available at: https://documents.worldbank.org/en/publication/documents-reports/documentdetail/737881468761945796. Accessed July 12, 2025.

Kitschelt, H., Mansfeldova, Z., Markowski, R., & Tóka, G. (1999). *Post communist party systems: Competition, representation, and inter party cooperation*. Cambridge University Press. https://doi.org/10.1017/CBO9781139175173

Kmezić, M. (2016). *EU Rule Of Law promotion: Judiciary reform in the Western Balkans*. Routledge. https://doi.org/10.4324/9781315580722

Lawson, M. L. (2013). *Foreign aid: International donor coordination of development assistance*. Congressional Research Service Report R41185. Washington, DC: Congressional Research Service. Available at: https://sgp.fas.org/crs/row/R41185.pdf. Accessed July 12, 2025.

Leftwich, A. (2010). Beyond institutions: Rethinking the role of leaders, elites and coalitions in the institutional formation of developmental states and strategies. *Forum for Development Studies*, *37*(1), 93–111. https://doi.org/10.1080/08039410903558327

Lin, J. Y. (2011). New structural economics: A framework for rethinking development. *The World Bank Research Observer*, *26*(2), 193–221. https://doi.org/10.1093/wbro/lkr007

Lin, J. Y. (2021). New structural economics: A framework for studying government and economics. *Journal of Government and Economics*, *2*, 100014. https://doi.org/10.1016/j.jge.2021.100014

Mazzucato, M. (2013). *The entrepreneurial state: Debunking public vs. private sector myths*. Anthem Press.

Mazzucato, M. (2021). *Mission economy: A moonshot guide to changing capitalism*. Allen Lane. https://doi.org/10.1007/s12115-021-00619-2

Meyer Sahling, J.-H. (2009). *The sustainability of civil service reforms in Central and Eastern Europe five years after EU accession*. SIGMA Paper No. 44. Paris: OECD Publishing. https://doi.org/10.1787/9789264063537-en

OECD. (2019). *Government at a glance: Western Balkans*. https://doi.org/10.1787/888934129030

OECD. (2022). *Assessing national digital strategies and their governance*. OECD Digital Economy Papers, No. 324. Paris: OECD Publishing. Available at: https://doi.org/10.1787/baffceca-en [Accessed 21 August 2025].

OECD. (2025). *Public administration in the Western Balkans 2024: Regional overview of assessments against the principles of public administration*, SIGMA monitoring reports, OECD Publishing, Paris, https://doi.org/10.1787/1ec4c18f-en. Accessed July 12, 2025.

Offe, C. (1996). *Modernity and the state: East, West*. Cambridge: Polity Press.

Ostrom, E. (1990). *Governing the commons: The evolution of institutions for collective action*. Cambridge University Press. https://doi.org/10.1017/CBO9780511807763

PDIA Network. (2017). *What Is PDIA?—Building state capability: Problem-driven iterative adaptation (PDIA)*. Harvard Kennedy School, Center for International Development. Available at: https://bsc.hks.harvard.edu/about/what-is-pdia/. Accessed July 15, 2025.

Provan, K. G., & Kenis, P. (2008). Modes of network governance: Structure, management, and effectiveness. *Journal of Public Administration Research and Theory*, *18*(2), 229–252. Available at. https://doi.org/10.1093/jopart/mum015

Radosevic, S. (1999). *International technology transfer and catch-up in economic development*. Edward Elgar.

Radosevic, S. (2011). Science–industry links in Central and Eastern Europe and the commonwealth of independent states: Conventional policy wisdom facing reality. *Science and Public Policy*, *38*(5), 365–378. https://doi.org/10.3152/030234211X12924093660435

Radosevic, S. (2017). Upgrading technology in Central and Eastern European economies. *IZA World of Labor*, *338*, https://doi.org/10.15185/izawol.338

Rhodes, R. A. W. (1997). *Understanding governance: Policy networks, governance, reflexivity and accountability*. Open University Press.

Rodrik, D. (2004). *Industrial policy for the twenty-first century*. Cambridge, MA: Harvard University, Kennedy School of Government. Available at: https://drodrik.scholar.harvard.edu/files/dani-rodrik/files/industrial-policy-twenty-first-century.pdf. Accessed June 4, 2025.

Rodrik, D. (2008). Second-best institutions. *American Economic Review: Papers & Proceedings*, *98*(2), 100–104. https://doi.org/10.1257/aer.98.2.100

Sabel, C., Zeitlin, J., & Helderman, J.-K. (2023). Transforming the welfare state, one case at a time: How Utrecht makes customized social care work. *Politics & Society*, *52*(2), 171–207. https://doi.org/10.1177/00323292221140710

Sabel, C. F., & Zeitlin, J. (2012). Experimentalist governance. In D. Levi-Faur (Ed.), *The Oxford handbook of governance* (pp. 169–183). Oxford University Press. https://doi.org/10.1093/oxfordhb/9780199560530.013.0012

Schmitter, P. C., & Karl, T. L. (1991). What democracy is ... and is not. *Journal of Democracy*, *2*(3), 75–88. https://doi.org/10.1353/jod.1991.0033

Stiglitz, J. E. (2015). *Industrial policy, learning, and development*. WIDER Working Paper 2015/149. Helsinki: UNU-WIDER. https://doi.org/10.35188/UNU-WIDER/2015/038-6

Teece, D. J., Pisano, G., & Shuen, A. (1997). Dynamic capabilities and strategic management. *Strategic Management Journal*, *18*(7), 509–533. https://doi.org/10.1002/(SICI)1097-0266(199708)18:7<509::AID-SMJ882>3.0.CO;2-Z

Wade, R. (1990). *Governing the Market: Economic Theory and the Role of Government in East Asian Industrialization*. Princeton University Press.

Wade, R. H. (2018). The developmental state: Dead or alive? *Development and Change*, *49*(2), 518–546. https://doi.org/10.1111/dech.12381

Williamson, J. (1990). 'What Washington means by policy reform', in J. Williamson (Ed.) *Latin American adjustment: How much has happened?*, (pp. 7–20). Washington, DC: Institute for International Economics. Available at: https://www.scirp.org/reference/referencespapers?referenceid=2230602. Accessed June 4, 2025.

World Bank. (2020). *Enhancing government effectiveness and transparency: The fight against corruption*. Washington, DC: World Bank. Available at: https://hdl.handle.net/10986/34533. Accessed July 12, 2025.

# Part II
# Sectoral Case Studies in Transitional Europe

This part of the book moves from conceptual foundations to empirical analysis. It shows how efforts to achieve economic and technological catch-up in the digital era are shaped by sector-specific governance dynamics in transitional European economies. The focus is on three Western Balkan countries: Kosovo, Albania, and North Macedonia, and how they manage the challenges of technological upgrading and structural transformation amid institutional fragmentation, limited state capacity, and significant donor influence.

Building on the Developmental Network State (DNS) model introduced in Part I, these case studies show that capability accumulation does not result from ideal planning or free-market forces. Instead, it emerges through adaptive coordination, embedded learning, and network-based experimentation. These processes vary across contexts, influenced by sectoral structures, political economy conditions, and the evolving pressures of digitalization and global integration.

Chapter 5 examines Kosovo's digital services and ICT sector, where diaspora networks, donor-supported incubators, and local government initiatives have created rich environments for entrepreneurial learning, even with minimal formal state backing. Chapter 6 analyses Albania's agri-food processing industry, where fragmented value chains and decentralized governance have produced both constraints and opportunities for capability upgrading through coordination and local innovation. Chapter 7 focuses on North Macedonia's automotive sector, where foreign direct investment, supplier development programs, and public–private partnerships demonstrate how strategic integration into global value chains can foster industrial upgrading when supported by coherent institutions and targeted learning mechanisms.

These chapters illustrate that catching up in the digital age is not about replicating best practices or adopting external policy templates. It is a governance challenge that depends on the ability to organize capability development within structural and institutional limits. Each case study shows that meaningful progress is possible, even in contexts with weak capacity and donor dependence, when governance systems effectively align actors, encourage experimentation, and institutionalize learning.

By situating the analysis within transitional Europe, Part II provides detailed insight into how the broader themes of the book—capabilities, governance, and industrial policy—manifest in sectors central to digital-era development. These cases form the empirical basis for Part III, which identifies cross-cutting patterns and examines their implications for managing structural transformation in complex and constrained environments.

# Chapter 5
# Digital Services and ICT in Kosovo

## 5.1 Introduction

Kosovo illustrates the challenges of pursuing development under tight constraints. As one of Europe's youngest and smallest states, it faces weak institutions, limited public finances, and continuing dependence on remittances and donor aid. These limitations are serious, yet beneath them lie important sources of potential that suggest alternative paths for progress.

Kosovo's advantages are clear. It has one of the youngest and most digitally literate populations in Europe, a large and well-connected diaspora engaged in the country's future, and proximity to major European markets. Under the right conditions, these factors could support a process of productive transformation. However, this transformation has not yet materialized. Industrial upgrading remains uneven and fragile, and promising initiatives often struggle to expand. The gap between potential and performance raises a key question: what kind of governance can convert opportunity into sustained progress?

This chapter approaches the question through the lens of the Developmental Network State (DNS) introduced earlier. Rather than depending on strong bureaucracies or fully liberalized markets, the DNS highlights three evolving governance functions—coordination, learning, and embeddedness—that must be continually cultivated and adapted.

In Kosovo, early forms of such governance are already emerging. Although often outside formal state structures, diverse actors—diaspora entrepreneurs, donor-supported innovation hubs, municipal authorities, and grassroots digital communities—are finding practical ways to share knowledge, solve problems, and collaborate. These efforts remain fragmented but point to a gradual shift in how governance operates in low-capacity environments.

The chapter is organized as follows. It first outlines Kosovo's industrial and governance context, then examines the information and communication technology



F. Sahiti, *Catching Up in the Digital Age*, Contributions to Economics,
https://doi.org/10.1007/978-3-032-17059-0_5

(ICT) sector's evolution and its role in capability building. Subsequent sections explore the influence of the diaspora, donor programmes, and municipal initiatives on digital transformation. The chapter concludes by assessing how these dynamics illustrate the principles of the DNS and what they reveal about the possibilities for digital-era development in constrained settings.

## 5.2 Industrial Underperformance and the Governance Gap

Kosovo's stalled economic catch-up exemplifies a common paradox among late-developing economies: structural advantages coexist with limited transformative outcomes. On paper, Kosovo possesses several promising assets—a young population, high digital connectivity, an active diaspora, and proximity to the European Union. In theory, these should provide a strong foundation for productive transformation. Yet in practice, they have not translated into sustained industrial upgrading.

The economy remains concentrated in low-value, low-complexity activities. Innovation systems are weakly developed and poorly integrated into production networks. Public and private actors often operate in isolation, constraining coordination and knowledge exchange. The challenge, therefore, extends beyond resource scarcity; it lies in governance—the absence of institutional mechanisms that can align efforts, coordinate across sectors, and embed learning processes essential for long-term capability building.

To address these issues, this section adopts the DNS framework; a perspective particularly relevant to contexts where authority is fragmented and state capacity is limited. Rather than relying on centralized bureaucracies or market-led coordination, this perspective highlights networked governance arrangements that link ministries, donors, firms, universities, and local initiatives in structured processes of problem-solving and mutual learning.

The analysis proceeds in three parts. First, it explores the structural constraints of Kosovo's industrial base and the absence of enablers for technological capability development. Second, it examines how low-complexity export patterns restrict opportunities for learning and upgrading. Third, it investigates institutional fragmentation as a central barrier to coordination, experimentation, and feedback.

### *5.2.1 Structural Constraints and the Capability Deficit*

Kosovo's industrial base remains narrow and technologically underdeveloped. Industry (excluding construction) accounts for just 18% of GDP, with manufacturing contributing only 9%—well below the EU average of 16%. Employment in industry is also limited, involving roughly 12% of the workforce, mainly in basic sectors such as metals, wood, and agri-food processing.

Crucially, investment in technological learning is minimal. Research and development spending is just 0.2% of GDP—far below the EU's 2.2% average. High-tech exports represent less than 1% of total trade. Despite near-universal broadband penetration, digital infrastructure has yet to support a shift toward knowledge-based production. University–industry collaboration remains weak and largely informal (European Commission, 2023; OECD, 2024b).

These indicators point to more than just a lack of capital or market scale. Kosovo's capability deficit is rooted in weak institutional mechanisms for learning and innovation. As Lall (1992) and Bell and Pavitt (1993) emphasize, technological capabilities do not emerge automatically. They must be built through deliberate policies, aligned institutions, and cumulative learning processes. In Kosovo, the disconnect between digital readiness and industrial performance reflects the absence of such mechanisms.

Table 5.1 presents Kosovo's structural profile relative to EU benchmarks, revealing a service-oriented economy characterized by limited manufacturing activity, negligible R&D investment, and shallow participation in complex value chains.

**Table 5.1** Kosovo's Economic Structure and Technological Enablers (2023)

| Indicator | Kosovo (2023) | EU average | Implication for technological capability |
|---|---|---|---|
| Sectoral Value Added (% of GDP) | | | |
| Industry (excluding construction)[1] | 18% | 25% | Narrow base limits scope for manufacturing-led upgrading |
| Manufacturing | 9% | 16% | Low complexity constrains productivity growth and innovation |
| Services | 55% | 65% | Service dominance with weak linkages to productive sectors |
| Agriculture | 7.4% | 1.5% | High share reflects persistent structural lag |
| Technological Capability Enablers | | | |
| R&D expenditure (% of GDP) | 0.2% | 2.2% | Critically low investment weakens national innovation systems |
| High-tech export share (% of manufactured exports) | <1% | 48% | Minimal integration into complex global value chains |
| Broadband penetration (households) | 95-97% | 92% | Strong infrastructure, underutilized for industrial transformation |
| University–firm collaboration[2] | Minimal (qualitative) | High | Weak linkages hinder applied learning and capability development |

*Notes* [1]Industry includes manufacturing, mining, and utilities, excluding construction; [2]Based on qualitative assessments from the EU Innovation Scoreboard and OECD reports
*Source* Kosovo Agency of Statistics (2023), Swiss Economic Report on Kosovo (2023), World Bank (2023), OECD (2024b), European Innovation Scoreboard (2025), and European Commission (2023)

### 5.2.2 Export Patterns and Low-Complexity Traps

Kosovo's export structure perpetuates its industrial stagnation. Over one-fifth of exports comprise base metals and scrap, with the remainder dominated by low-value wood and agri-food products. These semi-processed goods demand limited skills and provide few avenues for technological learning, while high-complexity exports such as machinery, chemicals, and electronics are largely absent.

Most firms lack the capabilities to compete in higher-value markets. Deficiencies in certification, quality standards, and marketing confine them to subcontracting and commodity-based trade (World Bank, 2023; European Commission, 2023; OECD, 2024b). Consequently, exports remain concentrated in low-value segments marked by weak innovation and high exposure to price volatility (Swiss Economic Report, 2023).

This configuration represents a developmental trap. The scarcity of complex products constrains organizational learning, technology transfer, and productivity growth. Firms remain small, fragmented, and under-resourced, unable to accumulate the collective capabilities needed for structural transformation.

As illustrated in Fig. 5.1, Kosovo's export basket remains heavily skewed toward primary and semi-processed goods, limiting prospects for upgrading and deeper integration into regional and global value chains.

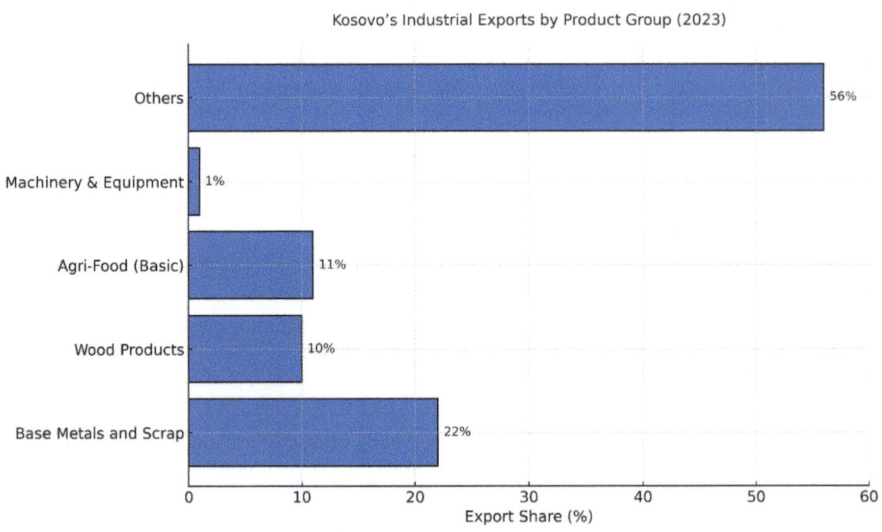


**Fig. 5.1** Kosovo's industrial exports by product group (2023). *Source* Author's elaboration based on data from the Kosovo Agency of Statistics (2023) and the Swiss Economic Report on Kosovo (2023)

### 5.2.3 Governance Failures and Institutional Fragmentation

Kosovo's industrial governance landscape is highly fragmented. Responsibilities are dispersed across multiple ministries, including those for economy, education, and industry, while donor programmes, diaspora networks, and business associations also play significant roles. Coordination among these actors remains limited. Most initiatives are project-based, short-term, and poorly integrated across sectors, leading to duplication and a loss of continuity.

Although strategic documents such as the *National Development Strategy* (2016) and the *Industrial Policy Concept Paper* (2022) articulate ambitions for industrial upgrading and skills development, implementation has been inconsistent. Institutional mechanisms for coordination are largely absent. There are no established platforms for cross-ministerial dialogue, no shared data systems to support policy alignment, and no feedback loops to enable collective learning and adjustment. Overlapping mandates and the absence of a designated lead agency further weaken policy coherence.

Donors continue to provide essential support in areas such as export promotion, digital infrastructure, and vocational training. However, many programmes operate outside national frameworks, following separate reporting and funding cycles. This fragmentation limits opportunities for institutional learning and hinders the consolidation or scaling of successful initiatives.

From the perspective of the DNS framework, these weaknesses reflect a failure to perform three essential governance functions: joint problem diagnosis, experimental solution-building, and iterative feedback. The DNS approach does not depend on a powerful central agency but on coordinated mechanisms that connect ministries, donors, firms, universities, and municipal actors in structured, continuous collaboration (Rodrik, 2008; Sabel & Zeitlin, 2012).

Some early signs of such collaboration are emerging. Innovation hubs, diaspora mentoring programmes, and local government initiatives have begun experimenting with new forms of engagement. Yet these efforts remain disconnected from one another and from national priorities. Establishing a governance architecture that links local experimentation with broader development goals through coordination units, feedback mechanisms, and learning platforms could help Kosovo move from fragmented initiatives toward a more adaptive and networked industrial strategy (Fig. 5.2).

The following section explores the emergence of DNS-inspired arrangements within Kosovo's digital services sector and considers how these nascent practices might be scaled and institutionalized to foster a more coherent approach to capability development.

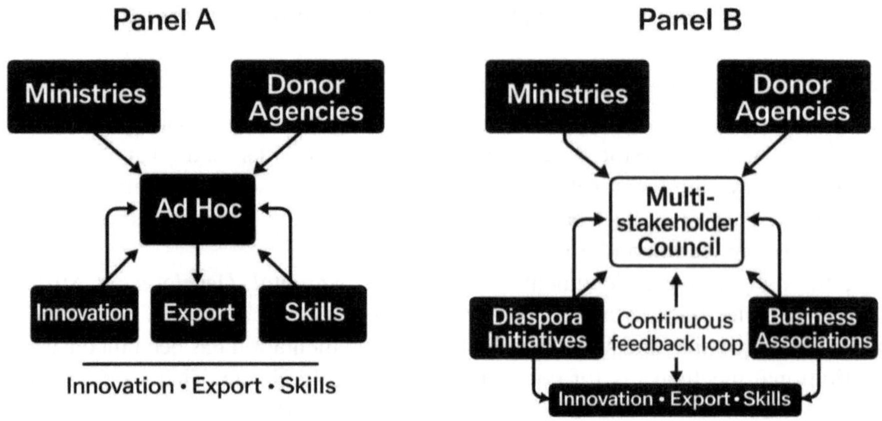


**Fig. 5.2** Comparative schematic of governance arrangements. *Source* Author's elaboration based on field data, sector reports, and stakeholder interviews (2024), generated with DALL·E using Microsoft Copilot (2025)

## 5.3 Emerging Industrial Subsectors and the Cross-Cutting Promise of ICT

Although Kosovo's industrial base remains limited, several subsectors such as wood processing, agri-food production, construction materials, and textiles have shown signs of gradual advancement. None has yet undergone deep structural transformation, but each holds potential for incremental upgrading and diversification if supported by stronger coordination and investment.

In wood processing, firms benefit from skilled craftsmanship, forest resources, and steady diaspora demand. Agri-food producers are making modest gains in niche, health-oriented markets, while parts of the construction materials sector, especially base metals, are slowly modernizing. In textiles, small firms target regional and diaspora markets but continue to rely heavily on subcontracting.

These gains remain fragile. Across all subsectors, firms face common challenges such as limited finance, skills shortages, outdated technologies, and weak policy support. Progress has largely been driven by individual entrepreneurs or donor initiatives rather than by a coherent industrial strategy. In the absence of sectoral councils, cluster initiatives, or mechanisms for collective learning, innovation remains fragmented and difficult to scale.

Within this landscape, the ICT sector stands out for its dynamism and cross-cutting potential. Leveraging strong diaspora ties, a digitally skilled youth population, and an expanding innovation ecosystem, ICT has begun to reshape entrepreneurship and export services. Beyond its own growth, it can enhance other industries by improving design, traceability, quality assurance, and market access. Yet integration across sectors remains limited, and capability gaps persist in areas such as artificial intelligence, cybersecurity, and digital infrastructure outside major cities.

Despite their differences, these subsectors share a common pattern: progress is partial and constrained by weak coordination and fragmented support systems. The ICT sector, however, offers a strategic entry point for overcoming these barriers. If effectively integrated into industrial policy, it could serve as a horizontal enabler of capability development across Kosovo's economy.

Table 5.2 summarizes the main characteristics of these subsectors, highlighting their export shares, key strengths, principal constraints, and the cross-cutting role of ICT as a potential driver of upgrading.

The figures in Table 5.2 illustrate the dual nature of Kosovo's industrial landscape: modest diversification alongside persistent structural weaknesses. The largest export share belongs to construction materials, reflecting the dominance of resource-based industries and regional trade in base metals. Wood processing and agri-food production each account for roughly one-tenth of exports, suggesting potential for upgrading through quality improvement and certification. Both remain constrained by technological gaps and fragmented logistics systems.

Textiles contribute a smaller but stable share, driven by cost advantages and vocational skills, though the sector remains confined to low-margin subcontracting. In contrast, the ICT sector, while smaller in employment terms, generates significant export revenue and increasingly functions as a horizontal enabler of innovation. Its digital strengths highlight the importance of linking technology-driven capabilities with traditional industries. Together, these patterns underscore the need

**Table 5.2** Key industrial subsectors in Kosovo—exports, strengths, and constraints

| Subsector | Export share (2023) | Strengths | Constraints |
|---|---|---|---|
| Wood processing | 10% (est.) | Resource base, skilled labour, regional demand | Technological upgrading, certification systems, market access |
| Agri-food processing (Non-Alc.) | 11% | High-quality water, diaspora networks, health product trends | Food safety compliance, fragmented supply chains, logistics infrastructure |
| Base Metals and Construction Materials | 22% (base metals) | Domestic demand, raw materials, regional export channels | Energy costs, outdated machinery, limited green compliance |
| Textile and apparel | 5% | Cost-competitive labour, vocational training, some FDI | Low automation, weak branding, poor cluster coordination |
| ICT sector (Enabler) | €284.2 million (2023) | Young digital workforce, global connectivity, tech entrepreneurship | Skill shortages (AI, cybersecurity), rural infrastructure gaps, weak industrial integration |

*Source* Author's elaboration based on data from the Kosovo Agency of Statistics (2023), Swiss Economic Report on Kosovo (2023), Kosovo Wood Association (2024), Kosovo Investment and Enterprise Support Agency (2024). Export shares are indicative and rounded. ICT exports are reported in value terms, reflecting their service-based nature.

for governance mechanisms that connect digital assets with broader industrial upgrading.

The next section examines the evolution of Kosovo's ICT sector in greater depth and explores how it can serve as a cornerstone of a DNS-based approach to industrial transformation.

## 5.4 ICT as a Driver of Digital-Age Capability Accumulation

Kosovo's ICT sector represents the most dynamic and internationally connected segment of its economy. While traditional manufacturing continues to face fragmentation, underinvestment, and weak learning systems, the ICT sector has expanded rapidly over the past decade. This growth has been supported by a digitally literate workforce, near-universal broadband access, and strong connections to the diaspora and global digital markets. Between 2013 and 2023, ICT service exports rose from €59.8 million to €284.2 million, while sectoral employment more than quadrupled (World Bank, 2024).

This transformation is distinctive because it did not result from formal industrial policy or centralized planning. Instead, it has evolved through decentralized processes of learning and adaptation. Freelancers have connected to global platforms, diaspora entrepreneurs have launched start-ups, and donor programmes have supported training and innovation. These dynamics reflect the core features of the DNS model, in which coordination, learning, and embeddedness emerge through networks of actors rather than hierarchical control.

This section examines how capability accumulation has taken root in Kosovo's ICT sector. It focuses on five interrelated dimensions: the expansion of exports and employment, the rise of platform-based freelancing, the role of the diaspora in start-up formation, the development of informal learning ecosystems, and the persistent constraints that continue to limit scaling and integration.

### *5.4.1 Growth Trajectory: Exports and Employment*

Over the past decade, Kosovo's ICT sector has experienced steady and substantial growth in both exports and employment. As illustrated in Fig. 5.3, ICT service exports increased nearly fivefold between 2013 and 2023, while employment rose from fewer than 3500 to more than 13,000 workers. This expansion has created new opportunities for upward mobility, particularly among young professionals, and demonstrates the sector's capacity to connect domestic talent with global digital markets.

A key driver of this growth has been the proliferation of online work platforms such as Upwork, Fiverr, and Freelancer. These platforms have enabled Kosovar freelancers to overcome the limitations of the domestic market and engage directly

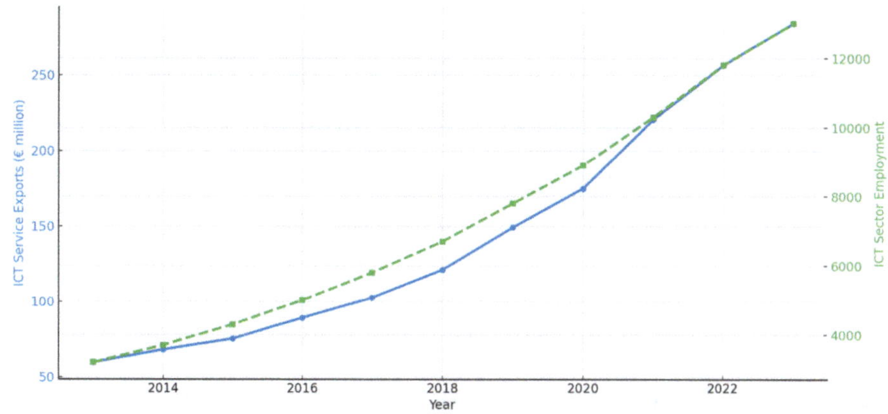


**Fig. 5.3** ICT export growth and employment trends in Kosovo (2013–2023). *Source* Author's elaboration based on data from World Bank (2024), Kosovo ICT Barometer (2023), and stakeholder interviews

with international clients, integrating into global value chains. However, while this digital leap has provided significant opportunities for income generation and skill acquisition, much of the learning remains individual and weakly embedded within local institutions. Consequently, the diffusion of capabilities across the broader economy remains limited.

### *5.4.2 Freelancing and Global Integration From Below*

Freelancing has become the most accessible entry point for young people in Kosovo to engage with the global economy. Through digital platforms, individuals offer services such as software development, graphic design, translation, and customer support. Entry barriers are low, requiring only basic internet access, self-taught skills, and proficiency in English.

Many freelancers start as individual contractors and gradually form teams or small firms, expanding their service portfolios and, in some cases, moving into product development. These decentralized work arrangements promote micro-level learning through direct client interaction, continuous feedback, and exposure to global performance standards. Freelancing also familiarizes participants with international workflows, digital tools, and quality requirements that are often absent from formal education systems.

Despite these advantages, the ecosystem remains fragile. In the absence of supportive legal frameworks, export facilitation, and access to tailored financing, much of its developmental potential remains underutilized. Figure 5.4 illustrates the flow of knowledge and skills within this evolving ecosystem, showing how informal, network-based governance can foster capability formation in low-capacity environments.

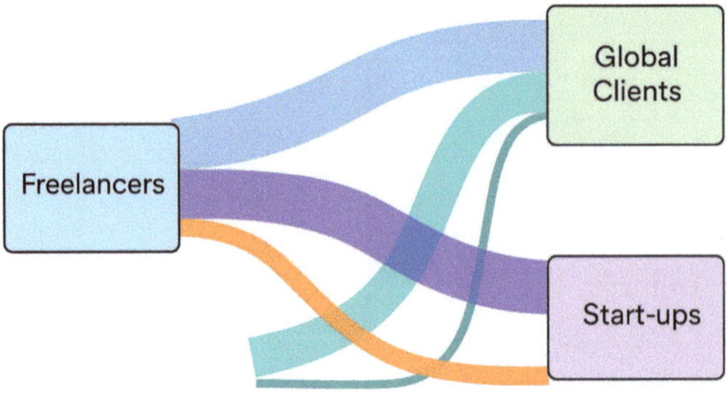


**Fig. 5.4** Skill flows in Kosovo's ICT freelancing ecosystem. *Source* Author's elaboration based on stakeholder interviews and platform data (2024), generated with DALL·E using Microsoft Copilot (2025)

### *5.4.3 Start-Up Growth and Diaspora-Fuelled Entrepreneurship*

Beyond freelancing, Kosovo's ICT sector has seen the emergence of software companies, software-as-a-service (SaaS) platforms, and business process outsourcing (BPO) ventures, many founded by diaspora returnees. Firms such as Solaborate, Gjirafa, and Kutia demonstrate how transnational networks can mobilize capital, expertise, and access to international markets.

Diaspora entrepreneurs often act as intermediaries between local talent and global ecosystems. They serve as mentors, investors, and advocates, exemplifying the DNS principles of distributed coordination and embedded learning. Support organizations including Innovation Centre Kosovo (ICK), VentureUP, and the Women in Tech Network complement these efforts by providing mentorship, workspace infrastructure, and early-stage financing. Although most of these initiatives rely on donor funding, they operate as hybrid institutions that link private firms, public agencies, and civil society actors.

Figure 5.5 traces the evolution of Kosovo's ICT ecosystem, illustrating how freelancer participation, diaspora-led start-ups, training academies, and donor programmes have gradually converged to form an increasingly self-sustaining digital environment.

The evolution of Kosovo's start-up ecosystem reflects a bottom-up process of capability formation. Growth has emerged not through state policy but through networked governance shaped by diaspora engagement, donor support, and community-based experimentation. This configuration has produced meaningful spillovers: returnees have launched ventures, mentored freelancers, and advocated for policy reform; donor platforms have provided infrastructure, training, and early-stage finance; and start-up events have fostered peer learning and exchange. Collectively, these elements form an emerging DNS architecture that functions pragmatically within a low-capacity environment.

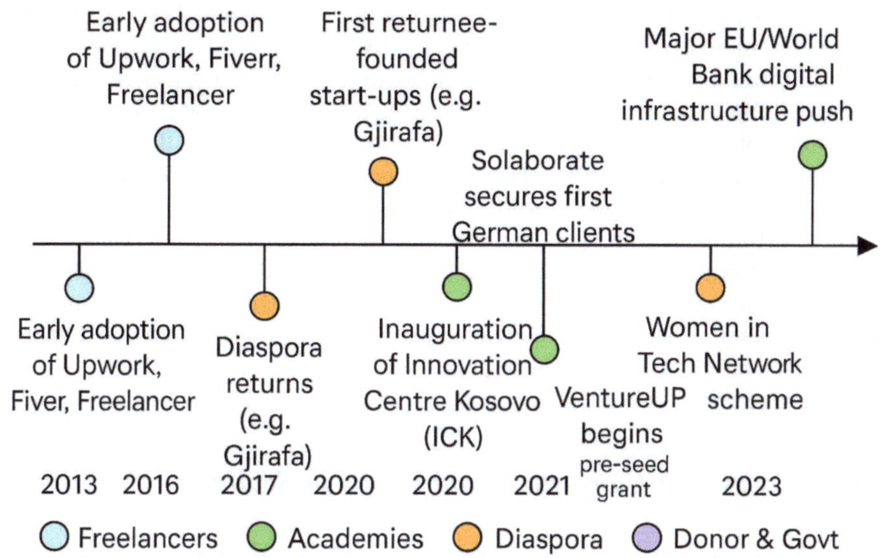


**Fig. 5.5** Timeline of key events in Kosovo's ICT start-up ecosystem. *Note* The timeline illustrates how freelancer participation, diaspora-led start-ups, and support platforms have sequentially contributed to the formation of a self-sustaining digital ecosystem. Each milestone represents a key function of the DNS: coordination, learning, or embeddedness. *Source* Author's elaboration based on interviews with founders, donor programme staff, and accelerator managers (2024), generated with DALL·E using Microsoft Copilot (2025)

Despite this progress, significant challenges persist. Many initiatives remain short-term and project-based, with limited alignment to national development priorities. Diaspora engagement, though valuable, is often informal and episodic, while coordination among support platforms remains weak. Without stronger consolidation and integration into a coherent governance framework, current momentum may prove difficult to sustain.

The next subsection examines the informal learning systems and peer networks underpinning this ecosystem and considers how they could evolve into more durable institutions for capability development.

### 5.4.4 *Informal Learning Ecosystems and Peer Networks*

Much of Kosovo's digital capability has developed through peer-driven and decentralized learning environments rather than formal education. Freelancers and entrepreneurs exchange knowledge on platforms such as Discord, GitHub, and Telegram, where they share resources, tools, and practical advice. These digital communities serve as a living infrastructure for continuous learning and collaborative adaptation.

Community events such as KosICT, BarCamp Prishtina, and Techstars Startup Weekend complement these online networks by offering in-person opportunities for mentoring, experimentation, and collaboration. Coding academies including JCoders, KODE Academy, and Cacttus Education provide modular training tailored to employer needs. Often led by diaspora professionals, these initiatives embody what Sabel and Zeitlin describe as *productive bricolage*: problem-solving through experimentation under institutional constraint.

These informal systems perform essential governance functions. They embed knowledge in practice, enable coordination through shared norms, and foster trust-based relationships. In doing so, they approximate the DNS model of capability formation, where learning and innovation evolve through distributed and adaptive mechanisms rather than hierarchical policy design.

### 5.4.5 Ecosystem Constraints and Limits to Scaling

Despite recent growth, Kosovo's ICT ecosystem faces structural constraints that limit its capacity to scale and generate wider economic transformation. Four key challenges persist.

First, advanced digital skills are scarce. While basic programming and web development are common, expertise in artificial intelligence, cybersecurity, and data science remains limited. Public universities are misaligned with industry needs and slow to revise curricula (Open Data Kosovo, 2020; IFME, 2020). Figure 5.6 illustrates this skills deficit.

Second, ICT activity is concentrated in Pristina, restricting opportunities for firms and individuals in other regions (ICT for Kosovo's Growth, 2022).

Third, financing for start-ups and innovation is fragmented. Early-stage investment is scarce, and no mechanism links public, private, and diaspora capital (GIZ and Ministry of Industry, 2022).

Fourth, cross-sector integration is weak. Although ICT could enhance sectors such as agri-food and manufacturing, few structured partnerships exist, limiting spillovers and developmental impact (IFME, 2020).

Addressing these challenges requires DNS-aligned interventions: multi-stakeholder councils to link education and labour markets, regional innovation hubs to widen access, blended finance platforms to connect investment sources, and cross-sector task forces to promote digital integration.

### 5.4.6 Toward a DNS-Compatible Digital Development Model

Kosovo's ICT sector already displays several features of a DNS. Coordination is driven by informal coalitions of diaspora mentors, training academies, and start-ups. Learning occurs through project-based work and peer exchange rather than

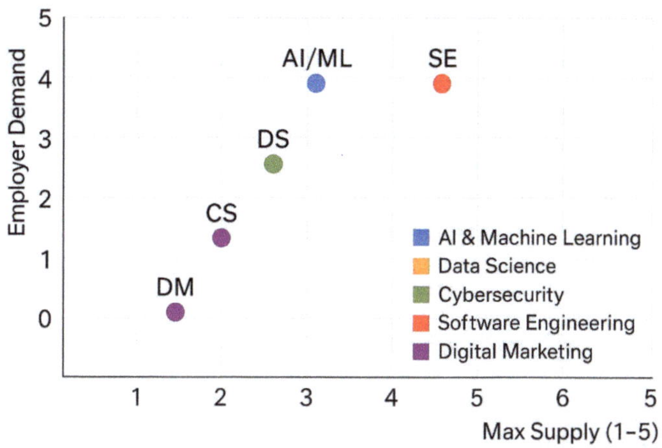


**Fig. 5.6** Skills-Gap Scatter—demand vs. supply in Kosovo's ICT Sector. *Note* Advanced skills in AI, cybersecurity and data science are in high demand but undersupplied, revealing weak alignment between education and industry. Basic development roles are better matched, though quality gaps remain. *Source* Author's elaboration based on stakeholder interviews, training data, and employer surveys (2024), generated with DALL·E using Microsoft Copilot (2025)

formal education, while embeddedness develops through dense networks linking local actors to global markets.

This governance configuration, however, remains fragile. The sector depends heavily on donor funding, is concentrated in Pristina, and remains weakly aligned with national development strategies. Without stronger institutional support, Kosovo risks entrenching a dual economy in which a globally integrated digital elite coexists with stagnant traditional sectors.

Consolidating recent gains requires institutionalizing existing informal mechanisms. Sectoral innovation councils could link ministries, firms, municipalities, and diaspora actors. Diaspora mentoring programmes should be embedded within national skills and enterprise initiatives. Public and private co-investment platforms could mobilize early-stage finance and distribute risk, while industrial and procurement policies should mainstream digital transformation to promote broad-based upgrading.

These measures build on current strengths and chart a path from fragmented experimentation toward a coherent and inclusive digital strategy. Figure 5.7 presents a coordination scorecard comparing effective DNS-like mechanisms such as diaspora engagement and responsive training systems with ongoing gaps in governance, planning, and finance.

Kosovo's experience illustrates that digital catch-up depends less on replicating external models than on connecting capabilities, actors, and strategic missions through adaptive and networked governance. As Andreoni and Chang (2019) note, successful upgrading rests on systems that learn, coordinate, and evolve.

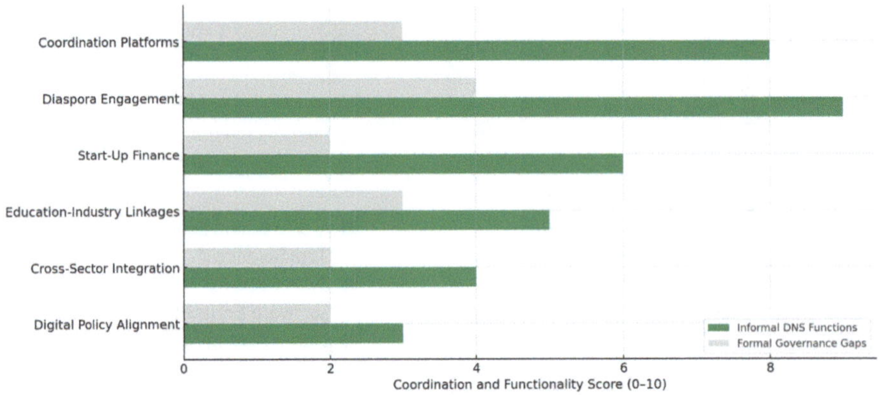


**Fig. 5.7** Informal and formal governance gaps. *Note* The figure contrasts effective informal mechanisms, such as diaspora engagement and training responsiveness, with formal governance gaps in strategic planning, cross-sector integration and financing. *Source* Author's elaboration based on stakeholder interviews, institutional assessments and policy reviews (2024)

The next sections examine how key stakeholders, particularly the diaspora, donors, and municipalities, are shaping this emerging trajectory.

## 5.5 Diaspora Networks and Entrepreneurial Ecosystems

Kosovo's diaspora has long played a central role in national development, initially through remittances and humanitarian assistance (World Bank, 2024). In recent years, this engagement has evolved toward direct contributions in investment, entrepreneurship, and knowledge exchange, particularly within the ICT sector. This shift marks a broader transformation in Kosovo's development trajectory, as the diaspora increasingly serves as a source of capabilities and informal governance consistent with the principles of the DNS (Kuznetsov and Sabel, 2006; Meyer & Brown, 1999).

This section analyses how returnees, mentors, and informal capital flows shape Kosovo's digital economy through personal networks, trust-based mentoring, and relational capital that compensates for institutional gaps.

### *5.5.1 Returnees as Entrepreneurial Catalysts*

A visible form of diaspora engagement is the return of skilled professionals. Many of Kosovo's leading ICT firms, including Solaborate, Gjirafa, and Formon, were co-founded by returnees from Germany, Switzerland, the United States, and the United

Kingdom (Emerging Europe, 2023). These individuals bring financial resources, technical expertise, and global perspectives that enrich the domestic business environment.

Returnees play a dual role: they establish globally connected firms and mentor emerging entrepreneurs. Their participation embeds international standards into local practices and facilitates transnational knowledge transfer (Sabel & Zeitlin, 2012). Some maintain active links with foreign accelerators and investors, while others divide their time between Kosovo and host countries, sustaining continuous exchanges of experience and innovation (Kuznetsov & Sabel, 2006).

### 5.5.2 Diaspora Mentoring and Transnational Learning

Beyond entrepreneurship, many diasporas professionals act as mentors, connectors, and brokers. Their engagement often takes the form of short visits, virtual advisory sessions, and participation in hackathons, pitch competitions, and bootcamps. These exchanges are typically informal and grounded in trust, focusing on strategic thinking and entrepreneurial mindset rather than purely technical skills (Leadbeater & Miller, 2004).

Platforms such as Germin, KosovoDiaspora.org, and Diaspora Flet have formalized parts of this mentoring ecosystem, yet the most impactful relationships remain personal and network-based. These interactions expand Kosovo's transnational embeddedness by linking local firms to global markets, clients, and support systems (Meyer & Brown, 1999). Mentoring thus functions as a governance mechanism that strengthens entrepreneurial capabilities through consistent, experience-based guidance that formal institutions rarely provide.

### 5.5.3 Remittance-Financed Entrepreneurship and Informal Capital

Remittances account for roughly 17.5% of Kosovo's GDP (World Bank, 2024). While much of this income supports household consumption, an increasing share is channelled into entrepreneurship, skills development, and informal investment in ICT (UNDP and Germin, 2023).

In many cases, remittances operate as patient capital, enabling individuals to start or join ventures, purchase equipment, or fund training without relying on banks or external investors (World Bank, 2021). Diaspora family members also invest directly in early-stage firms, often on the basis of trust rather than formal contracts and frequently combine financing with mentorship and client introductions (UNDP and Germin, 2023). These flows not only finance entrepreneurs but also strengthen ecosystem resilience, exemplifying a DNS principle: when formal institutions are weak, transnational trust networks become critical channels for capability formation.

### *5.5.4 Diaspora Institutions and the Limits of Formalization*

Kosovo has sought to formalize diaspora engagement through national strategies, investment incentives, and consular registries (Diaspora for Development, 2024; Germin, 2024; UNDP, 2023). However, these efforts have achieved limited results. Participation in registries remains low, mandates are fragmented, and implementation capacity is weak (Diaspora Engagement Mapping Kosovo, 2024).

By contrast, informal mechanisms such as co-founding companies, mentoring, and remittance-based support have produced more consistent outcomes with lower administrative overhead (UNDP and Germin, 2023). This contrast highlights a key DNS insight: effective governance relies not on replacing informal arrangements with formal institutions, but on reinforcing those that already function well.

Promising approaches include co-designed mentorship programmes linking diaspora professionals with training academies, joint investment funds managed through innovation centres, and standardized legal templates for trust-based investment. Such tools can connect effective informal practices to national frameworks without undermining their flexibility or responsiveness.

Figure 5.8 summarizes the four main channels through which diaspora actors contribute to Kosovo's ICT ecosystem: returnee entrepreneurship, mentoring, remittance-based investment, and formal policy initiatives. Each channel supports key governance functions, including embedded learning, relational coordination, and informal problem-solving.

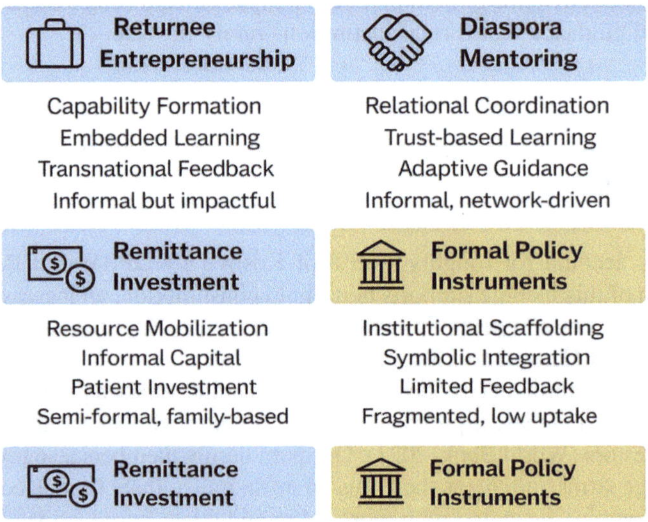


**Fig. 5.8** Channels of diaspora contribution to Kosovo's ICT ecosystem. *Source* Author's elaboration based on interviews with returnees, investors, and programme facilitators (2024), generated with DALL·E using Microsoft Copilot (2025)

Kosovo's diaspora has evolved from a source of remittances into a strategic partner in digital transformation. Through entrepreneurship, mentoring, and informal capital, diaspora actors fill institutional gaps and foster transnational learning. To realize this potential, the diaspora should be treated not as an external resource but as an integral participant in the governance of capability development.

These forms of engagement demonstrate that transnational networks are now central to Kosovo's digital evolution. By mobilizing knowledge, finance, and relationships, diaspora actors perform governance functions that formal institutions often struggle to sustain. Their activities show how learning, coordination, and resource mobilization can emerge through trust-based and adaptive mechanisms. To maximize developmental impact, these contributions must be aligned with domestic institutions and supported by local actors.

The next section examines how donors and municipalities can help bridge this gap and strengthen Kosovo's framework for digital capability development.

## 5.6 Donor Programs and Institutional Fragmentation

Donors have played a pivotal role in Kosovo's digital development. Through investments in training, infrastructure, and entrepreneurship, they have supported the early formation of digital capabilities and introduced models of agile, network-based governance. Despite these contributions, donor programmes often remain fragmented, short-term, and only loosely aligned with national strategies. Consequently, they struggle to generate sustained, system-wide transformation. The DNS framework offers a potential way forward by embedding donor initiatives within coordinated governance structures that promote learning, adaptability, and long-term alignment with development goals.

### *5.6.1 Donor Contributions to Digital Capability Formation*

Over the past decade, international donors including the EU, GIZ, USAID, SDC, SIDA, and the World Bank have invested substantially in Kosovo's ICT sector. Their programmes have focused on skills development, SME growth, export promotion, broadband expansion, start-up acceleration, and policy reform. Notable examples include SDC's *Enhancing Youth Employment (EYE)* programme, SIDA's support for the Innovation Centre Kosovo, and GIZ's *CETEP* project, which strengthened ICT skills, entrepreneurship, and export readiness. USAID's *EMPOWER* initiative expanded digital employment pathways, while EU programmes such as *IPA II* and *KODE* have advanced infrastructure development and e-governance.

These initiatives have produced visible results. Kosovo now hosts centres such as the Innovation Centre Kosovo (ICK) and VentureUP, alongside a growing ecosystem of bootcamps, hackathons, and vocational training programmes.

Donors have also introduced new governance tools, including challenge grants and agile implementation models, creating experimental spaces for innovation in a context of limited public capacity.

### *5.6.2 Fragmentation and Short-Termism*

Despite these achievements, donor programmes frequently operate in isolation. Each initiative follows its own mandate, funding cycle, and reporting framework, with limited coordination or strategic alignment with national development priorities (Bartlett et al., 2014; UNDP, 2025). Coordination mechanisms remain largely ad hoc, and opportunities for joint learning and institutional feedback are minimal (BCSDN, 2023).

As illustrated in Fig. 5.9, ministries, donor platforms, and implementing agencies often function in parallel, with weak linkages across programmes. Most projects lack feedback loops that would enable cross-initiative learning or long-term institutional adaptation. This fragmentation diminishes the systemic impact of donor investments and constrains the scaling of successful pilot projects.

Figure 5.9 illustrates three main funding streams: EU IPA II (economy), GIZ CETEP (education), and USAID EMPOWER (innovation). Each is channelled to

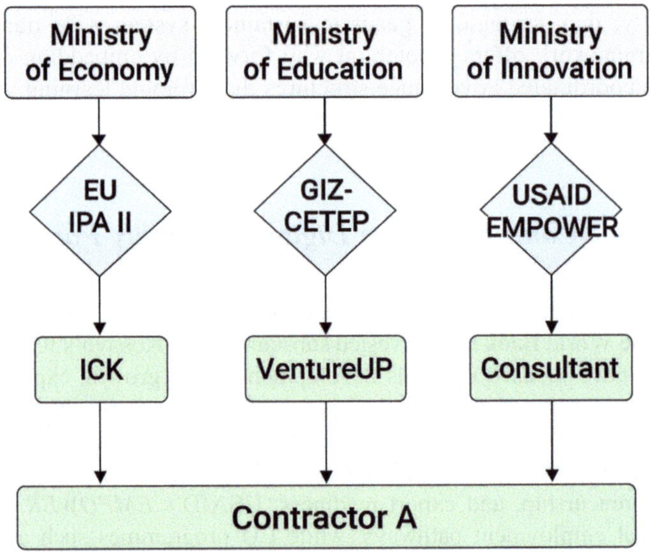


**Fig. 5.9** Institutional fragmentation in donor-funded ICT programs. *Note* This diagram reveals the siloed partnerships between ministries and donors and the resultant contractor bottleneck. *Source* Author's elaboration based on donor reports, stakeholder interviews, and program mapping (2024), generated with DALL·E using Microsoft Copilot (2025)

different implementing partners but ultimately converges on the same private contractor. This configuration exposes two structural weaknesses: weak coordination among public institutions and overreliance on a small group of contractors, which limits knowledge diffusion, reduces local ownership, and inhibits institutional learning.

Many initiatives are project-based and implemented by NGOs or consulting firms with minimal public-sector engagement. When projects conclude, networks dissolve, lessons remain undocumented, and policy linkages disappear. For instance, digital entrepreneurship programmes often operate separately from education reforms or national economic strategies. Although training activities have reached thousands, few are embedded in systems that enable sustained scaling or institutionalization.

This fragmentation also creates confusion for firms and entrepreneurs. Overlapping grants, duplicated training schemes, and inconsistent selection criteria foster short-term opportunism rather than strategic growth. The resulting support landscape remains scattered, preventing the accumulation of capabilities and coherent sectoral development.

### *5.6.3 DNS-Compatible Alternatives: Embedding Donor Learning*

The DNS framework offers a practical approach to enhancing the impact of donor programmes. Rather than functioning as isolated projects, donor initiatives can be embedded within governance systems that foster coordination, collective learning, and institutional development.

Three shifts are particularly important. **First**, programmes should be co-owned by at least two domestic actors. A ministry might partner with a municipal government, or a university could collaborate with an innovation centre. Joint design and implementation strengthen local ownership and improve cross-sector alignment. **Second**, continuous feedback mechanisms are essential. Task forces that bring together donors, ministries, and private actors can identify challenges, assess progress, and adapt interventions in real time. **Third**, support should follow a sequenced approach. A training initiative could lead to internships, which in turn connect to procurement opportunities or industrial upgrading policies. This gradual process encourages cumulative learning and sustained policy integration.

Figure 5.10 contrasts Kosovo's current fragmented donor landscape with a DNS-aligned model that emphasizes co-design, feedback, and system-wide coherence.

The left panel of Fig. 5.10 depicts Kosovo's current donor landscape, where projects operate in isolation and remain disconnected from national systems. The right panel presents a DNS-compatible structure that relies on multi-actor task forces, shared learning platforms, and cross-institutional ownership to enhance coherence and institutional development.

Kosovo's main challenge is not a shortage of donor funding but the absence of governance mechanisms capable of embedding donor efforts within a coherent national development strategy. DNS-oriented reforms can help bridge this gap. By linking donor initiatives with education, procurement, and industrial policy,

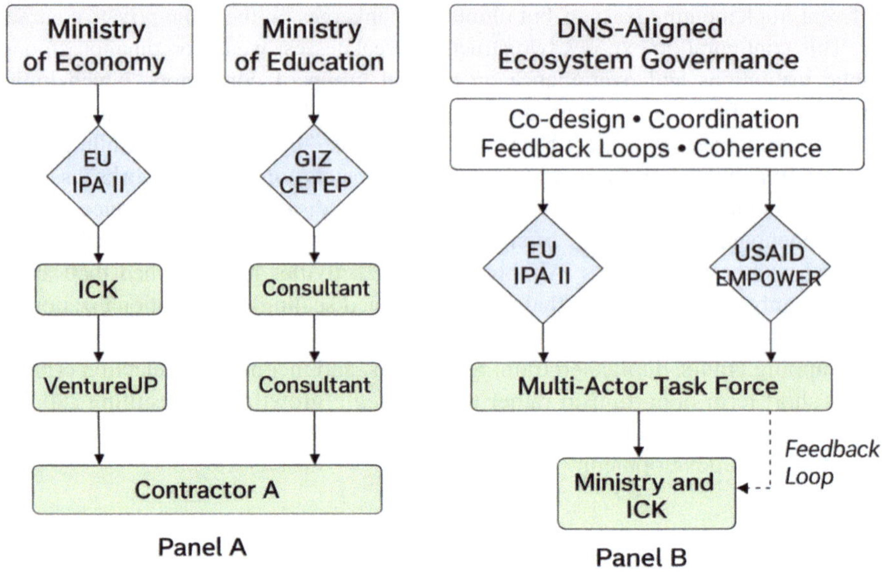


**Fig. 5.10** From project fragmentation to DNS-aligned ecosystem governance. *Source* Author's elaboration based on comparative donor governance models (2024), generated with DALL·E using Microsoft Copilot (2025)

Kosovo can move beyond isolated successes and build a more adaptive and resilient development model.

The next section turns to an often-overlooked yet critical actor in this process: municipal governments. Although frequently excluded from national planning and donor coordination, municipalities are well positioned to lead local experimentation, foster cross-sector collaboration, and advance digital transformation from the ground up.

## 5.7 Municipal Innovation Councils and Localized Learning

Across Kosovo, municipalities are emerging as key actors in the country's digital transformation. Although often excluded from national planning and donor coordination, local governments in Pristina, Prizren, Peja, and Gjilan are experimenting with ways to build capabilities, connect stakeholders, and promote digital inclusion. These initiatives, though modest and fragmented, embody the core principles of the DNS: collaboration, embedded partnerships, and continuous learning.

Pristina remains the centre of the digital economy, hosting most ICT firms, technology faculties, incubators such as the Innovation Centre Kosovo, and donor-supported programmes. The municipal government supports events, training initiatives, and civic technology projects that position the city as a facilitator within a broader digital ecosystem.

Other municipalities are pursuing similar approaches shaped by local strengths. Prizren has leveraged its creative economy to attract technology talent and host innovation festivals. Peja links ICT training to employment programmes, while Gjilan partners with businesses to expand vocational modules. These efforts have created new spaces for coordination and learning at the local level.

Despite this progress, Kosovo lacks a national framework to connect and sustain municipal innovation. Local governments, businesses, and donors often act independently, with limited coordination or knowledge exchange. Establishing municipal innovation councils could address this gap. With clear mandates, dedicated funding, and links to national strategies, such councils could align resources, coordinate stakeholders, and establish systematic feedback mechanisms.

Municipalities already perform many DNS functions by convening partners, adapting policy to local contexts, and promoting learning through practice. Yet their contributions remain scattered and under-recognized. With targeted support, they could become key nodes in a distributed innovation system that grounds Kosovo's digital transition in the realities of its cities and communities.

Local initiatives demonstrate that digital transformation can take root at the municipal level, where collaboration and experimentation foster learning and ownership. Sustaining and scaling these efforts, however, depend on broader system conditions. Persistent gaps in skills, finance, and institutional support continue to constrain progress. The following section examines these bottlenecks and their implications for Kosovo's capability development and industrial upgrading in the digital age.

## 5.8 Bottlenecks in Skills, Finance, and Scaling

Kosovo's ICT sector stands out as a dynamic outlier in an otherwise stagnant industrial landscape. Yet its long-term potential is constrained by three interrelated challenges: skills mismatches, weak absorptive capacity, and structural barriers to firm growth. This section examines how these limitations shape Kosovo's digital transition and considers how DNS-inspired governance can help address them through coordination, learning, and shared problem-solving.

### *5.8.1 Skills Mismatches and the Limits of Training Expansion*

Kosovo benefits from a young, digitally connected population with strong language skills (World Bank, 2023). However, education and training systems remain misaligned with the evolving needs of the digital economy. Public universities offer limited instruction in advanced fields such as artificial intelligence, cloud computing, and cybersecurity (Open Data Kosovo, 2020), while vocational schools often rely on outdated equipment and maintain weak industry links (IFME, 2020).

Private coding academies and bootcamps have partially filled this gap. Flexible and practice-oriented, they equip participants with employable skills but remain non-accredited and disconnected from formal education pathways, limiting their long-term impact (Kosovo ICT Barometer, 2023). As a result, many individuals possess basic digital literacy but lack readiness for high-value or innovation-driven roles.

A DNS-oriented approach would establish curriculum feedback councils linking training providers, employers, and public agencies to align education with labour market demand and foster cumulative learning (Open Data Kosovo, 2020).

### 5.8.2 *Infrastructure and Absorptive Capacity Gaps*

Despite high broadband penetration, digital adoption among firms remains limited. Many small and medium-sized enterprises continue to rely on analogue systems, particularly outside Pristina. Rural areas face uneven access to digital tools and services (ICT for Kosovo's Growth, 2022; World Bank, 2023). Public institutions, especially at the municipal level, lack dedicated staff or mechanisms to connect firms with ICT providers and training opportunities (UNDP, 2023).

The physical infrastructure exists but is not effectively mobilized for innovation or capability development. A DNS-compatible response would involve establishing municipal digital hubs that connect firms, trainers, and local governments in joint problem-solving, enabling contextual learning and local capacity building.

### 5.8.3 *Start-Up Growth and Scaling Constraints*

Kosovo's start-up scene is vibrant but constrained by limited access to finance and structural barriers to scaling. Venture investors are scarce, and commercial banks remain reluctant to lend to firms with intangible assets or minimal collateral (GIZ and MIET, 2022). Public procurement systems rarely prioritize digital innovation, restricting opportunities for start-ups to engage with government contracts (OECD, 2021).

Early-stage firms rely heavily on donor grants, remittances, and family funding but often lack mechanisms to transition from freelancing to product development and export growth (UNDP and Germin, 2023). Innovation support remains fragmented, and public R&D investment is among the lowest in Europe, below 0.1% of GDP (World Bank, 2023).

These conditions foster survival without scaling. A DNS-based approach would create co-investment platforms linking public, private, and diaspora capital, reform

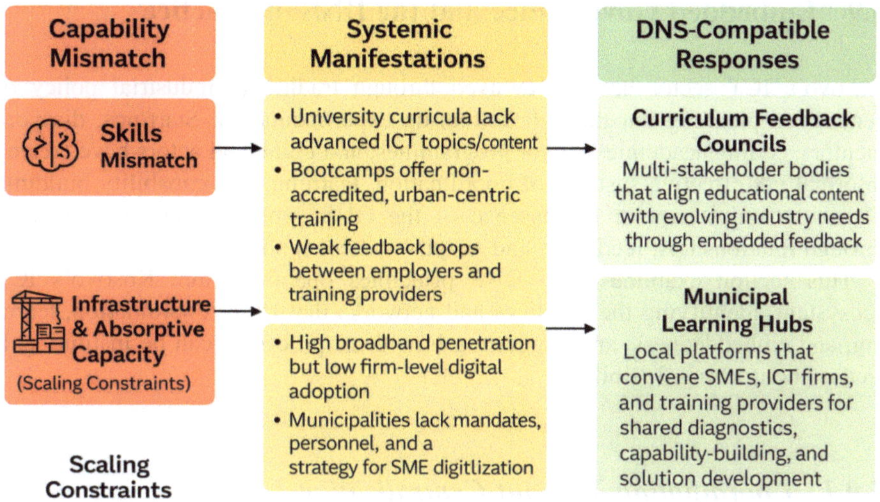


**Fig. 5.11** ICT bottlenecks and DNS-compatible responses in Kosovo. *Source* Author's elaboration based on sector analysis and DNS framework, generated with DALL·E using Microsoft Copilot (2025)

procurement rules to include digital enterprises, and strengthen export agency partnerships to help start-ups integrate into global value chains (Fig. 5.11).

### *5.8.4 Implications for DNS-Oriented Reform*

Addressing challenges in skills, infrastructure, and firm growth in isolation is unlikely to yield lasting results. A DNS-oriented model views them as interdependent parts of a broader learning system. Training must respond to enterprise needs, infrastructure must facilitate innovation, and firm growth must be supported by accessible finance, coherent policy, and market integration.

Kosovo's digital transition cannot be achieved through isolated projects or short-term reforms. It requires a governance system that connects actors, adapts over time, and embeds learning within institutions. The DNS framework provides a practical roadmap for building such a system—one capable of transforming fragmented initiatives into sustained capability development and long-term economic transformation.

## 5.9 Embedded Governance and the DNS in Practice

Kosovo's ICT sector has not evolved through traditional industrial policy or centralized planning but through bottom-up experimentation. Start-ups, diaspora mentors, coding academies, donor programmes, and municipal actors have created informal yet effective systems of coordination, learning, and capability building. These dynamics capture the essence of the DNS, where governance emerges through relationships, feedback, and adaptive problem-solving.

This section examines how DNS principles operate within Kosovo's ICT ecosystem, identifying the practices and networks that foster coordination, learning, and embeddedness, and suggesting how these processes can be institutionalized without losing flexibility.

### *5.9.1 Coordination Without Centralization*

Coordination in Kosovo's ICT sector occurs largely through informal networks. Diaspora returnees connect local start-ups with global clients and investors through trust-based professional ties. Coding academies collaborate with technology firms on training and recruitment without central oversight. Intermediaries such as the Innovation Centre Kosovo (ICK) and VentureUP act as conveners, linking firms, donors, educators, and community organizations. Though operating without formal mandates, these actors align interests and enable effective collaboration.

### *5.9.2 Learning by Doing and Embedded Feedback*

The sector advances through adaptive learning. Coding academies regularly update curricula in response to employer demand, client feedback, and diaspora input. Events such as hackathons and demo days create iterative spaces for experimentation and reflection. Governance depends less on formal planning than on continuous adaptation, consistent with the DNS principle of learning by doing.

### *5.9.3 Embeddedness Through Place and Transnational Ties*

DNS systems rely on embeddedness at both local and transnational levels. Municipalities foster coordination by hosting training programmes and local tech events, while diaspora professionals bridge Kosovo's ecosystem to global markets.

Through mentorship, partnerships, and informal investment, they transfer knowledge and business practices that link local actors to international networks of expertise and opportunity.

### *5.9.4 From Emergence to Institutional Possibility*

Kosovo already displays several features of DNS-oriented governance, although these remain fragmented and institutionally fragile. Strengthening them requires the development of light institutional scaffolding rather than the creation of new bureaucratic structures. Key priorities include: (i) recognizing diaspora mentorship within training and enterprise support programmes; (ii) establishing curriculum review councils that link employers and education providers; (iii) piloting multi-stakeholder municipal innovation councils; and (iv) creating task forces to connect start-ups with procurement and export opportunities. Collectively, these measures would transform informal governance arrangements into more resilient and coordinated systems while preserving the adaptability that underpins the sector's dynamism.

### *5.9.5 Mapping the Gaps: From Informal Practice to Formal Policy*

Kosovo's ICT sector illustrates that the core principles of the DNS, including coordination, learning, and embeddedness, can emerge even in the absence of strong formal institutions. These functions are already present, although informally and unevenly. The priority now is to stabilize and scale effective practices through governance arrangements that are adaptive, relational, and oriented toward continuous learning rather than through centralized control or large-scale investment.

The DNS framework offers a pathway for translating successful local experiments into system-wide development. By moving from emergence to institutionalization, Kosovo can transform its informal innovation networks into a durable foundation for long-term capability accumulation and digital transformation.

Figure 5.12 illustrates the persistent gap between informal practice and formal policy across six DNS-relevant domains. While informal coordination in areas such as mentoring, curriculum adaptation, and local innovation remains active and effective, the institutional mechanisms required to support, scale, and sustain these practices are still underdeveloped.

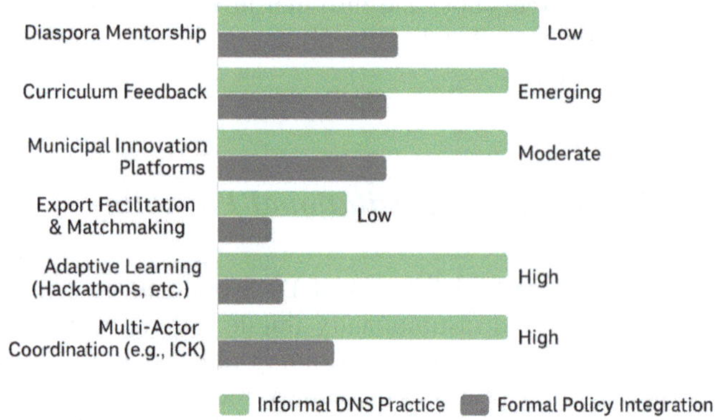


**Fig. 5.12** DNS functions vs. formal policy integration in Kosovo's ICT sector. *Note* The figure compares informal DNS activity (green) and formal policy presence (grey) across domains such as diaspora mentoring, curriculum feedback, municipal innovation, and export facilitation. *Source* Author's elaboration

## 5.10 Conclusion: Rethinking Digital Catch-Up Through DNS Insights

Kosovo's ICT sector demonstrates that meaningful development can emerge even under structural constraints. Despite limited resources, weak institutions, and fragmented policies, the country has built notable digital capabilities. This progress has not resulted from centralized planning or traditional industrial policy, but from adaptive, bottom-up coordination among entrepreneurs, diaspora actors, training providers, donors, and municipal authorities. These dynamics capture the essence of the DNS, where governance evolves through collaboration, feedback, and learning rather than through formal hierarchy. The Kosovo case shows that digital transformation can advance through distributed problem-solving and relational governance, even in low-capacity settings.

Coordination in Kosovo's digital economy has developed through relationships rather than mandates. Start-ups, coding academies, and technology intermediaries collaborate on skills development and recruitment. Diaspora returnees connect local firms to global markets, while donors and municipalities facilitate partnerships across sectors. These interactions, grounded in trust and shared purpose, have generated a flexible system of coordination that supports innovation without extensive bureaucracy.

Learning has progressed through practice. Coding academies continuously adapt curricula to employer needs and feedback from diaspora professionals. Hackathons, bootcamps, and start-up events provide spaces for experimentation and iterative learning. Donor programmes have similarly evolved, refining implementation models based on local experience. Together, these processes demonstrate how governance can rely on feedback and responsiveness rather than rigid planning.

Kosovo's digital actors are embedded in both local and transnational networks. Municipal initiatives foster proximity-based collaboration and contextual adaptation, while diaspora mentors and investors channel global knowledge, markets, and standards into the domestic ecosystem. This dual embeddedness strengthens the system by linking global learning with local experimentation.

Kosovo's ICT sector does not yet constitute a fully developed DNS, but it reveals its foundations in practice. The priority now is to consolidate what works without undermining the adaptability that has driven success. This requires recognizing the value of coding academies, diaspora mentoring, municipal innovation, and donor collaboration, while introducing light institutional scaffolding such as curriculum councils and export task forces to connect these efforts. Rather than replacing informal systems with heavy institutions, Kosovo can formalize coordination and learning mechanisms that already function effectively.

More broadly, Kosovo's experience offers lessons for other late-developing economies. Digital transformation depends less on institutional strength or abundant resources than on the capacity of systems to learn, coordinate, and evolve. The DNS framework provides both a conceptual lens and a practical roadmap for achieving this. Shaped by constraint but strengthened through cooperation, Kosovo's ICT ecosystem demonstrates that distributed governance can foster inclusive and resilient digital growth. The next task is to translate this emerging network of relationships into a durable foundation for long-term capability accumulation and structural transformation.

## References

Andreoni, A., & Chang, H. J. (2019). The political economy of industrial policy: Structural interdependencies, policy alignment and conflict management. *Structural Change and Economic Dynamics*, *48*, 136–150. Available at: https://doi.org/10.1016/j.strueco.2018.10.004

Barometer, K. I. C. T. (2023). *Annual review of digital activity and sectoral trends*. ICT Association of Kosovo (STIKK). Available at: https://stikk.org/publications. Accessed July 16, 2025.

Bartlett, W. (2020). International assistance, donor interests, and state capture in the Western Balkans. *Journal of Contemporary European Studies*, *29*(2), 184–200. Available at: https://doi.org/10.1080/14782804.2020.1794801

Bartlett, W., Kollias, P., Ahmetbasić, J., & Mijačić, D. (2014). The political economy of donor intervention in the Western Balkans and Turkey. *European Commission*. Available at: https://enlargement.ec.europa.eu/document/download/8d4388fe-1e8c-44d1-b10c-d30af274fcf9_en. Accessed July 17, 2025.

BCSDN. (2023). Mapping of donors active in the Western Balkans. *Balkan Civil Society Development Network*. Available at: https://kfos.org/storage/app/uploads/public/65a/fbd/4f7/65afbd4f7cd14056657063.pdf. Accessed July 17, 2025.

Bell, M., & Pavitt, K. (1993). Technological accumulation and industrial growth: Contrasts between developed and developing countries. *Industrial and Corporate Change*, *2*(2), 157–210. https://doi.org/10.1093/icc/2.2.157

Cohen, W. M., & Levinthal, D. A. (1990). Absorptive capacity: A new perspective on learning and innovation. *Administrative Science Quarterly*, *35*(1), 128–152. https://doi.org/10.2307/2393553

Diaspora for Development. (2024). Kosovo factsheet. Available at: https://diasporafordevelopment.eu/wp-content/uploads/2024/04/Kosovo-Factsheet-v.2.pdf. Accessed June 6, 2025.

Emerging Europe. (2023). IT sector in focus: Kosovo. Available at: https://emerging-europe.com/analysis/it-sector-in-focus-kosovo/. Accessed June 6, 2025.

European Commission. (2023). Kosovo 2023 report. *European Commission*. Available at: https://neighbourhood-enlargement.ec.europa.eu/kosovo-report-2023_en. Accessed July 16, 2025.

European Innovation Scoreboard. (2025). Directorate-general for research and innovation. Available at: https://research-and-innovation.ec.europa.eu/knowledge-publications-tools-and-data/publications/all-publications/european-innovation-scoreboard-2025_en

Feldman, M., & Zoller, T. (2012). Dealmakers in place: Social capital connections in regional entrepreneurial economies. *Regional Studies*, *46*(1), 23–37. https://doi.org/10.1080/00343404.2011.607808

Germin. (2024). Harnessing the potential of the Kosovar Diaspora's economic contributions. Available at: https://new.germin.org/wp-content/uploads/2024/01/Harnessing-the-Potential-of-the-Kosovar-Diasporas-Economic-Contributions-Research.pdf. Accessed June 6, 2025.

GIZ and Ministry of Industry. (2022). Kosovo ICT value chain study. Available at: https://mint.rks-gov.net/desk/inc/media/5A51D351-ADBF-472A-AFE2-8C360BCB2EE4.pdf. Accessed June 6, 2025.

Government of the Republic of Kosovo. (2016). *National development strategy 2016–2021*. Office of the Prime Minister. Available at: https://mapl.rks-gov.net/wp-content/uploads/2017/10/National_Development_Strategy_2016-2021_ENG.pdf

Government of the Republic of Kosovo. (2022). *Industrial policy concept paper*. Ministry of Industry, Entrepreneurship and Trade. Available at: https://mint.rks-gov.net/desk/inc/media/0824EBAC-476D-4C47-938B-C8041612DBE0.pdf

ICT for Kosovo's Growth. (2022). Project overview and sectoral insights. Available at: https://ictkosovo.eu/. Accessed June 6, 2025.

IFME. (2020). Comprehensive analysis of the ICT sector in Kosovo. Available at: https://ietl-oek.com/wp-content/uploads/2020/03/Report-Comprehensive-Analysis-of-ICT-Sector-in-Kosovo.pdf. Accessed June 6, 2025.

Innovation Centre Kosovo (ICK). (2024). *KosICT event archive and reports*. ICK. Available at: https://ickosovo.com/wp-content/uploads/2024/01/1._Startup_Ecosystem_Kosovo_-_Needs_Evaluation_Narrative_Report_-_Final_.pdf

Kaplinsky, R., & Morris, M. (2003). *A handbook for value chain research*. International Development Research Centre. Available at: http://www.globalvaluechains.org/docs/VchNov01.pdf. Accessed June 6, 2025.

KIESA. (2023). *Annual report 2023: Institutional activities and investment support for the year 2023*. Kosovo Investment and Enterprise Support Agency. Available at: https://kiesa.rks-gov.net/desk/inc/media/039C60AB-EE74-4CDE-8E49-7EDD70B5B0CA.pdf. Accessed July 16, 2025.

Kosovo Agency of Statistics. (2023). *Statistical yearbook of the republic of Kosovo 2023*. KAS. Available at: https://askapi.rks-gov.net/Custom/defdd9dd-aa69-43c2-ba43-8f9a3364cefd.pdf. Accessed June 6, 2025.

Kosovo Investment and Enterprise Support Agency. (2024). *Annual report 2024: Institutional activities and investment support for the year 2023*. KIESA. Available at: https://kiesa.rks-gov.net/desk/inc/media/039C60AB-EE74-4CDE-8E49-7EDD70B5B0CA.pdf. Accessed July 16, 2025.

Kosovo Ministry of Diaspora and Strategic Investments. (2023). *Annual report on Diaspora engagement 2023*. Government of Kosovo. Available at: https://diasporafordevelopment.eu/wp-content/uploads/2024/04/Kosovo-Factsheet-v.2.pdf

Kosovo Textile Association. (2023). *State of the textile and apparel industry in Kosovo*. Available at: https://kiesa.rks-gov.net/desk/inc/media/EB1B7901-8E34-4A84-8B39-D901D1531AA6.pdf

Kosovo Wood Association. (2024). *Annual industry performance report 2024*. Available at: https://www.kosovowood.org/Documents/GetDocumentsList?instanceId=132

Kuznetsov, Y., & Sabel, C. (2006). Global mobility of talent from a perspective of new industrial policy: Open migration chains and diaspora networks. *World Bank Institute*. Available at: https://doi.org/10.1093/acprof:oso/9780199532605.003.0004

Lall, S. (1992). Technological capabilities and industrialization. *World Development, 20*(2), 165–186. https://doi.org/10.1016/0305-750X(92)90097-F

Leadbeater, C., & Miller, P. (2004). *The pro-am revolution: How enthusiasts are changing our economy and society*. Demos. Available at: https://demos.co.uk/wp-content/uploads/files/proamrevolutionfinal.pdf. Accessed July 16, 2025.

Meyer, J.-B., & Brown, M. (1999). *Scientific Diasporas: A new approach to the brain drain*. UNESCO. MOST Discussion Paper Series No. 41. Available at: https://unesdoc.unesco.org/ark:/48223/pf0000116330. Accessed July 16, 2025.

Ministry of Education, Science, Technology and Innovation. (2023). *Statistical report on education and training infrastructure 2022/2023*. Government of Kosovo. Available at: https://masht.rks-gov.net. Accessed July 16, 2025.

OECD. (2024). *Western Balkans competitiveness outlook 2024: Kosovo chapter*. Organisation for Economic Co-operation and Development. Available at: https://www.oecd.org/south-east-europe/programme/wbco. Accessed July 16, 2025.

OECD. (2024a). *Western Balkans competitiveness outlook 2024: Regional profile*. Available at: https://doi.org/10.1787/170b0e53-en

OECD. (2024b). *Western Balkans competitiveness outlook 2024: Kosovo profile*. Available at: https://www.oecd.org/content/dam/oecd/en/publications/reports/2024/06/western-balkans-competitiveness-outlook-2024-kosovo_8d0f23ec/ff74ae0e-en.pdf. Accessed June 6, 2025.

Open Data Kosovo. (2020). The future workplace in the Kosovo ICT market. Available at: https://opendatakosovo.org/wp-content/uploads/2020/05/OPEN-DATA-Report_eng_preview.pdf

OpenAid. (2024). *Core support to innovation centre Kosovo (ICK)—Contribution overview*. Swedish International Development Cooperation Agency. Available at: https://openaid.se/en/contributions/SE-0-SE-6-12391. Accessed July 16, 2025.

Regulatory Authority of Electronic and Postal Communications. (2024). *Annual report 2023*. ARKEP. Available at: https://www.arkep-rks.org/repository/docs/ARKEP-Raporti-Vjetor-2023.pdf. Accessed July 16, 2025.

Rodrik, D. (2008). *Normalizing industrial policy*. Commission on Growth and Development Working Paper No. 3. World Bank. Available at: https://openknowledge.worldbank.org/handle/10986/28015. Accessed June 6, 2025.

Sabel, C. F., & Zeitlin, J. (2012). Experimentalist governance. In D. Levi-Faur (Ed.), *The Oxford handbook of governance* (pp. 169–183). Oxford University Press. https://doi.org/10.1093/oxfordhb/9780199560530.013.0012.

Swiss Cooperation Office Kosovo. (2023). *Swiss economic report on Kosovo 2023*. Embassy of Switzerland. Available at: https://www.eda.admin.ch/countries/kosovo/en/home/news/news.html/content/countries/kosovo/en/meta/news/2023/swiss-economic-report. Accessed June 6, 2025.

UNDP. (2023). Kosovo Diaspora and its role Amidst multiple crises. Available at: https://www.undp.org/sites/g/files/zskgke326/files/2023-05/Kosovo%20Diaspora%20and%20its%20Role%20Amidst%20Multiple%20Crises_ENG.pdf. Accessed June 6, 2025.

UNDP. (2025). Independent programme evaluation: Kosovo. United Nations Development Programme. Available at: https://www.undp.org/sites/g/files/zskgke326/files/2025-07/ipe-kosovo-full-report-final.pdf. Accessed July 17, 2025.

UNDP and Germin. (2023). Kosovo Diaspora and its role Amidst multiple crises. Available at: https://www.undp.org/sites/g/files/zskgke326/files/2023-05/Kosovo%20Diaspora%20and%20its%20Role%20Amidst%20Multiple%20Crises_ENG.pdf. Accessed June 6, 2025.
von Hippel, E. (2005). *Democratizing innovation.* MIT Press. Available at: https://mitpress.mit.edu/9780262002745/democratizing-innovation/
World Bank. (2018). *Project appraisal document: Kosovo Digital Economy Project (KODE).* Available at: https://documents.worldbank.org/curated/en/249951531020771941/pdf/Kosovo-KODE-PAD-06132018.pdf. Accessed July 16, 2025.
World Bank. (2021). Remittances—A gateway to sustainable development. Available at: https://env2.bqk-kos.org/edu/wp-content/uploads/2021/06/REMITTANCES-Eng-3.pdf. Accessed June 6, 2025.
World Bank. (2023). *Kosovo country economic memorandum: Breaking with the past.* Available at: https://documents.worldbank.org/en/publication/documents-reports/documentdetail/099350006012225430/null. Accessed June 6, 2025.
World Bank. (2024). *Kosovo country economic memorandum: Breaking with the past.* Available at: https://documents.worldbank.org/en/publication/documents-reports/documentdetail/099350006012225430/null. Accessed July 16, 2025.

# Chapter 6
# Agri-Food Processing in Albania

## 6.1 Introduction

This chapter examines Albania's development trajectory through the lens of industrial capability formation. Although Albania has achieved greater macroeconomic stability, lower donor dependency, and somewhat stronger institutional continuity than Kosovo, these advantages have not led to sustained structural transformation. Export growth and sectoral diversification have contributed only modestly to long-term upgrading or technological learning.

The economy remains heavily dependent on agriculture, tourism, and low-wage manufacturing.[1] Agri-food and textile production account for a large share of exports and employment, yet both sectors are constrained by informality, weak innovation systems, and limited coordination among public and private actors. Newer service sectors, including ICT and tourism, present promising opportunities but remain underdeveloped and only loosely linked to strategic development policies. Across all sectors, diaspora engagement has expanded, but its contributions are mostly informal and insufficiently embedded within national frameworks.

The central argument of this chapter is that Albania's fragmented governance landscape limits its capacity to transform isolated successes into a coherent and scalable development model. Using the Developmental Network State (DNS) framework introduced in Chap. 4, the chapter explores how dispersed actors and fragmented initiatives could be integrated into a more adaptive, capability-oriented system of governance.

[1] Tourism is a significant sector in Albania's economy. When direct and indirect effects are taken into account, it has contributed around one-fifth of GDP in recent years (INSTAT, 2024b). While it plays an important role in aggregate growth, this chapter focuses specifically on the agricultural sector as a domain for technological capability development, value addition, and industrial upgrading. The analysis concentrates on productive niches within agriculture, though agro-tourism is briefly discussed as an intersectional area where service-based activities complement rural economic development.



F. Sahiti, *Catching Up in the Digital Age*, Contributions to Economics,
https://doi.org/10.1007/978-3-032-17059-0_6

The chapter first traces the evolution of Albania's industrial sector from the pre-transition period through the post-socialist reforms to the years following 2000, highlighting how the legacy of central planning and the shocks of liberalization shaped its current structure. It then examines the agri-food and textile industries, which remain central to Albania's export base but continue to face persistent constraints related to informality, weak innovation, and limited coordination. The discussion turns to the ICT and tourism sectors, which represent emerging frontiers of growth but lack the institutional support and strategic coherence needed to realize their potential. The chapter also considers the broader governance and institutional bottlenecks that restrict capability formation across sectors. It concludes by assessing how the DNS framework can help address these challenges and by outlining lessons for building productive capabilities in settings marked by political fragmentation and limited state capacity.

## 6.2 Albania's Industrial Sector Before, During, and After Transition

Albania's current industrial underdevelopment can only be understood by examining its long and uneven historical trajectory. As the country entered the post-socialist period, it did so with one of the most autarkic and rigid economic systems in Europe. The industrial base, shaped by decades of central planning and economic isolation, collapsed rapidly in the early 1990s. Unlike other post-socialist economies that inherited more diversified or trade-integrated industrial structures, Albania faced a dual challenge: dismantling an inefficient system while lacking the institutional capacity to support new forms of industrial development.

This section traces the evolution of Albania's industrial sector across four key phases. It begins with the socialist era (1945–1990), moves through the collapse and post-communist transition of the 1990s, examines the contemporary industrial profile shaped by subcontracting and small-scale production, and concludes with an analysis of the structural and institutional bottlenecks that persist today. These phases illustrate the constraints and missed opportunities that continue to shape Albania's industrial economy.

### *6.2.1 Industrial Structure Under Socialism (1945–1990)*

During the socialist period, Albania pursued an extreme model of self-reliance. After breaking ties with the Soviet Union in 1961 and later with China, the country embraced economic isolation as a national ideology. Industrial policy focused on heavy industry, mining, energy, and chemicals, with limited attention to consumer goods or foreign trade (Kaser & Radice, 1985; Muço, 2001).

Between 1950 and 1980, industrial output expanded significantly, reaching nearly 40% of GDP by the late 1980s (World Bank, 2004). However, the sector was dominated by large state-owned enterprises that operated under political directives rather than market incentives. Many factories were located in remote regions to promote territorial balance, often at the expense of efficiency and infrastructure connectivity (Pano, 1992).

Technology remained outdated. Imports of foreign machinery were rare, and domestic production relied on obsolete equipment. Energy inefficiency, low labour productivity, and frequent technical breakdowns were widespread (UNDP, 2000). The education system reinforced this model, producing technicians through polytechnic schools and vocational centres designed to meet the needs of the planned economy. Yet it remained ideologically insular and disconnected from global scientific and industrial knowledge (Papapanagos & Sanfey, 2003).

By the late 1980s, industrial growth had stagnated. Many enterprises operated below capacity, infrastructure had deteriorated, and environmental damage was mounting. Despite these problems, the industrial sector remained central to urban employment and state legitimacy. When the regime collapsed in 1990–1991, this tightly controlled system disintegrated almost overnight, leaving behind obsolete assets and institutions unprepared for market competition.

### *6.2.2 Collapse and Transition (1990s to Early 2000s)*

The post-communist transition brought one of the steepest industrial declines in Eastern Europe. The shift to a market economy occurred without a coherent industrial strategy or institutional safeguards. Between 1990 and 2000, industry's share of GDP dropped from 39% to below 10%, while industrial employment fell from 38% to 12.6% of the labour force (World Bank, 2004; INSTAT, 2024a). These changes are illustrated in Fig. 5.1.

As state-owned enterprises lost subsidies and supply chains collapsed, most factories halted production. Rapid privatization followed, but it largely involved asset transfers without restructuring or new investment (Muço, 2001). Liberalization measures—such as tariff reductions, capital account liberalization, and currency convertibility—were introduced under pressure from international financial institutions but lacked proper sequencing and institutional support. As a result, they failed to revive industrial activity.

The social impact was severe. Industrial unemployment surged in cities such as Elbasan and Shkodër. Skilled workers emigrated in large numbers, and vocational schools lost both funding and relevance (UNDP, 2000). By the end of the 1990s, many former industrial workers had shifted into subsistence agriculture or informal services. Remittances became a crucial source of household income. What had once been the backbone of the Albanian economy was reduced to a marginal, fragmented, and largely informal industrial sector (Fig. 6.1).

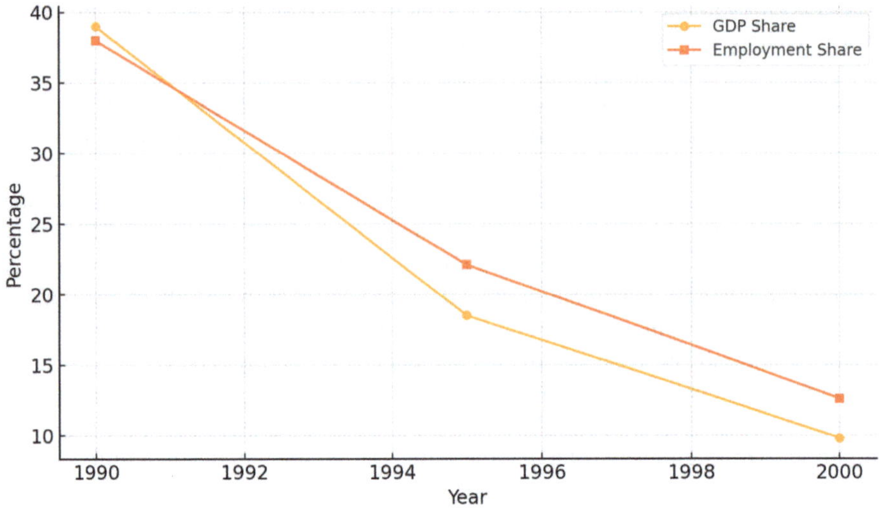


**Fig. 6.1** Collapse of Albania's industrial sector, 1990–2000. *Source* World Bank (2004); INSTAT (2024a). Author's illustration

### *6.2.3 Contemporary Industrial Profile (2000s to Present)*

Since the early 2000s, Albania has gradually rebuilt parts of its industrial base, though progress has been modest and largely shaped by external demand. Industry currently contributes about 23% to GDP and employs 22% of the labour force (INSTAT, 2024a). These figures include construction and utilities, meaning that the share of manufacturing itself remains limited.

The main export-oriented industries include textiles, footwear, wood processing, and construction materials (World Bank, 2022). A defining characteristic of Albania's industrial structure is its dependence on outward processing arrangements (*fason*), particularly in the textile and footwear sectors. Firms typically carry out basic processing of semi-finished goods imported from European clients and then re-export the finished products. This subcontracting model reflects Albania's structural dependence on foreign inputs and constrains domestic value creation (Proeksport Albania, 2023).

Table 6.1 summarizes the leading industrial subsectors, their principal products, export destinations, and modes of production. The data reveal a pattern dominated by small-scale subcontracting, limited innovation, and weak backward linkages to local suppliers.

Most firms remain positioned at the lower end of global value chains, with little control over design, branding, or marketing. Innovation and research activity are minimal, and domestic supplier networks remain underdeveloped. Raw materials and inputs are often imported, limiting opportunities for local linkages and knowledge transfer. The absence of mid-sized, capability-rich firms is particularly

**Table 6.1** Leading export-oriented industrial sub-sectors in Albania (2023)

| Subsector | Main products | Export destinations | Mode of production |
|---|---|---|---|
| Footwear | Leather shoes, soles | Italy, Germany | Outward processing (fason) |
| Textiles and apparel | Jeans, jackets, uniforms | Italy, Greece, Austria | Cut-make-trim contracts |
| Construction materials | Cement, tiles, plaster | Kosovo, N. Macedonia | Domestic capital, partial FDI |
| Wood processing | Doors, furniture parts | Italy, Montenegro | Mostly informal, SME-led |
| Metal processing | Basic aluminum, scrap iron | Turkey, Serbia | Small-scale, subcontracting |

*Source* Author's compilation based on INSTAT (2024a), World Bank (2022), Proeksport Albania (2023)

significant, as it restricts the development of industrial clusters and learning spillovers (Kaplinsky & Morris, 2003).

Institutionally, industrial policy remains fragmented. The Albanian Investment Development Agency (AIDA) provides investment promotion and limited support for exporters but lacks the mandate and instruments for strategic industrial upgrading. Donor-funded SME programmes continue to play a role in entrepreneurship and training, yet they operate largely in isolation from broader national capability-building efforts (OECD, 2024).

### 6.2.4 Legacy Constraints and Structural Bottlenecks

Three decades after transition, Albania's industrial sector remains constrained by historical legacies and persistent governance weaknesses. Fragmented ownership structures, shallow supply chains, and underdeveloped skills systems continue to limit the country's ability to strengthen and diversify its industrial base.

One of the most significant barriers is the absence of strong domestic anchor firms. In successful latecomer economies, such firms often play a central role in leading innovation, coordinating suppliers, and shaping policy dialogue (Evans, 1995). In Albania, the privatization process of the 1990s produced fragmented ownership and short-term investment patterns, discouraging the development of specialized, innovation-driven enterprises.

A second constraint is the "missing middle." The industrial landscape is dominated by micro-enterprises and a few subcontractors dependent on external buyers, while medium-sized firms capable of linking smaller producers to global markets are largely absent. As a result, critical functions such as tooling, logistics, and firm-level training remain weak or non-existent.

Human capital gaps further exacerbate these structural weaknesses. Albania's vocational education and training (VET) system has not kept pace with the needs of an open, export-oriented economy. Enrolment rates are low, curricula are outdated, and collaboration between firms and training institutions is rare. Only 15% of manufacturing firms report participating in formal skills development activities (World Bank, 2022).

Industrial policy is another area of fragility. The AIDA primarily focuses on investment promotion rather than long-term technological upgrading. Initiatives such as Smart Specialisation remain largely aspirational, and many industrial zones lack the infrastructure and institutional coordination required for effective cluster formation.

Participation in international markets remains concentrated in low-value segments. Assembly operations dominate, generating limited learning or innovation spillovers (Leti Tota et al., 2024). Albanian firms remain locked in contract manufacturing, unable to move into higher-value stages such as design, branding, or product development.

These challenges reinforce one another. Without anchor firms, supply chains do not deepen. Without functional training systems, firms cannot absorb new technologies. Without coordinated governance, capability development remains fragmented. Figure 6.2 illustrates how these interlocking constraints create a self-reinforcing "capability trap" that prevents Albania from achieving sustained industrial upgrading.

Despite relative macroeconomic stability and integration into global markets, Albania has yet to build the institutional and productive foundations necessary for

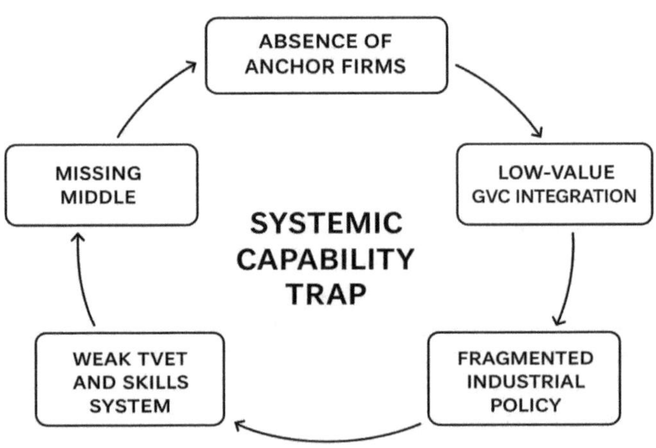


**Fig. 6.2** Feedback loops in Albania's industrial capability trap. *Source* Author's illustration based on Evans (1995), Rodrik (2008), and OECD (2024), generated with DALL · E using Microsoft Copilot (2025)

long-term transformation. Overcoming these barriers requires more than short-term competitiveness reforms. It calls for a governance model that prioritizes domestic learning, strengthens coordination across public and private actors, and aligns industrial policy with long-term capability development.

## 6.3 Agricultural Sector and Structural Transformation

More than three decades after the transition to a market economy, Albania's agricultural sector remains a cornerstone of national employment but continues to underperform in productivity and value creation. Agriculture employs more than one-third of the population yet contributes less than one-fifth of GDP. This persistent imbalance highlights a deep productivity gap and reflects broader structural weaknesses that continue to shape the country's economic development (World Bank, 2022; OECD, 2024).

### *6.3.1 Historical Legacy and Land Fragmentation*

The roots of Albania's current agricultural structure lie in the land reform of the early 1990s. Unlike other post-socialist countries that restored pre-communist property rights or relied on restitution-based privatization, Albania pursued an egalitarian model. Land was divided equally among rural households, irrespective of previous ownership. Although this approach helped prevent social unrest during the transition, it also led to extreme land fragmentation.

By 2023, more than 80% of farms were smaller than two hectares, with an average size of around 1.2 hectares (Cungu & Swinnen, 1999). Fragmentation was compounded by the absence of formal land titles. Many parcels were distributed without proper legal documentation, creating enduring barriers to consolidation, long-term investment, and access to credit. As a result, most farmers operate small, subsistence-oriented plots that cannot benefit from economies of scale. These institutional and structural legacies continue to constrain efforts to modernize and commercialize agriculture.

### *6.3.2 Productivity Gaps and Labour Allocation*

The productivity gap between agriculture and other sectors remains one of the most visible indicators of Albania's structural stagnation. In 2023, agriculture employed 36.4% of the labour force but generated only 18% of GDP. This imbalance, which has persisted for more than a decade, reflects the low technological base

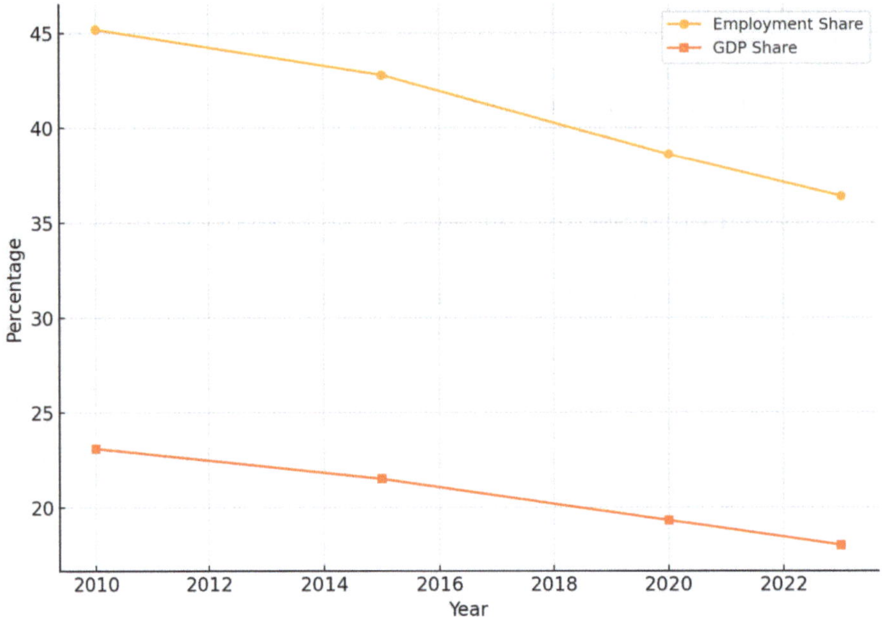


**Fig. 6.3** Agriculture in Albania—employment vs. GDP share (2010–2023). *Source* World Bank (2022); INSTAT (2024a)

of farming, limited access to finance, and weak integration into higher-value markets. Figure 6.3 illustrates this divergence between labour input and output, underscoring the need for coordinated policies to promote rural diversification and productivity growth.

Several factors contribute to this productivity gap. Farmers have limited access to modern inputs, machinery, and irrigation systems. Agricultural extension services are weak, and connections to formal value chains remain limited. Informality is widespread, with more than half of total agricultural output estimated to occur outside the formal economy (FAO, 2022). This restricts access to credit and investment, reduces incentives for technological upgrading, and hinders compliance with food safety and export standards.

### 6.3.3 Infrastructure and Market Access Constraints

Weak infrastructure continues to undermine agricultural productivity and competitiveness. Today, only around 40% of farmland is served by functional irrigation systems, compared to over 60% in the early 1990s (World Bank, 2022). Poor road networks, particularly in mountainous areas, make it difficult for farmers to reach regional markets and raise transport costs, further eroding profitability.

Storage and logistics systems remain underdeveloped. Post-harvest losses are high because of limited cold storage capacity and inadequate handling practices. These gaps discourage the cultivation of high-value crops and restrict Albania's ability to meet EU market standards. Although EU-funded IPARD programmes have sought to improve rural infrastructure, progress has been slow. Complex application procedures and the limited co-financing capacity of smallholders continue to limit participation (European Commission, 2023).

### 6.3.4 Institutional Coordination and Policy Fragmentation

Agricultural governance in Albania is fragmented. Responsibilities are divided among several institutions, including the Ministry of Agriculture, the Agency for Rural Development, and multiple donor-funded units. Coordination among them is weak, and policies often operate in isolation. The absence of a unified rural development strategy reduces the overall effectiveness of public investment and donor-supported initiatives (OECD, 2024).

Policy support has largely prioritized short-term subsidies rather than long-term investments in skills, research, and technological upgrading. Public spending on agricultural research, innovation, and education remains among the lowest in the region, accounting for less than 0.3% of agricultural GDP (FAO, 2022). This lack of sustained investment limits the sector's ability to modernize and compete in regional and global markets.

### 6.3.5 Structural Implications for Industrial Transition

The persistence of low-productivity agriculture has far-reaching consequences for Albania's broader economic transformation. A large share of the workforce remains trapped in subsistence-level activities, limiting the reallocation of labour into higher-productivity sectors such as manufacturing and services.

Linkages between agriculture and industry are weak. Agro-processing is small in scale and fragmented, and domestic value chains are poorly integrated. As a result, rural industrialization remains limited, and the potential for diversification through agriculture-led development is largely untapped.

These structural conditions reflect what Hausmann and Rodrik (2003) describe as a *low-capability equilibrium*—an environment in which firms have little incentive to invest in upgrading, while governments struggle to coordinate effective reforms. Without targeted institutional reforms and stronger governance mechanisms, Albania risks remaining locked in a development model characterized by high rural employment, low value-added output, and limited technological learning (Fig. 6.4).

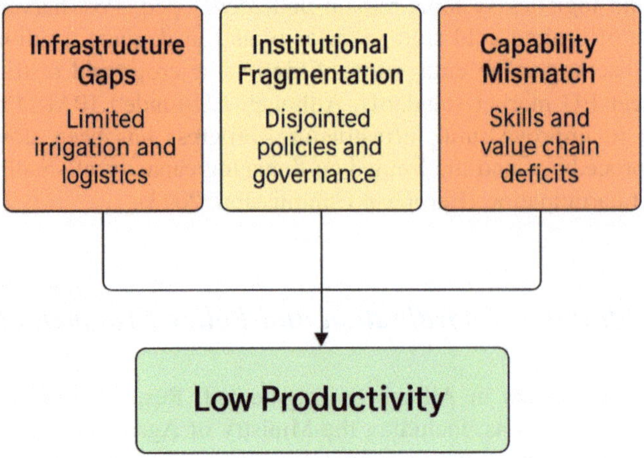


**Fig. 6.4** Structural bottlenecks in Albanian agriculture. *Source* Author's elaboration based on World Bank (2022), FAO (2022), OECD (2024), and European Commission (2023), generated with DALL · E using Microsoft Copilot (2025)

## 6.4 Upgrading Agri-Food Value Chains

Albania's agri-food sector holds considerable potential for rural income generation and value addition. The country benefits from favourable agro-climatic conditions and proximity to EU markets, creating opportunities in sub-sectors such as dairy, olive oil, fruits and vegetables, herbs, and wine. Yet this potential remains largely untapped. Fragmented production, capability gaps, and weak institutional coordination continue to limit the sector's role in structural transformation. This section explores the main opportunities for upgrading, the barriers that constrain growth, and the governance challenges that shape value chain development.

### *6.4.1 Sectoral Opportunities and Export Niches*

Several agri-food sub-sectors have demonstrated export-oriented growth. Olive oil exports, for example, increased by more than 80% between 2015 and 2022, supported by demand in Italy and Germany. Exports of medicinal and aromatic herbs such as sage, thyme, and lavender have also expanded, integrating Albanian producers into European supply chains through both formal contracts and informal collector networks (World Bank, 2022).

Vegetable production has grown in fertile regions such as Lushnjë and Fier, where logistics infrastructure is relatively well developed. In the dairy industry, mid-sized processors have begun investing in cold chains and product quality, particularly for packaged milk, cheese, and yogurt. These developments indicate the emergence of niche upgrading pathways within traditional sectors.

### *6.4.2 Certification and Compliance With EU Standards*

Meeting EU food safety and traceability standards remains a major challenge for Albanian producers. Certification schemes such as Protected Designation of Origin (PDO), Protected Geographical Indication (PGI), and organic labels have enabled a small group of producers to reach premium markets. For instance, certification of mountain tea (Çaj Mali) has facilitated exports to Austria and Switzerland (FAO, 2022).

Nevertheless, progress remains limited. As of 2023, fewer than 20 producers in Albania had achieved PDO, PGI, or organic certification (European Commission, 2023). The high costs of compliance, small production volumes, and weak enforcement mechanisms prevent most producers from accessing higher-value market segments.

### *6.4.3 Donor Support and Project-Based Modernization*

Donor-funded programmes have played an important role in supporting infrastructure, equipment, and advisory services. The EU's IPARD programme, along with initiatives funded by Switzerland and the World Bank, has provided support for irrigation, mechanization, and post-harvest processing.

However, these efforts remain limited in reach. Many smallholders struggle to meet co-financing requirements or navigate complex administrative procedures. Under IPARD II, approximately 32% of available funds were absorbed by 2022 (European Commission, 2023). The project-based nature of donor interventions, coupled with fragmented implementation, has restricted long-term learning and institutional capacity building.

### *6.4.4 Scaling Barriers and the Missing Middle*

A critical obstacle to value chain upgrading is the absence of mid-sized firms capable of aggregating output, coordinating logistics, and investing in branding and marketing. Most smallholders operate independently, with weak connections to processors or exporters. Cooperatives, where they exist, are often created to satisfy donor requirements rather than respond to market demand.

Many cooperative initiatives fail due to limited managerial skills, governance challenges, and a lack of trust among members. Informal intermediaries continue to dominate the collection of herbs and fruits, reinforcing short-term and extractive relationships that discourage quality upgrading and innovation (Lacroix et al., 2016).

### 6.4.5 Governance Challenges in Value Chain Development

Governance fragmentation remains one of the key barriers to upgrading. Responsibilities for production, land management, certification, trade, and investment are distributed across multiple ministries and agencies, with little coordination among them. The absence of a coherent national agri-food strategy weakens policy alignment between production support, export promotion, and industrial development.

The Ministry of Agriculture primarily focuses on farm-level assistance, while trade and investment promotion are handled by separate institutions. Donor-funded programmes often operate independently of these national frameworks, resulting in overlapping efforts and missed opportunities for strategic alignment (European Commission, 2023).

### 6.4.6 Emerging Islands of Learning

Despite systemic challenges, several successful examples of upgrading demonstrate the potential for progress. In the wine industry, producers such as Çobo Winery and Kantina Arbëri have invested in branding, quality improvement, and knowledge transfer. Their development has benefited from diaspora financing and targeted donor support.

In the dairy sector, cooperatives in regions such as Korça and Elbasan have established small-scale cold chain systems and launched locally branded products. Although these cases remain modest in scale, they show that when local leadership, institutional support, and external networks align, sustained upgrading is possible.

### 6.4.7 IPARD Disbursement Trends and Absorptive Capacity

The IPARD programme remains central to rural investment, but its implementation has faced persistent challenges. Under IPARD II, Albania received €94.6 million in funding, but by 2022 only around one-fifth to one-third of available funds had been absorbed, reflecting administrative complexity, limited outreach, and insufficient co-financing capacity among smallholders (European Commission, 2023). Common barriers include complex administrative procedures, limited outreach, and insufficient co-financing capacity among smallholders.

The launch of IPARD III increased Albania's allocation to €146.4 million for the 2021–2027 period. However, in 2023 the European Commission suspended disbursements following identified irregularities in procurement and contract management (SeeNews, 2023).These governance shortcomings have reduced trust among stakeholders and further constrained programme effectiveness.

### *6.4.8 Sub-sectoral Composition of Value Added*

A strategic approach to upgrading requires understanding which sub-sectors contribute most to value added. As shown in Fig. 6.5, dairy and olive oil dominate the sector, followed by fruits and vegetables, herbs and spices, and wine.

The strong performance of dairy and olive oil suggests that targeted policy support in these areas could generate significant multiplier effects. Smaller but dynamic subsectors, such as herbs and wine, which already attract donor and diaspora interest, may also benefit from focused industrial policies and cluster development strategies.

## 6.5 Light Manufacturing and Capability Challenges

Albania's light manufacturing sector occupies a modest but strategically important position in the national economy. Although it accounts for a relatively small share of GDP and employment, it generates a substantial portion of non-agricultural exports. The main subsectors include textiles and footwear, wood processing, construction materials, and basic metalwork. These industries expanded in the 1990s and 2000s, driven largely by foreign investment and contract manufacturing. However, the sector continues to face significant barriers, including low value-added, weak domestic linkages, and limited technological capabilities.

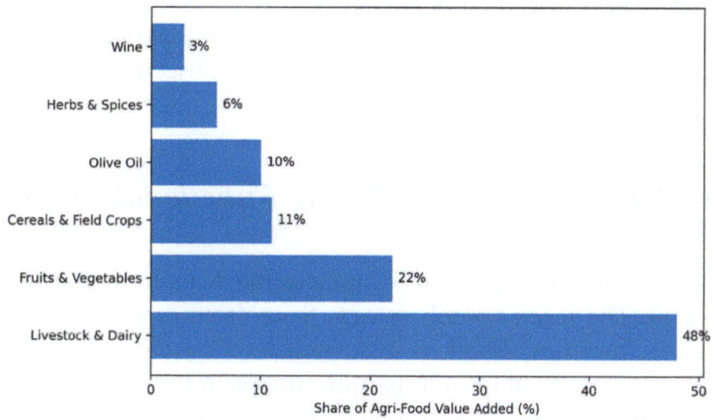


**Fig. 6.5** Agri-food value added by sub-sector in Albania, 2023. *Source* Author's compilation based on FAO (2023); INSTAT (2024b) and World Bank (2024)

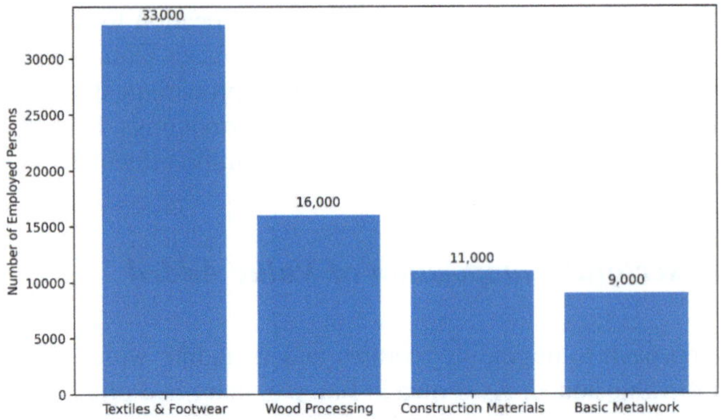


**Fig. 6.6** Employment in selected manufacturing subsectors in Albania, 2023. *Source* Author's estimates based on AIDA (2022) and INSTAT (2024a)

By 2023, light manufacturing, defined here as manufacturing activities excluding construction and utilities, contributed approximately 7.8% of GDP and employed around one-tenth of the labour force. Industrial activity is spatially concentrated in cities such as Durrës, Shkodër, Elbasan, and Berat, where infrastructure provision and labour supply are relatively favourable (INSTAT, 2024b; World Bank, 2022). Textiles and footwear dominate, accounting for more than half of total manufacturing exports.

Most firms operate under the *fason* model, importing semi-finished goods from EU clients, performing labour-intensive tasks such as cutting and assembly, and then re-exporting the final products. While this model has stabilized exports, it has confined Albanian firms to the lowest segments of global value chains.

The textile and footwear industry employs more than 30,000 workers, mostly under contracts with Italian and German buyers. Yet production is limited to assembly; design, branding, and distribution remain controlled abroad. The same pattern characterizes textiles, where Albania functions as a low-cost location within fast-fashion supply chains (EBRD, 2023). Figure 6.6 illustrates the concentration of employment across selected light manufacturing subsectors.

### *6.5.1 Low Value-Added and Missing Functional Upgrading*

A defining feature of Albanian light manufacturing is its limited progress beyond basic production. The *fason* model restricts firms from developing capabilities in design, branding, logistics, or client management. Consequently, domestic value capture remains minimal, and profit margins are narrow.

Published competitiveness assessments indicate that relatively few firms possess in-house design capabilities or export under their own brand (OECD, 2024).

Internal survey data from AIDA (2022, unpublished) similarly show that only a small minority of surveyed firms reported such capabilities. Most remain locked into buyer-driven chains with little institutional support for functional upgrading. This pattern reflects what Kaplinsky and Morris (2003) describe as a "race to the bottom" within global value chains.

### 6.5.2 *Supply Chain Fragmentation and Weak Backward Linkages*

The sector depends heavily on imported raw materials, machinery, and components, mainly from Italy, Turkey, and China. Few firms operate in upstream segments such as dyeing, printing, tanning, or parts manufacturing. This reliance weakens domestic value chains and heightens vulnerability to exchange rate shifts and external supply shocks (IFC, 2021).

Similar issues are evident in wood processing. Despite substantial forestry resources and a growing domestic market for furniture, most firms operate below capacity with outdated equipment. A 2023 report by the Association of Wood Processors of Kosovo found that technological and institutional constraints continue to hinder scaling and upgrading (AWPK, 2023).

### 6.5.3 *Skills and Workforce Constraints*

Technical and managerial skills shortages further limit competitiveness. Vocational education has declined in both enrolment and relevance, while training programmes are poorly aligned with industry needs. Firms frequently report difficulties finding qualified technicians, machine operators, and supervisors (OECD, 2024).

### 6.5.4 *Institutional Gaps and Policy Fragmentation*

Industrial policy in Albania remains fragmented and lacks strategic direction. The Ministry of Finance and Economy oversees industrial development, while AIDA focuses on investment promotion. Neither institution has a clear mandate to support sector-specific upgrading or long-term capability building.

Although strategic plans exist for tourism, energy, and agriculture, no comprehensive industrial development strategy has been adopted. Coordination among ministries, vocational institutes, and regional authorities is limited, and public programmes are often reactive, donor-dependent, and disconnected from firm-level needs (European Commission, 2023).

### 6.5.5 *Absence of Anchor Firms and Weak Clustering*

Albania's industrial ecosystem lacks large, domestically rooted firms that could coordinate supply chains and drive innovation. In successful late-industrializing economies, such anchor firms serve as focal points for clustering, promote standardization, invest in research, and engage in policy dialogue. Their absence in Albania leaves a gap in leadership and constrains opportunities for collective learning and technological upgrading (Evans, 1995). Figure 6.7 outlines the coordination and capability-building roles typically played by anchor firms.

### 6.5.6 *Strategic Constraints and Potential Pathways*

Despite these challenges, strategic opportunities exist. Albania's proximity to EU markets, rising labour costs in Asia, and the trend toward nearshoring have renewed investor interest in relocating certain production activities.

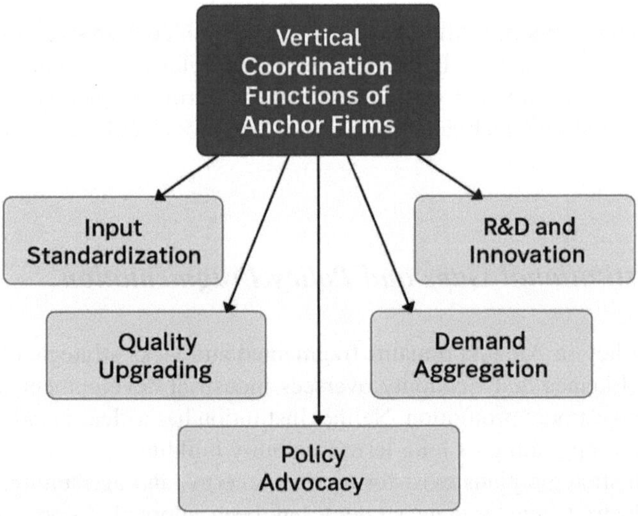


**Fig. 6.7** Vertical coordination functions of anchor firms. *Source* Adapted by author based on Altenburg (2011), and Sabel & Zeitlin (2012), generated with DALL · E using Microsoft Copilot (2025)

Some firms have begun experimenting with higher-value strategies such as niche product development, in-house design, and small-batch production for European clients. Although limited in scale, these efforts reveal latent potential.

To build on these trends, several policy measures could be prioritized:

- Support mid-sized firms seeking to expand into design, branding, and client management.
- Develop industrial parks with shared infrastructure, logistics, and sector-specific training.
- Strengthen public–private partnerships in vocational education aligned with industry demand.
- Reorient AIDA and related agencies toward capability development and sectoral upgrading.

When integrated into a broader industrial strategy, these measures could form adaptive coordination platforms that connect firms, training institutions, and public agencies. Such platforms would encourage joint problem-solving and sustained learning—key features of the DNS model.

## 6.6 Governance Networks and Diaspora Engagement

Albania's development has evolved within a fragmented institutional environment where limited state capacity has constrained the coordination of complex industrial upgrading. In this context, informal governance networks and the globally dispersed Albanian diaspora have played growing roles in shaping investment, knowledge transfer, and entrepreneurship. Yet these contributions remain weakly institutionalized and poorly integrated into national development strategies. This section explores how governance fragmentation and diaspora engagement interact, and how a more network-based approach could enhance coordination and learning.

### *6.6.1 Institutional Fragmentation and Coordination Failures*

Responsibility for industrial and agri-food development in Albania is spread across multiple institutions, including the Ministry of Finance and Economy, the Ministry of Agriculture, the AIDA, and several donor-funded project units. These bodies often operate independently, with overlapping mandates and little inter-agency collaboration (European Commission, 2023).

AIDA, for example, manages investment promotion and SME support but lacks programmes dedicated to sector-specific upgrading or sustained firm engagement. Rural development initiatives, such as IPARD, are run by stand-alone units that are poorly linked to national planning frameworks. This fragmentation weakens institutional learning, creates duplication, and undermines policy coherence.

National frameworks like the National Strategy for Development and Integration (NSDI) and the Smart Specialisation Strategy (S3) were designed to improve coordination but remain largely aspirational. Their implementation is limited by political turnover, administrative weaknesses, and insufficient engagement with the private sector and local governments (OECD, 2024).

### 6.6.2 Donor Influence and Parallel Structures

In the absence of strong domestic institutions, donor agencies have taken a leading role in implementing upgrading projects. Their programmes have improved infrastructure, training, and market access but often bypass national systems, reducing local ownership.

Swiss and EU-funded initiatives have supported cold chains, post-harvest facilities, and vocational training. However, once external funding ends, follow-up mechanisms are rarely sustained, and successful pilot projects struggle to scale. Coordination among donors is uneven, leading to duplication and regional disparities (World Bank, 2022).

The proliferation of such parallel structures limits long-term capability building within government and prevents the consolidation of institutional knowledge.

### 6.6.3 Emergence of Informal Networks and Hybrid Governance

Amid fragmented institutions, informal governance networks have gained importance. Business associations, diaspora entrepreneurs, municipal governments, and civil intermediaries often act as coordinators of upgrading efforts, disseminating information, connecting firms, and advocating for policy reforms.

Associations such as the Albanian Agribusiness Council and the Footwear Manufacturers Association have supported producers in export market access and certification. Yet their effectiveness depends largely on personal networks rather than formal mandates, making it difficult to sustain or scale their initiatives (Grindle, 2007).

Some municipalities, including Fier and Shkodër, have developed public–private partnerships to promote vocational training or export-oriented initiatives. Though limited in scope, these examples demonstrate the potential for local-level coordination when national leadership is weak or absent.

### 6.6.4 The Diaspora as a Strategic Network Resource

The Albanian diaspora—estimated at over 1.4 million people in Italy, Greece, Germany, the United Kingdom, and the United States—represents a major but underutilized development asset. While remittances contribute more than 9% of GDP (Bank of Albania, 2023), the diaspora's potential extends far beyond financial transfers.

Diaspora entrepreneurs have invested in agri-processing, wine production, and export-oriented consulting services. They bring valuable experience with EU standards, global customer networks, and modern business practices. However, their engagement with Albania remains sporadic. Bureaucratic hurdles, unresolved property disputes, and the lack of investment instruments discourage long-term commitment (Kuznetsov & Sabel, 2006).

Although some municipalities have signed cooperation agreements with diaspora chambers, these rarely evolve into operational partnerships. At the national level, no institutional platform systematically connects diaspora expertise with regional or industrial development strategies (Ministry of Diaspora, 2023).

### *6.6.5 Missed Opportunities for Strategic Coordination*

Diaspora engagement remains disconnected from Albania's broader industrial policy framework. Unlike countries such as Armenia or Vietnam, where diaspora networks are embedded in sectoral strategies, Albania's approach is mostly promotional.

Events such as diaspora summits and business forums raise visibility but are not backed by concrete policy instruments to address investment barriers, contract enforcement, or access to credit. As a result, opportunities for mobilizing diaspora capital, knowledge, and mentorship for industrial upgrading remain limited (Lacroix et al., 2016).

### *6.6.6 Toward Embedded Coordination*

The DNS framework offers an alternative path for overcoming coordination failures. Instead of relying on centralized control or fragmented donor projects, the DNS model encourages distributed problem-solving, mutual learning, and structured collaboration among diverse actors.

In Albania, one promising mechanism would be the creation of regional upgrading councils. These councils would not replace existing institutions but act as connective platforms linking municipalities, sectoral associations, training centres, diaspora intermediaries, and national agencies.

Fig. 6.8 visualizes how different actors could collaborate through joint structures that facilitate opportunity identification, align resources, and promote shared learning. Rather than building new bureaucracies, the focus would be on strengthening coordination among existing ones.

By linking local experimentation with diaspora expertise and national institutions, Albania could begin to overcome institutional fragmentation and strengthen

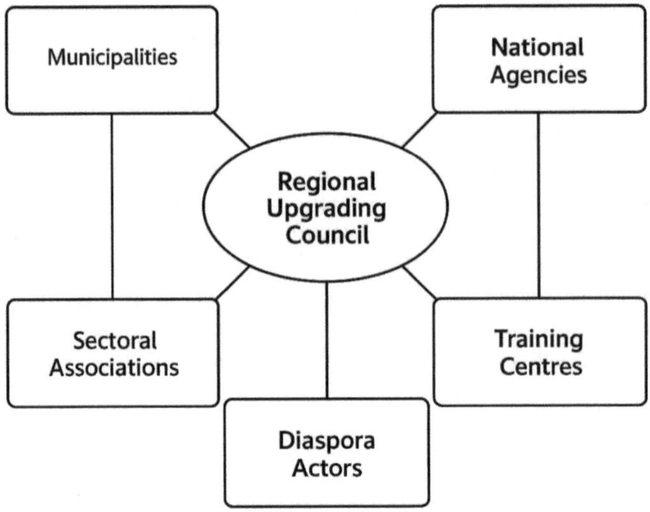


**Fig. 6.8** Developmental network governance for diaspora-driven upgrading. *Source* Author's illustration based on the DNS framework, generated with DALL·E using Microsoft Copilot (2025)

its capacity for coordinated industrial upgrading. This approach would enable more strategic use of diaspora networks and promote adaptive, inclusive forms of governance aligned with long-term development goals.

## 6.7 DNS Relevance and Constraints in Albania

The DNS offers a promising governance framework for countries such as Albania, where fragmented institutions, limited administrative capacity, and weak engagement of non-state actors continue to hinder long-term economic transformation. Unlike traditional developmental state models that depend on centralized authority and top-down coordination, the DNS emphasizes network-based collaboration, adaptive learning, and partnerships among public, private, and civic actors. This makes it especially relevant in contexts where formal structures are weak and political volatility disrupts sustained policy implementation.

### *6.7.1 Strategic Fit in a Fragmented Institutional Context*

Albania's governance environment shows many characteristics that make the DNS approach appropriate. Overlapping donor programmes, informal business networks, uncoordinated ministries, and inconsistent policy implementation reveal the limits of conventional governance models.

Instead of reinforcing centralized control, the DNS seeks to connect fragmented actors through iterative problem-solving platforms. It promotes capacity building through joint discovery among ministries, firms, vocational institutions, and diaspora networks (Andreoni & Chang, 2019; Rodrik, 2008).

Examples from earlier chapters highlight this relevance. In agri-food value chains, donor-led initiatives often operate separately from national planning and vocational education systems. In light manufacturing, diaspora entrepreneurship remains disconnected from institutional upgrading efforts. The lack of cross-sector platforms has weakened learning and prevented the formation of enduring development coalitions.

### 6.7.2 Gaps Between DNS Principles and Institutional Realities

Although the DNS framework aligns well with Albania's governance challenges, its implementation faces several constraints.

First, Albania lacks intermediary institutions that can coordinate across sectors and governance levels. Agencies such as AIDA and the Ministry of Agriculture have narrow mandates, limited resources, and little authority to convene diverse actors. Their ability to support joint discovery processes remains weak.

Second, formal mechanisms for embedded experimentation are largely absent. The Smart Specialisation Strategy has introduced regional consultations, but these are not linked to firm-level dynamics and lack continuity. Municipal capacities differ widely, and mechanisms for sustained collaboration among them are limited.

Third, political instability and frequent institutional turnover create further barriers. Leadership changes, politicized appointments, and low civil service continuity have eroded trust and undermined efforts to build adaptive, network-based governance systems (Grindle, 2007; Evans, 1995).

### 6.7.3 Emergent Prototypes and Institutional Possibilities

Despite these challenges, early signs of DNS-compatible governance are emerging. In municipalities such as Fier and Korça, local governments have begun collaborating with vocational schools, business associations, and diaspora actors to address development challenges. These initiatives remain small and informal but show that embedded coordination can arise from practical problem-solving.

In sectors such as medicinal herbs and footwear, producer groups have partnered with diaspora stakeholders to pursue certification, expand exports, and exchange knowledge. With proper support, these networks could evolve into regional upgrading platforms that connect public, private, and transnational resources.

Such platforms would not replace formal ministries or agencies but would act as connective infrastructure. Their purpose would be to coordinate bottleneck identification, resource mobilization, and institutional learning across fragmented governance layers.

### 6.7.4 Pathways for DNS-Oriented Reform

To realize the potential of the DNS framework in Albania, targeted reforms are needed at both institutional and policy levels.

First, regional upgrading councils should be established to connect municipalities, firms, training centres, and diaspora representatives. These councils should coordinate sector-specific initiatives, align donor funding with local priorities, and track progress through participatory monitoring.

Second, intermediary institutions such as AIDA and vocational education providers should create dedicated DNS units. These units would support stakeholder dialogue, promote joint problem-solving, and align public programmes with enterprise needs.

Third, learning mechanisms should be embedded in programme design. Pilot initiatives should include feedback loops, participatory evaluations, and processes for iterative adaptation. The Smart Specialisation Strategy and IPARD programme could serve as entry points for institutionalizing these practices.

Fourth, donor agencies should expand their focus beyond technical upgrading to include governance infrastructure. This would involve investing in platforms and mechanisms that strengthen cross-sector coordination and build long-term institutional capacity.

The DNS framework provides a pragmatic alternative to both technocratic central planning and laissez-faire liberalization. In Albania's context, it represents a realistic and incremental path toward building the institutional foundations necessary for sustained capability development and economic upgrading.

## 6.8 Conclusion—From Fragmented Progress to Networked Transformation

Over the past three decades, Albania's economic development has been marked by institutional fragmentation, limited industrial upgrading, and underutilized governance potential. Although the country has achieved relative macroeconomic stability and steady export growth in sectors such as agri-food, textiles, and footwear, these achievements have not led to deep structural transformation. Capability development remains uneven, and innovation is constrained by informality, donor dependency, and weak institutional coordination.

The agri-food sector illustrates both potential and constraint. Sub-sectors such as olive oil, dairy, and medicinal herbs show promise but remain hampered by smallholder fragmentation, inadequate infrastructure, and limited adoption of certification standards. Donor-supported modernization initiatives have produced some progress, yet scaling remains difficult in the absence of strong mid-tier firms, cooperative networks, and coherent policies.

In light manufacturing, Albania has maintained a place within European subcontracting chains through the fason model, but this integration is shallow. Most firms remain confined to low-value assembly activities, lacking the capabilities needed for design, branding, or supply chain management. Weak backward linkages, misaligned vocational training, and the absence of anchor firms limit upgrading potential. Institutional support remains fragmented, with agencies such as AIDA and sectoral ministries working in isolation and without a consistent strategic vision.

Across both agriculture and manufacturing, development has relied less on formal institutions than on informal networks, donor projects, and diaspora engagement. Local governments, business associations, and civic intermediaries have often stepped in to fill institutional voids, yet their initiatives tend to depend on personal relationships and remain detached from national planning frameworks. The diaspora contributes through investment, knowledge exchange, and mentoring, but these activities are rarely integrated into national industrial or regional strategies.

The result is a fragmented ecosystem of upgrading efforts driven by local experimentation but lacking the institutional framework needed to scale and sustain learning. Strategic coordination remains weak, and the state has struggled to provide a platform that aligns diverse actors around shared development goals.

The DNS framework offers an alternative to this pattern. Instead of pursuing coherence through centralized control or expecting coordination to emerge spontaneously from markets, the DNS model promotes collaborative problem-solving, adaptive governance, and the creation of institutional interfaces that connect public agencies, firms, training institutions, and diaspora networks. This approach aligns well with Albania's conditions, where formal capacity is limited but informal initiative, local innovation, and transnational linkages are active and resilient.

This chapter has highlighted emerging DNS-like practices in regional partnerships, sectoral associations, and diaspora-led initiatives. However, these remain fragile and insufficiently institutionalized. Albania's key challenge is not to create new institutions from scratch but to adapt existing ones into connective platforms that foster discovery, learning, and coordination across fragmented systems.

Targeted reforms are essential. Establishing regional upgrading councils, embedding DNS functions within intermediary bodies such as AIDA and vocational schools, and realigning donor programmes toward governance infrastructure rather than isolated projects would strengthen Albania's capacity for strategic coordination. These measures would allow the country to shift from fragmented progress toward networked transformation, building a more coherent, adaptive, and inclusive foundation for capability development and economic upgrading.

## References


AIDA. (2022). *Sectoral study of manufacturing firms in Albania*. Albanian Investment Development Agency. Available at https://aida.gov.al/en/sectors/manufacture/. Accessed 6 June 2025.

Altenburg, T. (2011). *Industrial policy in developing countries: Overview and lessons from seven country cases*, German Development Institute Discussion Paper, 4/2011. Available at: https://www.idos-research.de/uploads/media/DP_4.2011.pdf (Accessed: 8 June 2025).

Andreoni, A., & Chang, H.-J. (2019). The political economy of industrial policy: Structural interdependencies, policy alignment and conflict management. *Structural Change and Economic Dynamics*, *48*, 136–150. https://doi.org/10.1016/j.strueco.2018.10.007

AWPK. (2023). *Report on wood processing and furniture industry in the Western Balkans*. Association of Wood Processors of Kosovo. Available at https://kosovowood.org/Uploads/Page/Document/20/awpk_final_ENG.pdf Accessed 17 June 2025.

Bank of Albania. (2023). *Annual report 2023*. Bank of Albania. Available at https://www.bankofalbania.org/rc/doc/Annual_Report_2023_ENG.pdf. Accessed 18 June 2025.

Cungu, A., & Swinnen, J. F. M. (1999). Albania's radical agrarian reform. *Economic Development and Cultural Change*, *47*(4), 769–794. Available at https://www.jstor.org/stable/pdf/10.1086/452421.pdf. Accessed 6 June 2025

EBRD. (2023). *Transition report 2023–24: Structuring the future*. European Bank for Reconstruction and Development. Available at https://www.ebrd.com/home/news-and-events/publications/economics/transition-reports/transition-report-2023-24.html. Accessed 6 June 2025.

European Commission. (2023). *Albania 2023 report*. European Commission. Available at https://neighbourhood-enlargement.ec.europa.eu. Accessed 6 June 2025.

Evans, P. (1995). *Embedded autonomy: States and industrial transformation*. Princeton University Press. Available at http://www.jstor.org/stable/j.ctt7t0sr

FAO. (2022). *World Food and Agriculture – Statistical Yearbook 2022*. Food and Agriculture Organization of the United Nations. https://www.fao.org/3/cc2211en/cc2211en.pdf

Food and Agriculture Organization of the United Nations. (2023). *FAOSTAT: Agricultural value-added data* [Data set]. FAO. https://www.fao.org/faostat/en/#data/QV

Grindle, M. S. (2007). Good enough governance revisited. *Development Policy Review*, *25*(5), 553–574. https://doi.org/10.1111/j.1467-7679.2007.00385.x

Hausmann, R. & Rodrik, D. (2003). 'Economic development as self-discovery', *Journal of Development Economics*, *72*(2), pp. 603–633. https://doi.org/10.1016/S0304-3878(03)00124-X

IFC. (2021). *Creating markets in Albania: Country private sector diagnostic*. International Finance Corporation. Available at https://www.ifc.org

INSTAT. (2024a). *Statistical yearbook 2023*. Institute of Statistics of Albania. Available at https://www.instat.gov.al/media/12878/regional-statistical-yearbook-2023.pdf. Accessed 17 June 2025.

Institute of Statistics (INSTAT). (2024b). *National accounts and agricultural statistics* [Data set/statistical release]. INSTAT. https://www.instat.gov.al/en/themes/economy-and-finance/national-accounts/

Kaplinsky, R., & Morris, M. (2003). *A handbook for value chain research*. International Development Research Centre. Available at http://www.globalvaluechains.org/docs/VchNov01.pdf. Accessed 6 June 2025.

Kaser, M. C., & Radice, E. A. (Eds.). (1985). *The economic history of Eastern Europe, 1919–1975 (Vol. I: Economic structure and performance between the two wars)*. Clarendon Press.

Kuznetsov, Y., & Sabel, C. F. (2006). *Global mobility of talent from a perspective of new industrial policy: Open migration chains and diaspora networks*. WIDER Working Paper No. 2006/144. UNU-WIDER. Available at https://hdl.handle.net/10419/63609. Accessed 18 June 2025.

Lacroix, T., Levitt, P., & Vari-Lavoisier, I. (2016). Social remittances and the changing transnational political landscape. *Comparative Migration Studies, 4*(16). https://doi.org/10.1186/s40878-016-0032-0

Leti Tota, A., Spahija, S., & Shehi, E. (2024). Albanian garment and footwear leather industry: Shifting to own-brand production. *Journal of Integrated Engineering and Applied Sciences, 2* (1), 58–68. Available at https://www.researchgate.net/publication/379957971. Accessed 6 June 2025.

Ministry of State for Diaspora. (2023). *Albanian diaspora national strategy 2021–2025: Implementation review & mid-term report (Mid-2023).* Ministry of State for Diaspora. Available at https://akd.gov.al/wp-content/uploads/2020/12/STRATEGJIA-KOMBETARE-E-DIASPORES-2021-2025-ENG.pdf. Accessed 18 June 2025.

Muço, M. (2001). Albania. *Southeast European and Black Sea Studies, 1*(1), 119–131. https://doi.org/10.1080/14683850108454625

OECD. (2024). *Western Balkans competitiveness outlook 2024: Albania profile.* https://doi.org/10.1787/170b0e53-en

Papapanagos, H., & Sanfey, P. (2003). Emigration and the optimal speed of transition. *Review of International Economics, 11*(3), 541–554. https://doi.org/10.1111/1467-9396.00401. Accessed 6 June 2025.

Pano, N. C. (1992). *Albania.* St. Martin's Press / Pinter Publishers.

Proeksport Albania. (2023). *Sector maps: Footwear & apparel.* Proeksport Albania. Available at https://noafin.al/media/65d8ab56afca2.pdf. Accessed 6 June 2025.

Rodrik, D. (2008). *Normalizing industrial policy.* Commission on Growth and Development Working Paper No. 3. World Bank. Available at https://openknowledge.worldbank.org/handle/10986/28015. Accessed 6 June 2025.

Sabel, C.F. & Zeitlin, J. (2012) 'Experimentalist governance', in Levi-Faur, D. (ed.) *The Oxford Handbook of Governance.* Oxford University Press. Available at: https://doi.org/10.1093/oxfordhb/9780199560530.013.0012

UNDP. (2000). *Human development report: Albania 2000.* United Nations Development Programme. Available at https://docslib.org/doc/1096824/national-human-development-report-albania-2000. Accessed 6 June 2025.

World Bank. (2004). *Albania – sustaining growth beyond the transition: A World Bank country economic memorandum (Albanian).* World Bank. Available at http://documents.worldbank.org/curated/en/377631468741658428. Accessed 6 June 2025.

World Bank. (2022). *Albania country economic memorandum: Strengthening THE Sustainability of Albania's growth model.* World Bank Group. Available at http://documents.worldbank.org/curated/en/099845001312232607. Accessed 6 June 2025.

World Bank. (2024). World Development Indicators (WDI): Agriculture value added (% of GDP) [Data set]. World Bank. https://data.worldbank.org/indicator/NV.AGR.TOTL.ZS

# Chapter 7
# Automotive Supply Chains in North Macedonia

## 7.1 Introduction

This chapter explores how industrial upgrading and technological capability development have evolved in North Macedonia, a small post-socialist economy seeking structural transformation in an increasingly interconnected global market. It examines the governance conditions, institutional bottlenecks, and sectoral dynamics that influence the country's shift from enclave-driven growth toward a more adaptive and learning-oriented industrial base.

Since independence, North Macedonia has experienced uneven industrial restructuring. The economy has undergone significant deindustrialization, frequent policy shifts, and persistent reliance on foreign direct investment (FDI). Special Economic Zones (SEZs) have succeeded in attracting export-oriented manufacturers, yet their growth has reinforced a dualistic industrial structure. Firms operating within SEZs have achieved strong export performance, but domestic linkages remain limited, and learning processes tend to be shallow and confined to individual firms.

The automotive components sector provides a particularly revealing example of selective upgrading. As one of the most dynamic segments of North Macedonia's manufacturing industry, it illustrates how integration into European global value chains (GVCs) can simultaneously promote export growth and constrain domestic capability development. Multinational corporations such as Johnson Matthey, Lear Corporation, and Adient have played a central role in industrial expansion within SEZs. However, knowledge transfer is largely transactional and narrow in scope, and engagement with local suppliers remains minimal.

This chapter analyses these dynamics through the lens of supplier networks, knowledge flows, and the roles of public institutions and intermediary organizations. It identifies persistent governance weaknesses, including an underdeveloped innovation infrastructure, fragmented policy implementation, and the absence of



F. Sahiti, *Catching Up in the Digital Age*, Contributions to Economics,
https://doi.org/10.1007/978-3-032-17059-0_7

a coordinated supplier development strategy. Donor programmes have attempted to fill these institutional gaps, but their short-term and fragmented nature has limited their systemic impact.

To interpret these challenges, the chapter applies the Developmental Network State (DNS) framework introduced earlier in this volume. The DNS approach emphasizes embedded learning, coordinated upgrading strategies, and collaborative institutional arrangements that connect public agencies, firms, and knowledge providers. Without such governance capabilities, North Macedonia risks remaining trapped in a low-value-added and externally dependent growth path.

The chapter concludes by considering the broader relevance of the DNS framework for the Western Balkans (WB), where similar constraints such as institutional fragmentation, dependence on donor-driven reforms, and weak domestic linkages continue to shape the region's prospects for structural transformation.

## 7.2 Context of Industrial Transformation in North Macedonia

Since gaining independence in 1991, North Macedonia has followed a protracted and uneven path of industrial transformation. The country inherited a relatively diversified manufacturing base from Yugoslavia's self-managed socialist economy, which had been shaped by regional integration, public investment, and sectoral specialization. The dissolution of the federation, combined with domestic political instability and limited policy capacity in the 1990s, led to severe deindustrialization and the collapse of production linkages (World Bank, 2023). The early transition period was characterized by rapid privatization, widespread enterprise closures, and the liquidation of state-owned firms, often without restructuring strategies or viable pathways for industrial renewal.

Macroeconomic stabilization and liberal reforms in the early 2000s restored some balance, but industrial recovery remained partial and uneven. A dualistic structure now defines the industrial landscape. A small group of export-oriented firms, concentrated in SEZ, operate with high productivity and capital intensity, while a fragmented base of domestic firms struggles with outdated technology, limited market access, and weak institutional support. FDI has driven SEZ-based growth, particularly in the automotive components sector, but its wider developmental effects have been limited by weak domestic linkages and shallow learning processes.

Innovation capacity across the economy remains weak. Public and private investment in research and development (R&D) is low, institutional coordination is fragmented, and mismatches persist between workforce skills and industrial needs (OECD, 2024; European Commission, 2023). These challenges highlight the need for a more deliberate industrial strategy that integrates investment attraction with capability upgrading, supplier development, and system-wide learning.

This chapter uses the automotive sector as an analytical entry point to explore these dynamics. As North Macedonia's leading manufacturing export sector, it provides a useful lens for understanding both the opportunities and constraints of industrial upgrading in a small post-socialist economy. The following sections trace the evolution of the country's industrial structure, analyse the governance arrangements shaping its development path, and examine how integration into GVCs has produced selective gains without broader structural transformation.

### *7.2.1 Industrial Structure: Legacy and Transformation*

In 2023, industry accounted for approximately 23% of GDP and approximately 30% of employment in North Macedonia. Although this represents a modest recovery from early transition lows, it remains below the levels achieved during the socialist period (State Statistical Office of North Macedonia, 2024). The sector is sharply segmented. SEZ-based firms, which are mostly foreign-owned and export-oriented, drive manufacturing growth, while domestic firms remain disconnected and technologically stagnant.

Automotive components now represent the largest share of manufacturing output, contributing 31% of value added. This growth has been driven by FDI in SEZs such as Bunardzik, Štip, and TIDZ Tetovo, where multinational firms produce wiring systems, electronic assemblies, and mechanical components for export. However, these gains have not resulted in wider industrial upgrading. Domestic supplier engagement remains limited, and technology transfer is mostly transactional and confined to specific firms (Invest North Macedonia, 2023). Beyond automotive products, the export structure is shaped by electrical machinery (14%) and base metals (13%), which reflect an industrial base focused on intermediate goods and assembly-oriented activities with limited upgrading. Chemicals and plastics (12%) and textiles, apparel and footwear (10%) contribute to diversification but remain concentrated in standardised, low- to medium-value segments, while machinery and mechanical appliances (9%) show modest scale and fragmentation. Food, beverages and tobacco (8%) and other manufacturing (3%) play a marginal role, indicating untapped potential in higher-value processing. Overall, the figure points to moderate diversification but continued reliance on low- and mid-technology manufacturing outside the automotive sector, constraining broader productivity gains.

This industrial profile reveals a structural imbalance. SEZ-based firms are globally competitive but largely isolated from the domestic economy. Domestic firms remain under-resourced and lack institutional support. Without deliberate efforts to bridge this divide through supplier development, workforce upgrading, and coordinated learning, North Macedonia risks deepening a pattern of enclave industrialization (Fig. 7.1).

### *7.2.2 Structural Challenges of Industrial Transformation*

North Macedonia's industrial transition has been shaped by three interrelated structural constraints.

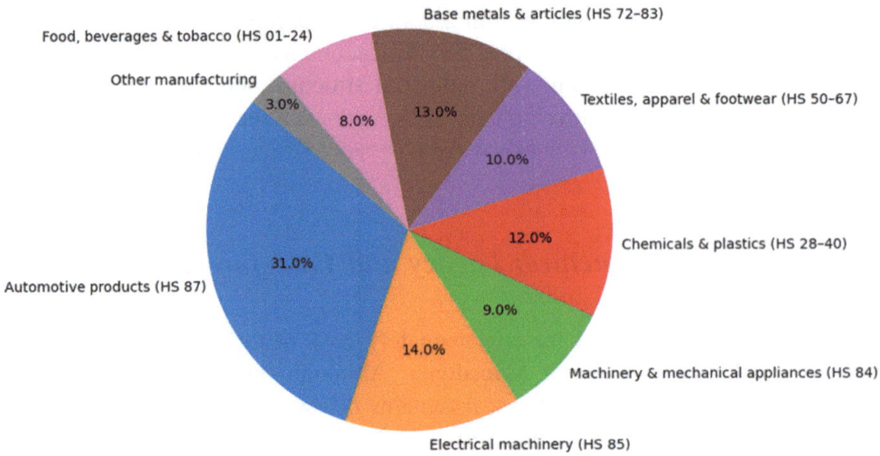


**Fig. 7.1** Structure of Manufacturing Exports by Product Group, North Macedonia (2023). *Note: Export data are reported according to the Harmonized System (HS). Source: State Statistical Office of the Republic of North Macedonia (2024).*

The first is the legacy of rapid deindustrialization. Between 1990 and 2000, industrial output declined by more than 50%, driven by mass layoffs, privatization without restructuring, and the collapse of state-owned enterprises. This dismantling of production capacity led to the erosion of technological capabilities, the loss of skilled labour, and the fragmentation of supplier networks (World Bank, 2023).

The second constraint is the limited accumulation of technological capabilities. Despite some modernization, the industrial sector remains technologically shallow. Investment in R&D is below 0.4% of GDP, reflecting both weak public funding and limited private engagement (UNESCO Institute for Statistics, 2023). Vocational training and higher education are poorly aligned with industrial needs, and collaboration between firms and research institutions remains minimal.

The third constraint is the enclave nature of industrial growth. FDI is concentrated in a few SEZs and rarely extends beyond production to include knowledge transfer or domestic supply chain development. While SEZs have become key drivers of export growth, they remain disconnected from the broader economy. This dualism restricts learning, innovation, and domestic upgrading (OECD, 2023).

North Macedonia's small market size and dependence on external actors such as donors, investors, and EU trade access further limit diversification and long-term planning. Institutional weaknesses compound these challenges, making it difficult to embed learning and develop adaptive governance capacity.

### *7.2.3 Industrial Policy and Governance Fragmentation*

Industrial policy in North Macedonia has developed in a fragmented and externally driven manner. Donor agendas and EU accession frameworks have heavily influenced national priorities, often at the expense of a coherent strategy. One of the few significant interventions has been the establishment of TIDZs in the early 2000s. These zones have successfully attracted FDI, particularly in the automotive sector, but their developmental impact has remained narrow and limited to enclave-based production (European Commission, 2023).

Policy implementation suffers from overlapping mandates and poor coordination. Key institutions, including the Directorate for TIDZs, the Ministry of Economy, and regional development agencies, often operate in parallel, resulting in jurisdictional competition and inefficiency. Donor agencies such as GIZ, USAID, and the EU Delegation have attempted to address gaps through project-based initiatives, but these are typically short-term and not well integrated into broader capability-building efforts (GIZ, 2023).

What is missing is a strategic vision that links FDI attraction with domestic capability development. Current policies do not adequately address supplier upgrading, skills formation, or the creation of innovation ecosystems. Without stronger institutional alignment and long-term investment in governance capacity, industrial policy risks reinforcing dependence rather than promoting transformation.

### *7.2.4 Framing the Automotive Sector as a Strategic Entry Point*

Within a fragmented and externally dependent industrial landscape, the automotive components sector stands out as North Macedonia's most dynamic manufacturing segment. Concentrated in SEZs and driven by FDI, the sector has become a key contributor to export growth and represents one of the few cases of successful integration into European production networks.

However, its contribution to domestic capability development remains limited. The sector's expansion raises important questions about how global integration can enable or constrain long-term upgrading. It therefore serves as a strategic entry point for analysing the country's broader industrial transformation and the governance structures that shape it.

The next section examines these dynamics in greater detail by analysing the sector's role within global value chains.

## 7.3 The Automotive Sector and Global Value Chains

Building on the next section, this part of the chapter examines the structure and dynamics of North Macedonia's automotive industry through the lens of GVCs. Although a relatively recent development, the sector illustrates the structural dualism and external dependence characteristic of post-socialist industrialization.

Under Yugoslavia's self-managed socialist system, North Macedonia's industrial base was centred on light manufacturing, including textiles, food processing, and basic machinery, with limited capacity for complex production. Following the federation's dissolution in the early 1990s, industrial output fell by more than 50% due to trade disruptions, institutional collapse, and transition policies that failed to support restructuring (World Bank, 2023).

By the early 2000s, the government adopted an export-oriented strategy focused on attracting FDI. A major milestone was the 2002 Law on TIDZs, which introduced tax incentives, customs exemptions, and simplified administrative procedures to encourage foreign investors (Directorate for TIDZs, 2023). These zones became the cornerstone of the emerging automotive industry. By the mid-2010s, multinational corporations such as Johnson Matthey, Lear Corporation, and Adient had established production facilities manufacturing catalytic converters, wiring harnesses, and seat components for European markets.

The sector has since expanded rapidly, driven largely by foreign capital. By 2023, it accounted for aproxamitaly 14% of manufacturing value added of GDP and 31% of total exports (State Statistical Office of North Macedonia, 2024). However, production remains concentrated within SEZs, while domestic firms are primarily engaged in packaging, warehousing, and logistics. Despite strong export performance, the sector's contribution to domestic capability development is limited. Employment growth, knowledge transfer, and supplier upgrading have not kept pace with production expansion. Without deliberate policies to strengthen backward linkages, embed learning mechanisms, and promote technology diffusion, the industry risks perpetuating an enclave model that increases exports but fails to foster structural transformation (Hausmann and Rodrik, 2003; Pietrobelli and Rabellotti, 2011).

### *7.3.1 GVC Integration: Trends, Drivers, and Constraints*

North Macedonia's integration into global value chains has become a defining feature of its industrial development strategy, particularly in the automotive sector. The country functions mainly as a Tier 2 and Tier 3 supplier within the European automotive production system, specializing in catalytic converters, wiring harnesses, electronic modules, and seat structures (UNCTAD, 2023; Gereffi et al., 2005). This positioning reflects the outsourcing strategies of major European original equipment manufacturers (OEMs) such as Volkswagen, BMW, and Renault, which increasingly procure medium-complexity components from lower-cost locations across Europe's periphery (Baldwin and Lopez-Gonzalez, 2015).

Figure 7.2 illustrates how SEZ-based automotive producers in North Macedonia are functionally integrated into European production networks through Tier 1 suppliers located primarily in Central and Eastern Europe. The country's role is shaped by its logistical proximity to major OEM hubs in Germany, Austria, and other core markets, as well as by its specialisation in cost-sensitive intermediate manufacturing.

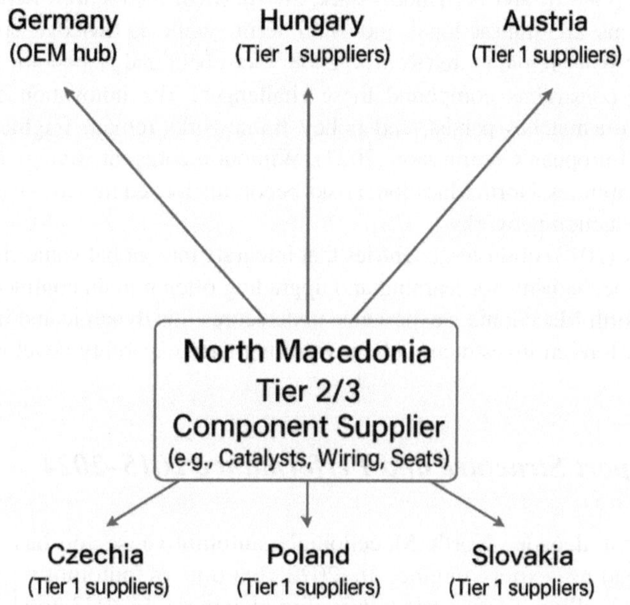


**Fig. 7.2** North Macedonia's Automotive Sector within European GVCs. *Source* Adapted from OECD (2024), European Commission (2023), and Invest North Macedonia (2023), generated with DALL · E using Microsoft Copilot (2025)

Four structural factors help explain North Macedonia's pattern of integration into global value chains.

First, geographic proximity to major European markets supports just-in-time and just-in-sequence delivery models that are essential in automotive production (European Commission, 2023).

Second, cost competitiveness continues to be a major attraction. With average monthly manufacturing wages of around €550, North Macedonia remains a low-cost location for component assembly (ILO, 2023; State Statistical Office, 2024).

Third, investment incentives have played a central role in attracting foreign investors. Tax exemptions, customs relief, and subsidized infrastructure in SEZs have drawn more than forty international automotive firms (Directorate for TIDZs, 2023).

Fourth, anchor firms such as Johnson Matthey, Lear Corporation, and Adient have established integrated production facilities that connect North Macedonia to regional supply chains, although these links have produced limited domestic spillovers (Invest North Macedonia, 2023).

Despite these advantages, integration remains functionally shallow. The country is concentrated in low- and mid-complexity production stages, with limited progress toward higher-value activities such as design, engineering, and research and development (Gereffi and Fernandez-Stark, 2016). Most interactions between foreign and local firms are transactional and short term, while knowledge spillovers and technology transfer remain rare (Rodrik, 2008; Pietrobelli and Rabellotti, 2011).

Structural constraints compound these challenges. The innovation ecosystem is weak, skills mismatches persist, and policy frameworks remain fragmented (World Bank, 2023; European Commission, 2023). Without a coherent strategy to strengthen domestic capabilities, North Macedonia risks becoming locked into low-value segments of global production networks.

As Stiglitz (2018) observes, countries that integrate into global value chains without institutional mechanisms for learning and upgrading often remain confined to subordinate roles. North Macedonia's experience underscores this dynamic and highlights the need to align foreign investment policy with long-term capability development.

### 7.3.2 Export Structure and Performance 2015–2024

Over the past decade, North Macedonia's automotive sector has become the country's leading export engine. In 2022, exports of automotive components reached €3.82 billion, representing 46% of total exports. In 2023, total merchandise exports were valued at $8.99 billion, with the automotive sector maintaining its dominant position.

The export portfolio is concentrated in high-demand intermediate components supplied to European manufacturers. In 2024, supported catalysts led the category, contributing $1.57 billion (18.6% of total exports), followed by wiring sets at $719.5 million (8.5%) and seat parts at $293.8 million (3.5%) (WTO, 2024). These products reflect North Macedonia's specialization in mid-complexity; high-volume components aligned with European production networks.

Export destinations are geographically concentrated. In 2023, Germany absorbed 44% of national exports, followed by Romania, Hungary, and Slovenia. Smaller volumes reached markets such as Mexico and Brazil, indicating limited diversification.

Employment in the sector has also grown. By 2019, the automotive industry employed around 28,000 people. Despite global disruptions caused by the COVID-19 pandemic, employment remained stable and even increased slightly, underscoring the sector's resilience.

Table 7.1 presents annual export values by product category between 2015 and 2024. The steady upward trend across all major product lines reflects deepening specialization and greater integration into European production networks.

While these figures demonstrate growing maturity in the automotive export sector, long-term competitiveness will depend on moving from assembly-based production toward deeper value creation. This shift requires targeted supplier development, institutional support for innovation, and coordinated policies that connect export success with domestic capability upgrading.

**Table 7.1** Automotive Export Structure in North Macedonia, 2015–2024 (€ million)

| Year | Supported catalysts (€ million) | Wiring sets (€ million) | Seat parts (€ million) | Total automotive exports (€ million) |
|---|---|---|---|---|
| 2015 | 1,200 | 450 | 200 | 1,850 |
| 2016 | 1,350 | 500 | 220 | 2,070 |
| 2017 | 1,500 | 550 | 240 | 2,290 |
| 2018 | 1,650 | 600 | 260 | 2,510 |
| 2019 | 1,800 | 650 | 280 | 2,730 |
| 2020 | 1,600 | 600 | 250 | 2,450 |
| 2021 | 1,700 | 650 | 270 | 2,620 |
| 2022 | 1,800 | 700 | 290 | 2,790 |
| 2023 | 1,900 | 750 | 310 | 2,960 |
| 2024 | 2,000 | 800 | 330 | 3,130 |

*Note* Export values are derived from HS-classified trade data. Investment-related information is used for contextual interpretation only.
*Source* Author's calculations based on WTO trade statistics and data from the State Statistical Office of the Republic of North Macedonia; contextual information from Invest North Macedonia.

### *7.3.3 Policy Framework on SEZs, Incentives, and Industrial Strategy Alignment*

The development of North Macedonia's automotive sector has been strongly influenced by a policy framework centred on FDI, SEZs, and export-led growth. The establishment of TIDZs in the early 2000s marked a turning point. These zones offer generous incentives to investors, including tax holidays of up to ten years, customs and VAT exemptions, subsidized infrastructure, and simplified administrative procedures (Directorate for TIDZs, 2023; OECD, 2024).

These incentives have attracted major multinational companies such as Johnson Matthey, Lear Corporation, and Adient. By 2023, more than forty foreign firms operated in TIDZs, most of them in the automotive sector. This concentration underscores the success of SEZs as engines of industrial recovery and investment attraction (Invest North Macedonia, 2023).

However, the broader industrial policy framework remains narrowly focused on attracting investment, with insufficient attention to building domestic capabilities. Mechanisms to strengthen local supplier networks, support SMEs, and foster innovation are limited in both scope and implementation. Although the *National Industrial Policy 2018–2027* outlines objectives for SME development and innovation, it lacks the institutional capacity and financial resources required to deliver systemic change.

Donor programmes led by the EU, GIZ, and USAID have supported SME upgrading through technical assistance and pilot initiatives. Yet their scale remains modest, and they often operate independently of national policy structures, limiting their long-term impact (European Commission, 2023).

Institutional fragmentation further constrains policy effectiveness. Key agencies, including the Directorate for TIDZs, the Ministry of Economy, the Directorate for Industrial Policy, and regional development authorities, frequently operate in isolation. Overlapping mandates, duplication of effort, and weak coordination undermine strategic coherence (OECD, 2024; Grindle, 2007).

As a result, North Macedonia has created a favourable environment for investment but not for learning or innovation. Without stronger institutional alignment and policies that link FDI to domestic upgrading, the current model risks entrenching enclave-based growth with limited spillovers into the broader economy.

### 7.3.4 Challenges in Local Value Addition, Technology, and Skills

Despite strong export performance, North Macedonia's automotive sector continues to face deep structural constraints that limit its contribution to sustainable upgrading. The most critical challenge is the low level of domestic value added. Production remains concentrated in assembly and processing, while most technologies, designs, and components are imported (Gereffi and Fernandez-Stark, 2016; OECD, 2024).

This dependence on foreign inputs has created a capability trap. Foreign investment has modernized manufacturing practices but has not generated substantial technology transfer or innovation diffusion. Multinational firms face few incentives to localize higher-value functions or to develop local suppliers. As a result, domestic firms remain confined to peripheral activities such as packaging, warehousing, and logistics (Rodrik, 2008; Pietrobelli and Rabellotti, 2011).

Workforce development represents another major challenge. The sector employed nearly 28,000 workers in 2023 (China-CEE Institute, 2021), but most positions involve low-skill, repetitive tasks. The education and vocational training systems have not adapted to the evolving requirements of the automotive industry. Persistent shortages of technicians, engineers, and specialists in fields such as robotics, quality control, and digital manufacturing constrain the sector's capacity for innovation (European Commission, 2023).

This skills gap is reinforced by weak collaboration between firms and training institutions. Apprenticeship programmes are limited, employers have little influence on curricula, and opportunities for lifelong learning or reskilling remain scarce. These weaknesses reduce the absorptive capacity of domestic firms and workers, hindering progress toward higher-value production.

In summary, these challenges reveal the structural vulnerabilities of North Macedonia's growth model. The automotive sector remains heavily dependent on foreign capital, focused on mid- and low-complexity production, and disconnected from domestic innovation systems. Without deliberate efforts to strengthen technological capabilities, enhance skills, and promote supplier upgrading, the sector is unlikely to move beyond its current position in European production networks.

To avoid stagnation, North Macedonia must reframe its industrial strategy. This involves embedding learning mechanisms, aligning investment incentives with upgrading objectives, and empowering institutions to link foreign investors with domestic actors. The DNS framework, discussed in Chap. 4, offers a potential roadmap for building a more connected, learning-oriented, and resilient industrial ecosystem.

## 7.4 Supplier Networks and Embedded Learning

North Macedonia's ability to move from enclave-based industrial growth to a more inclusive and capability-driven model depends largely on the strength of its supplier networks and the quality of learning mechanisms. Although FDI has driven export expansion and job creation, domestic linkages remain limited. Without strong local suppliers and institutionalized channels for knowledge transfer, the automotive sector risks remaining confined to low-value segments of GVCs.

This section examines the structure of the supplier base, the dynamics of knowledge exchange between foreign and domestic firms, and the role of intermediary institutions. It focuses on five interconnected dimensions: supplier structure, knowledge flows, firm-level capability building, institutional coordination, and systemic constraints related to skills, technology, and finance.

### *7.4.1 Mapping Supplier Networks: Structure and Gaps*

Despite deeper integration into European production networks, North Macedonia's domestic supplier base remains narrow and fragmented. Tier 1 firms such as Johnson Matthey, Lear Corporation, and Adient operate within SEZs and are fully foreign-owned. They assemble catalytic converters, wiring harnesses, and seat components using advanced quality systems and international certifications (OECD, 2024; Invest North Macedonia, 2023).

Domestic firms, by contrast, are mostly confined to Tier 3 activities such as packaging, logistics, and basic processing. Only a few participate in higher-value segments like engineered subcomponents or electronics. Most lack the technical capabilities, certifications, and process standards required by global clients. Table 7.2 summarizes the current supplier structure by ownership, capabilities, and estimated share.

Geographically, suppliers are concentrated in SEZs around Skopje, Štip, and Tetovo. Firms outside these zones face greater barriers, including limited access to technology, finance, and managerial expertise. The absence of coordinated supplier development programmes further limits integration.

**Table 7.2** Automotive suppliers in North Macedonia by Tier and capabilities

| Tier | Ownership structure | Capabilities | Share of total suppliers (%) |
|---|---|---|---|
| Tier 1 | 100% Foreign Owned | Advanced assembly, quality systems, compliance with global standards (ISO/IATF) | 5 |
| Tier 2 | Predominantly Foreign | Limited local sourcing, basic sub-assembly | 15 |
| Tier 3 | Mostly Domestic (SMEs) | Packaging, logistics, basic processing, limited certification | 80 |

*Source* OECD (2024); Invest North Macedonia (2023); author's synthesis

The result is a dualistic system in which foreign firms dominate high-value activities while domestic firms remain peripheral. Bridging this divide requires targeted support for capability upgrading and mechanisms that link local firms to regional and global production systems.

### *7.4.2 Learning Through Linkages and Knowledge Transfer*

Although integration into European GVCs has introduced international standards and production practices, the transfer of knowledge to domestic firms remains weak. Two main channels facilitate learning: direct interactions between multinational and local firms, and institutional programmes supported by donors (Altenburg, 2011; OECD, 2024).

At the firm level, relationships are mostly short-term and transactional. Multinational corporations tend to subcontract non-core services such as logistics or maintenance to local providers. Training is often limited to operational tasks and rarely extends to engineering or process innovation (China-CEE Institute, 2021).

Institutionally, North Macedonia lacks a formal supplier development programme for the automotive industry. Donor-led initiatives provide vocational training and technical assistance but remain fragmented and disconnected from firm-level upgrading needs (European Commission, 2023). Low trust, limited collaboration, and the absence of joint ventures or shared R&D platforms further restrict knowledge transfer (Rodrik, 2008). Figure 7.3 illustrates the weak and uneven flows of knowledge between foreign investors, local suppliers, and intermediary institutions.

Without institutional platforms that promote embedded learning, North Macedonia's participation in GVCs will remain shallow and transactional, offering limited opportunities for transformation.

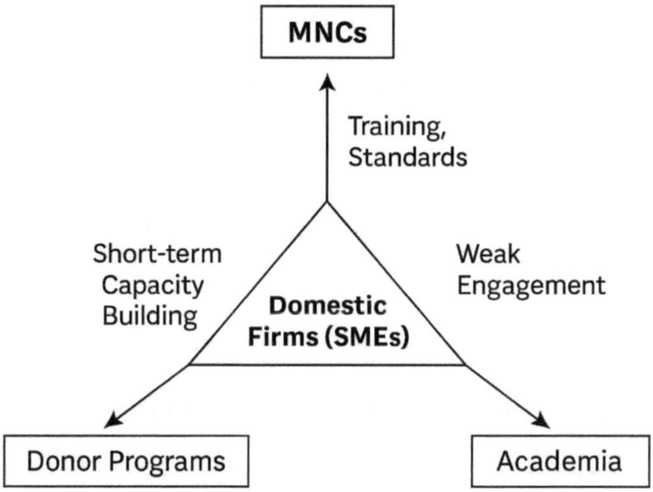


**Fig. 7.3** Knowledge flows in the automotive cluster. *Note* Conceptual diagram showing weak and strong knowledge transfer channels among SEZ-based foreign investors, local suppliers, and institutional actors such as vocational training centres and donor-funded programs. *Source* OECD (2024); European Commission (2023); Invest North Macedonia (2023), generated with DALL · E using Microsoft Copilot (2025)

### 7.4.3 *Capability Building in Domestic Firms: Successes and Gaps*

Despite these limitations, a small number of domestic firms have begun to develop basic capabilities. Some multinational corporations have subcontracted logistics and support services to local SMEs, creating limited but valuable learning opportunities. For example, Kemet Electronics Macedonia has collaborated with domestic providers and invested in workforce training, though its research and development (R&D) activities remain centralized abroad (OECD, 2024). Kostal Macedonia operates a large facility in Ohrid but relies little on local suppliers (European Commission, 2023).

Among fully domestic SMEs, only a few have achieved ISO certification or secured small contracts with multinationals. These gains are often donor-supported and remain isolated. Most firms continue to face barriers such as insufficient capital, limited managerial capacity, and weak technical expertise (Rodrik, 2008; Pietrobelli and Rabellotti, 2011).

Three systemic constraints persist, namely the absence of a national supplier development programme; limited access to finance for equipment, quality systems, and training; and weak innovation infrastructure, including a lack of R&D grants, prototyping centres, and technical extension services (World Bank, 2023; European Commission, 2023).

Even when firms are exposed to international best practices, many lack the absorptive capacity to convert this exposure into competitiveness (Cohen and Levinthal, 1990). Without sustained support, such progress will remain sporadic and unsustainable.

### 7.4.4 Intermediary Institutions and Missing Coordination Platforms

Intermediary institutions such as chambers of commerce, industry clusters, and technical associations can play an important role in developing capabilities and fostering collaboration. In practice, however, these institutions in North Macedonia remain underdeveloped and poorly aligned with national industrial goals.

The Automotive Cluster of Macedonia (ACM), established in 2012, was designed to promote supplier upgrading and linkages with multinational firms. Its activities have included networking events and promotional initiatives, but its impact has been limited due to narrow membership, inadequate funding, and weak implementation (OECD, 2024).

Other intermediaries, such as the Economic Chamber of North Macedonia, focus mainly on advocacy and regulatory issues. Their engagement in technical upgrading or innovation support is minimal. Coordination among these actors is limited, resulting in duplicated efforts and fragmented services (European Commission, 2023).

There is also no dedicated institution linking firms with applied research, technology services, or prototyping support. Although universities offer relevant programmes, collaboration with industry remains rare. Donor projects have piloted promising initiatives, but without institutional continuity, their impact has been temporary.

Strengthening intermediary institutions will require clear mandates, stable funding, and integration within a coherent industrial strategy. Without such coordination, the sector will remain fragmented and unable to support collective upgrading.

### 7.4.5 Constraints on Upgrading: Skills, Technology, and Finance

Three interconnected constraints continue to limit the sector's transformation: skills shortages, technological gaps, and limited access to finance.

The skills mismatch is the most pressing challenge. Although the automotive sector employs around 28,000 workers (China-CEE Institute, 2021), most are engaged in low-skilled, repetitive tasks. Engineering, digital manufacturing, and process innovation capabilities remain weak. Vocational education is outdated, and partnerships between firms and training institutions are limited (European Commission, 2023).

Technological upgrading faces similar obstacles. Many domestic firms lack access to modern machinery, process automation, and digital tools. The adoption of Industry 4.0 practices such as robotics, data-driven quality control, and lean manufacturing is minimal, reflecting both low awareness and limited capability (OECD, 2024).

Access to finance cuts across these challenges. SMEs face difficulties obtaining credit for upgrading equipment, staff training, or certification. Financial institutions remain cautious, and support instruments such as innovation grants or leasing schemes are fragmented and often donor-dependent (World Bank, 2023).

These constraints reinforce each other. Limited access to finance restricts investment in technology, which in turn reduces demand for skilled labour. Weak human capital then constrains innovation and firm growth. Without coordinated intervention, North Macedonia risks remaining in a low-skill, low-technology equilibrium.

Breaking this cycle requires integrated reforms that connect skills development, technological upgrading, and financial support within a coherent capability-building strategy (Hausmann and Rodrik, 2003; Rodrik, 2008). The next section explores how the DNS framework can provide a foundation for such transformation.

## 7.5 Governance Mechanisms Supporting Industrial Upgrading

As previously state, although North Macedonia has achieved notable export growth in the automotive sector, this success has not been matched by stronger governance capacity. Industrial development continues to take place within an institutional environment marked by fragmentation, donor dependence, and weak coordination. This section assesses the governance mechanisms that influence the sector's upgrading potential, focusing on the roles of public institutions, private actors, and intermediary organizations. It considers whether existing arrangements enable or constrain learning, capability accumulation, and the formation of productive networks.

### *7.5.1 Institutional Landscape and Weak Coordination*

The governance framework for industrial development in North Macedonia is dispersed and poorly integrated. Key institutions, including the TIDZs, the Ministry of Economy, and regional development agencies, operate with overlapping responsibilities and limited collaboration. This lack of coordination undermines policy coherence across investment promotion, SME support, and capability-building efforts (OECD, 2024; European Commission, 2023). Table 7.3 summarizes the core governance mechanisms influencing the automotive sector, highlighting their scope and *effectiveness*.

**Table 7.3** Key governance mechanisms in North Macedonia's automotive cluster

| Governance mechanism | Lead institution | Scope and focus | Status/Effectiveness |
|---|---|---|---|
| Technological Industrial Development Zones (TIDZs) | Directorate for TIDZs | FDI attraction, tax incentives, infrastructure | Effective for FDI attraction, limited in supplier development |
| SME support and quality certification | Ministry of economy, donor programs | Capacity building, quality standards, process upgrading | Project-based, fragmented impact |
| Supplier development programs | GIZ, EU IPA projects, ACM | Mentoring, audits, ISO training | Ad hoc, limited scale and sustainability |
| Cluster coordination (ACM) | Automotive cluster of Macedonia | Networking, matchmaking, events | Underdeveloped, low capacity |
| Industry-academia collaboration | Universities, select firms | Training, internships, limited joint research | Sporadic, weak institutionalization |
| Donor-driven technical assistance | EU, GIZ, USAID | Capacity building, policy advice | Valuable but short-term, donor-dependent |

*Source* OECD (2024); European Commission (2023); Invest North Macedonia (2023)

The Directorate for TIDZs has been effective in attracting foreign investment through fiscal incentives and infrastructure development. However, this narrow focus on FDI has not translated into stronger supplier networks or embedded learning. The Ministry of Economy oversees broader industrial policy but operates with limited resources and technical expertise. Regional authorities and chambers of commerce remain peripheral, contributing to duplication and policy fragmentation.

### 7.5.2 Donor-Led Governance and Policy Transfer

In the absence of strong national coordination, international donors have played a central role in shaping North Macedonia's industrial landscape. Programmes led by the EU, GIZ, and USAID have supported skills training, SME upgrading, and policy advice. While these initiatives have generated short-term results, they are typically project-based and poorly integrated into national strategies (Grindle, 2007; OECD, 2024).

The EU's Instrument for Pre-Accession Assistance (IPA) has funded SME certification and export readiness programmes, while GIZ has focused on supplier mentoring and workforce development. However, these interventions rarely lead to institutional continuity. They often operate independently, relying on external expertise rather than building local governance capacity.

Donor programmes tend to be most effective when embedded within broader policy frameworks. In North Macedonia, their fragmented nature has limited their ability to support systemic learning or long-term transformation.

### *7.5.3 The Limits of SEZ-Based Governance*

Special Economic Zones (SEZs) have become the cornerstone of North Macedonia's industrial governance model, with the Directorate for TIDZs serving as the main coordinating body. SEZs have succeeded in attracting foreign investors and expanding exports but operate largely in isolation from the domestic economy. Firms based in these zones have few incentives to engage in supplier development, innovation partnerships, or workforce upgrading beyond their own operations. Figure 7.4 illustrates the governance structure, showing strong vertical links between the state and foreign investors but weak horizontal connections to domestic firms, training institutions, and intermediary bodies.

The absence of coordination platforms and joint problem-solving mechanisms has created a fragmented system. SEZ-based firms act as isolated entities,

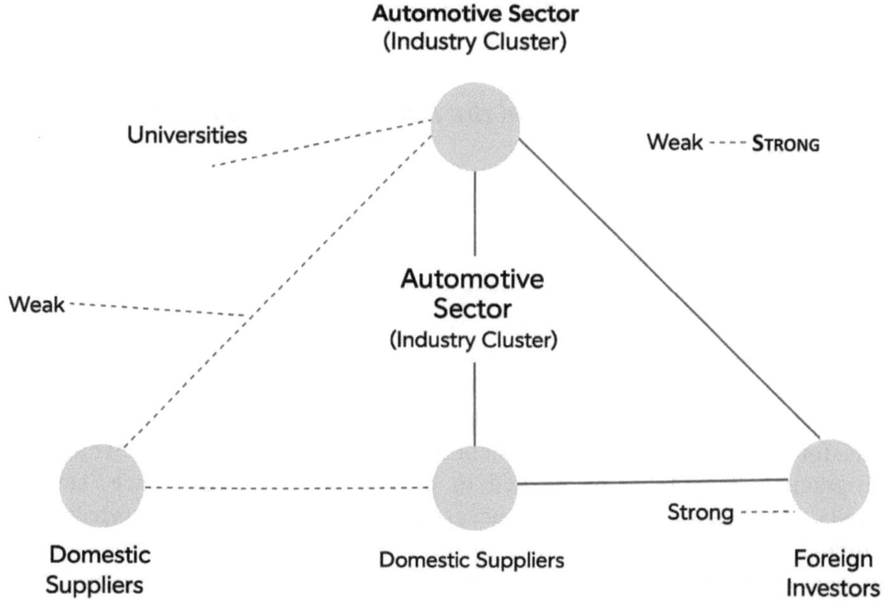


**Fig. 7.4** Governance network map: Actors, roles, and interactions. *Source* OECD (2024); European Commission (2023), generated with DALL · E using Microsoft Copilot (2025)

and opportunities for knowledge transfer or capability building are rarely institutionalized. Without stronger linkages between foreign investors and domestic stakeholders, the SEZ model risks reinforcing enclave-style development with limited local benefits.

### 7.5.4 Emerging Hybrid Governance Arrangements

Despite these structural weaknesses, some hybrid governance arrangements have started to emerge. Informal collaborations between firms and universities, donor-supported supplier development projects, and the initiatives of the Automotive Cluster of Macedonia (ACM) represent early attempts to build more networked and collaborative forms of governance.

While promising, these initiatives remain fragile. Most depend on donor funding and lack institutional mandates or stable financing. Their scale is limited, and continuity is uncertain. Without stronger public support, coordination mechanisms, and integration with national industrial strategies, these efforts are unlikely to evolve into lasting governance platforms.

Consolidating these experiments into formal structures that connect firms, public agencies, and training institutions across regions and sectors will be essential to strengthen systemic learning.

### 7.5.5 Governance Gaps and the Path to a Developmental Network State

The analysis above highlights the limits of North Macedonia's current industrial governance model. While SEZ-led development has generated exports and attracted investment, it has not produced the institutional learning or capability accumulation needed for sustained transformation. Overcoming these weaknesses requires a shift toward more embedded, coordinated, and adaptive governance, consistent with the principles of the DNS framework.

Several reforms could facilitate the transition toward a more integrated and transformative industrial development model. A national supplier development programme should be established to provide technical assistance, supplier audits, certification support, and access to industrial extension services. This initiative would strengthen the capabilities of domestic firms, enabling them to meet international standards and participate more effectively in global value chains.

Equally important is the creation of cross-sector coordination platforms that bring together firms, government ministries, training institutions, and donor agencies. These platforms would help identify key challenges in industrial upgrading and develop collaborative solutions that align diverse actors around shared objectives.

Encouraging stronger collaboration between foreign investors and domestic firms is another priority. Policy measures such as co-financing for research and development, tax incentives for local sourcing, and support for joint training initiatives could foster deeper linkages and knowledge transfer within the production system.

Finally, policy design should incorporate mechanisms for continuous learning and feedback. Regular monitoring, structured stakeholder consultations, and iterative policy adjustments informed by implementation experience would enhance policy coherence and adaptability over time (Hausmann and Rodrik, 2003; Rodrik, 2008).

A DNS approach does not rely on centralized control but on *connective capacity*—institutions and platforms that enable collaboration, build trust, and support continuous learning across the industrial ecosystem. For North Macedonia, this represents an essential step toward transforming enclave-based growth into an inclusive, adaptive, and capability-rich model of industrial development.

The next section situates North Macedonia's experience within a broader regional perspective and explores lessons for governance reform across the WB.

## 7.6 Lessons for DNS in Capability Building

This section synthesizes the findings from North Macedonia's automotive sector using the DNS framework. It evaluates how effectively the current governance system performs across key DNS functions: coordination, learning, embeddedness, and problem-solving. It also identifies reform priorities for transitioning toward a more capability-driven industrial model.

### *7.6.1 DNS Insights From North Macedonia*

North Macedonia's governance model shows significant weaknesses across the main functions of the DNS framework. Coordination is fragmented, with overlapping mandates and limited collaboration among ministries, agencies, and donors. Learning is short-term and confined to individual firms, with few mechanisms to embed knowledge within institutions. Embeddedness is weak because relationships between foreign investors, domestic suppliers, universities, and intermediary organizations remain transactional and lack continuity. Table 7.4 provides a diagnostic overview of DNS functions in the automotive sector and identifies areas for reform.

**Table 7.4** Diagnosing DNS functions in North Macedonia's automotive industry

| DNS function | Current status in North Macedonia | Challenges/Limitations | Opportunities for improvement |
|---|---|---|---|
| Coordination | Fragmented across TIDZs, Ministry, donors | Overlapping mandates, weak horizontal links | Establish sectoral platforms for joint problem-solving |
| Learning | Limited, firm-specific, shallow knowledge flows | Weak supplier development, poor industry-academia linkages | Create supplier development programs; embed learning in policy |
| Embeddedness | Weak, transactional ties between actors | Minimal trust, no joint projects, few partnerships | Incentivize long-term partnerships, build relational trust |
| Problem-Solving Orientation | Reactive, ad hoc, project-driven | Donor dependency, lack of adaptive policy capacity | Develop feedback loops, monitoring systems, and adaptive governance |
| Capability Accumulation | Enclave-based, low-value activities | Limited local value-added, minimal technology transfer | Link FDI incentives to local content and skill development |

*Source* Author's synthesis based on OECD (2024), European Commission (2023), and interviews

These findings point to the need for a strategic shift. Rather than focusing primarily on attracting investment, the state should evolve into an orchestrator of networks that support coordination, learning, and capability accumulation across institutions and firms.

### *7.6.2 Networked Governance for Embedded Learning and Upgrading*

North Macedonia's experience shows how fragmented governance structures limit industrial upgrading. Relationships among ministries, foreign investors, domestic suppliers, universities, and intermediaries are weak and often short-lived. Knowledge flows remain confined within firms or donor projects, with little institutional learning.

The DNS framework redefines the state's role as a convener and connector. Instead of trying to control outcomes, the state facilitates collaboration, supports experimentation, and builds long-term trust among economic actors. Practical examples include supplier development programmes that offer technical assistance, sectoral R&D alliances, and partnerships between firms and vocational institutions to align training with industry needs.

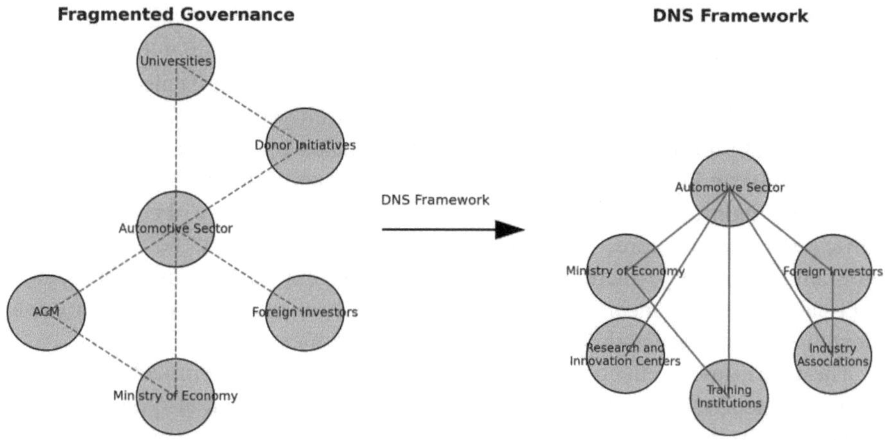


**Fig. 7.5** Strengthening automotive governance via DNS in North Macedonia. *Note* Dashed lines indicate weak coordination; solid lines indicate structured coordination. *Source* Author's synthesis based on OECD (2024), European Commission (2023), and interviews, generated with DALL · E using Microsoft Copilot (2025)

Without such embedded structures, upgrading efforts remain narrow, and the automotive sector risks being locked into low-value segments of global value chains. Figure 7.5 illustrates the contrast between North Macedonia's current fragmented governance system and a DNS-oriented model that promotes collaboration and iterative learning.

### *7.6.3 Policy Priorities for Capability-Driven Industrialization*

The analysis highlights several interconnected priorities for aligning industrial policy with the principles of the DNS framework. A central task is to link foreign direct investment more closely to domestic capability development. Incentive schemes should require foreign investors to engage in local supplier development, workforce training, and technology transfer to ensure that external investment contributes to long-term national learning and upgrading.

A second priority is the establishment of a national supplier development programme that offers technical assistance, certification support, process audits, and improved access to finance. This initiative should be institutionalized within public agencies rather than delivered solely through donor-funded projects, ensuring continuity and policy ownership.

Strengthening intermediary institutions is equally important. Organizations such as the Automotive Cluster of Macedonia require stable funding, expanded mandates, and technical upgrading. Their function as knowledge brokers and coordination platforms should be formally recognized within the industrial policy framework.

Institutionalizing collaboration between industry and academia also represents a critical step. Applied research centres, jointly developed training curricula, and public–private innovation initiatives should be scaled up and sustained to bridge the gap between knowledge creation and industrial application.

Finally, industrial governance must become more adaptive. Feedback loops, participatory evaluations, and policy experimentation should be embedded in programme design to facilitate real-time learning and continuous improvement. Such adaptive mechanisms would allow policies to evolve in response to implementation experience and changing industrial dynamics.

These priorities reflect a central principle of the DNS approach: successful upgrading depends not only on investment or liberalization but also on the institutional capacity to coordinate and learn continuously.

### *7.6.4 Transferability of DNS Principles in the Western Balkans*

North Macedonia's experience offers broader lessons for Western Balkan economies such as Serbia, Montenegro, and Bosnia and Herzegovina, which have also pursued FDI-led industrialization through Special Economic Zones and incentive-based policies. These countries face similar challenges, including underdeveloped supplier ecosystems, fragmented coordination, and limited integration among firms, academia, and public institutions.

The DNS model provides a framework for addressing these shared constraints by focusing on coordination, embedded learning, and institutional experimentation. It offers a pathway toward more inclusive and resilient growth. However, the application of DNS principles is not automatic.

Structural factors such as small market size, limited administrative capacity, and external dependencies related to EU accession and donor-driven reform shape the feasibility of change. Institutional transformation requires political commitment, inter-ministerial coordination, and sustained investment in public sector capabilities. DNS reforms must therefore be adapted to each country's governance realities and sectoral priorities.

The case of North Macedonia highlights a central insight: growth without learning is fragile. The DNS framework provides not only a set of policy tools but also a governance philosophy grounded in long-term institutional development. Its value for the WB lies in reframing industrial policy as a process of continuous learning, collaboration, and embedded coordination.

## 7.7 Conclusion: From Integration to Transformation

This chapter has explored the dynamics of North Macedonia's automotive sector through the DNS framework. Although the country has achieved significant export growth and integrated into European automotive value chains, this success has not been accompanied by the development of domestic industrial capabilities. The growth model remains dependent on foreign investment, focused on low- and medium-complexity production, and largely disconnected from the wider economy.

The analysis identified a dual structure within the industry. Foreign-owned firms in Special Economic Zones (SEZs) drive export performance but operate as isolated enclaves with limited connections to domestic suppliers, training institutions, or innovation systems. Local firms remain on the periphery of value chains, constrained by limited absorptive capacity, outdated technologies, and restricted access to finance. Governance mechanisms have been effective in attracting foreign direct investment but have not promoted coordinated upgrading or collective learning.

A central challenge lies in the fragmented institutional landscape. Policy responsibilities are divided among overlapping agencies, donor programs operate independently, and intermediary institutions often lack the capacity to coordinate or expand successful initiatives. Learning processes remain shallow and project-based, with few incentives for long-term partnerships between foreign and domestic actors.

The DNS framework provides an alternative approach by redefining the state's role as a convener, facilitator, and problem solver. It emphasizes the need for investment in coordination platforms, supplier development programs, and learning institutions that align diverse actors around common upgrading objectives.

North Macedonia's experience highlights a broader lesson: participation in global value chains alone does not guarantee structural transformation. Without mechanisms that promote embedded learning, local capability building, and institutional coherence, global integration can reinforce dependency instead of reducing it.

A transition toward a DNS-oriented approach would not require starting from zero. Local experimentation, hybrid initiatives, and emerging public–private collaborations already offer a foundation for change. What is needed is a coherent framework to consolidate, scale, and sustain these efforts. Only through such coordinated action can North Macedonia progress from enclave-driven growth toward a more inclusive and resilient model of industrial transformation.

## References

Altenburg, T. (2011) Industrial policy in developing countries: Overview and lessons from seven country cases, *German Development Institute Discussion Paper*, 4/2011. Available at: https://www.idos-research.de/uploads/media/DP_4.2011.pdf (Accessed: 8 June 2025).

Baldwin, R. & Lopez-Gonzalez, J. (2015). Supply-chain trade: A portrait of global patterns and several testable hypotheses. *World Economy*, *38*(11), 1682–1721. https://doi.org/10.1111/twec.12189

China-CEE Institute. (2021) *North Macedonia Economic Bulletin*. China-CEE Institute. Available at: https://china-cee.eu (Accessed: 8 June 2025).

Cohen, W. M. & Levinthal, D. A. (1990). Absorptive capacity: A new perspective on learning and innovation. *Administrative Science Quarterly*, *35*(1), 128–152. https://doi.org/10.2307/2393553

Directorate for Technological Industrial Development Zones (TIDZs). (2023). *Annual Report 2023*. Government of North Macedonia. Available at: https://fez.gov.mk/

European Commission. (2023). *North Macedonia 2023 Report*. European Commission. Available at: https://enlargement.ec.europa.eu/north-macedonia-report-2023_en (Accessed: 8 June 2025).

Gereffi, G. & Fernandez-Stark, K. (2016). *Global value chain analysis: A primer*, 2nd edn. Duke University, Center on Globalization, Governance & Competitiveness. Available at: https://hdl.handle.net/10161/12488 (Accessed: 8 June 2025).

Gereffi, G., Humphrey, J. & Sturgeon, T. (2005). The governance of global value chains. *Review of International Political Economy*, *12*(1), 78–104. https://doi.org/10.1080/09692290500049805

GIZ. (2023). *GIZ North Macedonia Project Portfolio*. Skopje: Deutsche Gesellschaft Für Internationale Zusammenarbeit (GIZ). Available at: https://www.giz.de/en/worldwide/301.html (Accessed: 8 June 2025).

Grindle, M. S. (2007). *Going local: decentralization, democratization, and the promise of good governance*. Princeton University Press. https://www.jstor.org/stable/j.ctt4cgd2m (Accessed: 8 June 2025).

Hausmann, R. & Rodrik, D. (2003). Economic development as self-discovery. *Journal of Development Economics*, *72*(2), 603–633. https://doi.org/10.1016/S0304-387(03)00124-X

ILO (2023) *Global Wage Report 2023–24*. International Labour Organization. Available at: https://www.ilo.org/sites/default/files/2024-11/GWR-2024_Layout_E_RGB_Web.pdf (Accessed: 8 June 2025).

Invest North Macedonia (2023). *Sector profile: Automotive industry*. Agency for Foreign Investments and Export Promotion. Available at: https://investnorthmacedonia.gov.mk/documents/ (Accessed: 8 June 2025).

OECD (2024) *Western Balkans competitiveness outlook 2024: Regional profile*. OECD Publishing. Available at: https://doi.org/10.1787/170b0e53-en

Pietrobelli, C. & Rabellotti, R. (2011). Global value chains meet innovation systems: Are there learning opportunities for developing countries?. *World Development*, *39*(7), 1261–1269. https://doi.org/10.1016/j.worlddev.2010.05.013

Rodrik, D. (2008). Normalizing industrial policy. *Commission on Growth and Development Working Paper*, No. 3. Available at: https://drodrik.scholar.harvard.edu/files/dani-rodrik/files/industrial-policy.pdf

State Statistical Office of North Macedonia (2024) *Statistical Yearbook of the Republic of North Macedonia 2024*. SSO. Available at: https://www.stat.gov.mk/

Stiglitz, J. E. (2018). From manufacturing-led export growth to a twenty-first-century inclusive growth strategy: Explaining the demise of a successful growth model and what to do about it. *WIDER Working Paper* 2018/176. Helsinki: UNU-WIDER. Available at: https://doi.org/10.35188/UNU-WIDER/2018/618-0

UNCTAD. (2023) *World Investment Report 2023: Investing in Sustainable Energy for All*. United Nations. Available at: https://unctad.org/publication/world-investment-report-2023 (Accessed: 8 June 2025).

UNESCO Institute for Statistics. (2023). *R&D Data by Country*. Available at: http://data.uis.unesco.org/ (Accessed: 8 June 2025).

World Bank. (2023). Macedonia—Moving to faster and more inclusive growth: Country economic memorandum, Vol. 2 of 2. World Bank. Available at: https://documents.worldbank.org/en/publication/documents-reports/documentdetail/118211468300831530/main-report-and-annex

World Trade Organization. (2024). Trade profiles: North Macedonia 2024. WTO. Available at: https://www.wto.org/english/res_e/statis_e/trade_profiles_list_e.htm (Accessed: 8 June 2025).

# Part III
# Conclusion Comparative Lessons and Future Pathways for Structural Transformation

This part of the book builds on the sectoral studies of Kosovo, Albania, and North Macedonia to explore a broader comparative question: what can late-industrializing states learn from differences in their capability development paths, and what forms of governance are feasible in contexts shaped by institutional fragmentation and donor dependence? The discussion extends the analytical reach of the Developmental Network State (DNS) framework, using it to understand how learning, coordination, and adaptation occur under real-world constraints.

Chapter 8 examines patterns of capability constraints and adaptive governance across three key industries—information and communication technologies (ICT), agri-food, and automotive manufacturing. It compares how formal policy tools, informal coordination mechanisms, and transnational actors influence learning processes and lead to different upgrading outcomes.

Chapter 9 turns to the role of digital transformation and artificial intelligence (AI), focusing on how digital and other general-purpose technologies reshape opportunities for technological upgrading. It explores how network-based governance can support capability formation in environments with limited absorptive capacity and uneven institutional support.

Chapter 10 looks ahead to the future of industrial policy, analysing the political economy of reform. It discusses how elite incentives, coalition structures, and external pressures influence the design and sustainability of adaptive institutions.

Taken together, these chapters provide a forward-looking perspective on how structural, technological, and political factors interact to shape the governance of industrial transformation in low-capacity and transitional economies.

# Chapter 8
# Cross-Cutting Patterns of Capability Constraints and Adaptive Governance

## 8.1 Introduction

The previous chapters examined how Kosovo, Albania, and North Macedonia have pursued industrial development under persistent constraints. Each country has followed a distinct path shaped by its history, political economy, and external alliances. Despite these differences, the sectoral studies reveal shared characteristics: fragmented institutions, weak coordination, and limited learning systems. These features reflect broader structural challenges common to many latecomer economies in transitional Europe, where governance capacity is limited and policy implementation uneven.

This chapter moves beyond individual cases to examine the cross-cutting patterns that connect them. The aim is not to overlook national specificities but to identify the systemic lessons they offer. The central questions are: which governance failures recur across contexts, where adaptive responses emerge despite institutional weakness, and how such responses can be organized into a framework that supports long-term capability development.

To explore these questions, the chapter applies the Developmental Network State (DNS) framework as its analytical lens. Introduced earlier in the book, the DNS highlights three essential governance functions for capability building: learning, coordination, and embeddedness. These functions are not confined to the state but emerge through interactions among public institutions, private firms, civic organizations, and diaspora networks. Governance, in this view, is less about command or deregulation and more about collective problem-solving through relationships, feedback, and mutual adjustment.

The analysis is organized around five core themes: institutional bricolage, coordination gaps, learning mechanisms, embeddedness and trust, and comparative synthesis.



F. Sahiti, *Catching Up in the Digital Age*, Contributions to Economics,
https://doi.org/10.1007/978-3-032-17059-0_8

In essence, this chapter begins from the recognition that development occurs under imperfect conditions. The DNS offers a pathway that emphasizes building governance functions capable of linking actors, learning from experience, and anchoring cooperation in trusted relationships, even when institutional capacity remains limited.

## 8.2 Institutional Bricolage and Governance Under Constraint

In many transitional economies, formal institutions are fragmented, under-resourced, or poorly aligned with developmental goals. Governance rarely follows a clear or coherent plan; instead, it often emerges from improvisation, negotiation, and creative adaptation. This process, known as institutional bricolage, describes how actors use available resources, navigate overlapping mandates, and develop temporary solutions to ongoing challenges (Andrews et al., 2017; Cleaver, 2012).

Across Kosovo, Albania, and North Macedonia, the case studies reveal numerous examples of such adaptive problem-solving. Progress often depends not on strong ministries or well-funded agencies, but on local actors who combine partial capacities from municipalities, donor programs, diaspora associations, and private firms to address coordination failures or promote capability-building initiatives. These responses may be limited in scope or sustainability, but they illustrate how governance evolves under constraint.

### *8.2.1 Understanding Institutional Bricolage in Transitional Contexts*

Bricolage challenges the idea that development can occur only through either a strong state or a fully liberalized market. It shows that progress can also arise from hybrid arrangements built on informal practices, embedded relationships, and institutional patchwork (Olivier de Sardan, 2011; Khan, 2018). In latecomer economies with weak bureaucracies and significant donor influence, such arrangements are not marginal—they often constitute the main mode of governance.

Bricolage is not disorder. It involves assembling workable arrangements from whatever tools or institutions exist, often within or alongside formal structures. This approach blurs the boundaries between state and non-state, legal and informal, planned and emergent systems. In the Western Balkans (WB), this dynamic is evident in project-based collaborations among underfunded ministries, international donors, and non-governmental organizations that step in to fill institutional gaps.

Examples illustrate this clearly. In Kosovo's ICT sector, municipalities, diaspora networks, and donor-funded innovation hubs have established coding academies and start-up accelerators despite the lack of a functional national innovation strategy. In Albania's agro-processing sector, cooperation between the public and private sectors often depends on intermediaries who bridge trust gaps and provide technical assistance to small farmers and local authorities. In North Macedonia, regional development agencies have acted as hybrid platforms, balancing central government mandates with donor priorities to deliver training and export support despite limited formal authority.

These cases demonstrate that governance under constraint does not mean the absence of agency. It shifts the focus from institutional design to the everyday practices through which development is made possible.

### *8.2.2 Mechanisms and Logics of Bricolage*

Three mechanisms stand out across the WB. First, repurposing institutional fragments, where actors adapt existing strategies, agencies, or regulations to new uses. Second, cross-boundary coalition building, in which alliances are formed across sectors and jurisdictions to bridge functional gaps and pool resources. Third, iterative adaptation, where approaches evolve through learning-by-doing in contexts of uncertainty or limited planning.

These mechanisms align with what Helmke and Levitsky (2004) call *informal institutional substitutions*, where informal practices compensate for weak formal structures. In transitional contexts, such substitutions are often not secondary solutions, but the primary means of moving forward.

### *8.2.3 The Limits and Risks of Bricolage*

While bricolage enables innovation under constraint, it also carries risks. It can deepen fragmentation by bypassing the very institutions that require strengthening. Donor-funded projects that operate through NGOs or municipalities may succeed locally but undermine national coherence. Temporary solutions can become entrenched, creating informal norms that block deeper reform. Reliance on personal networks and informal coalitions raises concerns about accountability, exclusion, and elite capture (Laws & Marquette, 2018).

Moreover, bricolage tends to be uneven. It flourishes where networks, funding, and trusted intermediaries exist, leaving other regions behind. The result is a patchwork of progress, with isolated hubs of innovation amid persistent stagnation. Without mechanisms to diffuse and institutionalize successful practices, their impact remains limited and short-lived.

### 8.2.4 Bricolage and the DNS Framework

Within the DNS framework, bricolage is not viewed as failure but as evidence of how governance actually operates in constrained environments. The DNS acknowledges that coordination does not have to come from a central authority. Municipalities, civil society groups, and business associations can all serve as engines of problem-solving when supported by enabling frameworks for collaboration, learning, and scaling.

For bricolage to contribute to broader capability development, it must be integrated into a structure that promotes feedback, alignment, and gradual upgrading. The DNS framework helps identify where bottom-up innovations are emerging, link them to wider policy goals, and ensure that their lessons are captured and applied rather than remaining isolated or donor-dependent.

### 8.2.5 Typology of Governance Under Constraint

The logic of bricolage can be illustrated through four governance modes that vary by institutional coherence and actor autonomy (Table 8.1).

Adaptive bricolage occupies a middle ground. It does not depend on ideal state capacity or unfettered market freedom but instead draws on moderate autonomy and fragmented yet usable institutional resources.

### 8.2.6 From Accidental to Strategic Bricolage

Institutional bricolage is both political and contextual. It highlights the creativity of actors working within structural constraints. However, when left uncoordinated, it risks remaining ad hoc, unsustainable, and dependent on external support.

**Table 8.1** Typology of governance modes in constrained contexts

| Governance mode | Institutional coherence | Actor autonomy | Typical form |
|---|---|---|---|
| Developmental hierarchy | High | Low | East Asian bureaucracies |
| Market-Led liberalism | Low | High | Neoliberal reform models |
| Institutional paralysis | Low | Low | Post-socialist stagnation |
| Adaptive bricolage (DNS) | Medium | Medium | Western Balkans experimentation |

*Source* Adapted by the author based on insights from Amsden (1989), Cleaver (2012), Andrews et al. (2017), Khan (2018), and Elster et al. (1998)

The challenge for transitional states is to move from *accidental* bricolage—improvised and local—to *strategic* bricolage that is institutionalized and scalable.

This shift requires identifying effective local practices, embedding them within stable institutional frameworks, and linking grassroots solutions to national strategies. The DNS framework provides a means to achieve this transformation by accepting fragmentation as a reality while building mechanisms to turn it into a source of adaptive integration.

Transitional states cannot wait for perfect governance conditions. They must treat governance as an iterative, learning-based process where capabilities evolve through purposeful coalitions, feedback, and experimentation rather than through one-time comprehensive reforms.

## 8.3 Coordination Gaps and Policy Incoherence

In many transitional European economies, efforts to build technological and industrial capabilities often falter on a familiar obstacle: the inability to align actors, policies, and instruments around a shared strategic vision. Official development plans frequently emphasize cross-sectoral coordination and integrated frameworks, yet the reality is usually fragmented, reactive, and siloed.

This section explores the roots and implications of such coordination failures in Kosovo, Albania, and North Macedonia. Rather than viewing them as simple administrative shortcomings, it examines them as outcomes of deeper political and institutional dynamics shaped by post-socialist transitions and a high degree of donor dependence. Through the lens of the DNS framework, the section also considers more adaptive ways of fostering alignment under constraint.

### *8.3.1 Fragmentation by Design: Institutional Overlaps and Donor Silos*

A persistent feature across the region is the proliferation of agencies with overlapping mandates and few mechanisms for horizontal coordination. In Kosovo, for instance, digital skills development is managed simultaneously by the Ministry of Education, the Ministry of Economy, and a variety of municipal and donor-led programs. Each operates independently, with its own budget, priorities, and reporting systems. The result is duplication, inefficiency, and lost opportunities for shared learning.

Albania's agri-food sector reflects a similar pattern. Although the Ministry of Agriculture is nominally responsible for rural development, practical implementation is dispersed among the Investment Development Agency, EU IPARD programs, and municipal authorities. Coordination tends to occur through sporadic consultations rather than structured collaboration, leaving little space for institutional learning or policy feedback. North Macedonia faces comparable challenges, as export promotion and SME upgrading remain fragmented among donor projects and multiple ministries.

These arrangements are not accidental. They arise from a governance environment where donor agendas, political rivalries, and bureaucratic fragmentation prevent coherent strategy formation. Ministries often compete for visibility and control over external funding, while donors pursue narrow, sector-specific programs with short implementation cycles that discourage joint planning.

### *8.3.2 Coordination as a Political Problem*

Coordination failures are not merely technical issues that can be solved through better procedures. They are rooted in politics. In states with weak administrative traditions, ministerial competition often mirrors broader patterns of patronage and factionalism. In both Kosovo and Albania, rival political factions control different ministries, leading to turf battles, parallel delivery systems, and reluctance to share authority or information.

Even when coordination councils or inter-ministerial committees exist formally, they often lack the power, resources, or legitimacy to ensure cooperation. Meetings are irregular, and agendas tend to follow donor requirements rather than national priorities. Local governments and regional development agencies, which could serve as bridges between actors, are typically underfunded and excluded from national planning.

The underlying problem is not simply the absence of coordination mechanisms but the lack of incentives to use them. In these contexts, working in silos can be safer than collaborating. Ministries fear losing control over budgets, and donor-funded projects often reward alignment with external rather than domestic partners.

### *8.3.3 Implications for Capability Development*

Coordination gaps have far-reaching effects on the process of capability building. Fragmentation erodes institutional memory and prevents the accumulation of shared knowledge. Donor projects and government programs often produce valuable data and lessons, but these remain isolated and rarely inform broader reforms. The result is a pattern of disjointed progress—training initiatives unlinked to export promotion, or SME programs disconnected from innovation strategies.

This fragmentation also undermines adaptability. Without integrated planning and feedback systems, governments struggle to revise strategies or respond to changing conditions. In fast-evolving sectors such as ICT or advanced manufacturing, where system-wide learning is essential, this rigidity can be particularly damaging. Lacking coherent links between education, industrial policy, and local innovation, many countries risk falling into capability traps—collections of small successes that never scale into structural transformation.

### 8.3.4 Networked Coordination Under the DNS

The DNS framework offers a pragmatic alternative to the idea that coordination must rely on strong central planning. Instead, it views alignment as a process of task-specific collaboration, iterative feedback, and trust-building among diverse actors. Coordination becomes a continuous exercise in negotiation and joint learning rather than a one-time institutional design.

Key principles guide this approach. Task-oriented coalitions unite ministries, municipalities, firms, and civil society organizations around specific challenges. Joint ownership and budgeting align incentives by encouraging shared program design and monitoring. Interface platforms—such as innovation councils, donor–government steering committees, or municipal forums—serve as coordination hubs that connect actors and facilitate learning. Digital tools enhance this process by improving data exchange, planning, and real-time evaluation (Table 8.2).

This approach does not eliminate fragmentation, but it turns it into a space for engagement. Coordination becomes a negotiated process where institutions learn from each other and adapt together.

### 8.3.5 Illustrative Examples

Kosovo's ICT skills ecosystem began as a collection of disconnected donor and municipal projects. Over time, co-financed working groups involving the Ministry of Economy, diaspora-led firms, and GIZ developed a joint pilot platform with shared budgets and feedback loops. This eventually informed the national Digital Economy Strategy, demonstrating how networked coordination can grow from fragmented beginnings.

**Table 8.2** From fragmentation to networked coordination

| Feature | Traditional governance | DNS-Oriented coordination |
|---|---|---|
| Primary logic | Ministerial control or donor silo | Problem-focused alignment |
| Coordination unit | Interministerial councils | Cross-sectoral task forces |
| Actor participation | Ministries or donors only | Ministries, municipalities, firms, CSOs |
| Monitoring | Fragmented and ex-post | Iterative and feedback-driven |
| Adaptability | Low | Medium to high |

*Source* Author's elaboration based on, Bartlett (2020), Andrews et al. (2017), Khan (2018), and empirical cases from Kosovo and North Macedonia

In North Macedonia, the establishment of the Fund for Innovation and Technological Development (FITD) created a hybrid institution capable of convening diverse stakeholders, coordinating funding calls, and aligning donor initiatives with national SME policies. Although challenges remain, FITD exemplifies how intermediary institutions can bridge silos and promote systemic learning.

These examples illustrate that policy coherence cannot be achieved through formal mandates alone. It requires shared incentives, institutional flexibility, and mechanisms for continuous feedback. The DNS provides a practical pathway for building such coherence in environments where resources are limited and political complexities persist.

Lasting alignment in these settings will emerge not from command but from collaboration. The task ahead is to design arrangements, build trust, and institutionalize monitoring systems that allow cooperation to evolve into systemic coherence.

## 8.4 Learning Mechanisms and Feedback Loops in Practice

Building technological and industrial capabilities depends not only on sound policy design and effective coordination but also on the capacity to learn from implementation. In many transitional European economies, where institutions are fragmented and reforms are externally driven, learning remains undervalued and weakly institutionalized. Mechanisms such as iterative feedback, reflexive planning, and institutional memory are essential for avoiding repeated mistakes, scaling successful initiatives, and adapting strategies to changing conditions.

This section examines the presence and absence of such learning mechanisms in Kosovo, Albania, and North Macedonia. It uses the DNS framework to interpret these findings, emphasizing learning as a central governance capability rather than a technical afterthought.

### *8.4.1 Learning Without Feedback and the Limits of Project-Based Reform*

Across the WB, policy learning is frequently confined to donor-financed project cycles. Monitoring and evaluation systems are designed primarily to meet reporting obligations rather than to promote adaptive learning. In Kosovo, for instance, youth employment and digital skills programs implemented by GIZ, USAID, and Swisscontact have produced numerous evaluations, yet few of these findings have informed national policy. Ministries receive final reports, but without coordination platforms, analytical capacity, or political incentives, lessons rarely translate into reform.

In Albania, vocational education and training reform has been heavily supported by EU IPA and Swiss programs. Although tracer studies and employer surveys are conducted, their findings are seldom synthesized or used to update curricula. Donors often emphasize short-term outputs over system-level learning, creating fragmented knowledge and limited feedback (ETF, 2021). Even well-designed evaluations tend to remain external exercises, disconnected from domestic policy dialogue.

North Macedonia offers a partial exception. The FITD conducts internal reviews and organizes post-funding reflection sessions with grantees. However, these insights generally stay within the Fund and are not systematically shared with other institutions. Across all three countries, learning occurs in isolated pockets without meaningful integration into national planning processes.

### *8.4.2 Structural Barriers to Policy Learning*

Several structural factors explain the weakness of feedback mechanisms in these settings.

First, evaluation systems are primarily designed for donor accountability. While many studies are methodologically sound, they often fail to generate actionable insights for domestic policymakers. Their technical focus, external authorship, and limited follow-up reduce their practical relevance (Andrews et al., 2017).

Second, institutional discontinuity is widespread. High staff turnover, political appointments, and poor archiving practices erode institutional memory. Few ministries maintain dedicated units with the mandate and skills to consolidate lessons from past interventions.

Third, there is almost no structured pathway for bottom-up feedback. Municipalities, NGOs, and firms often possess valuable local knowledge, yet they lack formal channels to communicate this to central policy bodies.

Finally, in globally integrated sectors such as automotive components and agri-food exports, learning remains largely transactional. Firms focus on meeting compliance and certification requirements for lead firms, with little diffusion of knowledge beyond their boundaries. As a result, the state and supporting institutions have limited access to firm-level insights that could inform broader strategies.

These barriers collectively undermine the emergence of adaptive governance and make it difficult to scale successful initiatives or sustain reform momentum.

### *8.4.3 Learning in the DNS Framework*

Within the DNS framework, learning is not an auxiliary task but a central function of governance. It is through continuous learning that states build the capacity to adapt, coordinate, and innovate. Effective learning requires well-structured feedback loops, open communication across institutional levels, and a willingness to experiment and revise. Rather than relying exclusively on formal monitoring and evaluation systems, DNS-compatible governance embeds learning into the everyday routines of policy formulation, implementation, and review.

This approach resonates with the concept of *dynamic capabilities* in public institutions. As Kattel and Mazzucato (2018) emphasize, governments must be able to sense emerging trends, adapt to evolving conditions, and actively shape their policy environments. Such adaptive capacity depends on mechanisms that combine anticipation and reflection—ranging from horizon scanning and real-time monitoring to collaborative evaluation among multiple actors.

In this context, a DNS-oriented learning system can be seen as an interactive architecture that connects experimentation with institutionalization. It integrates diverse forms of knowledge and promotes shared responsibility for improvement. Four elements stand out as particularly important:

1. *Feedback loops* in which pilot programs are explicitly designed for testing, reflection, and adaptation rather than to demonstrate predetermined success.
2. *Joint learning platforms* that convene ministries, municipalities, firms, and civil society organizations to share experiences, assess outcomes, and adjust implementation strategies.
3. *Knowledge intermediaries* such as innovation councils, applied research centres, or development agencies that translate localized lessons into policy-relevant insights.
4. *Reflexive planning cycles* in which national strategies are continuously revised based on evidence and feedback, rather than being adjusted only during formal mid-term reviews.

**Table 8.3** Contrasting learning regimes in transitional governance

| Dimension | Project-based governance | DNS-compatible learning |
|---|---|---|
| Primary purpose | Donor accountability | Institutional improvement and system learning |
| Ownership of knowledge | External implementers | Shared among public, private, and civic actors |
| Learning frequency | End-of-project reporting | Iterative and real-time |
| Institutionalisation | Weak or non-existent | Embedded in planning and budgeting cycles |
| Outcome | Documentation | Strategic recalibration and capability building |

*Source* Author's elaboration based on Andrews et al. (2017), Kattel and Mazzucato (2018), and case evidence from Kosovo, Albania, and North Macedonia

These mechanisms collectively redefine learning as a systemic process rather than a procedural step. They create the institutional conditions for continuous improvement, enabling governments to move from static compliance toward adaptive governance. To illustrate how DNS-compatible learning contrasts with conventional, project-based models, Table 8.3 summarizes key differences across major dimensions of governance practice.

### *8.4.4 Examples of Emerging Practice*

Despite limitations, there are encouraging examples of adaptive learning in the WB. In Kosovo, the Ministry of Economy has begun integrating lessons from donor-funded digital training initiatives into a national framework. These review sessions bring together municipalities, industry representatives, and diaspora actors, creating an early model of collective learning.

In Albania, the National Agency for Vocational Education and Training has initiated a tracer study system to monitor graduate employment outcomes. Though still at an early stage, it represents a pathway for linking training provision with labour market demand.

In North Macedonia, the FITD has established knowledge exchange forums where grantees share challenges and experiences. These forums have started to inform the design of new support schemes, moving towards a more iterative approach to policy learning.

While these cases remain partial and experimental, they demonstrate the feasibility of embedding learning even in low-capacity environments.

In the absence of structured feedback systems, development efforts risk becoming static and disconnected from real conditions. Without learning, reform fatigue sets in, and the same mistakes are repeated. The DNS framework provides a way to design governance systems that institutionalize learning, turning reflection and adaptation into regular practice.

For transitional states, progress should not be measured by replication of donor models but by the capacity to learn and adapt. Scaling through learning—rather than simple expansion—is essential for sustained capability development and long-term transformation.

## 8.5 Embeddedness and Relational Trust Across Ecosystems

Effective governance for capability development depends not only on formal institutions or well-crafted strategies but also on the quality of relationships among actors, the depth of mutual trust, and the degree to which institutions are anchored in their surrounding economic, social, and knowledge ecosystems. As discussed in earlier chapters, institutions that are not embedded in these networks struggle to coordinate effectively, gather feedback, or scale successful initiatives.

In many latecomer and transitional economies, policies often remain detached from the everyday realities of firms, municipalities, and intermediary organizations. When this disconnection persists, implementation becomes fragmented and adaptive learning is constrained. This section explores how embeddedness and relational trust function in Kosovo, Albania, and North Macedonia and how they enable, or limit, the practice of governance compatible with the DNS framework. It also considers the role of transnational actors, including donors and diaspora organizations, whose interventions can either strengthen or weaken embeddedness depending on their alignment with domestic systems.

### *8.5.1 Types and Levels of Embeddedness*

Evidence from the WB reveals three distinct forms of embeddedness that shape how governance operates in practice.

First, symbolic embeddedness occurs when participation is more formal than substantive. Consultation platforms may exist, but feedback is selectively incorporated or ignored. In Albania, for instance, regional development processes occasionally invite private sector participation, yet this input rarely influences the final policy design or resource allocation.

Second, transactional embeddedness is based on short-term, incentive-driven cooperation, often tied to donor project cycles. In Kosovo, firms engage in donor-funded digital skills programs but typically disengage once funding ends. These forms of collaboration are useful for short-term objectives but seldom build durable institutions or trust. Diaspora-led initiatives, while often more responsive to local needs, also risk remaining disconnected from national frameworks if they lack formal recognition or state partnership.

Third, relational embeddedness develops through repeated interaction, mutual adaptation, and shared goals. In North Macedonia, the FITD has cultivated such embeddedness by maintaining open communication, transparent selection criteria, and consistent engagement with universities, innovation hubs, and firms. Over

**Table 8.4** Typology of embeddedness in developmental governance

| Type of embeddedness | Defining features | Implications for governance |
|---|---|---|
| Symbolic | Formal inclusion without substantive influence | Low trust, limited feedback integration |
| Transactional | Instrumental cooperation based on external incentives | Partial coordination, unsustainable alignment |
| Relational | Trust-based, iterative collaboration with shared goals | High embeddedness, learning-oriented governance |

*Source* Author's elaboration based on Granovetter (1985), Evans (1995), and field evidence from Kosovo, Albania, and North Macedonia time, these practices have built trust and encouraged a culture of joint learning and problem-solving. The distinctions among these forms of embeddedness are summarized in Table 8.4.

This typology illustrates how deeper relational embeddedness generates not only greater trust but also more effective governance, enabling learning and sustained collaboration.

### *8.5.2 Relational Trust and Capability Formation*

Relational trust is central to coordination, experimentation, and capability formation. In settings characterized by limited administrative capacity and institutional volatility, formal rules alone cannot secure cooperation. Trust acts as a substitute for missing enforcement mechanisms by lowering transaction costs, fostering shared understanding, and encouraging actors to take risks on collaborative ventures (Kattel & Mazzucato, 2018).

In Kosovo, the Innovation and Training Park in Prizren provides an example of trust-based cooperation. Long before formal agreements were signed, diaspora entrepreneurs, local authorities, and donor representatives worked together on the basis of personal relationships and reputational credibility. These informal ties enabled sustained collaboration that extended beyond specific projects.

In Albania, efforts to establish dual vocational education and training (VET) systems have struggled precisely because trust between training providers and firms is weak. Public institutions often view private partners as self-interested, while firms see public providers as rigid and disconnected from market realities. Without credible intermediaries to bridge these perceptions, engagement remains shallow and inconsistent.

By contrast, North Macedonia's FITD has strengthened trust by ensuring transparency, responsiveness, and technical professionalism in its operations. Even unsuccessful applicants report willingness to remain engaged, which contributes to cumulative learning and enhances the legitimacy of the institution.

### *8.5.3 Embedding Governance in Ecosystems: Implications for DNS*

Within the DNS framework, embeddedness is not an abstract goal but a practical condition for effective governance, particularly in low-capacity environments. Where hierarchical institutions are weak, relational infrastructures—networks of trust, collaboration, and feedback—serve as the foundation for adaptive coordination.

Three principles guide this process:

1. Proximity over centralization. Governance becomes more effective when it is close to the problems it seeks to address. Local innovation councils, regional task forces, and municipal clusters create the dense interaction networks necessary for trust to grow.
2. Intermediaries as trust brokers. Chambers of commerce, diaspora groups, and research centers can act as bridges across sectors, aligning diverse interests and maintaining continuity through political change. Their effectiveness depends on credibility and neutrality as much as on formal mandates.
3. Time-consistent engagement. Trust requires continuity. Programs designed for repeated interaction and long-term collaboration are more likely to foster shared learning than short-term, project-based engagements.

These principles shift the focus from institutional design to institutional behaviour. Embeddedness is not about the existence of formal structures but about how institutions interact, adapt, and learn within their ecosystems.

Across the WB, embeddedness and trust remain underdeveloped but essential. Where relational capacity is weak, symbolic and transactional engagement dominate, leading to short-lived initiatives, limited feedback, and low institutional credibility. Strengthening relational embeddedness therefore demands more than procedural reform—it requires investing in processes that build trust through transparency, reciprocity, and repeated engagement.

The DNS framework treats embeddedness as a developmental asset: a means of transforming fragmented institutions into collaborative networks capable of collective learning and sustained transformation.

## 8.6 DNS in Practice and Comparative Reflections

The previous sections show that even in fragmented institutional environments, transitional economies can generate experimentation, partial learning, and moments of coordination. This section revisits the DNS framework and applies it to Kosovo, Albania, and North Macedonia. The aim is to assess how far its core governance functions—learning, coordination, and embeddedness—are emerging in practice, and to identify the pathways, mechanisms, and limits of networked governance under constraint.

None of the three countries represents a fully developed DNS. Instead, they display evolving and partial configurations of DNS-compatible practices. These practices do not arise from a single institutional design. They emerge from the cumulative interaction of actors, experiments, and relational infrastructures that enable problem solving across organizational boundaries.

The discussion proceeds in four parts. First, it outlines the operational pillars of the DNS as a benchmark. Second, it compares the three countries across these dimensions. Third, it identifies enabling and constraining conditions. Fourth, it reflects on broader lessons for capability development and governance reform in transitional contexts.

### 8.6.1 Operationalizing the DNS Through Coordination, Learning, and Embeddedness

The DNS is not a fixed institutional model. It is an analytical tool for identifying three interdependent governance functions.

Coordination is the capacity to align goals, actors, and resources across fragmented policy areas and institutional levels. It involves joint planning, problem-focused task forces, and multi-actor platforms that connect central and local government, the private sector, and civil society.

Learning is the ability to generate, absorb, and act upon feedback. It depends on adaptive planning, iterative evaluation, and mechanisms for knowledge exchange across sectors. Learning is both a technical and a political capability that strengthens institutional responsiveness.

Embeddedness is the relational dimension of governance. It describes how institutions connect to their wider ecosystems, sustain trust through repeated engagement, and adapt through networks that foster accountability and collective learning.

These functions evolve together. Weakness in one area constrains the others. The DNS framework therefore focuses on their interaction under conditions of limited capacity and political complexity.

### 8.6.2 Comparative Patterns Across Kosovo, Albania, and North Macedonia

All three countries demonstrate elements of DNS-compatible governance, although with different scope and intensity.

In Kosovo, the most dynamic developments are in ICT and digital skills. Initiatives such as the Innovation and Training Park in Prizren and the Kosovo Digital Economy Project show how municipalities, diaspora entrepreneurs, and donors can form collaborative ecosystems. Coordination is uneven but improving where joint financing and multi-actor working groups are used. Learning remains weakly institutionalized, although national digital strategies and inclusive evaluations indicate progress. Embeddedness is strongest where diaspora actors sustain long-term partnerships and trust-based networks. Without state mechanisms to integrate these lessons, part of this potential remains untapped.

**Table 8.5** Comparative assessment of DNS functions in practice

| Country | Coordination | Learning | Embeddedness |
|---|---|---|---|
| Kosovo | Municipal-donor-diaspora alignment in ICT and skills pilots | Weakly structured, improving via digital strategy efforts | Strong in diaspora-linked initiatives |
| Albania | Fragmented sectoral initiatives, weak horizontal coherence | Isolated pockets in VET sector, limited feedback use | Predominantly symbolic or transactional |
| North Macedonia | FITD as coordination hub in innovation policy | Structured feedback loops in innovation ecosystem | Relational trust building through FITD and academic networks |

*Source* Author's elaboration based on field evidence, strategy reviews, and programme assessments

Albania presents a more fragmented landscape. In agri-food and vocational education, donor dependence has encouraged project-based coordination with limited cross-sector coherence. Pilot projects are often short lived and disconnected from institutional feedback. DNS-like practices appear when donor objectives align with national strategies. Where alignment is absent, duplication and fragmentation persist.

North Macedonia offers the most consolidated example in innovation policy. The FITD acts as a coordination hub that links ministries, firms, and universities. It integrates feedback into funding cycles and collaborates with domestic and international partners without relying on a single donor. This approach is not yet widespread across policy areas, but it shows that institutional innovation is possible under constraint.

The comparative analysis of Kosovo, Albania, and North Macedonia can be summarized through the lens of the three DNS functions: coordination, learning, and embeddedness. Table 8.5 synthesizes these dimensions to show how each country exhibits different degrees of progress. It highlights areas where network-based governance is beginning to take root, as well as where fragmentation, weak feedback systems, and limited trust continue to constrain capability development.

### *8.6.3 Enabling and Constraining Conditions*

DNS-compatible practices reflect underlying political economy dynamics rather than chance. Several enabling factors stand out.

Credible intermediaries help bridge gaps between public and private actors. FITD in North Macedonia, diaspora organizations in Kosovo, and selected donor programs in Albania have provided platforms for alignment and learning.

Relational continuity allows trust and institutional memory to accumulate. In Kosovo, diaspora networks sustain long-term collaboration. In North Macedonia, stable staffing at FITD supports deeper relationships.

Strategic focus on innovation and digitalization creates space for experimentation. These domains are often less politicized than others and have enabled coalition building in Kosovo's digital initiatives and North Macedonia's SME innovation support.

Diaspora engagement provides trusted brokerage between global expertise and domestic institutions. When supported by municipal authorities or donor partnerships, these networks strengthen collaborative problem solving and knowledge transfer.

Several constraints limit the diffusion of DNS practices. Donor-driven fragmentation, short project cycles, and rigid compliance frameworks discourage coordination and local learning. Ministries are incentivized to pursue funds independently rather than through shared platforms. Donor initiatives may meet project targets but can weaken domestic ownership when success is measured by deliverables rather than institutional development. Political instability and patronage disrupt institutional learning and weaken intermediary bodies through turnover and politicized appointments. Lack of institutionalized feedback channels prevents lessons from pilots from informing broader reforms. Reports are produced but seldom discussed, and coordination meetings lack follow through. Global value chain dynamics in sectors such as automotive components and agri-food focus firms on compliance with lead-firm standards. Without mechanisms to translate firm-level experience into public strategy, learning remains isolated and fragmented.

These tensions illustrate the gap between pressures for modern governance and systems that reward short-term compliance over long-term coordination and learning.

### *8.6.4 Governing Under Constraint: Comparative Reflections*

The comparative evidence suggests that the DNS should be seen as an evolving logic of governance rather than a fully operational model. Its value lies in identifying where coordination, learning, and embeddedness take root, and where they remain absent. The framework helps capture incremental progress, institutional improvisation, and relational innovations within imperfect systems.

DNS-compatible governance often emerges from mid-level actors rather than top-down design. Municipal officials, donor liaisons, civil servants, and intermediary institutions connect otherwise separate parts of the system. Their effectiveness depends on informal trust and negotiation as much as on formal mandates.

Strategic sectors such as ICT, digital transformation, and innovation can serve as entry points for networked governance. These areas tend to be less burdened by legacy institutions and more open to collaborative experimentation. They provide spaces where DNS principles can be tested, refined, and extended to other sectors.

The DNS framework offers a practical way to govern under constraint. It does not promise to remove fragmentation. It works through it by emphasizing intermediaries, adaptive learning platforms, and trust-based collaboration. Donors, diaspora networks, and firms can strengthen or weaken these dynamics depending on how well their actions are embedded in national systems. Recognizing these interdependencies is essential for designing feasible, capability-oriented pathways to industrial transformation.

## 8.7 Conclusions: Meta-Capabilities and Development Under Imperfection

This chapter has shown that governance in the WB does not follow ideal institutional models. Instead, it operates through partial, adaptive, and context-specific arrangements. By moving from sectoral case studies to cross-cutting patterns, the analysis has examined how Kosovo, Albania, and North Macedonia coordinate, learn, and build trust in environments where administrative capacity is limited. These observations have been interpreted through the DNS framework, which views governance not as a fixed institutional design but as a dynamic system of interdependent functions.

The central argument is that capability development in late-industrializing economies requires a rethinking of what effective governance means. In contexts characterized by institutional fragmentation, strong donor influence, and uneven state capacity, the goal is not to replicate textbook versions of the developmental state. Rather, it is to cultivate governance functions that enable problem solving within imperfect conditions. Coordination, learning, and embeddedness should be understood as practical capabilities that can be designed, tested, and strengthened through experimentation and collaboration.

The WB cases demonstrate that institutional weakness alone does not prevent development. The real challenge lies in the absence of mechanisms that help fragmented actors align their actions, adapt their strategies, and engage in sustained, trust-based cooperation. Coordination remains limited not because collaboration is impossible, but because there are few institutional platforms to support it. Learning is underdeveloped not for lack of data, but because feedback systems are weak and continuity is fragile. Embeddedness is constrained not by unwillingness to cooperate, but by the absence of credible intermediaries and long-term engagement.

Each country nevertheless provides examples of emerging DNS-compatible governance. In Kosovo, diaspora-led digital initiatives have shown how municipalities, private actors, and donors can collaborate to create shared development platforms even without strong central coordination. In Albania, vocational education reforms have begun to institutionalize learning through tracer studies and curriculum reviews. In North Macedonia, the Fund for Innovation and

Technological Development has served as a coordinating hub that combines cross-sector trust with adaptive policy implementation.

These examples are not full models but hybrid forms of governance. They depend on the creativity of actors who find ways to collaborate despite political, administrative, or financial constraints. Together, they illustrate how governance in transitional settings evolves through what can be described as meta-capabilities.

Meta-capabilities are higher-order capacities that allow governance systems to integrate, adapt, and evolve across sectors and institutions. They are not confined to a single domain but operate at the system level, enabling governments to coordinate complex processes and respond to uncertainty. Within the DNS perspective, three meta-capabilities stand out.

- *Problem-driven coordination:* The ability to mobilize and align diverse actors around shared challenges through platforms, incentives, and monitoring systems that cross traditional boundaries.
- *Iterative learning:* The capacity to absorb feedback, learn from mistakes, and adjust policies based on evidence and reflection. This requires reflexive planning, transparent monitoring, and intermediaries that can translate knowledge into actionable insights.
- *Relational embeddedness:* The cultivation of trust-based relationships through repeated engagement, shared goals, and credible institutions that act as bridges between sectors.

When these meta-capabilities reinforce each other, governance systems become more flexible in responding to change, more coherent in scaling successful practices, and more adaptive in reorienting strategies as new challenges emerge.

The key insight is that development does not depend on perfect institutions, but on institutions capable of continuous improvement. Imperfection is not a barrier but a starting point. Although transitional states often lack strong bureaucracies, stable political coalitions, or extensive resources, they still possess actors, experiences, and experiments that can be built upon.

The DNS framework recognizes this reality. It does not call for strong state autonomy or donor withdrawal but for relational and adaptive governance embedded in networks of practice. Such governance must coordinate without relying solely on command, learn without excessive bureaucracy, and embed itself in social and economic ecosystems without falling into capture.

In this sense, the DNS should be understood not as a rigid model but as a vocabulary for describing how transformation occurs under constraint. It emphasizes the need for mechanisms that support local experimentation, institutions that connect distributed actors, and feedback systems that anchor learning within policy processes.

A recurring theme in this chapter is the paradox of fragmentation. While fragmentation weakens coherence, it also creates space for innovation and decentralized problem solving. The challenge is to connect these scattered initiatives through learning platforms, strategic coordination, and trust-based engagement. Without meta-capabilities, such efforts remain isolated and temporary. With them, they can form the basis for systemic upgrading.

The experiences of Kosovo's digital initiatives, Albania's donor-supported reforms, and North Macedonia's innovation ecosystem suggest that the components of a DNS can emerge even under imperfect conditions. The task ahead is to connect these components and transform them into enduring structures for capability development.

Achieving this will require policy communities that think beyond individual projects, donors that invest in governance processes rather than only technical outputs, and public institutions that treat collaboration and learning as central responsibilities.

Ultimately, the DNS framework helps identify and strengthen the governance capacities that make industrial transformation, skills upgrading, and innovation sustainable. It points to a pathway for development under constraint by acknowledging imperfections and turning them into opportunities for learning, adaptation, and systemic progress.

## References

Amsden, A. H. (1989). *Asia's next giant: South Korea and late industrialization*. Oxford University Press. Available via Oxford Academic. https://academic.oup.com/book/10201

Andrews, M., Pritchett, L., & Woolcock, M. (2017). *Building state capability: Evidence, analysis, action*. Oxford University Press. Available at https://bsc.cid.harvard.edu/book/building-state-capability

Bartlett, W. (2020). International assistance, donor interests, and state capture in the Western Balkans, *Journal of Contemporary European Studies*, *29*(2), 184–200. https://doi.org/10.1080/14782804.2020.1794801

Cleaver, F. (2012). *Development through bricolage: Rethinking institutions for natural resource management*. Routledge. https://doi.org/10.4324/9781315094915

Elster, J., Offe, C., & Preuss, U. K. (1998). *Institutional design in post-communist societies: Rebuilding the ship at Sea*. Cambridge University Press. https://doi.org/10.1017/CBO9780511628351

ETF. (2021). *Key indicators on education, skills and employment 2021: Western Balkans*. European Training Foundation. Available at https://www.etf.europa.eu/sites/default/files/2021-11/kiese_2021.pdf. Accessed 19 July 2025.

Evans, P. (1995). *Embedded autonomy: States and industrial transformation*. Princeton University Press.

Granovetter, M. (1985). Economic action and social structure: The problem of embeddedness. *American Journal of Sociology*, *91*(3), 481–510. https://doi.org/10.1086/228311

Helmke, G., & Levitsky, S. (2004). Informal institutions and comparative politics: A research Agenda. *Perspectives on Politics*, *2*(4), 725–740. https://doi.org/10.1017/S1537592704040472

Kattel, R., & Mazzucato, M. (2018). Mission-oriented innovation policy and dynamic capabilities in the public sector. *Industrial and Corporate Change*, *27*(5), 787–801. https://doi.org/10.1093/icc/dty032

Khan, M. H. (2018). Political settlements and the analysis of institutions. *African Affairs*, *117* (469), 636–655. https://doi.org/10.1093/afraf/adx044

Laws, E., & Marquette, H. (2018). *Thinking and working politically: Reviewing the evidence on the integration of politics into development practice over the past decade*, ODI Working Paper. Available at https://odi.org/en/publications/thinking-and-working-politically-reviewing-the-evidence-on-the-integration-of-politics-into-development-practice-over-the-past-decade/. Acces sed July 2025.

Olivier de Sardan, J. P. (2011). The eight modes of governance: Informal governance in the real world. *IDS Bulletin*, *42*(2), 22–31. https://doi.org/10.1111/j.1759-5436.2011.00208.x

# Chapter 9
# Digital Technologies, AI, and New Frontiers in Technological Upgrading

The global pace of technological change is accelerating. Digitalization, artificial intelligence (AI), and platform-based business models are reshaping how industries produce, trade, and innovate. For latecomer economies, these transformations bring both opportunity and risk. They offer new avenues for productivity growth and innovation but also carry the potential to deepen dependency, widen skills gaps, and reinforce structural inequalities.

In the Western Balkans (WB), digital transformation is taking place within fragmented industrial systems and modest state capacity. Public institutions often struggle to coordinate across sectors, while firms face obstacles in accessing finance, knowledge, and technology. These conditions make digitalization a double-edged process: it can create pathways for integration into global markets but also entrench peripheral participation in global value chains if learning and capability development do not advance at the same pace.

This chapter explores how countries in the region can navigate this tension and turn digital transformation into a driver of development. It examines how global technological trends, particularly digitalization and AI, are reshaping the possibilities for industrial upgrading in latecomer economies. It considers the kinds of capabilities that firms and institutions must develop to use these technologies effectively and investigates how governance systems can foster coordination, learning, and adaptation in the face of rapid technological change.

The central argument is that digital transformation is not only a technological process but also a governance challenge. Infrastructure investment and regulatory reform, while important, are insufficient on their own. What is required is a form of adaptive governance that links digital investment to capability formation, encourages experimentation, and builds mechanisms for feedback and collaboration. Drawing on the Developmental Network State (DNS) framework introduced earlier in the book, this chapter presents adaptive governance as a practical approach to managing technological change through coordination, learning, and institutional responsiveness.



F. Sahiti, *Catching Up in the Digital Age*, Contributions to Economics,
https://doi.org/10.1007/978-3-032-17059-0_9

The discussion begins by analysing global patterns of technological change and their implications for capability development in latecomer economies. It then examines how AI and digital platforms can serve as enablers of learning and innovation while also creating new forms of dependency. The chapter goes on to develop the concept of adaptive governance for emerging technologies and explores how it might be applied in the WB. It concludes by proposing the idea of a learning state that integrates digitalization into long-term strategies for inclusive and sustainable development.

## 9.1 Technological Change and Implications for Capabilities

Digital technologies, including AI, data-driven business models, and global platforms, are transforming how value is created, captured, and distributed (Baldwin, 2019; Brynjolfsson & McAfee, 2014). These shifts are accelerating productivity growth, reorganizing global value chains (GVCs), and creating both opportunities and new pressures for late-industrializing economies (UNCTAD, 2021).

For the WB, where industrial structures remain fragmented, state capacity is limited, and innovation systems are still developing, the digital transition presents a familiar paradox. On one hand, it can lower barriers to market entry, open global niches for innovation, and allow firms to bypass traditional constraints to upgrading. On the other hand, it can deepen dependency on external platforms, reinforce low-value positions in GVCs, and widen gaps in skills and institutional capacity (Yoruk et al., 2023).

The notion of "leapfrogging" has often been used to describe the idea that latecomer economies can skip traditional stages of industrialization by adopting advanced technologies (World Bank, 2021). While attractive, this view often underestimates the structural foundations needed for sustained progress. Without consistent investment in education, infrastructure, and institutional coordination, leapfrogging can reproduce inequality rather than reduce it (Gereffi, 2019). Platform-based business models and proprietary AI systems add further risks, such as data dependency, market concentration, and the erosion of local innovation ecosystems (Kenney & Zysman, 2016; Srnicek, 2017).

This section examines how digital transformation affects capability development in the WB. It identifies four foundational conditions that determine whether technological change promotes upgrading or reinforces marginalization: human capital, institutional coherence, infrastructure readiness, and firm-level absorptive capacity. These reflect the perspective of the DNS, which views governance as a meta-capability. In this framework, the key determinant of progress is not simply the presence of technology, but the ability to adapt, coordinate, and embed innovation within broader development strategies.

Digital tools can enhance productivity, stimulate innovation, and expand market access, especially in services, logistics, and manufacturing (Baldwin, 2019;

Brynjolfsson & McAfee, 2014). In the WB, digital platforms have connected freelancers and micro-enterprises to international clients, while early applications of AI are emerging in e-governance and language technologies (UNCTAD, 2021). These developments have raised hopes that digitalization can accelerate structural transformation.

Yet, the benefits remain unevenly distributed. Firms and individuals with access to infrastructure, institutional support, and skilled labour are best positioned to benefit (Yoruk et al., 2023). Others risk being left behind. According to the Regional Cooperation Council and OECD (OECD, 2025; RCC, 2022), while more than 85% of the WB population has internet access, approximately 34% possess basic digital skills such as using spreadsheets or collaborating online. Rural populations are especially disadvantaged due to weak connectivity, affordability issues, and lower digital literacy (World Bank, 2021).

Firm-level differences compound these inequalities. Larger, export-oriented, and foreign-owned firms are far more likely to adopt digital tools and participate in digital GVCs. In contrast, many domestic SMEs lack the resources, knowledge, or incentives to digitalize. This has created a fragmented technological landscape, with large disparities in productivity, innovation, and market participation (Gereffi, 2019; OECD, 2023).

Platform economies add another layer of complexity. Digital work platforms such as Upwork and Fiverr have expanded income opportunities, yet they centralize control, impose opaque rules, and extract a large share of value. For freelancers and entrepreneurs in the WB, these platforms enable market access but offer little scope for local learning or value capture (Kenney & Zysman, 2016; Srnicek, 2017).

Table 9.1 summarizes this duality, showing how digitalization can create opportunities for innovation and inclusion, while also posing risks of dependency and exclusion if capability-building strategies are absent.

In summary, digital transformation in the WB presents both promise and peril. Without sustained investment in institutions, skills, and governance systems that promote inclusion, new technologies may reinforce existing divides. The challenge

**Table 9.1** Digital transformation in the WB, opportunity vs. risk

| Enabling potential | Constraining risks |
|---|---|
| Low entry barriers and scalability | Digital divide and unequal access |
| Global market access via digital platforms | Platform dependency and market asymmetry |
| Leapfrogging traditional stages of industrial growth | Skills gaps and low absorptive capacity |
| Niche innovation with modest capital requirements | Structural lock-in and limited local value capture |
| AI-enhanced productivity in services and logistics | Proprietary algorithms and data sovereignty concerns |

*Source* Author's synthesis based on key sources including Brynjolfsson and McAfee (2014), Gereffi (2019), UNCTAD (2021), and OECD (2023)

is not only to adopt digital tools, but to embed them in governance frameworks that foster coordination, learning, and broad-based capability development.

## 9.2 Digitalization and Its Implications for Capability Development

The promise of digitalization depends on more than access to technology. It requires the ability to build and continuously upgrade the capabilities that make technology productive. For the WB, this means long-term investment in four interconnected domains: human capital, institutional coherence, infrastructure readiness, and firm-level absorptive capacity. Without progress in these areas, digitalization is likely to entrench existing structural weaknesses rather than overcome them.

These four domains are mutually reinforcing. Skills development underpins technological adoption, while institutional and infrastructural readiness provide the framework and tools through which firms can innovate. Absorptive capacity determines whether firms can translate access to technology and knowledge into sustained productivity growth. Finally, integration into GVCs provides the context in which these capabilities interact, shaping whether digitalization drives upgrading or dependency.

### *9.2.1 Human Capital and Skills Development*

A shortage of skilled workers is one of the most immediate obstacles to digital transformation. Education systems in the region have been slow to respond to the demands of a digital economy, and skills mismatches are common, especially in AI-related fields such as data science, programming, and cybersecurity (ETF, 2023). Although internet use is widespread, only about one-third of the population has basic digital skills (RCC, 2022).

Performance varies across countries. Kosovo and North Macedonia perform slightly better (35–36%) than Albania (29%), but all remain far below the EU average of 56%. Figure 9.1 illustrates these disparities, showing how far the region lags behind EU benchmarks.

Skill gaps are widest among older citizens, rural populations, and disadvantaged groups. VET systems are underfunded and poorly aligned with labour-market needs. Initiatives such as the Regional Challenge Fund support work-based learning, but outdated curricula, limited teacher training, and inadequate digital infrastructure continue to slow progress. Without targeted investment in education and lifelong learning, the divide between digital insiders and outsiders will continue to grow.

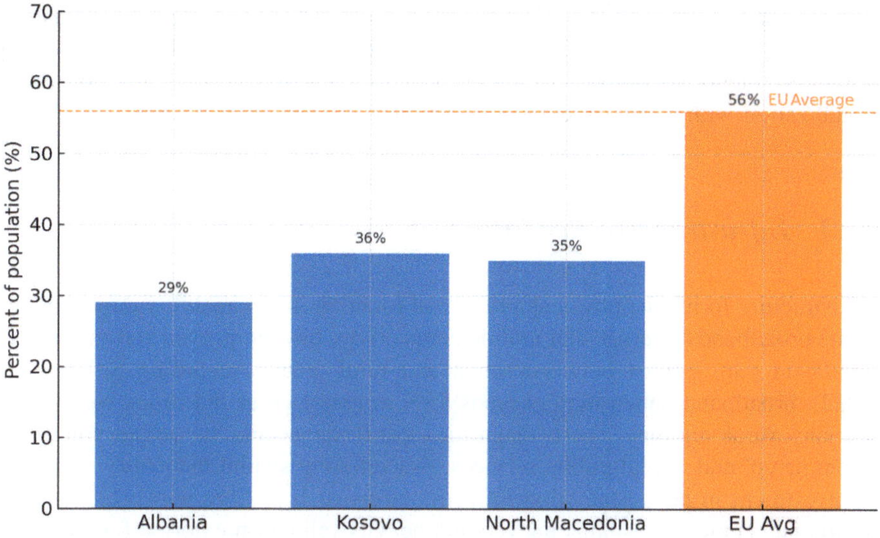


**Fig. 9.1** Basic digital skills in the Western Balkans. *Source* RCC (2022), Western Balkans Digital Economy and Society Index (WB DESI) Report. Available at: https://www.rcc.int/pubs/159

### *9.2.2 Institutional Coherence*

Institutional coherence refers to the degree to which policies, regulations, and governance structures operate in a coordinated and adaptive manner to support technological transformation. In the WB, fragmented governance and overlapping mandates often undermine digitalization efforts. Ministries responsible for economy, education, innovation, and ICT frequently operate in silos, resulting in inconsistencies between digital strategies, industrial policies, and skills initiatives (OECD, 2023). The absence of effective coordination mechanisms limits policy learning and the ability to align investment priorities with long-term development goals.

Several economies in the region have adopted digital strategies aligned with EU frameworks such as the Digital Agenda for the WB and the EU's Digital Single Market. However, implementation has been uneven. Weak inter-ministerial coordination, limited fiscal space, and short political cycles hinder continuity. For example, while Serbia and North Macedonia have established innovation funds and e-governance bodies, their integration with industrial and education policies remains limited (World Bank, 2021).

Institutional coherence also involves engaging firms, universities, civil society, and local governments in collective learning processes. In the WB, these linkages remain underdeveloped. Policy design tends to be top-down, with limited consultation or feedback mechanisms. Strengthening coherence therefore requires more than administrative reform; it calls for governance systems capable of coordination, adaptation, and experimentation—core attributes of what the DNS framework defines as meta-capabilities. Building such systems is essential for embedding digitalization within inclusive and sustainable development strategies.

### *9.2.3 Infrastructure Readiness*

Infrastructure forms the physical and digital foundation of capability development. While broadband coverage and mobile connectivity have improved across the WB, significant gaps persist between urban and rural areas. According to the RCC (2022), broadband penetration exceeds 85% in major cities but drops below 50% in many rural regions. These disparities constrain access to online education, e-commerce, and digital public services, exacerbating spatial inequality.

Investment in next-generation infrastructure—such as fibre networks, 5G, and secure data centres—remains uneven and heavily reliant on external funding. The European Bank for Reconstruction and Development's *Go Digital in the Western Balkans* initiative (EBRD, 2025) represents an important step toward closing connectivity gaps and supporting SME digitalization. However, private-sector participation is often limited by small market size, high investment risks, and weak regulatory incentives.

Beyond connectivity, infrastructure readiness includes data governance, cybersecurity, and cloud capacity. Many WB countries lack national data centres and depend on foreign cloud providers, raising concerns about data sovereignty and privacy (OECD, 2023). Public-sector digital infrastructure—such as e-government platforms—has expanded, but interoperability and security standards vary widely. Addressing these challenges requires long-term public investment, effective regulatory frameworks, and partnerships that ensure equitable access to infrastructure benefits.

### *9.2.4 Firm-Level Absorptive Capacity*

Firm-level absorptive capacity—the ability to acquire, assimilate, and apply new knowledge—is a crucial determinant of how digital transformation translates into productivity gains and innovation. In the WB, this capacity is highly uneven. Larger, export-oriented, and foreign-owned firms are generally more capable of adopting advanced digital tools, engaging in R&D, and integrating into digital global value chains (Reiter & Stehrer, 2021). By contrast, many domestic SMEs operate with limited managerial capabilities, weak technological bases, and minimal engagement with research or training institutions (Cirera et al., 2022).

Low levels of investment in skills and innovation reduce firms' ability to benefit from digitalization. Surveys indicate that fewer than 20% of SMEs in the region use cloud computing or advanced analytics, compared with over 40% in the EU (OECD, 2023). Financial constraints, information gaps, and risk aversion further discourage experimentation. Even when foreign direct investment brings technology spillovers, weak supplier linkages and limited local R&D capacity prevent broad diffusion.

Building absorptive capacity requires policies that strengthen firm-level learning mechanisms. This includes expanding access to digital advisory services, incentivizing collaboration between firms and universities, and supporting cluster-based initiatives that encourage knowledge sharing. Within the DNS perspective, firm-level learning is not an isolated process but one embedded in wider governance systems that coordinate investment, build trust, and sustain continuous upgrading. Without such embeddedness, digitalization risks deepening the divide between a small group of competitive firms and a larger pool of technologically marginalized enterprises.

### *9.2.5 Integration Into Global Value Chains*

Integration into GVCs remains a central pathway for technology diffusion and capability upgrading in the WB. However, participation alone does not guarantee learning or structural transformation. Most WB firms occupy low-value segments of GVCs—primarily in assembly, subcontracting, and routine services—where opportunities for technological upgrading are limited (Reiter & Stehrer, 2021). Foreign direct investment has supported some technology transfer, but weak linkages between MNEs and local suppliers have constrained broader spillovers (Cirera et al., 2022).

The benefits of GVC participation depend critically on domestic absorptive capacity and the strength of local innovation systems. When firms possess the skills, managerial competencies, and institutional support to internalize external knowledge, integration can foster diversification, learning, and productivity growth. In the absence of these capabilities, however, digitalization may reinforce dependency on foreign technologies and platforms, deepening structural asymmetries.

Policies that link GVC participation with capability development are therefore essential. This includes promoting supplier-development programmes, supporting R&D partnerships between MNEs and domestic firms, and aligning investment incentives with upgrading objectives. Regional cooperation mechanisms, such as the Common Regional Market initiative and EU-supported value-chain projects, can also enhance regional integration and attract knowledge-intensive investment (OECD, 2023).

From the perspective of the DNS framework, GVC integration should not be seen as an end in itself but as a governance challenge—one that requires coordination across firms, institutions, and sectors. Effective governance can align industrial, education, and innovation policies to ensure that participation in global production networks contributes to the development of dynamic capabilities rather than reinforcing peripheral dependence.

In summary, these five subsections indicate that the digital transformation of the WB hinges not merely on technology adoption but on the capacity to govern, learn, and coordinate across multiple levels. Human capital, institutional coherence, infrastructure readiness, and firm-level learning form the foundation upon which successful GVC integration and sustained upgrading can occur. Building these meta-capabilities is essential for turning digitalization from a temporary opportunity into a foundation for long-term, inclusive development.

## 9.3 AI and Digital Platforms as Capability Enablers

AI and digital platforms are reshaping the global economy by transforming how value is created, distributed, and captured. As general-purpose technologies, they can enhance productivity, stimulate innovation, and open new forms of participation in global markets. For smaller firms and latecomer economies, they offer tools to overcome traditional barriers to growth. However, their benefits are unevenly distributed and depend on the presence of key foundations: skilled human capital, robust digital infrastructure, coherent institutions, and adaptive governance (Brynjolfsson & McAfee, 2014; UNCTAD, 2021).

In the WB, where economies are still shaped by the legacies of post-socialist transition and fragmented policymaking, AI and digital platforms present both opportunities and risks. They can help firms enter international markets, automate labor-intensive processes, and innovate in data-driven niches without the heavy investment typical of traditional industries (World Bank, 2021; OECD, 2023). Yet capturing these benefits requires capabilities that remain underdeveloped across much of the region, particularly in skills, infrastructure, and institutional coordination (Yoruk et al., 2023).

The rise of global platforms such as Amazon, Meta, and Upwork has redefined how firms and workers in the WB access markets and generate income. These platforms offer visibility and flexibility but also impose asymmetrical relationships. Their algorithms determine visibility and pricing, their fees reduce local earnings, and their dominance limits opportunities for domestic value retention and innovation (Kenney & Zysman, 2016; Srnicek, 2017). AI technologies pose similar dilemmas: proprietary algorithms, costly infrastructure, and data dependence often reinforce reliance on firms in the Global North (UNCTAD, 2021).

The key question for the WB is not whether to adopt AI and platforms but how to govern them strategically. What institutional, policy, and learning frameworks can ensure that these technologies foster capability development and inclusion rather than deepen dependency? The answer lies in strengthening absorptive capacity—the ability of firms and institutions to acquire, adapt, and apply external knowledge productively (Crespi & Zuniga, 2012; Yoruk et al., 2023).

This section analyses the evolving landscape of AI and platform use in the WB. It argues that while these technologies can enable upgrading, their transformative potential will only be realized through coordinated investment in education, infrastructure, policy coherence, and innovation systems. Without these, digitalization risks reinforcing existing structural weaknesses.

### *9.3.1 Current Landscape of AI and Digital Platforms in the Western Balkans*

AI adoption across the WB remains limited and fragmented. Most initiatives are exploratory, often donor-funded or driven by diaspora-led startups rather than embedded in national innovation systems.

North Macedonia has made the most structured progress. Its National AI Strategy (2022) outlines goals for AI use in public administration, education, healthcare, and industry (OECD, 2023). The NGO AI NOW has been pivotal in promoting AI literacy and ethical standards, developing the first open-source large language model (LLM) for the Macedonian language. This initiative demonstrates how investment in localized data and applied research can generate indigenous innovation capacity (AI NOW, 2023).

Kosovo's AI ecosystem is largely informal, led by diaspora-founded startups working on translation, predictive maintenance, and marketing analytics. These firms benefit from donor support but operate without a national AI strategy or coordinating body, limiting their scalability and sustainability (RCC, 2022).

In Albania, AI experimentation has emerged mainly within civil society and the public sector. The Albanian Institute of Science has piloted AI tools to enhance transparency in public procurement. Yet without a coherent national AI policy, such initiatives remain small and disconnected (OECD, 2023; World Bank, 2024).

A critical barrier across all three countries is weak data infrastructure. AI development relies on large, clean, and interoperable datasets, but data systems in the WB are fragmented and poorly governed. Limited investment in data management, privacy regulation, and interoperability constrains the creation of locally relevant AI applications (UNCTAD, 2021; OECD, 2023).

Nonetheless, momentum is building. EU programmes such as the *Digital Europe Programme* and the *EU4Digital initiative for the Western Balkans* provide funding and technical assistance to strengthen digital capacity, infrastructure, and skills development. The challenge now is less about accessing support and more about developing the institutional and political capacity to use it effectively. Table 9.2 summarizes the comparative position of the three economies.

**Table 9.2** Comparative overview of AI adoption in the WB (2024)

| Country | National AI strategy | Notable initiatives | Data ecosystem status | Institutional coordination |
|---|---|---|---|---|
| North Macedonia | ✓ Published (2022) | AI NOW; Macedonian LLM | Weak but improving | Moderate |
| Kosovo | ✗ None | Diaspora-led startups; AI for translation | Fragmented and donor-reliant | Low |
| Albania | ✗ None | AIS procurement transparency pilots | Fragmented and underdeveloped | Low |

*Source* Author's synthesis based on OECD (2023); RCC (2022, 2023); World Bank (2024); AI NOW (2023)

## 9.3.2 *Challenges in Leveraging AI and Digital Platforms*

The potential of AI and digital platforms to foster capability development in the WB is limited by three systemic challenges: infrastructure deficits, regulatory and ethical gaps, and shortages of skilled human capital.

### 9.3.2.1 Infrastructure and Connectivity

Connectivity remains uneven. While broadband and mobile coverage have improved in urban centres, rural areas lag by up to 30 percentage points (RCC, 2022). This gap restricts access to education, digital services, and innovation (OECD, 2023). The European Bank for Reconstruction and Development's "Go Digital in the Western Balkans" programme, launched in 2025 with a budget of €377 million ($417 million), aims to accelerate SME digitalisation, automation, and green innovation, supported by EU grants, (EBRD, 2025). However, progress has been slow due to bureaucratic hurdles, overlapping responsibilities, and weak local implementation capacity. Investments are concentrated in urban areas, which risks deepening spatial inequality.

### 9.3.2.2 Regulatory Frameworks and Ethical Considerations

Regulatory frameworks across the region are outdated and fragmented. Data protection laws are inconsistently enforced, and few mechanisms exist for ethical oversight of AI use. Platform workers typically operate outside formal labour protections (ILO, 2023). Efforts to align with EU regulations, including the AI Act and the Digital Services Act, are ongoing but hindered by limited expertise and institutional coordination.

Governance of data infrastructure remains a major weakness. Few standards exist for data ownership, consent, or cross-border sharing, which limits the development of trustworthy and context-specific AI systems (Yoruk et al., 2023).

#### 9.3.2.3 Skills and Human Capital

AI and platform use depend heavily on a skilled workforce. Yet education systems across the WB have not kept pace with technological change. Curricula are outdated, practical training opportunities are scarce, and cooperation between universities and industry is limited (ETF, 2023). Some universities in Kosovo and North Macedonia now offer AI-related courses, but participation remains small and concentrated in major cities.

Talent retention is another major challenge. Many qualified professionals emigrate for better career opportunities, leaving domestic institutions understaffed and reliant on foreign expertise (World Bank, 2024). Table 9.3 summarizes these structural constraints.

### *9.3.3 Strategic Opportunities for Capability Development*

Although the WB face significant structural challenges, these barriers are not insurmountable. Well-designed and inclusive policies can build the foundations for digital transformation that benefits the wider population. Inclusion in this context means ensuring that all social groups—across gender, geography, and socioeconomic lines—participate in and benefit from technological change.

Three interlinked areas are central to capability development: education and training, innovation ecosystems, and regional cooperation. These are mutually reinforcing and together form the basis of an inclusive digital strategy.

#### 9.3.3.1 Enhancing Education and Training

Education and training are the cornerstones of digital transformation. Across the WB, education systems remain poorly aligned with labour market needs, and

**Table 9.3** Structural challenges to AI and digital platform adoption in the WB

| Challenge area | Core issues | Core issues |
|---|---|---|
| Infrastructure & connectivity | Rural-urban digital divide; limited broadband and data infrastructure | Excludes peripheral regions; undermines equitable digital access |
| Regulatory & ethical gaps | Absence of AI laws, weak data protection, no institutional oversight | Increases risk of misuse, algorithmic bias, and technological lock-in |
| Skills & human capital | AI talent shortages; outdated curricula; brain drain | Limits domestic innovation; deepens dependency on foreign expertise |

*Source* Author's synthesis based on OECD (2023); RCC (2022); UNCTAD (2021); World Bank (2024); ETF (2023)

digital and AI literacy are unevenly developed (OECD, 2023; ETF, 2023). Curriculum reform should integrate computational thinking, digital problem-solving, and applied skills at all levels of education.

Pilot initiatives, such as university AI programmes in North Macedonia, represent progress but remain small-scale. Expanding these efforts requires stronger partnerships between education providers, private firms, and public institutions. These partnerships can align curricula with market demand, expand internships and apprenticeships, and link learning with clear career pathways.

Informal training models such as ICT bootcamps in Kosovo have helped address short-term needs but are donor-dependent and weakly connected to formal education systems (RCC, 2022). Long-term transformation requires national frameworks that integrate these initiatives and ensure recognition of skills through modular certifications and micro-credentials.

#### 9.3.3.2 Fostering Innovation Ecosystems

Innovation ecosystems convert skills into productivity and entrepreneurship. Innovation hubs, incubators, and research centres are vital for linking knowledge to application. North Macedonia's Fund for Innovation and Technological Development (FITD) and Kosovo's Innovation and Training Park (ITP) are early examples of this approach. Yet the region lacks the institutional scale, financing, and policy coherence needed to sustain such ecosystems (OECD, 2023).

Building a robust AI entrepreneurship ecosystem requires targeted incentives such as tax credits, R&D grants, and access to venture capital. Collaboration between startups, universities, and established firms can stimulate joint learning and accelerate technology transfer. Regional cooperation can further amplify these benefits by pooling resources and harmonizing fragmented policies (European Commission, 2022).

#### 9.3.3.3 Strengthening Regional Cooperation

Given the small size of national markets, regional cooperation is essential for achieving scale in digital transformation. Shared frameworks for AI adoption and digital governance can help harmonize regulations, pool expertise, and attract investment.

Initiatives like the *Digital Agenda for the Western Balkans* and the *Berlin Process* provide platforms for collaboration on infrastructure, skills, and policy alignment (European Commission, 2022). A region-wide AI ethics framework could strengthen accountability and align the WB with EU standards, while regional innovation platforms and cloud infrastructures could support cross-border experimentation.

A WB AI Observatory could monitor trends, map capability gaps, and coordinate donor activities. Similarly, an annual Digital Innovation Forum under the RCC could promote peer learning and dialogue among policymakers, firms, and researchers.

Regional cooperation is not optional but fundamental. It reduces duplication, spreads costs, and enhances the region's bargaining power with global platforms and international partners.

Education reform, innovation ecosystem development, and regional cooperation form the essential foundations for inclusive digital transformation in the WB. Implementing these measures requires a governance approach capable of coordinating fragmented institutions, managing uncertainty, and promoting continuous learning. The next section introduces adaptive governance as a flexible framework that can help countries with limited administrative capacity steer technological change through experimentation, coordination, and feedback.

## 9.4 Adaptive Governance for Emerging Technologies

The preceding analysis shows that AI and digital platforms offer real opportunities for technological upgrading in the WB, yet their integration is constrained by gaps in infrastructure, regulation, and human capital. In this environment, conventional industrial policy models that rely on centralized coordination and long planning cycles often fall short. They assume stable conditions and strong institutions, which are rarely present where technologies and markets change quickly.

This section introduces adaptive governance as a complementary framework to the DNS. It explains how governments with limited administrative capacity can still engage productively with emerging technologies by fostering experimentation, promoting cross-sector coordination, and investing in institutional learning. Adaptive governance does not replace strategy with improvisation. It provides a flexible and iterative process that allows the DNS functions of learning, coordination, and embeddedness to operate under conditions of uncertainty and fragmentation.

### *9.4.1 Conceptual Foundations of Adaptive Governance*

Latecomer economies struggle to match the speed and uncertainty of technological change. Rapid shifts in AI, platform economies, and data-intensive systems expose the limits of fixed policy blueprints and static institutions.

Adaptive governance offers an alternative. It is a flexible, iterative mode of policymaking that prioritizes learning, experimentation, and responsiveness (Rodrik, 2008; Sabel & Zeitlin, 2012). Rather than assuming clear goals and predictable outcomes, it accepts the ambiguity that surrounds emerging technology sectors. Policy evolves through pilot programs, stakeholder engagement, feedback loops, and cross-sector collaboration.

This approach contrasts with passive adoption strategies that import regulatory models, follow donor templates, or rely on market self-correction. Such practices often lead to shallow implementation, weak local ownership, and missed learning opportunities (UNCTAD, 2021). Adaptive governance requires an active, evolving state role, even if that role is provisional and distributed.

Its relevance is strongest in fast-moving domains such as AI, platform economies, and digital labour markets, where technical complexity intersects with unresolved ethical and social questions. Static regulations quickly lag behind, either constraining innovation or failing to manage risk. Adaptive systems create structured space for trial and error, timely feedback, and collective revision (Kenney & Zysman, 2016; European Commission, 2022).

The framework aligns closely with the DNS. The DNS provides the structural scaffolding for networked development. Adaptive governance supplies the procedural tools for implementation under uncertainty. Both reject the notion of an omniscient state and instead view governance as embedded experimentation in which policy evolves through collaboration and continuous learning. This is well suited to the WB, where institutional fragmentation coexists with active municipalities, diaspora networks, universities, and private firms.

In short, adaptive governance is not a substitute for strategic vision. It is the means by which a capability-cantered model like the DNS can operate in complex, resource-constrained environments. It enables flexibility without loss of direction and responsiveness without disorder, allowing states to shape technological change while building trust, institutional capacity, and resilience over time.

## 9.4.2 Challenges of Governing in Weak-Capacity Contexts

The case for adaptive governance in the WB is strong, but application faces clear obstacles. Governance systems still reflect legacies of post-socialist transition. They are formally decentralized, yet fragmented, donor-dependent, and uneven in execution. These limitations are acute in digital policy, where effective action depends on agility, technical expertise, and cross-sector coordination that are not evenly distributed (OECD, 2023).

Institutional fragmentation is a central constraint. Ministries responsible for the economy, education, labour, digitalization, and public administration often hold overlapping mandates and lack a shared strategic vision. National digital agendas, skills strategies, and AI frameworks are developed in parallel, which produces duplication and weak alignment. Political turnover disrupts continuity, reduces reform momentum, and discourages bureaucratic learning. Many initiatives stay tied to short project cycles rather than becoming part of institutional routines.

Donor fragmentation compounds these issues. External assistance has supported important reforms, yet it is frequently project-based, externally designed, and weakly integrated with national plans. Pilots in skills training, digital infrastructure, and regulatory reform have produced useful results, but scale-up and institutionalization are rare (RCC, 2022). Without coordinated donor frameworks, opportunities for system learning and sustained reform are lost.

Mechanisms for policy experimentation and feedback are also scarce. Regulatory sandboxes, pilot schemes with clear exit criteria, and learning-oriented monitoring are the exception. Once adopted, digital strategies tend to remain static, with little scope for course correction. In domains like AI and platform work, rigidity quickly produces outdated policies that cannot respond to new developments.

The costs of inaction or inflexible responses are high. Without adaptive mechanisms, governments risk policy paralysis or lock-in to outdated approaches, which reinforces dependence on low-value activities in global value chains and digital ecosystems. Many firms remain confined to outsourced services or platform-based freelancing with limited opportunities for upgrading (Gereffi, 2019; World Bank, 2024). Over time, reliance on external technologies and standards further limits the ability of states to steer innovation.

These challenges point to a needed shift in mindset and method, from rigid planning toward a governance culture that values collaboration, feedback, and continuous learning.

### *9.4.3 Principles of Adaptive Governance for Digital Transformation*

Adaptive governance gives latecomer states a practical way to engage with digital transformation through approaches that are iterative, inclusive, and context sensitive. The following four principles are particularly relevant for the WB.

Iterative learning. Digital policy should evolve through cycles of experimentation, feedback, and adjustment. Pilot programs, performance monitoring, and real-time evidence allow strategies to adapt as conditions change (Sabel & Zeitlin, 2012). Regulatory sandboxes can test AI applications in controlled settings before wider deployment. In North Macedonia, an open-source language model pilot generated insights on technical design, institutional readiness, and public engagement. In Kosovo, skills bootcamps and diaspora-led accelerators have adjusted curricula in response to employer feedback. Embedding similar mechanisms into national strategies would strengthen responsiveness across the region.

Multi-actor coordination. Collaboration among ministries, firms, universities, donors, and civil society is essential in fragmented systems. Digital skills councils that align vocational training with labour market needs, diaspora entrepreneurship hubs that link global expertise to local firms, and municipal innovation forums can reduce duplication, build trust, and turn isolated pilots into institutional routines (OECD, 2023).

Institutional flexibility. Digital strategies must be adjustable. Fixed targets without mid-course review stall progress. Allowing for local experimentation, for

**Table 9.4** Principles of adaptive governance in the Western Balkans

| Principle | Core focus | Western Balkans Example |
|---|---|---|
| Iterative Learning | Experimentation, feedback loops, pilot-based governance | Kosovo's digital skills bootcamps; North Macedonia's AI LLM pilot |
| Multi-Actor Coordination | Cross-sector collaboration and inclusive co-creation | Digital skills councils (North Macedonia); diaspora-driven ICT hubs |
| Institutional Flexibility | Avoiding policy rigidity; allowing for contextual adjustment | Albania's e-procurement pilot reforms; local-level tech labs |
| Strategic Foresight | Horizon scanning, scenario planning, anticipatory policy | Digital Agenda for WB foresight efforts; AI NOW awareness programs |

*Source* Author's synthesis based on OECD (2023); RCC (2022, 2023) World Bank (2024); AI NOW (2023); Sabel and Zeitlin (2012)

example municipal service pilots or donor-supported innovation labs, encourages agility. Practices such as prototyping, short iteration cycles, and user feedback loops improve public service design without requiring comprehensive reform.

Strategic foresight. Public institutions should invest in tools that anticipate risks and opportunities, including horizon scanning, scenario planning, and policy labs. Many current strategies are static and do not address developments such as generative AI or platform monopolization. National observatories, interdisciplinary advisory councils, and a regional Digital Futures Forum could help identify disruptive trends early and support proactive responses (UNCTAD, 2021; European Commission, 2022). Table 9.4 summarizes these principles and illustrates examples from the region.

In summary, adaptive governance offers a politically feasible and technically grounded pathway for the WB to manage digital transformation under constraint. By institutionalizing iterative learning, fostering inclusive coordination, enabling policy flexibility, and developing strategic foresight, governments can not only respond to rapid technological change but also shape it, reinforcing the broader vision of the DNS as a capable, learning-oriented state.

## 9.5 Operationalizing Adaptive Governance in the Western Balkans

Turning adaptive governance from principle into practice requires approaches suited to fragmented and low-capacity institutions. Across the WB, ministries often operate in silos, donor coordination is inconsistent, and policy cycles are short and reactive. Under these conditions, adaptive governance must evolve through incremental and context-specific actions that strengthen coordination, promote local experimentation, and embed learning into institutional routines.

Figure 9.2 outlines a concentric-ring framework with four core entry points for operationalizing adaptive governance in the region. At its centre are adaptive learning loops, surrounded by three mutually reinforcing layers: national coordination mechanisms, regional harmonization platforms, and local experimentation. These are supported by foundational functions and sustained through long-term institutional culture change.

### 9.5.1 National Digital Transformation Units

The inner ring highlights the importance of central coordination bodies capable of scanning emerging trends, promoting cross-sector collaboration, and ensuring evidence-based policy adjustment. One key step is the creation of national digital transformation units, ideally located in the Prime Minister's Office or a cross-cutting ministry.

These units would monitor technological developments, integrate digital priorities across sectors, and serve as repositories for adaptive policy learning.

In Kosovo, for instance, the Ministry of Economy leads digital policy but lacks formal authority to coordinate other ministries. Locating a transformation unit at the centre of government could align diaspora-led technology initiatives, donor programs, and education reforms within a single strategic framework. Experiences from Estonia and the United Kingdom show the value of such units, though their design must reflect WB administrative realities and resource constraints.

### 9.5.2 Western Balkans AI Governance Observatory

The regional layer of the framework envisions a WB AI Governance Observatory to facilitate policy alignment, collective learning, and foresight across borders.

This body could support governments in aligning with EU digital regulations such as the AI Act, share lessons from municipal and national pilots, and advise on algorithmic transparency and ethical procurement. The Observatory could be hosted by the Regional Cooperation Council or structured as a consortium involving governments, academia, and civil society. Its main purpose would be to institutionalize learning, reduce duplication, and promote consistency in AI and digital policy implementation.

### 9.5.3 Local Experimentation and Horizontal Learning

The local layer emphasizes the role of municipal-level pilots and horizontal learning as catalysts for innovation when national reforms progress slowly. Local governments, universities, and civic organizations can lead in piloting AI-based services, digital inclusion projects, and challenge-based learning initiatives.

Examples already exist. In Kosovo, diaspora-supported coding academies and freelance networks have pioneered flexible training models that could be scaled through public procurement. In Albania, local administrations have tested data-driven approaches to service delivery, though most remain isolated experiments. Challenge funds and microgrants could expand such initiatives and enable successful models to spread across municipalities through peer learning and open platforms.

### 9.5.4 Foundational Functions for Learning and Coordination

The outer ring identifies three foundational capabilities that must be embedded within digital governance systems:

1. Monitoring and evaluation—Systems should move beyond tracking outputs to focus on user experience, institutional adaptation, and learning outcomes.
2. Donor coordination—External support must be aligned with national strategies to prevent parallel systems and reinforce local ownership.
3. Multi-stakeholder engagement—Regular forums should bring together small enterprises, diaspora professionals, universities, and civil society to co-create and monitor digital transformation agendas.

These functions ensure that experimentation contributes to collective learning and that local innovations are integrated into national and regional policy frameworks.

### 9.5.5 Institutional Culture Change and DNS Enablers

Sustaining adaptive governance requires cultural transformation. Moving from compliance-based planning to learning-oriented governance depends on nurturing reflexivity, openness, and iterative problem-solving. Such change cannot be imposed by law but can be encouraged through leadership, incentives, and repetition in practice.

Finally, adaptive governance in the WB relies on core enablers from the DNS framework: investment in interoperable data infrastructure, alignment with evolving regulatory standards, and continuous development of digital skills. These elements allow coordination, learning, and embeddedness to function as system-wide capacities rather than isolated project outcomes.

Figure 9.2 synthesizes these insights into a multi-layered model for designing adaptive governance in the WB—linking experimentation, coordination, and learning into a coherent pathway for digital transformation

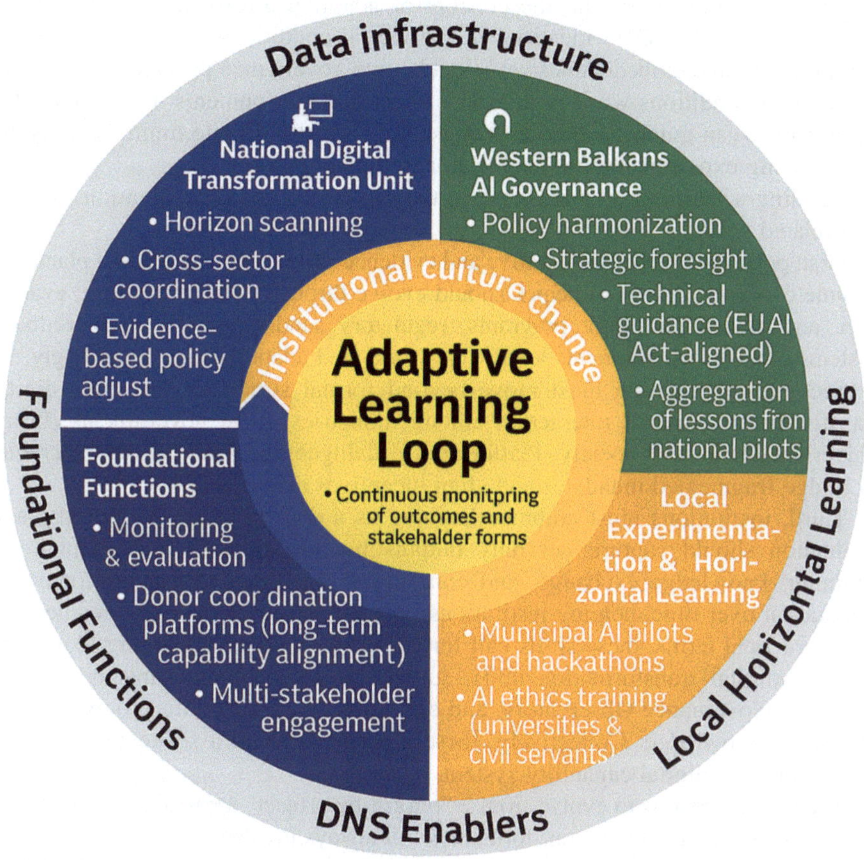


**Fig. 9.2** Adaptive governance in the Western Balkans. *Source* Author's elaboration, generated with DALL · E using Microsoft Copilot (2025)

## 9.6 Conclusion: Toward a Learning State for Digital Futures

The discussion throughout this chapter has shown that digital transformation in the WB presents both an opportunity and a challenge. Artificial intelligence, data-driven platforms, and digital infrastructure have the potential to drive productivity, innovation, and regional integration. Yet these same technologies can deepen dependency, reinforce inequality, and expose institutional weaknesses if not governed strategically.

The key insight is that technology by itself does not produce development. What matters is the governance capacity to use, adapt, and embed technology in ways that strengthen long-term learning and coordination. In contexts where formal institutions remain fragmented and resources are limited, transformation depends less on comprehensive reform and more on the gradual accumulation of practical capabilities.

The DNS framework and the concept of adaptive governance together offer a way forward. The DNS identifies the structural conditions needed for learning, coordination, and embeddedness, while adaptive governance provides the tools to make these conditions work in fluid and uncertain environments. In the WB, this combination can guide governments to act strategically despite limited means, by emphasizing experimentation, feedback, and collaboration.

Building a learning-oriented state in the digital era requires attention to three interrelated shifts.

First, policy must become iterative and evidence-driven. Instead of rigid plans that assume certainty, digital strategies should evolve through cycles of testing, evaluation, and adjustment. Pilot programs, regulatory sandboxes, and user feedback systems can help governments learn what works and adapt policies accordingly.

Second, coordination must move beyond formal structures. Effective digital transformation requires interaction among ministries, local governments, firms, universities, and civil society. Platforms for dialogue and joint action are crucial to bridge fragmented mandates and align incentives across actors.

Third, institutions must embrace learning as a core function. Monitoring and evaluation should capture not only outputs but also lessons and adaptations. Training, knowledge exchange, and communities of practice can reinforce this orientation over time, helping institutions become more reflective and resilient.

In practical terms, these shifts call for embedding adaptive learning loops into national digital transformation units, supporting regional mechanisms such as a WB AI Governance Observatory, and empowering municipalities to experiment and share knowledge. Collectively, these measures can turn scattered initiatives into a coherent digital capability system.

The broader goal is to evolve from a "reform by project" approach to a system of continuous learning. Digital transformation will always involve uncertainty, but adaptive governance allows governments to engage with it constructively rather than reactively. By building the capacity to learn and adapt, WB states can transform technological change from an external pressure into an internal driver of development.

Ultimately, becoming a learning state does not mean possessing all the answers. It means developing the institutional intelligence to ask the right questions, experiment responsibly, and adjust policies in real time. This orientation is essential not only for navigating the digital era but also for ensuring that innovation contributes to inclusive, sustainable, and locally grounded development across the WB.

## References

AI NOW. (2023). *AI NOW Macedonia reports and LLM pilot summary*. AI NOW Initiative. Available at https://github.com/AI-now-mk/MK-LLM. Accessed 19 February 2025.

Baldwin, R. (2019). *The globotics upheaval: Globalization, robotics, and the future of work*. Oxford University Press. Available at https://global.oup.com/ushe/product/the-globotics-upheaval-9780197518618. Accessed 9 June 2025.

Brynjolfsson, E., & McAfee, A. (2014). *The second machine age: Work, progress, and prosperity in a time of brilliant technologies*. W.W. Norton. Available at https://wwnorton.com/books/9780393239355
Cirera, X., Comin, D., & Cruz, M. (2022). Bridging the technological divide: Technology adoption by firms in developing countries. World Bank. Available at https://coilink.org/20.500.12592/q0bzfv. Accessed 23 October 2025.
Crespi, G., & Zuniga, P. (2012). Innovation and productivity: Evidence from six Latin American countries. *World Development*, *40*(2), 273–290. Available at https://doi.org/10.1016/j.worlddev.2011.07.010
EBRD. (2025). *Go digital in the Western Balkans: Investment programme overview*. European Bank for Reconstruction and Development. Available at https://www.ebrd.com/home/news-and-events/news/events/go-digital-in-the-western-balkans-.html. (Accessed 9 June 2025).
ETF. (2023). *Jobs and skills in the Western Balkans: Highlights from the digital training gap*. European Training Foundation. Available at: https://www.etf.europa.eu/en/news-and-events/news/etf-survey-jobs-skills-western-balkans-highlights-digital-training-gap
Gereffi, G. (2019). *Global value chains and development: Redefining the contours of twenty-first century capitalism*. Cambridge University Press. Available at https://doi.org/10.1017/9781108559423
ILO. (2023). Global Wage Report 2023–24. Geneva: International Labour Organization. Available at: https://www.ilo.org/sites/default/files/2024-11/GWR-2024_Layout_E_RGB_Web.pdf (Accessed: 8 June 2025).
Kenney, M., & Zysman, J. (2016). The rise of the platform economy. *Issues in Science and Technology*, *32*(3), 61–69. Available at https://issues.org/the-rise-of-the-platform-economy
OECD. (2023). *Digital Transformation in the Western Balkans: Policy challenges and opportunities*. OECD Publishing. Available at https://www.oecd.org/en/about/programmes/digital-transition-in-the-western-balkans.html
OECD. (2025). Economic Convergence Scoreboard for the Western Balkans 2025, OECD Publishing, Paris, https://doi.org/10.1787/bc0babf3-en
RCC. (2022). *Western Balkans digital economy and society index (DESI) 2022 report*. Regional Cooperation Council. Available at https://www.rcc.int/pubs/159
RCC. (2023). *Digital skills and platform work in the Western Balkans: Trends and Gaps*. Regional Cooperation Council. Available at https://www.rcc.int/pubs/169
Reiter, O., & Stehrer, R. (2021). *Learning from tumultuous times: An analysis of vulnerable sectors in international trade in the context of the corona health crisis*. The Vienna Institute for International Economic Studies (wiiw). Available at https://hdl.handle.net/10419/240654
Rodrik, D. (2008). Second-best institutions. *American Economic Review*, *98*(2), 100–104. Available at https://doi.org/10.1257/aer.98.2.100
Sabel, C. F., & Zeitlin, J. (2012). Experimentalist governance. In D. Levi-Faur (Ed.), *The Oxford handbook of governance*. Oxford University Press. Available at https://doi.org/10.1093/oxfordhb/9780199560530.013.0012
Srnicek, N. (2017). *Platform capitalism*. Cambridge: Polity Press. Available at https://www.politybooks.com/bookdetail/?isbn=9781509504862
UNCTAD. (2021). *Technology and innovation report 2021: Catching technological waves*. United Nations Conference on Trade and Development. Available at https://unctad.org/webflyer/technology-and-innovation-report-2021
World Bank. (2021). *World development report 2021: Data for better lives*. World Bank. Available at https://www.worldbank.org/en/publication/wdr2021

World Bank. (2024). *Western Balkans regular economic report no. 26: Retaining the growth momentum*. World Bank. Available at https://documents1.worldbank.org/curated/en/099101424043012347/pdf/P17920510ad45290105de14b0e18d531049127312370.pdf. Accessed 9 June 2025.

Yoruk, E., Radosevic, S., & Fischer, B. (2023). Technological profiles, upgrading and the dynamics of growth: Country-level patterns and trajectories across distinct stages of development. *Research Policy*, *52*(8), 104847. Available at https://doi.org/10.1016/j.respol.2023.104847

# Chapter 10
# Rethinking Industrial Policy for the Digital, Green, and Geopolitical Transitions

## 10.1 Introduction

The preceding chapters have shown that fragmented institutions, donor dependence, and limited capabilities continue to shape policy outcomes in the Western Balkans (WB). Yet within this difficult environment, there are encouraging signs of change. In Kosovo, ICT-based entrepreneurship is creating new opportunities for small firms. In Albania, donor-supported agri-food upgrading is helping to form new clusters of innovation. In North Macedonia, supplier development initiatives are strengthening industrial linkages. Across these examples, governments, firms, and civic actors are beginning to coordinate, learn, and experiment in ways that echo the principles of the Developmental Network State (DNS). However, these efforts remain uneven, short-lived, and vulnerable to external pressures.

Chapter 9 examined how the region can approach emerging technologies, particularly artificial intelligence and digital platforms, through adaptive forms of governance. It argued that success depends less on formal state capacity and more on the ability to experiment, coordinate, and learn in uncertain conditions. By framing governance as a learning infrastructure for technological transformation, the chapter provided a foundation for applying similar principles to industrial policy.

This chapter argues that latecomer economies such as those in the WB must rethink their industrial policy frameworks in response to three interconnected global shifts: digitalization, the green transition, and geopolitical restructuring. These transformations are redefining competitiveness, altering patterns of value creation, and limiting the effectiveness of uncoordinated or reactive reforms. They also expose the fragility of systems that depend on fragmented donor agendas, low-value integration into global value chains, and weak national ownership of reform.

At the same time, these global trends offer a strategic opportunity. They encourage movement away from static models of industrial policy—based on fixed targets, subsidies, or rigid plans—toward more adaptive and network-based approaches.



F. Sahiti, *Catching Up in the Digital Age*, Contributions to Economics,
https://doi.org/10.1007/978-3-032-17059-0_10

Adaptive industrial policy, guided by DNS principles, is not a prescriptive blueprint but a dynamic process. It seeks to build institutions that can coordinate across sectors, learn from experience, engage international partners, and respond flexibly to shifting technological and market conditions.

The sections that follow examine how digitalization, the green transition, and geopolitical realignments are reshaping the environment for industrial development in the WB. They then discuss how governance systems can evolve to manage these changes and propose a framework for adaptive industrial policy as an institutional infrastructure for learning, coordination, and strategic upgrading. The chapter concludes that latecomer states can guide structural transformation most effectively not through centralized control or imitation of external models, but through continuous learning, experimentation, and coalition building across public and private domains.

## 10.2 Digitalization and the Changing Landscape of Industrial Policy

Digitalization has become central to industrial policy, transforming how value is created, governed, and distributed across sectors and regions. For latecomer economies such as those in the WB, the rise of digital platforms, data infrastructures, and artificial intelligence (AI) integration presents both strategic opportunities and structural challenges. These technologies enable upgrading in digital services and digitally enhanced manufacturing, yet they also create risks of technological dependence, regulatory asymmetry, and value capture by external actors.

Three interrelated trends drive this transformation. The first is the phantomization of economic coordination, where firms and workers increasingly interact through digital marketplaces, global productivity tools, and algorithmically managed systems. The second is the datafication of production and services, in which competitiveness depends on the ability to generate, control, and analyse large datasets. The third is the integration of AI and automation, reshaping processes across sectors, from logistics and predictive maintenance in manufacturing to chatbots and personalized services in customer-oriented industries (Kenney & Zysman, 2016; Srnicek, 2017).

These developments are dissolving traditional sectoral boundaries. As discussed in Chap. 8, emerging hybrid sectors such as logistics-tech, agri-tech, and manufacturing-as–a-service demand both production and digital capabilities. Competitiveness now depends not only on cost and quality, but also on the ability to integrate cloud services, digital workflows, and platform visibility into operations (Brynjolfsson & McAfee, 2014; Baldwin, 2019).

For WB economies, this convergence creates both opportunity and vulnerability. Digital tools have lowered entry barriers for freelancers, start-ups, and small and medium-sized enterprises (SMEs). In Kosovo's ICT sector, for instance, platform-based work enables participation in global markets without large industrial infrastructure (UNCTAD, 2021; RCC, 2022). Yet such participation is mediated by external platforms with opaque governance, pricing, and algorithms. This produces new forms of technological lock-in, where domestic firms depend on foreign infrastructures and lack the bargaining power to influence standards or capture learning benefits (Srnicek, 2017; Yoruk et al., 2023).

The risk is a form of path-dependent digitalization. Without strong domestic capability-building, digital transformation may entrench existing dependencies rather than foster innovation. Firms may optimize for short-term visibility on global platforms instead of long-term technological learning, while governments may focus on access indicators rather than the foundational systems such as public data infrastructure, secure cloud services, or AI regulatory frameworks needed for sustained upgrading (OECD, 2022).

This tension is evident in recent policy experiences. In Kosovo and Albania, donor- and diaspora-supported digital skills programmes have provided useful tools and training but often remain disconnected from national policy frameworks and institutional learning processes. North Macedonia's development of an open-source large language model in Macedonian represents a rare example of strategic alignment between local data resources, language sovereignty, and applied research, but such initiatives remain exceptional.

Avoiding digital dependency requires a strategic approach to digital industrial policy that embeds digitalization within broader systems of capability development. This involves investing in national data infrastructure and governance, supporting cross-sectoral digital platforms that strengthen SMEs and local ecosystems, aligning education, research, and public procurement with long-term upgrading goals, and creating feedback mechanisms linking platform users, regulators, and policymakers.

From a DNS perspective, digitalization should be governed through coordinated learning and institutional collaboration. Governments can establish cross-ministerial digital task forces, launch pilot programmes that evolve through user feedback, and create platforms connecting firms, regulators, and civil society (Andrews et al., 2017; Bartlett, 2020). DNS-compatible digital policy focuses not merely on access but on embedding learning and strategic coherence across fragmented systems.

In conclusion, digitalization is a defining test for industrial policy in latecomer economies. It holds transformative potential, but this potential can only be realized through adaptive governance, sustained investment in capabilities, and a commitment to strategic autonomy. Without these foundations, the promise of digital leapfrogging may instead lead to new forms of marginalization within the global digital economy.

## 10.3 Green Transition and Capability Constraints

The green transition represents one of the most significant transformations of industrial policy since the post-war period. In Europe, initiatives such as the EU Green Deal, the Carbon Border Adjustment Mechanism (CBAM), and related climate frameworks are reshaping how firms operate, invest, and trade. For the WB, these developments have systemic implications. They affect trade access, investment eligibility, donor alignment, and domestic governance. Although they create opportunities for green upgrading, they also reveal the structural limitations of latecomer economies. The key challenge is to design governance systems that enable compliance with environmental standards without hindering innovation or long-term capability development.

The EU Green Deal, launched in 2019, sets a roadmap for climate neutrality by 2050, with influence extending beyond EU borders through trade, finance, and regulatory spillovers. CBAM, one of its central instruments, applies a carbon price to selected imports, initially in sectors such as steel, aluminium, cement, and fertilizers, based on the EU's Emissions Trading System. For Western Balkan exporters, carbon intensity has become a condition for market access rather than a purely environmental issue (European Commission, 2023).

International donors and financial institutions have linked development finance to environmental conditionalities. The World Bank, GIZ, and the European Bank for Reconstruction and Development (EBRD) now embed environmental benchmarks into loans, grants, and technical assistance programmes. While this supports global climate objectives, it often creates a double constraint: governments must meet ambitious external standards without having sufficient institutional capacity to design, implement, and coordinate green industrial strategies (Bartlett, 2020; OECD, 2023).

This problem is particularly evident in the WB, where industrial legacies, donor fragmentation, and institutional silos intersect. Ministries in Kosovo, Albania, and North Macedonia often pursue parallel projects with little coordination. In Albania, renewable energy initiatives are divided among the Ministry of Infrastructure, the Investment Development Agency, and EU IPARD-related rural funds, each with separate timelines and benchmarks. In North Macedonia, green SME support has been partly integrated into innovation policy through the Fund for Innovation and Technological Development (FITD), but it remains weakly aligned with broader decarbonization strategies. The outcome is a fragmented governance landscape in which compliance risks becoming procedural rather than developmental.

The main governance tension lies between short-term compliance and long-term learning. Donor programmes often emphasize measurable outputs, such as the number of solar panels installed or tonnes of carbon reduced, rather than systemic reforms that build domestic climate-industrial capabilities. Ministries may pursue targets as funding opportunities rather than as elements of a coherent capability-building agenda. The result is a form of climate policy substitution, where green reforms are externally managed and financed but not embedded within national policy processes (Andrews et al., 2017).

This trajectory, however, is not inevitable. Some cases suggest emerging forms of selective reintegration, where donor influence is aligned with national strategies. In North Macedonia, green finance tools have been incorporated into FITD's SME programmes, linking donor goals with domestic innovation policy. In Kosovo, diaspora-led renewable energy start-ups have collaborated with municipal governments and GIZ to pilot off-grid solutions that meet environmental targets while developing local technical skills. In Albania, the Ministry of Finance has begun to explore green bonds and climate budgeting as part of a domestically driven sustainability agenda.

Scaling such approaches requires three interconnected governance shifts. First, climate finance must be integrated into national policy planning, connecting green conditionalities with industrial and innovation strategies. This means moving beyond isolated projects, encouraging ministries to share ownership of donor-funded initiatives, and embedding monitoring mechanisms into public systems (OECD, 2023). Second, coordination must bridge ministries, municipalities, and implementing agencies, since climate objectives cut across energy, transport, agriculture, industry, finance, and environmental policy. As discussed in Chap. 8, adaptive governance tools such as inter-ministerial climate task forces, regional observatories, and foresight labs can support this process. Third, learning and feedback systems must take precedence over compliance reporting. Green transitions are uncertain and politically complex, requiring institutions that enable experimentation, adaptation, and course correction. This includes funding for pilot programmes, iterative reviews of green public procurement, and open access to environmental data for public scrutiny and research.

From a DNS perspective, the green transition is not only an environmental imperative but also a test of whether fragmented, resource-constrained states can manage structural change in a coordinated and adaptive way. Industrial policy under climate pressure must evolve from narrow subsidies and tax incentives toward a systemic capability agenda that integrates green technologies, regulatory foresight, transnational cooperation, and institutional resilience.

If approached strategically, the green transition can become a developmental opportunity. By strengthening domestic institutional capacity, aligning donor support with national reform priorities, and embedding learning mechanisms into green investments, Western Balkan governments can move from reactive compliance toward proactive industrial transformation. The DNS framework provides both the conceptual foundation and practical tools for pursuing this path.

## 10.4 Geopolitical Shifts and Strategic Autonomy

The COVID-19 pandemic and the Russian invasion of Ukraine have exposed the fragility of global production networks and prompted a major rethinking of supply chain resilience, economic security, and geopolitical interdependence. Questions that were once technical aspects of trade logistics have become central to national strategy and regional autonomy. In this environment, industrial policy is being redefined not only to promote competitiveness and innovation but also to enhance strategic autonomy and reduce vulnerability to external shocks.

For latecomer economies in the WB, these changes bring both risks and opportunities. Their peripheral position within global value chains, often as subcontractors, service outsourcers, or low-cost assemblers, leaves them highly exposed to fluctuations in supply and demand. At the same time, proximity to the European Union (EU), combined with growing interest in reshoring and nearshoring, offers a strategic opening for reintegration into new industrial geographies.

Across Europe, the pandemic revealed the dangers of excessive dependence on distant suppliers for essential goods such as medical equipment, electronics, and food. In response, the European Commission's revised Industrial Strategy for Europe and its Strategic Dependencies Review emphasize the creation of diversified, secure value chains in sectors considered critical, including semiconductors, batteries, pharmaceuticals, and green technologies (European Commission, 2021). The war in Ukraine has intensified this agenda, motivating EU institutions and member states to prioritize resilience through regionalization and supply chain restructuring.

This shift has already led to the development of new industrial corridors in Central and Eastern Europe, with countries such as Poland, Hungary, and Slovakia becoming preferred nearshore destinations for production and logistics. While the WB are not yet fully integrated into these networks, they are increasingly viewed as adjacent, cost-competitive regions that could complement European production hubs if capability and infrastructure gaps are addressed. The European Bank for Reconstruction and Development (EBRD) notes that the post-war reconstruction of Ukraine, combined with Europe's pursuit of energy security and resilience in critical raw materials, presents new opportunities for Western Balkan economies to integrate into emerging east–west industrial corridors (EBRD, 2023).

The policy implications are twofold. First, governments must strengthen institutional capacity to manage and regulate incoming investment. This includes aligning national regulations with EU standards, streamlining permitting processes, and improving mechanisms for dispute resolution. Second, industrial upgrading should be embedded in broader capability-building agendas rather than treated solely as investment attraction. Policies on foreign direct investment (FDI) should aim to promote supplier upgrading, workforce development, and research linkages instead of focusing only on reducing transaction costs.

Structural vulnerabilities persist. The prevailing logic of global value chain participation often confines latecomer economies to low-value-added roles as component assemblers or service subcontractors. These positions limit their ability to shape standards, retain learning, or transition into design- or technology-intensive activities. Although such roles can be profitable in the short term, they increase exposure to external shocks and restrict the strategic autonomy of domestic institutions (Pietrobelli & Rabellotti, 2011; Gereffi, 2019). The World Bank (World Bank, 2022) has emphasized that while Europe's ongoing supply chain restructuring offers a window of opportunity for the WB, institutional readiness is essential. Without coherent policy coordination and predictable governance, the region risks being overlooked in favour of more stable Central and Eastern European partners.

A DNS-compatible approach to industrial policy requires more than regulatory alignment. It calls for strategic positioning within industrial ecosystems that are evolving under geopolitical pressure. This involves identifying competitive niches in European strategic sectors such as battery storage, renewable energy components, and digital logistics. It also requires designing conditional FDI instruments that ensure local capability spillovers, investing in corridor-linked infrastructure including transport and data networks with built-in redundancy, and engaging in foresight exercises and scenario planning through EU regional platforms.

Strategic autonomy in this context does not mean self-sufficiency but rather the capacity to shape development trajectories, manage external dependencies, and engage selectively with transnational production systems. For the WB, this implies a shift from reactive participation in global value chains to negotiated integration supported by learning-oriented governance.

The DNS framework provides an institutional model for this transition. Industrial policy agencies should act as network coordinators rather than administrative gatekeepers. Transformation units and interface platforms can align objectives across ministries and engage a wide range of stakeholders, including foreign investors, domestic firms, and research institutions. Learning coalitions involving diaspora actors, regional donors, and local organizations can build institutional trust and enhance strategic foresight.

Early examples of this approach are beginning to emerge. In North Macedonia, the Innovation Fund is implementing supplier development programmes aligned with EU export requirements. In Kosovo, diaspora-led ICT clusters are advocating for regional data infrastructure to connect with EU digital corridors. In Albania, logistics improvements supported by GIZ and the EU are being linked to broader corridor development strategies, although these initiatives remain at an early stage.

These efforts are still partial and weakly institutionalized, but they demonstrate that geopolitical restructuring does not have to reinforce marginalization. With DNS-compatible governance and regional coordination, the WB can reposition themselves not as peripheral zones of low-cost labour but as strategic partners within a reconfigured European industrial landscape.

## 10.5 Policy Ownership, Donor Alignment, and Learning Coalitions

In transitional economies such as those of the WB, the boundary between domestic policymaking and external support is often unclear. Donors play a central role in funding, designing, and sometimes implementing reforms. While this engagement provides valuable financial and technical assistance, it also creates a recurring challenge: the replacement of national policy processes with donor-driven agendas. Reforms are often carried out in parallel to state institutions, which weakens policy ownership, distorts incentives, and limits institutional learning.

This challenge is particularly evident in settings with fragmented bureaucracies and weak coordination across ministries. As noted in Chap. 7, development initiatives in Kosovo, Albania, and North Macedonia often take the form of isolated projects designed to match the objectives and timelines of individual funding agencies. In Kosovo, for example, digital skills programmes have been funded simultaneously by the EU, GIZ, USAID, and Swisscontact, with limited coordination of target groups, outcomes, or monitoring systems. In Albania, vocational training and agri-food reforms have been implemented through a patchwork of ministries, donors, and municipalities, each operating independently. This proliferation creates vertical accountability to external funders while undermining horizontal coherence within the state.

The problem is not only administrative but also political. Ministries frequently compete for control over donor-funded portfolios, which bring both visibility and access to resources. Donors, meanwhile, often maintain direct relationships with specific ministries or sectors rather than engaging in slower, more complex cross-ministerial coordination. The result, described by Bartlett (2020) as "donor-driven disarticulation," is a situation in which governments act as implementing agencies for externally defined priorities rather than as strategic policy leaders.

This fragmentation also hampers learning. As discussed in Sect. 7.5, monitoring and evaluation systems are typically designed for donor accountability rather than for policy feedback. Reports are written for external funders rather than integrated into national learning processes. Ministries often lack the capacity, mandate, or incentives to synthesize lessons across projects. North Macedonia's Innovation Fund (FITD) provides one of the few exceptions, having begun to institutionalize feedback cycles and peer learning. However, such cases remain limited, and knowledge from donor programmes often remains fragmented or lost once projects conclude.

Despite these constraints, opportunities are emerging to embed donor engagement within nationally owned and adaptive governance frameworks. Section 8.4.4 identified several institutional entry points, including transformation units, regional observatories, and challenge funds, that could be used to improve donor alignment and coalition-building. The goal is not to remove donor influence but to integrate it within national systems in ways that strengthen capability and promote policy coherence.

### *10.5.1 Institutionalizing Donor Coordination as a Governance Function*

Donor coordination should be treated as a formal function of governance rather than an ad hoc or diplomatic activity. Governments can embed coordination into national planning through interministerial steering committees, digital project-mapping platforms, and jointly agreed investment frameworks. Kosovo's Digital Economy Project, which created co-financed task forces involving ministries, donors, and diaspora representatives, provides an example of effective coordination that overcomes donor silos and supports a DNS approach.

### 10.5.2 Embedding Learning Coalitions Within Reform Platforms

Donor engagement should take place within learning coalitions rather than through one-off consultation events. Learning coalitions are iterative platforms where ministries, municipalities, donors, and firms jointly assess and adjust strategies. As Andrews et al. (2017) argue, such coalitions are essential for building state capability under constraint. North Macedonia's FITD illustrates how donor-funded initiatives can evolve into learning platforms when supported by transparent evaluation, stakeholder participation, and internal feedback loops. Scaling such models requires ministries to have both the mandate and resources to integrate lessons through dedicated learning units, evaluation budgets, and spaces for experimentation. Donors can support this process by co-investing in learning infrastructure instead of focusing only on project outputs.

### 10.5.3 Aligning Donor Metrics With Institutional Capability Goals

Many donor programmes still measure success through short-term outputs, such as the number of trainees, laws enacted, or facilities built, rather than through long-term institutional outcomes. Governments should negotiate performance frameworks that assess progress in terms of coordination, systems learning, and policy feedback. Where donors already use adaptive approaches such as outcome-based funding or policy-based lending, these should be explicitly aligned with government-led and DNS-compatible strategies.

Implementing these reforms requires a cultural shift for both governments and donors. Governments must move from passively accepting donor blueprints to actively setting priorities and shaping implementation. Donors, in turn, should shift from project delivery toward co-creation of institutional capabilities. When these conditions are met, donor–government relationships can evolve into genuine learning partnerships rather than remain defined by fragmented conditionalities.

Positive examples are beginning to appear. The World Bank's support for Albania's Public Finance Management reform includes adaptive elements that promote cross-ministerial coordination. GIZ has introduced long-term advisory models that embed technical experts within ministries to encourage knowledge transfer. The European Commission's WB Investment Framework has also begun to emphasize coherence and regional alignment, encouraging joint planning between donors and governments.

The DNS framework provides a coherent way forward. It views external actors not as threats to sovereignty but as potential partners in networked governance, provided that their engagement is iterative, embedded, and aligned with domestic learning systems. Donor fragmentation remains a serious challenge, but with the right institutional structures it can be transformed into a source of policy experimentation, diversity, and resilience.

## 10.6 The Role of Diaspora in Strategic Upgrading

Diaspora engagement in the WB has traditionally been understood in terms of remittances, humanitarian assistance, and symbolic nation-building. While these functions remain significant, the region's current development challenges require a more strategic approach. In the context of digitalization, the green transition, and shifting geopolitical dynamics, diasporas can play a far more active role as partners in innovation, foresight, and capability development. The task for the region is to move from transactional interactions to sustained and institutionalized collaboration between diaspora actors and the state.

This shift is already visible in countries such as Kosovo and North Macedonia. In Kosovo, diaspora networks have been instrumental in building the ICT ecosystem, establishing coding academies, and connecting freelancers to international clients. The Innovation and Training Park in Prizren, supported by diaspora entrepreneurs in partnership with local authorities, donors, and private firms, illustrates this potential. Its importance lies not only in financial contributions but also in the relational trust and continuity of engagement among stakeholders (Sect. 7.6; Granovetter, 1985; Evans, 1995).

In North Macedonia, the diaspora has contributed to the development of the national innovation system. The Fund for Innovation and Technological Development (FITD) has collaborated with diaspora-founded firms and researchers to design competitive calls, mentoring programmes, and matchmaking events. These initiatives facilitate knowledge exchange and create networks that connect diaspora expertise with national priorities. In both cases, diaspora actors function as intermediaries embedded within the learning and coordination systems characteristic of DNS governance.

Despite these examples, success remains uneven and often dependent on individual initiatives. Most countries in the region lack a coherent strategy for integrating the diaspora into industrial transformation. Institutional responsibilities are fragmented, funding mechanisms are inconsistent, and platforms for collaboration are underdeveloped. Ministries of diaspora affairs, where they exist, typically focus on cultural promotion or diplomacy rather than on innovation, industrial upgrading, or knowledge transfer. As a result, much of the potential for diaspora-led development remains unrealized.

To address these shortcomings, diaspora engagement should be treated as a core element of national industrial strategy. Three areas are particularly important.

### *10.6.1 Diaspora and Strategic Foresight*

As discussed in Chap. 8, industrial policy under conditions of uncertainty depends on continuous learning, horizon scanning, and anticipatory governance. Diaspora networks can provide valuable strategic intelligence, offering insights into global technology trends, regulatory changes, and emerging business models. This contribution is particularly significant for small states with limited research and analytical capacity. For example, Kosovo's diaspora communities in Switzerland, Germany, and the United States include professionals in policy analysis, technology, and research who could support foresight platforms or advisory councils if structured mechanisms for engagement were in place.

National innovation councils or transformation units, such as those proposed in Sect. 8.4.4, could institutionalize these contributions. Diaspora foresight panels could act as permanent advisory bodies contributing to sectoral strategies, digital skills roadmaps, and climate transition plans. The objective is to incorporate diaspora knowledge into formal policy processes rather than treat it as occasional or external input.

### *10.6.2 Diaspora and Innovation Ecosystems*

Diasporas can also serve as connectors between global and local innovation systems. They can link domestic start-ups with venture capital, introduce international standards, and provide mentorship in business development. In North Macedonia, FITD's cooperation with diaspora networks has partially achieved this role, though implementation remains inconsistent. In Albania, some municipalities have established diaspora advisory boards, but these lack financial resources and formal integration with national innovation policy.

To expand these efforts, governments could establish diaspora innovation platforms that include co-financing schemes for diaspora-led start-ups, research grants for returning professionals, and mentorship programmes in incubators and technology parks. Such mechanisms do not need to rely solely on donor support. They could be financed through diaspora bonds, sovereign wealth funds, or blended finance instruments integrated into national innovation and industrial strategies.

### *10.6.3 Diaspora and Development Finance*

Remittances remain a key source of income across the WB, but they rarely contribute to productive investment. With appropriate governance mechanisms, part of diaspora savings could support long-term development goals. Instruments such as diaspora bonds, digital crowd-financing platforms, and regional investment vehicles are often discussed but rarely implemented in practice.

The barriers are not only financial but institutional. Weak policy credibility and fragmented governance discourage engagement. As highlighted in Chap. 7, trust and relational embeddedness are essential. Diaspora investors are unlikely to commit to environments characterized by opaque bureaucracies or limited coordination. When trusted intermediaries such as chambers of commerce, business councils, or hybrid institutions like FITD act as brokers, participation becomes more likely. Kosovo's co-funded technology initiatives and North Macedonia's innovation matchmaking events demonstrate the benefits of this approach.

From the perspective of the DNS, diasporas are integral components of distributed governance networks that promote learning, experimentation, and coordination. Effective engagement requires the same principles that guide DNS-compatible reform: embeddedness, iterative learning, and collaboration among multiple actors. States must invest not only in outreach but also in platforms that enable diaspora actors to co-design and co-own national strategies. This could include regular foresight summits, formal representation in innovation policy bodies, and funding schemes that reward sustained involvement. Responsibility for diaspora policy should extend beyond ministries of foreign or diaspora affairs to include economic development and industrial policy institutions.

The next phase of diaspora engagement in the WB should move from symbolic diplomacy to strategic capability development. When institutionalized through mechanisms such as foresight panels, innovation platforms, and investment partnerships, diaspora actors can help bridge global knowledge networks with domestic capability-building. Their participation can enhance the governance reforms discussed in previous sections, including donor coordination, global value chain integration, and the green transition. To achieve this, diaspora engagement must become an integral part of a broader shift toward learning-oriented, networked governance that strengthens the region's strategic autonomy and developmental capacity.

## 10.7 Adaptive Governance as Industrial Policy Infrastructure

Throughout this chapter, adaptive governance has appeared as a central theme, encompassing digitalization, donor alignment, climate policy, and diaspora engagement. It is more than a coordination mechanism or implementation tool. Adaptive governance should be recognized as a distinct method of industrial policy, particularly relevant for latecomer economies that face severe constraints. Rather than replacing industrial strategy, it serves as the institutional foundation that enables learning, coherence, and strategic upgrading when traditional state capacity is limited (Andrews et al., 2017).

As discussed in Chap. 8, adaptive governance relies on iterative feedback, experimentation, and learning by doing. It provides a way to govern in complex, uncertain, and rapidly changing contexts, especially those marked by fragmented authority, donor dependence, and volatile global conditions. Its value extends beyond digital transformation to include industrial modernization, supply chain repositioning, climate transition, and capability development.

The DNS framework provides the conceptual basis for this approach. It is not a rigid institutional blueprint, but a heuristic organized around three core functions: coordination, learning, and embeddedness. Adaptive governance supplies the operational language through which these functions are institutionalized. It shapes how task forces are organized, how feedback is processed, how inter-ministerial routines are adapted, and how trust is maintained among public, private, and civic actors (Sabel & Zeitlin, 2012).

The DNS–adaptive governance relationship offers an alternative to two ineffective approaches: reliance on hierarchical planning agencies, which transitional states often lack, and dependence on market coordination or donor-led reforms, which typically produce fragmentation and policy substitution. Instead, it provides a way to govern under imperfect conditions by building lightweight, iterative, and trust-based governance infrastructures suited to low-capacity environments (Andrews et al., 2017).

Evidence from Kosovo, Albania, and North Macedonia suggests that elements of such infrastructures are already emerging (OECD, 2023). Examples include task-based working groups in digital skills policy, innovation funds that incorporate stakeholder feedback into programme design, and platforms that connect municipal authorities with diaspora networks. However, these practices remain fragmented and insufficiently institutionalized. To expand and sustain them, adaptive governance must be intentionally embedded within industrial policy design.

Building adaptive governance capacity in fragmented or low-capacity contexts requires practical institutional mechanisms that translate strategic intent into coordinated action. Three such instruments are particularly important: cross-sectoral task forces, transformation units, and structured pilot programmes. Each addresses a distinct coordination challenge—horizontal, vertical, or experimental—while together forming the connective infrastructure of the DNS.

### *10.7.1 Cross-Sectoral Task Forces*

Rather than relying on permanent inter-ministerial committees that often lack authority or operational focus, governments can create task-specific coordination platforms dedicated to defined developmental challenges such as supplier upgrading, industrial greening, SME digitalization, or innovation financing. These task forces can bring together ministries, municipalities, donors, firms, and civic actors in a collaborative problem-solving mode.

Section 7.4 described how this approach was tested in Kosovo's digital skills ecosystem. Initially driven by GIZ, diaspora-led firms, and the Ministry of Economy, it was later integrated into national strategy through budgetary alignment. In North Macedonia, the Fund for Innovation and Technological Development (FITD) serves as an informal task force hub for innovation and SME support, convening stakeholders around programme cycles rather than bureaucratic structures.

Effective task forces share three key features, namely, a shared problem definition rather than jurisdictional ownership; joint budgeting or pooled funding to prevent fragmented implementation; and embedded feedback loops that allow results to inform policy adjustments (OECD, 2023).

### 10.7.2 Transformation Units Within Central Government

Adaptive industrial policy requires a permanent reflexive core: a small unit within central government with the authority and capacity to convene actors, monitor global trends, and integrate lessons across initiatives. These transformation units do not design every reform but instead create the conditions for experimentation, link disparate initiatives, and ensure that learning is fed back into policy processes.

As outlined in Sect. 8.4.4, such units can be located within prime ministers' offices or ministries of economy and tasked with: (i) scanning global technology and market trends, (ii) facilitating donor coordination and diaspora engagement, and (iii) tracking reform pilots and maintaining institutional memory.

Examples from Estonia's Government CIO Office and the United Kingdom's Central Digital and Data Office demonstrate how these units can promote policy coherence and foster adaptive learning (Sabel & Zeitlin, 2012).

### 10.7.3 Pilot Programmes With Structured Learning Protocols

Pilot programmes are common in transitional contexts, yet they are often driven by external donors, detached from national systems, and evaluated only through formal monitoring and evaluation reports. Adaptive governance requires a different approach. Pilots should be designed from the outset as structured experiments, comparable across cases, and continuously refined in response to emerging evidence.

For example, Albania's early digital procurement reforms and Kosovo's smart municipal infrastructure pilots could become replicable models if they were designed with: open-ended objectives and flexible timeframes; mixed stakeholder governance involving ministries, donors, and end users; and, transparent data-sharing and institutionalized peer learning.

The purpose of pilots is not merely to "test before scaling," but to function as organizational laboratories that help states build capability through practical engagement (Andrews et al., 2017).

These three institutional instruments, task forces, transformation units, and structured pilot programmes, should not be viewed as isolated innovations. Together, they form interconnected components of an adaptive governance architecture that can be integrated into industrial policy frameworks. When applied in combination, they create the connective capacity required to coordinate across sectors, embed feedback into decision-making, and sustain collaborative problem-solving under constraint.

Table 10.1 summarizes these instruments, highlighting their core functions, links to the DNS's foundational logics, and examples from emerging practice in the WB.

In combination, these instruments position adaptive governance as a form of infrastructure for industrial policy. It is not a replacement for strategy but the connective system that enables it to function across conditions of fragmentation,

**Table 10.1** Adaptive governance instruments for industrial policy in the WB

| Instrument | Core function | DNS Logic | Western Balkan example |
|---|---|---|---|
| Task Forces | Cross-sectoral coordination around problems | Embedded coordination | Digital skills ecosystem (Kosovo) |
| Transformation Units | Strategic scanning and learning infrastructure | Feedback + foresight | Proposed PM office models |
| Pilot Programmes | Experimental policy design with adaptation | Iterative learning | E-procurement (Albania, GIZ) |

*Source* Author's elaboration based on OECD (2023); field evidence from Kosovo, Albania, and North Macedonia

uncertainty, and limited resources. The DNS framework elevates this approach from a collection of good practices to a systemic necessity, enabling coordination without hierarchy, learning without technocracy, and transformation without centralization.

The key conceptual shift lies in moving from the assumption that governance capacity must be fully developed before reform can begin, to recognizing that capacity is built through the reform process itself. States need not wait for ideal conditions. They can strengthen capability through iterative, embedded, and feedback-rich processes. This reframes industrial policy as an evolving process of capability accumulation rather than a static technocratic blueprint.

As the final section will argue, this approach goes beyond addressing immediate challenges. It offers a sustainable method for managing long-term transformation, grounded in realism, shared responsibility, and the co-creation of future possibilities.

## 10.8 Conclusion: Governing Industrial Transformation Under Constraint

This chapter has examined how global shifts in digital technology, environmental sustainability, and geopolitical realignment are reshaping the context in which industrial policy operates in the WB. Rather than addressing these as separate domains, the analysis has considered their combined effects on policy space, institutional capacity, and the strategic dilemmas faced by latecomer economies.

Digitalization offers both opportunities and risks. It can enable new forms of service-led upgrading, platform participation, and AI-driven efficiency, but it also introduces vulnerabilities linked to proprietary technologies, data sovereignty, and uneven skill bases. As shown in Sect. 9.2, without solid foundations in skills, infrastructure, and absorptive capacity, digital transformation risks deepening existing inequalities. At the same time, the strategic integration of diaspora actors, learning systems, and innovation hubs, discussed in Chaps. 8 and 9.6, points to a pathway toward inclusive digital industrialization.

The green transition, explored in Sect. 9.3, introduces new conditionalities through EU mechanisms such as the Green Deal and the Carbon Border Adjustment Mechanism. These frameworks require domestic industries to meet higher environmental standards but also open access to climate finance and preferential integration for those that comply. To make these opportunities developmental, governance systems must balance external compliance with domestic innovation, turning conditionality into a learning process. Donors such as GIZ, the World Bank, and the EBRD can serve as strategic allies when their involvement aligns with nationally defined priorities.

Geopolitical disruptions, including the COVID-19 pandemic and the war in Ukraine, have reshaped global supply chains and created new openings for the WB. As discussed in Sect. 9.4, trends such as reshoring, nearshoring, and the creation of industrial corridors represent not only trade shifts but also governance opportunities. Countries that demonstrate reliability, coordination, and reform credibility can reposition themselves within new industrial geographies. Doing so requires institutions capable of anticipating change, aligning diverse actors, and responding quickly. These are capacities central to DNS-oriented governance.

Across these domains, successful industrial transformation depends less on institutional perfection than on the accumulation of meta-capabilities: the ability to coordinate across sectors, learn from partial implementation, and sustain relationships of trust and reciprocity. Sect. 9.5 showed how donor engagement can either weaken or strengthen these capabilities depending on whether it supports nationally owned learning coalitions. Sect. 9.6 extended this logic by showing how diaspora actors, when institutionally integrated, can function as transnational nodes of capability, linking global knowledge networks with domestic reform processes.

The discussion in Sect. 9.6 demonstrated that adaptive governance is not simply a tool for digital policy but a foundational infrastructure for industrial transformation. Whether through cross-sectoral task forces, centrally embedded transformation units, or pilot programmes with structured learning protocols, adaptive governance provides the scaffolding for governing under constraint. It is not a temporary substitute for institutional strength but a practical method for building capability in fragmented and resource-limited settings.

The central insight is that industrial transformation in the WB is constrained less by structural disadvantage than by the absence of institutional mechanisms able to manage fragmentation, integrate feedback, and align local initiatives with strategic priorities. The DNS framework shows that such mechanisms can be built even in environments marked by donor dominance, political volatility, and fiscal constraint, provided governance is reoriented toward iterative learning, distributed leadership, and collaborative problem-solving.

This approach does not reject strategic planning; it redefines it as adaptive strategy. It does not idealize the state; it recasts it as a platform for coordination, experimentation, and capability-building. Nor does it exclude external actors; it embeds them within networked governance systems that prioritize learning over compliance.

In doing so, it prepares the ground for the theoretical synthesis in Chap. 10, which consolidates the conceptual contributions of the DNS, assesses its wider applicability beyond the WB, and considers its implications for rethinking development theory in the twenty-first century.

## References


Andrews, M., Pritchett, L., & Woolcock, M. (2017). *Building state capability: Evidence, analysis, action*. Oxford University Press. Available at https://bsc.cid.harvard.edu/book/building-state-capability. Accessed 14 July 2025.

Baldwin, R. (2019). *The Globotics Upheaval: Globalization, Robotics, and the Future of Work*. Oxford University Press. Available at: https://global.oup.com/ushe/product/the-globotics-upheaval-9780197518618. (Accessed: 9 June 2025).

Bartlett, W. (2020). International assistance, donor interests, and state capture in the Western Balkans. *Journal of Contemporary European Studies*, *29*(2), 184–200. https://doi.org/10.1080/14782804.2020.1794801. Accessed 8 June 2025.

Brynjolfsson, E. & McAfee, A. (2014). *The Second Machine Age: Work, Progress, and Prosperity in a Time of Brilliant Technologies*. W.W. Norton. Available at: https://wwnorton.com/books/9780393239355

EBRD. (2023). *Rebuilding Ukraine and enhancing regional resilience: Supporting economic recovery, integration, and regional connectivity*. European Bank for Reconstruction and Development. Available at https://www.ebrd.com/publications/rebuilding-ukraine-and-regional-resilience

European Commission. (2021). *Updating the 2020 new industrial strategy: Building a stronger single market for Europe's recovery*. https://ec.europa.eu/commission/presscorner/detail/en/ip_21_1884

European Commission. (2023). *Enlargement Package: Western Balkans Progress Reports*. Directorate-General for Neighbourhood and Enlargement Negotiations (DG NEAR).

Evans, P. (1995). *Embedded autonomy: States and industrial transformation*. Princeton University Press.

Granovetter, M. (1985). Economic action and social structure: The problem of embeddedness. *American Journal of Sociology*, *91*(3), 481–510. https://doi.org/10.1086/228311

Kenney, M., & Zysman, J. (2016). The rise of the platform economy. *Issues in Science and Technology*, *32*(3), 61–69. Available at https://issues.org/the-rise-of-the-platform-economy

OECD. (2022). *SME policy index: Western Balkans and Turkey 2022: Assessing the Implementation of the Small Business Act for Europe*. OECD Publishing. Available at https://doi.org/10.1787/b47d15f0-en. Accessed 20 July 2025.

OECD. (2023). *Global Trends in Government Innovation 2023. OECD Public Governance Reviews*. OECD Publishing. https://doi.org/10.1787/0655b570-en

Pietrobelli, C., & Rabellotti, R. (2011). Global value chains meet innovation systems: Are there learning opportunities for developing countries? *World Development*, *39*(7), 1261–1269. https://doi.org/10.1016/j.worlddev.2010.05.013

RCC. (2022). *Western Balkans digital economy and society index (DESI) 2022 Report*. Regional Cooperation Council. Available at https://www.rcc.int/pubs/159

Sabel, C. F., & Zeitlin, J. (2012). Experimentalist governance. In D. Levi-Faur (Ed.), *The Oxford handbook of governance*. Oxford University Press. Available at https://doi.org/10.1093/oxfordhb/9780199560530.013.0012

Srnicek, N. (2017). *Platform capitalism*. Polity Press. Available at https://www.politybooks.com/bookdetail/?isbn=9781509504862

UNCTAD. (2021). *Technology and innovation report 2021: Catching technological waves*. United Nations Conference on Trade and Development. Available at https://unctad.org/webflyer/technology-and-innovation-report-2021

World Bank. (2022). *Western Balkans regular economic report No. 22: Investing in resilient recovery*. World Bank. Available at https://www.worldbank.org/en/region/eca/publication/western-balkans-regular-economic-report

Yoruk, E., Radosevic, S., & Fischer, B. (2023). Technological profiles, upgrading and the dynamics of growth: Country-level patterns and trajectories across distinct stages of development. *Research Policy*, *52*(8), 104847. Available at https://doi.org/10.1016/j.respol.2023.104847

# Part IV
# Conclusion and Policy Directions

Part IV brings together the conceptual, empirical, and policy insights developed throughout the book, offering a forward-looking synthesis that connects theory with practice. It revisits the Development Network State (DNS) not only as a conceptual innovation but as a governance strategy suited to the realities of late-developing, low-capacity, and donor-dependent economies. Drawing on evidence from Kosovo, Albania, and North Macedonia, the DNS is presented as a pragmatic framework for advancing technological upgrading and institutional transformation under constraint.

Chapter 11 provides a theoretical synthesis by distilling the three core functions of the DNS, namely coordination, learning, and integration, and linking them to observed practices in the Western Balkans. It situates the DNS within wider debates in institutional economics, innovation systems, and experimental governance. The chapter argues that effective development policy must prioritize adaptive capabilities and continuous learning rather than fixed institutional forms. It also proposes the DNS as an analytical framework for understanding how development governance evolves in constrained environments, bridging theoretical reflection with empirical evidence.

Chapter 12 translates these conceptual findings into strategic policy directions for governments, donors, and development practitioners. It emphasizes the need to build coalitions that support capacity development, enhance institutional learning, and invest in infrastructures that enable reflection and adaptation. The chapter sets out practical pathways for designing adaptive governance mechanisms that can sustain industrial transformation over time. Instead of prescribing rigid policy models, it promotes a flexible and iterative approach grounded in learning, coalition building, and context-sensitive experimentation.

Part IV concludes that successful development in the digital age requires more than the imitation of policies or alignment with donor agendas. It calls for a fundamental rethinking of how governance is conceived, designed, and implemented. The DNS framework provides a pathway for this transformation by linking developmental ambition with institutional feasibility, even in contexts often described as ungovernable. It shows that progress under constraint is possible when governance is understood as a dynamic capability that enables societies to learn, coordinate, and adapt amid uncertainty.

# Chapter 11
# Synthesis and Theoretical Contributions

## 11.1 Introduction

This book set out to explain why structural transformation in the Western Balkans (WB) has remained limited despite decades of reform, market integration, and targeted sectoral initiatives. The central argument is that the main obstacle is not the shortage of capital, technology transfer, or market access, but the weakness of technological capabilities and, more specifically, the lack of governance arrangements that can develop, coordinate, and sustain them.

The preceding chapters have shown that capability formation in the region is influenced by the interaction between sector-specific dynamics and the broader strategic environment. Rapid advances in digital technologies, tighter environmental standards, and the reorganization of global production networks have reshaped the conditions under which firms compete and states intervene. These changes affect how value is created and captured, how markets are accessed, and how production systems are structured. They also place new demands on governance systems to mobilize resources, coordinate actors, and adapt to ongoing transformations.

The sectoral studies in Chaps. 4, 5, 6 revealed how these pressures expose the fragility of the region's capability base. Kosovo's ICT industry, while dynamic, remains heavily dependent on external platforms and diaspora networks. Albania's agri-food and light manufacturing sectors have achieved operational competence in specific niches but struggle to move up the value chain. North Macedonia's automotive components sector has achieved structured integration into global supply chains yet remains constrained by weak linkages and limited knowledge transfer from foreign investors. Across all three cases, the governance functions required to convert isolated gains into systemic upgrading, such as learning, coordination, and embeddedness, are partial, fragmented, or reliant on temporary coalitions.

This synthesis chapter consolidates the evidence from these sectoral cases and from the thematic analyses in Chaps. 8, 9, 10 to refine the Developmental Network



F. Sahiti, *Catching Up in the Digital Age*, Contributions to Economics, https://doi.org/10.1007/978-3-032-17059-0_11

State (DNS) framework. It demonstrates how a new model of governance, based on adaptive coordination, can offer a practical approach for managing capability development under conditions of constraint. The discussion begins by revisiting the central analytical puzzle, then distils the main empirical insights and advances the conceptual framework in light of the findings. It concludes by situating these refinements within broader debates on governance, industrial policy, and development theory, and by linking them to the strategic policy directions discussed in Chap. 12.

## 11.2 Restating the Analytical Puzzle

This book has been guided by a central challenge: how to govern structural transformation when state capacity is limited, authority is fragmented, and external incentives often conflict with domestic priorities. In the WB, this challenge is intensified by dependence on donors, the legacies of post-socialist institutions, and the combined pressures of digitalization, the green transition, and geopolitical restructuring. These forces create opportunities for upgrading but also deepen existing vulnerabilities.

The analysis has developed around several interconnected themes. One has examined how governance systems in donor-dependent, post-socialist contexts influence the development of technological, organizational, and institutional capabilities, and how learning occurs through evolving coalitions, digital tools, and policy mechanisms. Another has explored the conditions that enable or hinder coordination, adaptation, and problem-solving when administrative resources are scarce and political incentives diverge. A third theme has focused on the governance functions that can sustain upgrading in polycentric environments where authority is dispersed and bureaucratic autonomy is weak. Across these themes, the use of digital tools, from data platforms to regulatory sandboxes, has raised the question of how technological possibilities can be integrated into governance frameworks to accelerate capability formation.

These lines of inquiry point to three core challenges that define the analytical puzzle of the book.

The first concerns why fragmented, donor-dependent states struggle to achieve structural transformation. Weak horizontal coordination, limited institutionalized learning, and the instability of strategic initiatives hinder the embedding of sectoral reforms within a coherent development trajectory.

The second relates to why traditional models of state-led or market-led development have proven inadequate. Developmental state models, as exemplified by East Asian catch-up experiences (Amsden, 1989; Wade, 1990; Wade, 2018), relied on cohesive bureaucracies and long-term planning horizons that are largely absent in transitional economies. Market-liberal approaches, by contrast, have often reinforced dependency by locking firms into low value-added positions within global value chains (Pietrobelli & Rabellotti, 2011; Gereffi 2019), without building the domestic capabilities required for upgrading.

The third challenge asks how a new model of governance can provide a viable alternative. Centred on the interrelated functions of coordination, learning, and embeddedness, the DNS reframes governance as the orchestration of adaptive and networked coalitions rather than as either centralized control or laissez-faire facilitation. This approach emphasizes distributed leadership, iterative experimentation, and sustained engagement with firms, municipalities, civil society, and transnational actors.

The remainder of this chapter brings together the evidence from the WB to examine how these functions operate under constraint, how they can be institutionalized through adaptive governance, and what this implies for both theory and practice.

## 11.3 Key Empirical Insights

The empirical foundation of this book rests on three sectoral studies: Kosovo's ICT industry (Chap. 4), Albania's agri-food and light manufacturing sectors (Chap. 5), and North Macedonia's automotive components sector (Chap. 6). These cases reveal, in distinct contexts, how technological capabilities are built, constrained, and at times eroded, and how governance arrangements shape these trajectories in decisive ways.

The central aim is to demonstrate that capability outcomes do not arise solely from market forces or firm-level efforts. They emerge from continuous interaction among firms, public agencies, donors, and other actors within governance systems that can enable, distort, or block the processes of learning, coordination, and embedded engagement. While sectoral histories and global linkages define the starting conditions, it is the quality and configuration of governance functions that determine whether operational competencies evolve into higher-order capabilities or remain limited in scope.

Even in contexts marked by weak institutions and scarce resources, the analysis identifies moments and mechanisms through which capabilities can advance. Yet, without institutional arrangements to consolidate and expand these advances, progress remains fragile and episodic. The empirical contribution of this book lies in identifying these mechanisms and showing how they can be institutionalized through a new approach to governance.

Although the sectors differ in history, market structure, and global integration, two consistent findings emerge. First, technological capabilities remain partial, uneven, and vulnerable to external shocks, even in the most dynamic subsectors. Second, governance functions—coordination, learning, and embeddedness—are often absent, fragmented, or dependent on temporary coalitions, preventing capability gains from becoming systemic.

The following subsections revisit each case using the tiered capability framework introduced in Chap. 2 (operational, intermediate, and advanced) to examine how governance has enabled or constrained their developmental trajectories.

## 11.4 Kosovo ICT: Digital Expansion Without Deep Upgrading

Kosovo's ICT sector has become one of the most dynamic in the WB, showing consistent export growth and initial integration into global digital markets.

At the operational level, capabilities are relatively well developed. Skills such as coding proficiency, agile project management, and effective communication with international clients are widespread. These competencies allow Kosovar developers and service providers to compete in software development, web services, and outsourcing.

Intermediate capabilities, including the adaptation of global tools to local contexts, localization of products for client needs, and limited product development, are beginning to emerge. They are concentrated among a smaller group of firms, many led by diaspora entrepreneurs who bring process knowledge, market insights, and innovation-oriented business practices.

Advanced capabilities, such as original product design, proprietary software development, and scalable platform creation, remain rare. Only a few firms have achieved this level, typically those with access to patient capital or long-term partnerships with demanding international clients. Most companies continue to operate as service providers, implementing client specifications rather than leading innovation.

### *11.4.1 Mechanisms of Capability Formation*

Three main mechanisms have shaped the sector's growth and capability profile.

First, diaspora linkages have been the most consistent driver of capability formation. Entrepreneurs and professionals abroad connect local firms to international markets, transfer tacit knowledge, and sometimes invest directly in expansion.

Second, platform-mediated work through marketplaces such as Upwork and Fiverr has reduced entry barriers, allowing individuals and small firms to access global opportunities without major capital investment. However, these platforms also create dependency on external governance rules, algorithms, and fee structures.

Third, donor-supported training programs, provided by organizations such as GIZ, USAID, and Swisscontact, have expanded the pool of entry-level professionals in coding, design, and digital marketing. Yet these initiatives are typically short-term and project-based, lacking the institutional continuity required for sustainable capability development.

Although each mechanism contributes to growth, learning remains highly individualized and weakly shared across firms. Freelance work improves execution skills but rarely strengthens design or innovation capacity. Donor programmes often measure success by the number of trainees rather than by long-term sectoral impact.

### 11.4.2 Governance Functions

Governance in Kosovo's ICT sector operates through a loosely connected network of municipalities, diaspora entrepreneurs, and donor agencies. Coordination is mostly informal and relies on personal relationships rather than institutionalized mechanisms. The Kosovo Digital Economy Project has made progress in bringing together public institutions, private actors, and donors, but its structures remain early-stage and vulnerable to shifting priorities.

Learning processes are sporadic, often initiated by donor projects or municipal programmes, and rarely embedded within feedback loops that connect successful initiatives to national policy. Embeddedness—the depth of trust-based relationships between actors—is stronger in Kosovo than in Albania or North Macedonia due to the density of diaspora networks. However, these relationships are not systematically mobilized by the state for sector-wide upgrading.

### 11.4.3 Implications for the Developmental Network State

The Kosovo ICT case illustrates both the potential and the fragility of bottom-up adaptive governance. The combination of diaspora entrepreneurship, platform-based market participation, and donor-supported skills development demonstrates that technological capabilities can emerge even in resource-constrained environments. These dynamics highlight the capacity of non-state actors and transnational networks to drive learning and innovation where formal institutions remain weak. However, the absence of institutional mechanisms to coordinate actors, consolidate learning, and direct resources toward firms capable of developing advanced capabilities limits the transformative potential of these initiatives. In their current form, such gains tend to remain isolated, short-lived, and insufficiently connected to systemic upgrading.

A strategy consistent with the DNS approach would seek to institutionalize these emerging dynamics within a more coherent governance framework. This would involve establishing a permanent coordination platform linking municipalities, ministries, donor agencies, and diaspora networks in order to facilitate strategic dialogue and resource alignment. Equally important would be the creation of structured mechanisms to capture, codify, and disseminate lessons from high-performing firms so that individual successes can inform broader capability development. Finally, targeted support should be directed toward firms positioned to transition from intermediate to advanced capabilities, particularly those developing proprietary products, digital platforms, and intellectual property.

Embedding technological capability development as a central objective of governance, rather than treating it as a by-product of market participation, could enable Kosovo to move beyond a service-oriented and externally dependent growth model.

By institutionalizing adaptive coordination and learning, the country could begin to chart a more autonomous, innovation-driven development trajectory aligned with the principles of the DNS.

## 11.5 Albania's Agri-Food and Light Manufacturing Gains and Traps

Albania's agri-food and light manufacturing sectors present a picture of gradual operational progress alongside enduring structural weaknesses. In agri-food, operational capabilities are most visible in niche export segments such as olive oil, dairy products, and medicinal herbs. A small number of firms have achieved compliance with basic EU quality and safety standards, allowing them to access specific market niches. Intermediate capabilities, including process adaptation, packaging innovation, and modest product differentiation, are concentrated among a few export-oriented firms, often supported by donor funding or technical assistance. Advanced capabilities, such as new product development, branding, and integration into higher-value global chains, remain rare and are typically limited to isolated success stories.

In light manufacturing, particularly textiles and footwear, operational competencies in assembly work are well established and consistently applied within subcontracting arrangements. However, intermediate and advanced functions such as design, brand creation, integrated logistics, and direct marketing are largely absent. This has left the sector confined to low-value segments of global value chains, with limited prospects for upgrading.

### *11.5.1 Mechanisms of Capability Formation*

Three mechanisms have been central to capability development in these sectors.

The first is donor-funded modernization. Programmes such as the EU's IPARD scheme and GIZ-supported initiatives have financed equipment upgrades, quality certification, and compliance with export standards. Although these interventions have improved firm-level operations, they have not generated broader knowledge diffusion or institutionalized learning mechanisms across the sector.

The second mechanism involves cluster initiatives. Donor or NGO-led projects have occasionally promoted knowledge exchange among firms, but most supplier networks remain fragmented. The absence of mid-tier coordinators, firms or institutions capable of linking smaller producers to export markets, has severely limited scaling and collective upgrading.

The third mechanism is vocational education and training (VET). The VET system remains outdated, poorly aligned with industry needs, and disconnected from the private sector. Curricula rarely reflect modern production technologies or market requirements, and opportunities for work-based learning are scarce.

Collectively, these mechanisms tend to address immediate operational or compliance gaps rather than fostering adaptive capabilities that allow firms to respond to changing market conditions. Upgrading often occurs in short bursts, tied to donor project cycles, and lacks the institutional continuity required for sustained progress.

### 11.5.2 Governance Functions

Governance across Albania's agri-food and light manufacturing sectors is characterized by fragmentation and weak coordination. Ministries responsible for agriculture, trade, and vocational training operate in isolation, while donor agencies run parallel programmes with limited communication or integration.

Learning processes are largely externalized. Monitoring and evaluation frameworks are designed primarily to satisfy donor reporting requirements rather than to inform domestic policy learning. Lessons from these interventions are seldom synthesized or used to refine national strategies, and systematic feedback mechanisms are almost entirely absent.

Embeddedness, understood as the degree of relational trust and collaboration among actors, is particularly weak. Farmer cooperatives are few and institutionally fragile, while manufacturing supply chains are dominated by transactional relationships with little incentive for joint upgrading. The trust deficit between public institutions and private actors further inhibits collective initiatives or problem-solving efforts that could support sectoral upgrading.

### 11.5.3 Implications for the Developmental Network State

The Albanian case demonstrates the limitations of donor-driven upgrading in the absence of systemic governance frameworks. Donor interventions have generated visible operational improvements within selected firms, yet these achievements have not evolved into cumulative capability development at the sectoral level. Without effective coordination and institutionalized learning, upgrading remains fragmented, and progress often dissipates once project funding ends.

A strategy consistent with the DNS approach would seek to integrate these fragmented efforts into a more coherent system of governance. This would involve establishing multi-actor coordination platforms that bring together ministries, donors, and private sector representatives to align upgrading strategies, share information, and avoid duplication. Reform of the vocational education and training system should be co-designed with leading firms to ensure that curricula, facilities, and work-based learning reflect real market needs. In parallel, trust-building initiatives within supplier networks, particularly in agri-food clusters, should promote cooperation through cooperative development, buyer and supplier partnerships, and targeted public support for collaborative innovation.

By embedding these measures within a broader governance framework focused on learning, coordination, and embeddedness, Albania could begin to overcome its current capability traps. Such an approach would allow its agri-food and light manufacturing sectors to move beyond donor dependency and toward a trajectory of sustained, innovation-oriented upgrading within regional and global markets.

## 11.6 Automotive Integration and Capability Ceilings in North Macedonia

The automotive components sector in North Macedonia represents one of the most strategically integrated manufacturing activities in the WB. It has achieved sustained export growth through its participation in European and global automotive value chains. At the operational level, firms demonstrate strong capabilities in quality assurance, lean production, and process control, meeting the rigorous standards of original equipment manufacturers (OEMs).

Intermediate capabilities are evident in supplier development practices and the ability to adapt production processes to specific OEM requirements. These competencies have enabled some domestic firms to sustain long-term supplier relationships and compete in quality-sensitive markets.

Advanced capabilities, such as component design, participation in research and development, and the creation of proprietary technologies, remain concentrated among foreign lead firms. Domestic companies continue to occupy lower-tier supplier roles, performing contract manufacturing without contributing significantly to product design or innovation strategy.

### *11.6.1 Mechanisms of Capability Formation*

Three key mechanisms have shaped capability development in this sector.

The first is foreign direct investment (FDI) within Special Economic Zones (SEZs), which has introduced advanced manufacturing practices, quality management systems, and compliance with EU and OEM standards. These developments have improved operational performance among participating firms, but their benefits have not extended widely across the national industrial base.

The second mechanism is the set of innovation programmes managed by the Fund for Innovation and Technological Development (FITD). These initiatives have co-financed collaborative projects linking domestic firms with universities, research institutions, and, in some cases, foreign investors. They have created opportunities for experimentation and incremental innovation, although the impact remains limited in scope.

The third mechanism involves targeted training provided by foreign investors and lead firms, particularly in quality management, process optimization, and health and safety. While these programmes have strengthened operational and intermediate capabilities, high-value functions such as product design, research and development, and strategic decision-making are still retained in investors' home countries. Many domestic suppliers continue to face skill shortages, limited infrastructure, and restricted access to finance. As a result, SEZs function largely as enclaves, with weak connections to local supply networks.

### 11.6.2 Governance Functions in WB

Compared with Kosovo and Albania, North Macedonia has developed more structured coordination mechanisms in its automotive sector. The Fund for Innovation and Technological Development acts as a key intermediary, linking firms, academic institutions, and government agencies through targeted programmes for innovation and upgrading.

Learning processes are embedded within FITD's evaluation and monitoring cycles, generating feedback on project outcomes and informing future funding decisions. However, these mechanisms are not yet fully integrated into the broader industrial strategy, which limits their potential to shape policy across sectors.

Embeddedness between SEZ-based foreign firms and domestic suppliers remains shallow. Relationships are largely driven by compliance with technical and quality standards rather than shared innovation agendas or collaborative investment in upgrading. As a result, supplier integration is limited, and opportunities for knowledge transfer remain underdeveloped.

### 11.6.3 Implications for the Developmental Network State

The North Macedonian case demonstrates how hybrid governance institutions such as the Fund for Innovation and Technological Development can partially fulfil the functions of the DNS. FITD bridges the state, private sector, and knowledge institutions, promoting collaborative innovation and learning. Yet the sector's upgrading potential remains constrained by limited spillovers from foreign investors and by the absence of mechanisms that integrate Special Economic Zone activity into the wider economy.

A strategy consistent with the DNS would aim to extend FITD's role and strengthen domestic linkages. This would include expanding its mandate and resources to support supplier development programmes focused on upgrading local firms' technological and managerial capabilities. Strengthening absorptive capacity through skills development, increased research funding, and strategic infrastructure investment would also be essential. In addition, linking SEZ-based production with national industrial strategies through corridor and cluster initiatives could ensure that participation in global value chains contributes to domestic capability accumulation rather than reinforcing enclave patterns.

By aligning SEZ activity with a national upgrading agenda and embedding learning across the sector, North Macedonia could move from a model of externally driven integration constrained by capability ceilings toward one based on innovation-led growth and deeper domestic value capture.

## 11.7 Comparative Patterns

The three sectoral cases reveal both shared constraints and distinct developmental pathways shaped by each sector's structure and actor configuration.

Across all three countries, governance fragmentation remains a central challenge. Ministries, municipalities, and donors often operate in parallel with limited coordination. Donor dominance in programme design is widespread, with external actors setting priorities and timelines that can undermine locally owned strategies. Institutional learning is sporadic and rarely incorporated into domestic policymaking, while weak embeddedness within supply chains limits trust, cooperation, and opportunities for long-term upgrading.

Despite these shared obstacles, each sector displays a distinct trajectory. Kosovo's ICT sector demonstrates high dynamism, driven by diaspora entrepreneurship and digital integration into global markets, but remains constrained by informal and fragile governance arrangements. Albania's agri-food and light manufacturing sectors show operational competence in selected niches, yet progress is heavily tied to donor projects and seldom sustained once funding ends. North Macedonia's automotive components sector exhibits a more structured upgrading path, supported by hybrid institutions such as FITD, but faces persistent capability ceilings due to limited spillovers from foreign investors and weak domestic integration of SEZ activities.

Across the three cases, elements consistent with the DNS approach are beginning to emerge. Municipal and diaspora partnerships in Kosovo, donor–firm cluster initiatives in Albania, and FITD's multi-actor innovation programmes in North Macedonia each represent early forms of adaptive and networked governance. If these practices were scaled and institutionalized, they could provide the foundation for a more coherent system of capability development across the WB.

**Table 11.1** Comparative capability–governance profiles of sectoral cases

| Sector & country | Technological capability profile | Governance features | DNS potential |
|---|---|---|---|
| Kosovo ICT | Operational: Strong in coding, project management, client-facing communication. Intermediate: Emerging in diaspora-led start-ups. Advanced: Rare, limited proprietary design or scalable platforms | Coordination: Informal, recent national frameworks. Learning: Episodic, limited policy integration. Embeddedness: Strong diaspora ties, weak institutional leverage | High if diaspora networks integrated into national frameworks and firm learning scaled |
| Albania Agri-food & Light Manufacturing | Operational: Solid in niche agri-food exports, assembly in manufacturing. Intermediate: Limited process adaptation in select firms. Advanced: Rare in branding, product development, high-value chain integration | Coordination: Minimal, siloed ministries and donors. Learning: Externalized to donor reporting. Embeddedness: Weak cooperatives, transactional supply chains | Moderate if donor programmes embedded in coordinated upgrading platforms and VET reformed |
| North Macedonia Automotive Components | Operational: Strong in quality assurance, lean production. Intermediate: Some supplier development, adaptation to OEM standards. Advanced: Concentrated in foreign lead firms; limited domestic R&D or design | Coordination: Stronger via FITD. Learning: Embedded in FITD evaluation cycles but not systemic. Embeddedness: Shallow links between SEZ firms and domestic suppliers | High if FITD role expanded to embed SEZ activity in domestic innovation systems |

*Source* Author's elaboration based on Chaps. 4, 5, 6

These comparative patterns are summarized in Table 11.1, which outlines the capability profiles, governance features, and DNS potential of each sector. This table serves as a reference point for the cross-case discussion that follows.

In addition, Fig. 11.1 plots each sector's current position in relation to both technological capability maturity and governance functionality maturity. This visual representation of the "capability–governance gap" illustrates why governance compatible with the DNS framework is essential for guiding sectors toward the upper-right quadrant, where high capability and high governance functionality coincide. Movement toward this quadrant signals a transition to self-sustaining transformation, in which learning, coordination, and embeddedness reinforce one another over time.

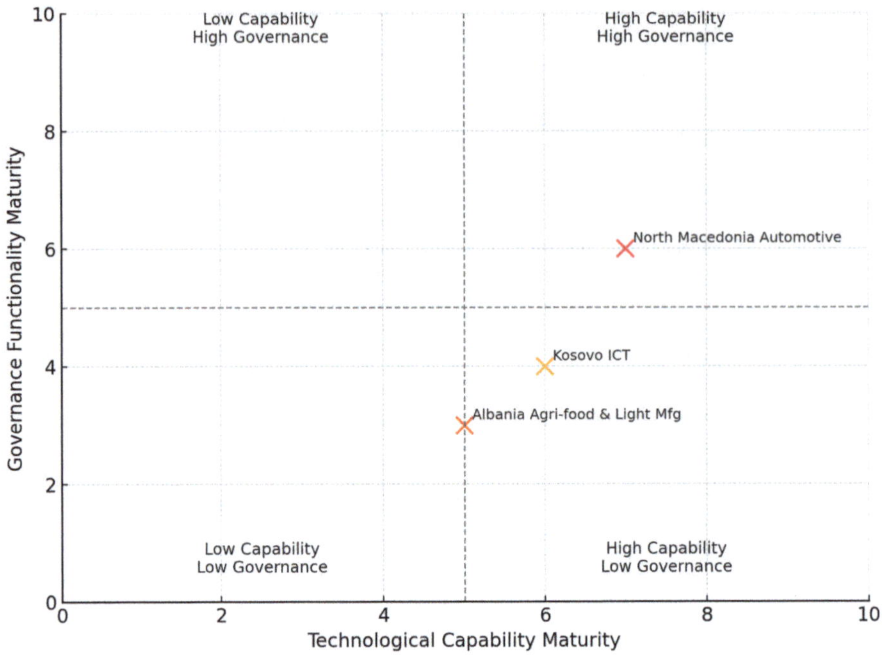


**Fig. 11.1** Capability–governance gap in sectoral cases. *Note* This diagram positions the three sectoral cases according to their current levels of technological capability maturity and governance functionality maturity. The vertical and horizontal lines divide the space into four quadrants, highlighting the gap between present positions and the upper-right quadrant, where high capability and high governance functionality combine to create self-sustaining transformation. *Source* Author's elaboration based on Chaps. 5, 6, 7

Across the three cases, a shared set of structural weaknesses continues to constrain capability accumulation. Governance remains fragmented, donor agendas dominate reform priorities, institutional learning is sporadic, and embeddedness in supply chains is shallow. These constraints reduce the ability of firms and public institutions to coordinate effectively or sustain upgrading beyond isolated interventions.

Despite these common limitations, each sector follows a distinct developmental trajectory shaped by its actors and institutional configurations. Kosovo's ICT industry displays strong entrepreneurial dynamism driven by diaspora linkages but lacks consistent governance support. Albania's agri-food and light manufacturing sectors maintain operational competence in selected niches yet struggle to achieve sustained upgrading once donor programmes conclude. North Macedonia's automotive components industry benefits from more structured coordination through the Fund for Innovation and Technological Development (FITD), but its progress remains restricted by limited spillovers from foreign investors and the enclave nature of Special Economic Zone production.

These contrasting experiences demonstrate that while the DNS model is only partially realized across the WB, important elements of DNS-compatible practice are already visible. Municipal and diaspora partnerships in Kosovo, donor–firm cluster initiatives in Albania, and multi-actor innovation programmes in North Macedonia each represent early forms of adaptive and networked governance. Together, they offer a foundation for scaling governance arrangements that can embed learning, strengthen coordination, and support long-term capability development across the region.

## 11.8 The DNS Framework: Refined

Part I introduced the DNS as an alternative governance model for latecomer economies, particularly those facing institutional fragmentation, donor dependence, and limited administrative capacity. At its core, the DNS is built on three interdependent meta-capabilities: learning, coordination, and embeddedness. These capabilities represent mutually reinforcing processes that enable actors to align strategies, adapt through feedback, and sustain trust-based collaboration across public, private, and civic domains.

Evidence from Kosovo's ICT sector, Albania's agri-food and light manufacturing sectors, and North Macedonia's automotive components sector both confirms and extends this model. While the three meta-capabilities remain foundational, the comparative analysis highlights the institutional instruments, actor configurations, and scaling mechanisms that can make DNS principles operational in contexts of limited state capacity. It also highlights the importance of transnational actors, who function not as external enablers but as integral components of governance networks.

### *11.8.1 Meta-Capabilities as the Foundation of Transformation*

The case evidence confirms that coordination, learning, and embeddedness are indispensable for building and deepening technological capabilities. In Kosovo's ICT sector, coordination through informal diaspora networks supported rapid export growth, but the lack of institutionalized learning prevented firm-level successes from scaling. Embeddedness was strong in terms of relational trust yet underutilized by public institutions. In Albania's agri-food and light manufacturing sectors, limited embeddedness in supply chains and weak learning systems meant that donor-funded operational improvements remained isolated achievements. North Macedonia's automotive components sector achieved stronger coordination through the Fund for Innovation and Technological Development (FITD), but embeddedness between foreign firms in Special Economic Zones and domestic suppliers was shallow, restricting opportunities for knowledge transfer and spillovers.

### 11.8.2 Institutional Instruments for Low-Capacity Contexts

The research identifies three types of institutional instruments that are particularly relevant for implementing DNS functions in contexts where administrative resources are scarce and governance systems are fragmented. Each instrument convenes diverse actors, structures collaboration, and embeds learning within the implementation process.

The first are task forces, or problem-focused coalitions that bring together ministries, agencies, municipalities, and non-state actors around a clearly defined challenge. They are most effective when they have a fixed mandate, dedicated coordination capacity, and a direct link to decision-making forums. In Kosovo's growing digital skills ecosystem, for example, municipalities, diaspora entrepreneurs, and donors collaborated to align training provision with market needs, creating a shared platform for workforce upgrading.

The second are transformation units, small and strategically positioned teams that possess both convening authority and analytical expertise. These units act as connectors across policy domains and can be embedded within ministries, development agencies, or specialized institutions. The Fund for Innovation and Technological Development in North Macedonia demonstrates this function by linking financing instruments with innovation support and supplier development, bridging the priorities of public institutions and private firms.

The third are structured pilots, time-bound and iterative initiatives designed as much for learning as for achieving immediate outcomes. These pilots generate evidence on what works, strengthen trust among participants, and create foundations for scaling interventions. In Albania, donor-supported cluster projects, although limited in scope, showed how embedded experimentation can enhance cooperation within value chains when linked to a broader industrial strategy.

When combined, these instruments give low-capacity states practical means to perform DNS functions without relying on large central bureaucracies. They facilitate coordination across institutional boundaries, embed continuous learning, and nurture relationships that support sustained capability upgrading.

### 11.8.3 Transnational Actors as Embedded Nodes

Transnational actors play a decisive role in shaping capability trajectories across all three countries. Diaspora entrepreneurs in Kosovo act as market brokers and carriers of knowledge. Foreign investors in North Macedonia transfer advanced manufacturing practices and standards. Donor–firm partnerships in Albania enable compliance upgrades and access to niche export markets. Their long-term contribution depends on whether governance systems integrate these actors into feedback loops, align their activities with domestic priorities, and position them as partners in cumulative capability development rather than as isolated contributors (Fig. 11.2).

In summary, the refined DNS framework retains the centrality of coordination, learning, and embeddedness while introducing a concrete operational architecture tailored to the realities of low-capacity and donor-dependent states. By identifying practical instruments, clarifying the role of transnational actors, and emphasizing scaling and sequencing mechanisms, this refinement bridges the gap between an abstract governance ideal and the practical challenges of managing industrial transformation under constraint.

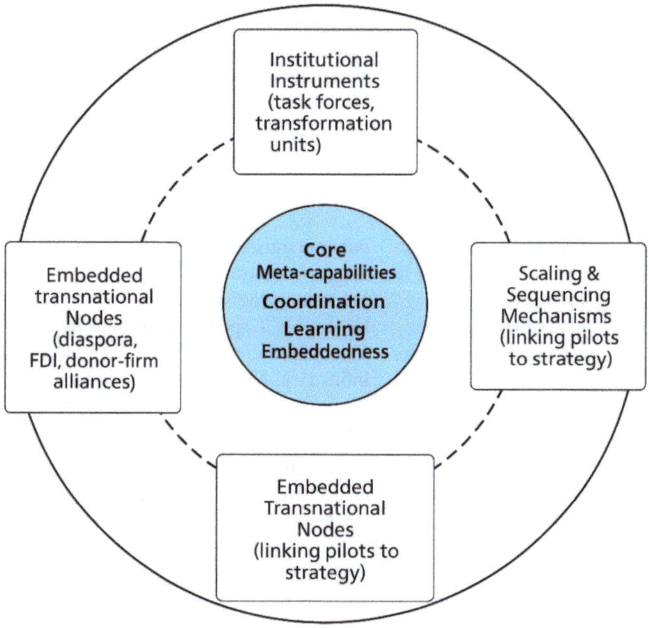


**Fig. 11.2** Refined Developmental Network State model. *Note* The diagram places the three core meta-capabilities, coordination, learning, and embeddedness, at the centre. Surrounding them are three operational refinements: institutional instruments (task forces, transformation units, structured pilots), embedded transnational nodes (diaspora networks, foreign investors, donor–firm alliances), and scaling and sequencing mechanisms linking pilots to national strategies. The outer ring represents the overarching goal of sustained capability accumulation under constraint. *Source* Author's elaboration based on Chap. 5, 6, 7, generated with Microsoft Copilot (DALL · E, Microsoft, 2025)

## 11.9 Theoretical Contributions

This book makes four interrelated contributions to the study of governance, development, and political economy in latecomer economies. Each engages with established scholarship while reframing it through the lens of the DNS and comparative evidence from the WB. Together, these contributions form a coherent theoretical agenda linking meta-capabilities, systemic capability building, value chain positioning, and reform processes.

**Table 11.2** Theoretical contributions, evidence, and gaps

| Theoretical contribution | Conceptual shift | Empirical illustrations | Gap addressed in literature |
|---|---|---|---|
| Governance Theory Adaptive governance as industrial policy infrastructure | From hierarchical, high-capacity state models to meta-capabilities (coordination, learning, embeddedness) as industrial policy infrastructure in low-capacity contexts | Kosovo ICT hubs, diaspora accelerators, donor skills programmes; Albania light manufacturing supplier programmes; North Macedonia SEZ-linked supplier pilots | Extends adaptive governance theory to fragmented, donor-dependent settings where bureaucratic depth is limited |
| Development Theory From sectoral upgrading to capability systems | From narrow, sector-specific upgrading to interconnected capability systems enabling cross-sector learning and spillovers | Albania agri-food niche exports constrained by processing/logistics gaps; Kosovo ICT spillovers into fintech and creative industries; North Macedonia automotive supplier integration pilots | Reframes development theory to prioritize systemic capability building over isolated sectoral success |
| Global Value Chain Literature Embedding state capability in GVC analysis | From firm- and lead-firm-centric GVC analysis to embedding state capability and network governance in shaping upgrading trajectories | North Macedonia SEZ automotive enclaves with weak supplier integration; Albania garment/footwear low-value subcontracting; Kosovo ICT peer learning and export readiness programmes | Bridges GVC and state capability literatures by analysing domestic governance as a determinant of upgrading outcomes |
| Policy Transfer Literature Embedded and iterative reform processes | From wholesale institutional transplantation to embedded, iterative reform processes co-designed with domestic actors | Kosovo ICT policy adapted from EU strategies via local co-design; Albania vocational reforms piloted in regional clusters; North Macedonia industrial policy selectively integrated into SEZ governance | Refines policy transfer literature by operationalizing iterative, context-sensitive reform in low-capacity settings |

*Source* Author's synthesis based on conceptual framework and empirical case evidence developed in this book

Table 11.2 summarizes these contributions, the conceptual shifts they represent, illustrative case evidence, and the specific gaps they address in the literature. The discussion below elaborates on each contribution in turn.

### *11.9.1 Building Industrial Policy Infrastructure Through Governance*

Foundational studies on the developmental state (Johnson, 1982; Amsden, 1989; Evans, 1995) associated economic transformation with strong, centralized bureaucracies capable of long-term planning and policy coherence. More recent work (Rodrik, 2004; Sabel & Zeitlin, 2012; Andreoni & Chang, 2019) has shifted attention toward adaptive and experimentalist governance, though these approaches have largely been examined in high-capacity settings.

This book extends the debate by showing that even in fragmented and donor-dependent contexts, governance can operate as industrial policy infrastructure when conceived as a meta-capability—the ability to coordinate, learn, and embed. The DNS model demonstrates that a large, centralized bureaucracy is not the only form capable of steering transformation.

The case studies show how these meta-capabilities can be mobilized through different configurations of actors. In Kosovo's ICT sector, municipal innovation hubs, diaspora-led accelerators, and donor-backed skills programmes formed a loosely connected but effective growth network. In Albania's light manufacturing sector, supplier upgrading programmes were linked to vocational reforms that matched skill development with firm-level needs. In North Macedonia's automotive components industry, supplier development pilots connected Special Economic Zone investors with domestic firms and technical schools, enabling knowledge transfer without reliance on a dominant central agency.

### *11.9.2 Development Theory: From Sectoral Upgrading to Capability Systems*

Classic contributions to development theory (Gerschenkron, 1962; Lall, 1992; Bell & Pavitt, 1993) identified capability accumulation as the foundation of latecomer growth but often treated it as a sector-specific process. This book reframes catch-up development as the creation of capability systems—interconnected technological, organizational, and institutional capacities that circulate across sectors, enabling learning, spillovers, and sustained transformation.

The case studies illustrate how these systems evolve or stall. In Albania's agri-food exports, promising niches such as medicinal plants and fresh produce were constrained by missing processing facilities, logistics networks, and certification bodies, preventing spillovers into related industries. Kosovo's ICT sector demonstrated how digital design, coding, and project management skills could extend into fintech, e-commerce, and creative industries once governance actors established cross-sector connections. In North Macedonia, advanced manufacturing capabilities remained concentrated in foreign-owned automotive plants, with only limited diffusion through targeted supplier integration initiatives.

### *11.9.3 State Capability in Global Value Chain Analysis*

The global value chain (GVC) framework (Gereffi et al. 2005) transformed the study of global production by mapping inter-firm relationships and upgrading trajectories. Yet it often underestimates the role of domestic state capability in shaping upgrading outcomes.

This book integrates GVC analysis with perspectives on state capability and network governance. It shows that the effectiveness of value chain participation depends not only on firm-level strategies but also on how domestic governance systems enable coordination, learning, and embeddedness.

In North Macedonia, SEZ-based automotive production achieved high technical standards but failed to develop strong domestic supplier linkages due to weak coordination among SEZ agencies, ministries, and training providers. Albania's garment and footwear industries remained locked into low-value subcontracting because institutions supporting design, branding, and marketing were absent. In contrast, Kosovo's ICT firms leveraged peer learning networks, diaspora mentorship, and export-readiness programmes to reach higher-value niches in digital services.

### *11.9.4 Policy Transfer Literature: Embedded and Iterative Reform Processes*

Research on policy transfer (Dolowitz & Marsh, 2000; Evans, 2004; Peck & Theodore, 2015) has long cautioned against importing "best practices" without adapting them to local contexts. The WB cases show why externally designed reforms often fail: they fragment capability systems by neglecting local conditions and political incentives.

The DNS approach proposes an alternative based on embedded and iterative reform. This involves co-designing policies with domestic actors, piloting them in targeted contexts, and scaling them gradually through sequenced steps that build institutional commitment. In Kosovo, ICT strategies inspired by EU frameworks only gained traction after being adapted to local realities and linked to diaspora networks. In Albania, vocational education reforms were most effective when piloted within regional industry clusters before national adoption. In North Macedonia, industrial policy tools derived from East Asian models delivered results only when integrated into SEZ governance with input from both foreign and domestic firms.

In summary, the DNS framework brings these four contributions together into a context-sensitive model for enabling structural transformation in the digital age. It acknowledges the realities of limited capacity, fragmented institutions, and donor influence while offering a practical governance architecture for capability accumulation and adaptive industrial policy.

## 11.10 Implications Beyond the Western Balkans

Although the DNS framework was developed in response to the institutional and economic realities of the WB, its relevance extends to many other latecomer economies in Sub-Saharan Africa, Southeast Asia, and Latin America. These regions share several structural constraints, including fragmented governance systems, small domestic markets, shallow integration into global value chains, and significant donor influence over policy priorities.

In Sub-Saharan Africa, countries such as Rwanda, Ghana, and Ethiopia have pursued forms of adaptive governance in sectors including ICT services, agro-processing, and light manufacturing. The DNS framework could help align donor support with domestic industrial strategies by strengthening capability building and coordination mechanisms. Success would depend on three key factors: political commitment, credible anchor nodes such as diaspora networks or industry associations, and financing aligned with coordinated pilot projects. However, risks remain. Fragile political settlements, fragmented donor programmes, and shortages of skilled facilitators capable of sustaining collaboration can all limit impact.

In Southeast Asia, economies such as Cambodia, Laos, and Myanmar are attempting to move from low-cost manufacturing toward higher-value production. The DNS approach could help link foreign investment with domestic supplier upgrading and integrate feedback mechanisms into industrial policy without requiring a large, centralized bureaucracy. Effective application would depend on active investment promotion agencies, partnerships between lead firms and local suppliers, and local or municipal entry points for coordination. Constraints include the persistence of enclave foreign investment, limited absorptive capacity among small firms, and weak legitimacy for newly established coordination bodies.

In Latin America, countries such as Paraguay, Honduras, and several in the Andean region face similar challenges. DNS principles could guide the adaptation of industrial policy tools to local institutional contexts through embedded and iterative reform processes. These could support capability accumulation in agribusiness, light manufacturing, and niche service industries. Key enablers would include trusted intermediaries such as business chambers and universities, decentralized but connected regional clusters, and flexible development finance mechanisms. Likely obstacles include resistance from entrenched interests, political instability at the subnational level, and weak systems for monitoring and learning.

Applied in these diverse contexts, the DNS framework provides a flexible yet structured approach to building technological and institutional capabilities under constraint. Rather than replicating institutional forms from other regions, it focuses on strengthening the governance functions of coordination, learning, and embeddedness. Where enabling conditions exist and political challenges are effectively managed, the DNS offers a pathway for incremental but cumulative transformation that can align development goals with local realities.

## 11.11 Conclusions: Linking to Policy Directions

The theoretical synthesis presented in this chapter is not an end in itself but a guide for practical action. The governance framework developed here, informed by both theory and comparative evidence, is designed to serve as more than an analytical tool. It provides a foundation for action in contexts where structural transformation is both necessary and constrained by political and institutional realities.

By focusing on governance functions rather than on replicating institutional forms, the DNS approach offers a practical way to mobilize coordination, foster learning, and strengthen embeddedness, even in settings with limited administrative capacity and fragmented institutions. The preceding analysis has shown how these functions operate in the WB, how they can be adapted to other latecomer regions, and what enabling conditions and limitations shape their effectiveness.

The lessons emerging from this synthesis are not purely descriptive. They point to concrete policy choices that governments, donors, and private sector actors can make to reinforce capability systems, deepen participation in higher-value segments of global markets, and sequence reforms in ways that are politically feasible and institutionally sustainable.

The next chapter moves from diagnosis to prescription. It translates the insights on meta-capabilities, capability systems, value chain governance, and iterative reform into a set of strategic policy directions. These directions are presented not as a fixed blueprint but as a flexible roadmap supported by practical tools, sequencing guidance, and actor-specific strategies. The aim is to help policymakers, development partners, and civic actors navigate the complexity of transformation under constraint by bridging the analytical depth of the DNS framework with the operational realities of policy design, aligning ambition with capacity and strategy with context.

# References


Amsden, A. H. (1989). *Asia's next giant: South Korea and late industrialization*. Oxford University Press.

Andreoni, A., & Chang, H. J. (2019). The political economy of industrial policy: Structural interdependencies, policy alignment and conflict management. *Structural Change and Economic Dynamics*, *48*, 136–150. Available at https://doi.org/10.1016/j.strueco.2018.10.004

Bell, M., & Pavitt, K. (1993). Technological accumulation and industrial growth. *Industrial and Corporate Change*, *2*(2), 157–210. https://doi.org/10.1093/icc/2.2.157

Dolowitz, D. P., & Marsh, D. (2000). Learning from abroad: The role of policy transfer in contemporary policy-making. *Governance*, *13*(1), 5–23. https://doi.org/10.1111/0952-1895.00121

Evans, P. (1995). *Embedded autonomy: States and industrial transformation*. Princeton University Press. Available at https://www.jstor.org/stable/j.ctt7t0sr. Accessed 12 July 2025.

Evans, M. (2004). *Policy transfer in global perspective*. Routledge.

Gereffi, G., Humphrey, J., & Sturgeon, T. (2005). The governance of global value chains. Review of International Political Economy, 12(1), 78–104. https://doi.org/10.1080/09692290500049805

Gereffi, G. (2019). *Global value chains and development: Redefining the contours of twenty-first century capitalism*. Cambridge University Press. Available at https://doi.org/10.1017/9781108559423

Gerschenkron, A. (1962). *Economic backwardness in historical perspective: A book of essays*. Belknap Press of Harvard University Press. https://www.hup.harvard.edu/catalog.php?isbn=9780674226005

Johnson, C. (1982). *MITI and the Japanese miracle: The growth of industrial policy, 1925–1975*. Stanford University Press. https://doi.org/10.1515/9780804765602

Lall, S. (1992). Technological capabilities and industrialization. *World Development*, *20*(2), 165–186. https://doi.org/10.1016/0305-750X(92)90097-F

Peck, J., & Theodore, N. (2015). *Fast policy: Experimental statecraft at the thresholds of neoliberalism*. University of Minnesota Press. https://doi.org/10.5749/minnesota/9780816677306.001.0001

Pietrobelli, C., & Rabellotti, R. (2011). Global value chains meet innovation systems: Are there learning opportunities for developing countries? *World Development*, *39*(7), 1261–1269. https://doi.org/10.1016/j.worlddev.2010.05.013

Rodrik, D. (2004). *Industrial policy for the twenty-first century*. Harvard University, Kennedy School of Government. Available at https://drodrik.scholar.harvard.edu/files/dani-rodrik/files/industrial-policy-twenty-first-century.pdf. Accessed 4 June 2025.

Sabel, C. F., & Zeitlin, J. (2012). Experimentalist governance. In D. Levi-Faur (Ed.), *The Oxford handbook of governance* (pp. 169–183). Oxford University Press. https://doi.org/10.1093/oxfordhb/9780199560530.013.0012

Wade, R. (1990). *Governing the market: Economic theory and the role of government in East Asian industrialization*. Princeton University Press.

Wade, R. H. (2018). The developmental state: Dead or alive? *Development and Change*, *49*(2), 518–546. https://doi.org/10.1111/dech.12381

# Chapter 12
# Strategic Policy Directions

## 12.1 Introduction

The comparative analysis in the previous chapter showed that even in contexts marked by fragmentation, donor dependence, and limited state capacity, governance can still evolve toward sustained capability development. The Developmental Network State (DNS) framework, synthesized from the Western Balkans (WB) cases of Kosovo, Albania, and North Macedonia, demonstrates that transformation does not depend on replicating institutional forms but on cultivating three core governance functions: learning, coordination, and embeddedness.

This chapter translates those analytical insights into a strategic agenda for implementation. Its objective is to show how the DNS framework can be operationalized within real-world constraints where resources are scarce, authority is dispersed, and reform must be negotiated among multiple stakeholders. Rather than prescribing a single reform model, it offers principles, instruments, and sequencing strategies that can be adapted to different institutional contexts.

The approach rests on three interrelated considerations. First, feasibility: what can realistically be achieved given prevailing political and administrative conditions. Second, sequencing: how to structure reforms so that early wins build momentum and manage risk. Third, scalability: how to expand pilot initiatives into system-wide capability development. These dimensions shape the structure of the chapter, which moves from institutional mechanisms that make DNS functions tangible, to strategic directions for capability accumulation, and finally to lessons for governing under constraint.

The intended audience includes both academic researchers and practitioners—policymakers, donor representatives, and civic actors—interested in how adaptive and networked governance can generate cumulative capability development. The following section begins by examining how the DNS meta-capabilities can be made operational through institutional design.



F. Sahiti, *Catching Up in the Digital Age*, Contributions to Economics,
https://doi.org/10.1007/978-3-032-17059-0_12

## 12.2 Operationalizing the DNS in Practice

The three meta-capabilities at the core of the DNS, learning, coordination, and embeddedness, constitute the functional capacities that enable governance systems to align diverse actors, adapt policies through feedback, and sustain trust-based relationships that support upgrading. The purpose of this section is to move from defining these capabilities to demonstrating how they can be translated into institutional practice, particularly in settings where administrative resources are scarce, authority is fragmented, and external actors have a strong influence on policy design.

Translating the DNS into practice begins with recognizing that these functions require institutional mechanisms through which they can operate. Without structures that convene actors, embed routines, and organize continuous interaction, coordination remains ad hoc, learning becomes episodic, and embeddedness stays superficial. Comparative evidence from Kosovo, Albania, and North Macedonia indicates that three institutional instruments have proven especially useful for realizing the DNS functions in low-capacity environments: task forces, transformation units, and structured pilots. These instruments do not replicate institutional forms from high-capacity states but instead adapt existing administrative and political arrangements to promote learning and collaboration across sectors.

However, the presence of these instruments alone is not sufficient. Their effectiveness depends on a set of enabling conditions. The first is political commitment. High-level support is essential to grant coordination platforms the authority to convene stakeholders, overcome bureaucratic resistance, and maintain continuity across political cycles. The second condition is the existence of credible anchor nodes, meaning organizations or networks that command trust among diverse actors and connect domestic capability systems to global markets and knowledge flows. In Kosovo, diaspora networks have played this role in the ICT sector; in Albania, export-oriented agribusiness firms have acted as anchors in value chains; and in North Macedonia, foreign investors have served as conduits for knowledge transfer and supplier upgrading.

A third enabling condition is aligned financing. In fragmented policy landscapes, donor funding often dominates capability-building efforts. When uncoordinated, these initiatives risk duplication and short-lived impact. Aligning external assistance with national priorities and channelling it through DNS instruments enhances coherence and multiplies developmental returns. The fourth condition involves identifying and strengthening institutional entry points within ministries, agencies, or municipal administrations that can host coordination platforms, absorb lessons from pilot projects, and translate them into durable policy frameworks. These entry points ensure that experimentation contributes to the institutional memory of the state rather than remaining isolated.

The interaction among functions, instruments, enabling conditions, and developmental outcomes can be visualized through an action map of the DNS. Figure 12.1 illustrates how the three meta-capabilities link to specific institutional instruments, supported by political, financial, and organizational conditions that enable them to

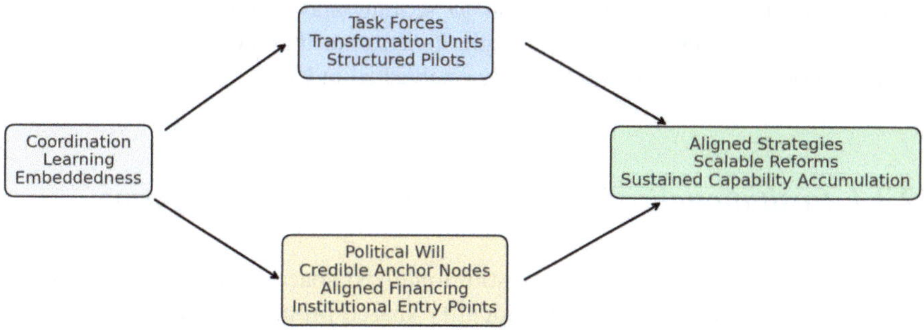


**Fig. 12.1** DNS action map: from functions to outcomes *Source* author's elaboration based on case study evidence from Kosovo, Albania, and North Macedonia

function effectively. The figure emphasizes that capability accumulation is not a linear process but a dynamic and iterative cycle in which feedback and learning progressively reinforce institutional performance and policy coherence.

The purpose of this mapping is to provide a conceptual framework for understanding how abstract governance functions are translated into concrete institutional forms. It shifts the discussion from general appeals for stronger coordination or improved learning to the practical domain of institutional design. By specifying the mechanisms through which DNS functions can be operationalized and identifying the enabling conditions that sustain them, the analysis offers a structured pathway from conceptual formulation to practical implementation.

By clarifying this pathway, the section establishes the foundation for the strategic policy directions that follow. The next section builds on these operational insights to outline how late-developing economies can sequence and scale capability-driven reforms under constraint.

## 12.3 Strategic Directions for Capability-Driven Transformation

The operational mapping in the previous section identified the institutional instruments and enabling conditions through which the meta-capabilities of coordination, learning, and embeddedness can be applied. Building on those insights, this section outlines six interrelated strategic directions that together form a framework for capability-driven transformation under constraint. These directions are not discrete policy interventions but interconnected processes that reinforce one another through feedback and learning. They represent an adaptive approach to state capability building that evolves through experimentation, reflection, and recalibration.

The framework builds on the adaptive policy perspectives developed by Rodrik (2004), Sabel and Zeitlin (2012), and Andreoni and Chang (2019), while adapting them to the fragmented and donor-dependent governance environments of late-developing economies. Each direction corresponds to one or more DNS meta-capabilities, moving from coordination and experimentation to scaling and institutional learning. The discussion below focuses on their strategic logic rather than detailed case narratives, as the empirical foundations were already established in Chap. 9.

### 12.3.1 Institutionalize Multi-Actor Coordination Platforms

Effective coordination depends on institutionalized spaces where public agencies, firms, and knowledge providers can identify shared problems and align resources. In low-trust environments, formal authority alone is insufficient; credibility and continuity are built through repeated interaction and transparent procedures. Coordination platforms, whether sectoral councils, transformation task forces, or municipal–diaspora networks, function best when anchored in legitimate institutions with a mandate to convene stakeholders and influence policy direction. Their design should balance inclusivity with focus, combining diverse representation with decision-making authority. As shown in the WB experience, hybrid structures that combine political endorsement, professional facilitation, and co-financing from domestic and external sources are most likely to sustain engagement and learning over time.

### 12.3.2 Embed Structured Experimentation

Structured experimentation enables governments to learn by doing, linking pilot projects to broader sectoral or national strategies. When experimentation is embedded within institutional frameworks rather than pursued as ad hoc projects, lessons can accumulate and inform policy adjustment. In contexts of limited capacity, pilots provide a controlled environment to test policy innovations and refine coordination mechanisms. The strategic task is to design pilots with replication potential and ensure that feedback from implementation informs decision-making. Transformation units, cross-ministerial working groups, or donor coordination platforms can serve as vehicles for integrating experimental learning into formal policy cycles. Over time, these arrangements help transform uncertainty from a source of paralysis into a driver of adaptive capability development.

### 12.3.3 Target Supplier and Skills Upgrading

Industrial competitiveness depends on the co-evolution of firm-level capabilities and workforce skills. Fragmenting these agendas weakens both. Supplier development and vocational upgrading should therefore be pursued jointly, linking training systems to the needs of upgrading firms and supply chains. This can be achieved through joint training centres, applied research partnerships, and fiscal incentives for firms that invest in workforce and supplier development. Effective coordination between training institutions, industry associations, and innovation agencies helps align education, production, and technology objectives. The strategic priority is not to scale training programmes indiscriminately, but to embed capability upgrading within the micro-dynamics of production and learning.

### *12.3.4 Leverage Transnational Nodes*

Diaspora networks, foreign lead firms, and donor organizations are often treated as external actors, yet they are integral components of domestic capability systems. When appropriately embedded, these transnational nodes can expand access to markets, technology, and finance. Their contribution depends on institutional mechanisms that align external resources with domestic upgrading goals, such as diaspora–firm matchmaking, supplier development partnerships, or investment agreements linked to capability targets. The strategic challenge is to translate transient external engagement into durable learning relationships that build local institutional capacity and reduce dependence on external intermediaries.

### *12.3.5 Integrate SEZ and GVC Activity Into Domestic Economies*

Special Economic Zones (SEZs) and participation in global value chains (GVCs) can accelerate structural change, but their developmental impact depends on the extent of domestic integration. Without deliberate linkage strategies, SEZs risk becoming enclaves disconnected from local firms and knowledge systems. Integration requires proactive policies that support supplier upgrading, promote local sourcing, and foster joint research and innovation projects between foreign investors and domestic enterprises. Coordination between SEZ authorities, industry associations, and innovation agencies ensures that global production networks become platforms for domestic capability accumulation rather than substitutes for it.

### *12.3.6 Institutionalize Learning in Policy Cycles*

Transformation is sustainable only when learning becomes an institutionalized feature of governance. This requires establishing formal review and feedback mechanisms that connect programme evaluation with policy design and budgeting. Ministries, coordination platforms, and planning offices should be required to review performance data regularly and incorporate lessons into subsequent planning cycles.

Institutionalizing learning reduces dependence on external technical assistance and strengthens domestic policy autonomy. Over time, such routines embed adaptability within state structures, making governments more capable of responding to shifting economic and political conditions.

Table 12.1 summarizes the six strategic directions, showing how each operationalizes specific DNS functions and contributes to cumulative capability development. The table emphasizes their interdependence: coordination platforms create the trust and information channels that make experimentation and learning possible; embedded experimentation generates knowledge that informs scaling and linkage strategies; and institutionalized learning consolidates the gains, feeding back into coordination and system-wide adaptation.

In summary, these strategic directions illustrate how the DNS framework can be implemented through iterative and context-sensitive processes of coordination, learning, and scaling. They also demonstrate that capability accumulation in late-developing economies does not rely on replicating external models, but on cultivating domestic systems that can learn, adapt, and evolve. The next section turns to the question of sequencing and political feasibility, examining how these strategic orientations can be introduced and sustained in environments where reform space is constrained.

**Table 12.1** Summary of strategic directions for capability-driven transformation

| Strategic direction | Core aim | Illustrative example | Implementation horizon |
|---|---|---|---|
| Institutionalize Multi-actor coordination Platforms | Establish credible spaces for joint problem-solving and resource alignment | Kosovo ICT municipal–diaspora networks; North Macedonia FITD | Medium to long term |
| Embed structured experimentation | Link pilots to strategies and embed feedback loops for scaling | ICT and education pilots aligned with export promotion strategies | Short to medium term |
| Target supplier and skills upgrading | Integrate firm upgrading with workforce development | Supplier and vocational upgrading in SEZ-linked sectors | Medium term |
| Leverage transnational nodes | Align external actors with domestic capability goals | Diaspora–firm linkages and FDI–supplier partnerships | Short to long term |
| Integrate SEZ and GVC activity into domestic economies | Build domestic linkages and spillovers from SEZs and GVC participation | Automotive SEZ integration in North Macedonia | Medium term |
| Institutionalize learning in policy cycles | Embed adaptive feedback into policymaking | Programme evaluation and reform cycles in innovation agencies | Ongoing |

*Source* Author's elaboration based on case study evidence from Kosovo, Albania, and North Macedonia, and synthesis of relevant literature

## 12.4 Sequencing and Political Feasibility

The six strategic directions outlined above cannot be implemented simultaneously in low-capacity and politically fragmented contexts. Reform design must therefore follow a deliberate sequencing strategy that builds coalitions and institutional capability over time. Sequencing is not simply a matter of project phasing, but a political and learning process that determines how reform gains are consolidated and scaled. This approach reflects Rodrik's (2004) principle of gradualism and self-discovery, and aligns with the problem-driven iterative adaptation model developed by Andrews et al. (2017), which emphasizes starting from feasible entry points and evolving through feedback and adjustment.

### *12.4.1 Entry Points and Demonstration Effects*

Evidence from the WB cases suggests that politically feasible reforms tend to begin where resistance is low and where early, visible results can shift expectations. In Kosovo's ICT sector, municipal–diaspora training partnerships and export-readiness initiatives progressed rapidly because they aligned with donor priorities and avoided disruption of entrenched rent networks. In Albania's agri-food sector, quality certification and niche export programmes succeeded because they delivered tangible benefits to producers without challenging established intermediaries. In North Macedonia, supplier development pilots advanced by framing upgrading as export standard compliance rather than as interference with SEZ governance.

These experiences illustrate M.H. Khan's (2010) argument that reform is most viable when initial steps impose minimal costs on powerful actors while generating demonstration effects that expand the space for subsequent change. Sequencing, in this sense, is not merely technical prioritization but a method of managing political risk through visible problem-solving and cumulative credibility.

### *12.4.2 Sequencing Logic*

A pragmatic sequencing pathway begins with targeted pilots and coordination platforms in specific sectors or regions. These initial initiatives should aim to produce quick, observable results that build trust among actors and generate learning about what works under local conditions. Once credibility and capability accumulate, the second phase involves institutionalizing coordination mechanisms and scaling successful pilots within national strategies. The final phase consolidates sectoral achievements into system-level reforms, linking learning platforms, investment strategies, and regulatory adjustments that reinforce capability accumulation.

**Fig. 12.2** Sequencing pathway for capability-driven reform *Note* The figure presents a three-phase pathway for implementing capability-driven reform in low-capacity, politically fragmented contexts. Phase 1 targets low-resistance entry points such as pilot initiatives and coordination platforms that deliver early results and build trust. Phase 2 consolidates these gains by institutionalizing coordination bodies, scaling successful pilots, and embedding them within sectoral and national strategies while managing emerging resistance and institutional competition. Phase 3 extends toward system-level reform, linking sectoral progress through cross-sector learning, coordinated investment, and regulatory adaptation. Feedback loops across all phases ensure that reform remains adaptive, cumulative, and politically feasible over time. *Source* Author's elaboration based on case study evidence from Kosovo, Albania, and North Macedonia, and synthesis of relevant literature

This phased approach mirrors Sabel and Zeitlin's (2012) insight that moving from demonstration to consolidation requires both political capital and technical capacity. It avoids overloading fragile institutions by sequencing reform in ways that allow experience, legitimacy, and institutional trust to develop gradually. Figure 12.2 summarizes this logic.

### *12.4.3 Navigating Political Economy Constraints*

Sequencing must respond to the political economy structures that shape reform incentives. Entrenched interests often resist measures that alter established rents or resource flows. In Kosovo, sections of the procurement system opposed supplier integration clauses that challenged existing contracting practices. In Albania, agricultural intermediaries resisted cooperative models that could bypass their control. In North Macedonia, some SEZ management bodies hesitated to deepen domestic linkages for fear of jeopardizing investor relations. Managing such resistance requires aligning reform with the incentives of influential actors, offering compensatory benefits, or reframing initiatives as opportunities rather than threats. This reflects Khan's (2018) notion of rent management as a pragmatic tool for navigating power relations while advancing developmental goals.

Donor fragmentation compounds these challenges. As seen in all three cases, uncoordinated donor programmes can erode national policy coherence and overwhelm limited administrative capacity. Embedding donor activities within nationally led coordination platforms helps align external support with domestic objectives and strengthens local ownership. Institutional competition among ministries and agencies presents another recurrent obstacle. Overlapping mandates for industrial policy, innovation, and skills development have generated duplication and rivalry, particularly where donor funding or political visibility is at stake. Clarifying responsibilities, formalizing joint decision mechanisms, and ensuring high-level political mediation are essential to prevent reform paralysis.

### *12.4.4 Balancing Short-Term Gains and Long-Term Transformation*

Political feasibility improves when reforms deliver tangible outcomes within the political cycle while laying foundations for sustained capability building. Early wins are important, but they must be designed as stepping stones toward cumulative learning and institutionalization. The sequencing challenge is to combine the urgency of visible progress with the patience required for structural transformation. Reforms that demonstrate problem-solving capacity early on, without overpromising systemic change, can strengthen credibility, attract new partners, and expand reform coalitions. Over time, these iterative cycles of experimentation, consolidation, and institutional learning transform constraint itself into a resource for adaptive governance.

## 12.5 Implementation Roadmap

The six strategic directions developed in this chapter bring together the analytical and practical foundations of capability-driven reform. They provide an operational pathway for late-developing economies to build cumulative capability under political and institutional constraint. The roadmap presented here is not a prescriptive manual but a structured synthesis that links reform intent to implementation strategy. It demonstrates how coordination, experimentation, and learning can evolve into self-reinforcing governance functions when embedded in credible institutions and adaptive policy processes.

**Three guiding principles shape this roadmap**

First, institutional anchoring: each reform component must be rooted in organizations capable of sustaining coordination and learning beyond electoral or donor cycles.

Second, adaptive sequencing: reforms should start where resistance is low and demonstration effects can generate momentum, expanding incrementally through feedback and coalition building.

Third, reflexive learning: mechanisms for monitoring, evaluation, and review should transform lessons into continuous policy adjustment, allowing institutions to evolve with changing circumstances.

Table 12.2 summarizes how these principles translate into an integrated framework for action. It identifies the key functions, indicative sequencing, primary

**Table 12.2** Implementation roadmap for capability-driven reform

| Strategic direction | Core implementation focus | Indicative sequencing | Key institutional actors | Typical risks | Adaptive responses |
|---|---|---|---|---|---|
| Institutionalize Multi-actor coordination Platforms | Establish sectoral councils, regional upgrading committees, or municipal–diaspora partnerships with clear mandates and budgets | Medium to long term | Ministries, municipalities, business associations, diaspora organizations | Elite capture, institutional fatigue, donor dependency | Transparent membership rules, co-financing, balanced participation |
| Scale embedded experimentation | Design pilots with replication potential, link them to national strategies, and develop transformation units to manage learning feedback | Short to medium term | Line ministries, innovation agencies, donor partners, universities | Fragmentation, political discontinuity | Cross-ministerial coordination, iterative evaluation mechanisms |
| Target supplier and skills upgrading | Integrate vocational and supplier development; incentivize firm-based training and applied research collaboration | Medium term | Industry associations, training agencies, SEZ authorities | Skills mismatch, SME exclusion, migration of skilled workers | Employer feedback loops, SME-tiered support, retention incentives |
| Leverage transnational nodes | Build structured diaspora–firm linkages, align donor and FDI projects with upgrading strategies, and promote co-financing | Short to long term | Investment promotion agencies, diaspora offices, donor organizations | External dependence, misaligned incentives | Institutionalized partnerships, multi-year agreements |
| Integrate SEZ and GVC activity into domestic economies | Strengthen local supplier linkages, fund joint R&D, and align SEZ governance with national industrial policy | Medium term | SEZ authorities, ministries of trade, supplier networks | Shallow linkages, power asymmetry | Local content monitoring, supplier development programmes |
| Institutionalize learning in policy cycles | Embed monitoring and review processes into planning and budgeting; preserve institutional memory and ensure accountability for implementation | Ongoing | Planning ministries, coordination councils, statistical agencies | Data gaps, tokenistic reviews, loss of institutional memory | Integrated M&E systems, knowledge repositories, continuity mechanisms |

*Source* Author's elaboration based on case study evidence from Kosovo, Albania, and North Macedonia, and synthesis of relevant literature actors, and recurrent risks associated with each strategic direction. The table should be read not as a checklist of interventions but as a dynamic representation of how interdependent processes of coordination, upgrading, and learning combine to produce systemic transformation.

The roadmap illustrates that capability development does not advance through isolated projects but through recursive interaction among coordination, learning, and experimentation. Reformers can use this framework to assess where institutional anchoring is weak, where feedback systems are missing, and where reform sequencing can be recalibrated to expand political feasibility. Over time, the interplay between these functions can generate the adaptive resilience necessary to sustain transformation in uncertain environments.

## 12.6 Epilogue: Governing Under Constraint

This book has explored how development can proceed under conditions of structural constraint, limited state capacity, and external dependence. Its central argument is that the possibilities for transformation lie not in overcoming constraint but in governing within it. The DNS framework has shown that even fragmented polities can develop cumulative capability when governance focuses on coordination, learning, and embeddedness rather than on replicating institutional forms from elsewhere.

Across the WB cases, moments of progress did not emerge from wholesale institutional reform or the transplantation of best practices. They arose when reformers built connective tissue between state agencies, firms, and knowledge institutions, often through modest, experimental, and politically negotiated arrangements. These mechanisms, coordination platforms, structured pilots, and embedded learning systems, illustrate how capability can grow in spaces of partial autonomy and persistent dependence. The key to such progress lies in institutionalizing adaptability: designing systems that can learn from error, realign incentives, and extend networks of cooperation across political divides.

Governing under constraint requires a political economy of patience. It recognizes that reform is not a linear trajectory from weakness to strength but a series of negotiated advances, reversals, and recalibrations. The state's developmental role is therefore not to control the market or to retreat from it, but to convene actors, broker cooperation, and sustain an environment in which experimentation becomes cumulative. In this sense, the DNS represents not an alternative to the developmental state but its renewal under contemporary conditions.

The broader implication is that transformation in the twenty-first century will depend less on institutional imitation and more on institutional learning. Countries that can build the capacity to experiment, coordinate, and adapt will not only manage constraint but convert it into a source of strategic advantage. The lesson of this book is that development remains possible even where resources are scarce and authority is dispersed, provided that governance learns to evolve purposefully within its limits.

The arguments advanced in this book emerge from contexts where ambition and limitation coexist. They affirm that development is not the privilege of stability or abundance, but the outcome of collective learning under pressure. The capacity to govern under constraint is not a second-best substitute for ideal conditions; it is a distinctive form of statecraft that redefines what is possible within them. If the DNS offers one enduring insight, it is that institutions evolve not by transcending uncertainty but by learning to act purposefully within it. The future of development will belong to those who turn constraint into a source of creativity, cooperation, and adaptive resolve.

## References

Andreoni, A., & Chang, H.-J. (2019). The political economy of industrial policy: Structural interdependencies, policy alignment and conflict management. *Structural Change and Economic Dynamics*, *48*, 136–150. https://doi.org/10.1016/j.strueco.2018.10.007

Andrews, M., Pritchett, L., & Woolcock, M. (2017). *Building state capability: Evidence, analysis, action*. Oxford University Press. Available at https://bsc.cid.harvard.edu/book/building-state-capability

Khan, M. H. (2010). Political settlements and the governance of growth-enhancing institutions. In D. North, J. Wallis, S. Webb, & B. Weingast (Eds.), *The shadow of violence: Politics, economics, and the problems of development* (pp. 285–323). Cambridge University Press. Available at https://www.researchgate.net/publication/265567069. Accessed 15 May 2025.

Khan, M. H. (2018). Political settlements and the analysis of institutions. *African Affairs*, *117*(469), 636–655. https://doi.org/10.1093/afraf/adx044

Rodrik, D. (2004). Industrial policy for the twenty-first century, *CEPR Discussion Paper No. 4767*. Centre for Economic Policy Research. Available at https://drodrik.scholar.harvard.edu/publications/industrial-policy-twenty-first-century. Accessed 14 July 2025.

Sabel, C. F., & Zeitlin, J. (2012). Experimentalist governance. In D. Levi-Faur (Ed.), *The Oxford handbook of governance* (pp. 169–183). Oxford University Press. https://doi.org/10.1093/oxfordhb/9780199560530.013.0012

# Index





F. Sahiti, *Catching Up in the Digital Age*, Contributions to Economics,
https://doi.org/10.1007/978-3-032-17059-0

MIX
Papier aus verantwortungsvollen Quellen
Paper from responsible sources
FSC® C105338

If you have any concerns about our products,
you can contact us on
**ProductSafety@springernature.com**

In case Publisher is established outside the EU,
the EU authorized representative is:
**Springer Nature Customer Service Center GmbH**
**Europaplatz 3, 69115 Heidelberg, Germany**

Printed by Libri Plureos GmbH
in Hamburg, Germany